The Well-Tended
Perennial Garden

The Well-Tended Perennial Garden

PLANTING & PRUNING TECHNIQUES

by Tracy DiSabato-Aust

Timber Press
Portland, Oregon

All photographs are by the author unless otherwise noted.
Black-and-white illustrations are by Beth Ann Daye.

Copyright © 1998 by Tracy DiSabato-Aust. All rights reserved.

Published in 1998 by

Timber Press, Inc.
The Haseltine Building
133 S.W. Second Avenue, Suite 450
Portland, Oregon 97204, U.S.A.

Twenty-first printing 2003

Printed in Hong Kong

Library of Congress Cataloging-in-Publication Data

DiSabato-Aust, Tracy.
    The well-tended perennial garden : planting and pruning techniques / by Tracy
DiSabato-Aust.
        p.   cm.
    Includes bibliographical references (p.   ) and index.
    ISBN 0-88192-414-8
    1. Perennials. I. Title.
SB434.D37   1998
635.9'32—dc21   97-29768
                                                                         CIP

To

Jim and Zachary

For their love and support and for the magic they give to my life

Contents

Color plates follow pages 64 and 144

Foreword

THE popularity of herbaceous perennial plants has fluctuated greatly over the last century in North America. Catalogs from the early 1900s illustrate the many perennials that were available during the period, but following the first quarter of the twentieth century the interest in perennials lessened. Until the early 1980s the use of perennials in North America was limited largely to estate gardens and to the highly interested home gardener. Woody plant materials and annuals or bedding plants were the talk of the trade, with a few perennials dotting the landscape.

In the early 1980s a reawakening occurred with a new awareness of herbaceous perennials by the gardening public. The Perennial Plant Association was formed in 1983, other area and regional associations concerned with perennials were formed, and symposium after symposium was offered on this "new found" palette of plant materials. In 1980 one could count the number of books about perennials on one hand. What a difference a few years can make! There are now dozens of books available on nearly any aspect of perennials. We can find books on individual species, design, color combinations, edible perennials, perennials in the fall, encyclopedic treatments of genera, and many others. Garden writers have recently asked: "Is there any perennial topic that has not been covered?" I can answer with a resounding "Yes." One area where a complete coverage has not been made is that of maintenance and long-term care of perennials.

Fortunately, Tracy DiSabato-Aust has produced for gardeners—and for professionals—an excellent horticultural account of the care and maintenance of perennials. *The Well-Tended Perennial Garden* provides a straightforward, no-holds-barred look at creating a perennial border or bed, from the beginning stage of soil preparation to planting, with specific pruning techniques to promote long bloom and long enjoyment of the garden.

The highlight of *The Well-Tended Perennial Garden* lies in the meticulous care taken to provide very specific information on perennial maintenance. Sections relating to maintenance in previous books on perennials too often are general in nature. Tracy has either experimented with each practice or has done a careful review and interviewed dozens of notable perennial experts to arrive at the specific suggestions that highlight this book. Practical applications obtained from over 20 years of work in Belgium, England, Canada, and Ohio have provided Tracy with many experiences to share with the reader. This book is destined to become the reference for home gardeners and professionals seeking answers for species-related maintenance questions.

The perennials industry has waited a long time for a work of high quality and accuracy on the subject of maintenance of perennials. Tracy DiSabato-Aust has provided this work with *The Well-Tended Perennial Garden*.

Dr. Steven M. Still
Department of Horticulture
The Ohio State University

Preface

WHEN I was first asked to write about pruning perennials many years ago I didn't have any idea it would take me to this point, nor that it would prove to be such a fascinating, exciting, and challenging area of perennial gardening. As I continued to write and lecture about pruning, as well as to lecture about bed preparation and maintenance of perennial gardens in general, I was thrilled and encouraged by the vast amount of interest in these areas exhibited by my readers and by people attending my lectures. Their enthusiasm and expression of the need for such information in a book was my inspiration for this work and continues to be my light. I hope this book will be a valuable contribution to the horticulture industry for professionals and home owners as well as students.

I often feel a bit as though I am "bursting the perennial bubble" by focusing on the maintenance of perennials, since so many people choose herbaceous perennials for their gardens with the idea that they won't have to do maintenance anymore. Although many lower maintenance perennials are available, most perennials require some maintenance to perform their best. This book is intended to help gardeners experience success with their perennials by providing knowledge for how to properly care for them. It is not a book about enslaving the gardener or about a neat-nik, regimented approach to creating a garden void of any seedheads or dying foliage. It is meant to increase awareness of the many attributes of pruning perennials and to provide some basic guidelines. It is also viewed as a pioneer project in this area, with endless possibilities for continued experimentation, research, and sharing of ideas among gardeners and industry professionals.

I have tried to blend the academic and practical gardener in me to provide the information—which can be rather technical at times—in a digestible form. My experience in the landscape industry and in my own gardens is the basis of the book, although many gardeners from across the country have generously offered insight into their different techniques for pruning perennials. The chapters in the first two sections of the book offer important general information about pruning and maintenance to provide a base, and the Encyclopedia of Perennials in Section Three gives specifics in a species-by-species fashion.

I hope this book is useful to you in the never-ending joy of perennial gardening.

Acknowledgments

A WORK of this kind would not be possible without the help and support of many people. I cannot thank everyone enough for all they have done. Even though this book is dedicated to my husband, Jim, and my son, Zachary, I want to thank them again for their constant patience, support, and understanding of my "obsessive" horticulture passion. A special thanks also goes to Denise Adams, my fellow indomitable spirit, for proofreading, endless encouraging, and always believing in this book. Also to Beth Ann Daye for her beautiful illustrations, computer assistance, and most of all her untiring support. Thank you to my parents Therese and Louis DiSabato and to my in-laws Jeanne and Jim Aust for their help in so many ways. Thanks to Dr. Steven Still, my mentor, for "forcing" me into this whole pruning business, and for everything else he has done. To my editors Josh Leventhal and Neal Maillet and everyone at Timber Press for giving me the opportunity to write this book. To Team HC&C (Horticultural Classics & Consultations, my old crew), especially: Chad Morrison, Tom Ahlstrom, Richard Fenwick, Betsy Parker, Char Steelman, and Linda Fling for all their hard work, from preparing numerous perennial beds to posing for pruning photographs. To Bettyann Boleratz and Amy Collins, who suffered through hours of data entry and miscellaneous other "un-fun" book tasks. And to my clients for allowing me the joy of creating and maintaining gardens for them and for permitting me to print some of the photographs in this book.

The following people have helped in a variety of ways, from reviewing chapters to offering suggestions or generously sharing their knowledge; one of the biggest pleasures of writing this book was getting to know and spend time with these people. Many thanks to: Allan Armitage, Elsa Bakalar, David Beattie, Leo Blanchette, Denny Blew, Allen Bush, Caroline Burgess, Art Cammeron, Rose Marie Casale, Arla Charmichael, Charles Cresson, Dr. Chuck Darrah (CLC Labs), Neil Diboll, Mike Epp, Galen Gates, Judy Glattstein, John Greenlee, Ed Higgins (Yoder Brothers), Dr. Harry Hoitink, Gerry Hood (Canadian Sphagnum Peat Growers), Roy Klehm and staff members Debbie Chalk and Maryann Metz, Mary-Beth Mahne, Ed McCoy, Sarah Price, Joanna Reed, Rita Riehle, David Schultz, Roger Seely, Holly Shimizu, Jim Super and the Kurtz Brothers staff, Nadean and Jeff Traylor, Rod Tyler, Susan Urshal, Mark Viette, and Van Wade.

CHAPTER 1

Design and Its Relationship to Maintenance

THE amount of maintenance a garden requires depends precisely on how the garden was designed or planned. The chosen setting, style, size, and shape of the garden as well as the plant selection, arrangement, and spacing all intertwine to determine the type of care needed. Questions to be asked before the design stage include: How much time and money can be devoted to the upkeep? Who is going to do the maintenance—the owner, a professional crew, or a combination of the two? Whoever is doing it, do they know how to care for the plants chosen? Even the best designed garden never lives up to what its creator visualized if it is poorly maintained.

There is no question that the planning stage of any perennial garden is thrilling; there are so many great plants from which to choose. The fact that many perennials require maintenance to one degree or another usually is overlooked at this stage, placed far away in the back of one's mind behind all the fantastic colors, cut bouquets, butterflies, fragrance, and other anticipated attractions. Such selective memory is not just the province of beginners; this thinking is true of my mindset as well when I'm planning gardens. Nonetheless, I don't feel that a garden should be planned solely around the premise of maintenance—this would be too limiting and inhibiting. I do believe in a balance, however, and this balance is going to be different for different people. For some, gardening 4 hours a week constitutes low maintenance; for others, anything over 30 minutes moves into the high-maintenance category. (Based on a 9-month period, I average 16 to 20 hours of gardening each month in my own gardens, which are about 4600 square feet—of course certain months see more work than others.) Still, some gardeners are willing to invest time for maintenance in the spring, but prefer a golf club or a tennis racket to a pair of pruners in the summer. Such preferences need to be considered during the planning stages. For practical purposes we'll make the "mid-maintenance" garden the one to strive for in this book. Even better, let's not think of it as maintenance but as *gardening!* How much gardening are you or your clients willing to do?

In this chapter I will present general points that should be considered when planning a garden. The following chapters offer more specifics on the ins and outs of the various aspects of planting and maintenance. See Section Three of this book, Encyclopedia of Perennials, for information on specific plants, as well as the extensive lists provided in the appendices to find out which plants are best for certain conditions and requirements.

THE SITE

Let's look at some aspects of a garden and how they relate to maintenance, starting with the site. Considerations such as contour of the land, conditions of the existing soil, light exposure, and moisture conditions fall under this category. Before thinking about personal objectives, such as garden style or color and plant preferences, you must recognize that the site directly affects all these variables. Unfortunately, the site is not always given this preferential treatment, I suppose because it isn't really a "fun" thing to think about. You might visualize a vibrantly colored perennial garden full of fragrant dianthus and perhaps bright red beebalm, when in actuality the site is too shady to support either of these plants or these bright colors (most shade-loving plants bloom in the soft pastel colors).

You need to take into account existing vegetation, buildings or structures, sun patterns, winds, soil conditions, and microclimates before you can start thinking about anything else. Are there trees that will compete with the perennials for moisture and sun? Is there an overhang on the house that will prevent rainfall or sun from reaching a 2- or 3-foot area of the garden? It's a waste of valuable resources to try to maintain moisture-loving plants in a dry location. Perennials such as *Epimedium*, *Lamium*, and *Symphytum grandiflorum* will compete with trees for moisture without requiring large amounts of supplemental watering. And the solution for moisture-blocking overhangs is to start the planting out from underneath the overhang, which can also provide a useful 2-ft. catwalk for maintenance along the back of the border. There are perennials suited for just about any location, so you simply need to make the correct choices.

Soil Conditions

What is the soil like where you want to plant the garden? Is it wet or dry? Clay or sand? Can organic matter be incorporated in the soil to improve the conditions and meet the needs of the plants you are interested in growing? Most perennials prefer a well-draining soil, and most garden sites need to be modified to meet this need. We all need to consider biodiversity when planning gardens. If you have a spot that is extremely wet or extremely dry, rather than trying to fight it by significantly changing the site to grow plants not suited to the natural conditions, why not grow plants that will take the conditions you have? Turn a wet clay area into a beautiful prairie or meadow full of plants native to those conditions. Neil Diboll of Prairie Nursery has an extensive list of natives that he refers to as "clay busters" (see Appendix C, list 3). A wooded setting would be a good spot for woodland natives. If you have an area that is constantly dry, select drought lovers. Remember that you can find perennials for almost any soil condition. I believe in using a variety of plantings—perennial gardens, herb gardens, mixed borders, and vegetable gardens, as well as areas devoted to prairies, meadows, and woodlands and a reduction in the amount of area devoted to turf. If you understand the natural growing condition of a plant, you can better understand the setting and the maintenance that suit it best. Do keep in mind, though, that when it comes to soil just about all plants, be they native or exotic, would prefer to have a soil high in organic matter for establishment and further growth. I discuss soil in detail in the next chapter, and I urge you to read this information before preparing your garden.

Light Conditions

How much sun does the proposed garden area receive? People are too often "in the dark" when it comes to this question. They think an area receives full sun when in actuality the area only receives sun in the late afternoon, which happens to be the time they are home from work. Most often people just haven't taken the time to think about light conditions. Sometimes they are simply deceived by sun-blocking trees or buildings. Whenever existing trees, buildings, and other structures or the angle of the house raise questions about the amount of light exposure, I have my clients observe what I call sun patterns, or I do so for them. This involves tracking sunlight on an area throughout an entire day. It is the only way to truly evaluate light conditions. Sometimes such a survey can uncover some pretty complex patterns, particularly in large gardens with existing scattered mature trees. I have seen cases where areas of a garden that are in full sun for a good part of the day are directly next to areas that are in shade for most of the day (Plate 33). It is also important to remember that 3 hours of cool morning sun are quite different from 3 hours of hot afternoon sun. To me, knowing the amount of sun an area receives is crucial in planning for the proper perennials for a site. If the wrong plant is selected for a shady area, it can lead to leggy plants that may not flower and will require pruning or staking for height control or support. In an overly sunny area, scorched plants might need pruning to remove damaged leaves or require more water in an effort to grow against the odds. All this means more maintenance than would have been necessary had the sun patterns been determined initially. It is best to evaluate the sun patterns during the growing season, as the angle of the sun in late autumn or winter is very different from the angle of the sun during the summer.

Other Factors To Keep in Mind

Winds also can be an important factor in considering a site. If your gardens are exposed to high winds, as some of mine are, tall perennials that are noted for not requiring staking may in fact need support in your windy site. *Boltonia asteroides* 'Snowbank' and *Rudbeckia nitida* 'Herbstsonne' are two such perennials that require staking or pruning in my gardens to keep them from falling over, while they are happy to stand on their own with no supplemental treatment in several of my clients' gardens.

You may be dealing with several different soil conditions and sun patterns in a single garden as well as a variety of microclimates. Learn which areas are sheltered and warmed by the morning sun, for instance, and which areas are frost traps that remain colder than others. The sheltered sites are great for experimenting with tender perennials that perhaps are not normally hardy to your growing zone. The known cold areas should be devoted to reliably hardy species.

When evaluating the site take note of heat pumps, air conditioners, and any other eyesores that need to be hidden. Take photographs to work with later while designing; pictures help you to avoid ignoring such considerations. They also make great "before" shots for record keeping and self-satisfaction to see your accomplishment, or as additions to a professional portfolio of client "before" and "afters" as you see in this book (see the color plate section).

Beds and Borders

Will you create a border or island bed? A border is a garden that is bordered by a wall, fence, or hedge; see Plates 12–20 for a variety of examples of border gardens. As I mentioned before, it is a good idea to leave a 2-ft. catwalk at the back of the border to assist with maintenance. Otherwise it can be difficult to reach the plants in the back, and these same plants often will lean over the shorter ones in front for light. Plants can also suffer from disease as a result of lack of air circulation in the back of the border. With the catwalk, an 8-ft.-wide border gives you 6 ft. of growing space that can easily be reached from either side of the bed, preventing excess compaction on any one side. The only problem is that 6 ft. isn't really much space when you start putting a garden together. So, as with many design "rules," this one is sometimes meant to be broken—but such rules do give the beginner a place from which to start. You will invariably step into your garden while working or cutting flowers anyway, so you might as well make the bed a bit wider. You can reduce the incidence of compaction by avoiding stepping on the bed while it's wet, or use small pieces of wood to step on and distribute your weight. I design small paths of stepping stones or mulch into large beds to assist with maintenance. You can also aerate the bed by light forking or hoeing if it has received a good deal of traffic.

The island bed—surrounded by lawn or maybe pavement (see Plates 11 and 49)—was popularized by English perennial aficionado Alan Bloom. Many gardeners have observed that plants grown in island beds are sturdier and less susceptible to disease because of more even sunlight and air movement. According to the "rules," an island is supposed to be three times as long as it is wide. So, for example, a 6-ft.-wide bed would be approximately 18 ft. long. For proportion the tallest plant in the center ideally should be one-half the width of the bed, so a 6-ft.-wide bed would have about a 3-ft. plant for its tallest inhabitant. Again, this gives you somewhere to start from, but have fun experimenting.

You may not have an area for either an island bed or a border, but the garden may be an area in a naturalized setting (an area of existing trees and native plants). Congratulations! Utilize that natural space for cultivated woodland perennials or introduce other natives or use a combination of the two. This is a garden style in itself (Plate 34).

It goes without saying that the larger the garden, the more time and effort is required for maintenance. Of course, a large garden can be very rewarding. It is easier to achieve a long season of interest in a large garden, and plenty of space allows you to follow many of the standard design principles, such as repetition and rhythm (see Plates 35–36). If you only have a small lot, you can overcome limitations by devoting the entire space to plants and do away with the lawn. Some of my favorite garden creations are no larger than 20 ft. × 20 ft. or 30 ft. × 16 ft. (Plates 21–24 and 37). Small gardens require more prudent plant selection. Each plant needs to provide a long season of interest to earn a place in a small garden.

My favorite garden style is a mixed border combining perennials with shrubs, disease-resistant shrub roses, vines, grasses, pockets of unusual annuals, bulbs (especially the small or minor bulbs), and small trees where appropriate (Plate

38). Utilize the entire space by planting in layers and using any vertical space available: bulbs tucked under shrubs, vines growing on walls or in shrubs for support, and early season perennials that can be cut back to make room for later bloomers are all good uses of space. Most of the gardens I design are not simply for visual beauty but are also for cutting, for attracting butterflies and birds, and for providing fragrance. After all, these are the garden experiences that most of us want. By utilizing a variety of plant materials and having a decent amount of space with which to work, I'm easily able to accomplish these goals.

Massed plantings (large amounts of a limited number of different species) are often billed as low maintenance. But this depends entirely on the species selected. The massed style can be rather boring and limiting and is not appropriate in every situation. It is also frequently misused. This style can be appropriate in a commercial setting, in large gardens with large beds, or for a site located far from the house or prime viewing area where larger masses are needed to carry the garden and provide proper scale (Plates 39–40).

SELECTING PLANTS

There are so many things to consider when selecting plants for the garden. Desirable traits include long flowering, attractive foliage, and low or lower maintenance. For many plants that are billed as long flowering, long flowering can only be achieved through deadheading or cutting back. The gardener must be willing to do this chore to extend the plants' season of interest.

Another point to consider when selecting plants is that when a perennial needs to be cut back in order to rebloom the plant will reflower at a shorter height than its original size. This trait can make possible interesting design combinations, pairing shorter plants with rebloomers during their second flush.

All too often we focus on flowers to the exclusion of other desirable qualities. When selecting plants, ask questions like: Does the plant have attractive foliage? Does it die down gracefully, easily hidden by other plants after its decline? Does it need to be cut back to maintain decent foliage? It is important to think about what the plant looks like through the entire growing season. Foliage may change to scarlet or yellow in autumn on some perennials, and on others the foliage will hold its summer color into the winter. Many plants simply need to be cut back once per season to maintain their attractive foliage. Others have foliage that is unattractive even with pruning. This needs to be considered at design time.

Maintenance Factors

Is the perennial low or rather "lower" maintenance? A number of variables determine what level of maintenance, high or low, a perennial will require. Regional differences in climate and soil conditions dramatically affect a plant's performance. For example, moonshine yarrow (*Achillea* 'Moonshine') may do beautifully in a northern garden but is considered high maintenance in a southern garden where it will melt out from the humidity. A perennial can be high maintenance in one area because it grows like a weed, while in another region it can be high maintenance because it languishes in the cold winters. Then there are those plants that are high or low maintenance no matter where they are grown. So the "higher" and "lower" maintenance designations (such as is provided in Appendix C, lists 4 and 5) should be considered general guidelines only.

To my dismay, the first perennials that a beginning gardener wants in his or her border, often because of gorgeous pictures seen in English perennial books, are high-maintenance "traditional" perennials, such as the giant Pacific hybrid delphiniums. These delphiniums, for instance, generally are not cold, wet, or heat hardy; they are subject to a long list of disease and insect problems; they need to be staked, thinned, deadheaded, and cutback for best performance; and they require summer fertilizing to maintain any vigor.

All perennials need some form of maintenance, and we would have a pretty short list of perennials from which to choose if we insisted that they possess all the characteristics of easy care. The typical lower maintenance perennial will have most (approximately four-fifths) of the following traits:

- Life span of 5 or more years
- Cold hardiness
- Heat, humidity, and moisture tolerance
- Doesn't require frequent division
- Doesn't require daily deadheading
- Doesn't require staking
- Insect and disease resistance or tolerance
- Doesn't require numerous prunings to maintain acceptable foliage or habit
- Not invasive
- Doesn't require heavy fertilizing

A perennial that lives 5 or more years is considered a long-lived perennial. Some perennials are tolerant of extreme cold temperatures but are killed by wet soil conditions over the winter. Likewise, many perennials tolerate heat well but can be weakened or killed by summer humidity. Silver-foliaged plants are particularly susceptible to high humidity and can rot.

Four years or more before division is needed is what to look for in a lower maintenance perennial. Some perennials don't ever need division and may even resent it.

Many *Coreopsis lanceolata* and *C. grandiflora* cultivars require daily dead-heading to look their best. To call this high maintenance is an understatement. A better selection would be the *C. verticillata* cultivars, particularly 'Moonbeam', which can be sheared once for continual bloom for most of the summer.

Staking is an unpopular aspect of perennial gardening and consequently it is often put off to the last minute, when it is usually too late. Select a lower growing cultivar if possible, or prune to reduce the need for staking. For example, *Gaura lindheimeri* 'Whirling Butterflies' would be a better choice than the straight species because it is more compact, and also because it is sterile so it doesn't reseed like the species type.

Perennials should be chosen that are resistant to disease and insects, or at least tolerant to the point that either they are not bothered to any great degree or they can be pruned to help recover from the problem rather than being sprayed. Spraying is an area where I will not compromise. I love gardening, but I hate spraying chemicals for pest control for many reasons. So I don't. I would rather do anything else as far as maintenance goes. This is an area where proper plant selection is critical.

If a plant requires cutting back more than once or twice a season to look its best (above and beyond normal spring or winter clean-up), it moves into the higher maintenance category. Some plants do best if cut back before flowering for height control. They may also require frequent deadheading. And then they may need cutting back once or twice to maintain a decent habit and to rebloom after flowering. This can involve a lot of work. You need to decide whether growing the plant is worth the extra work.

Perennials that need heavy feeding and a supply of supplemental nutrients through the season means additional maintenance. A rich, high-organic soil and possibly a light spring fertilization is all that most perennials require.

An invasive plant can take over the world (or at least the garden) before you know it! Or at least it can seem that way when your *Monarda*, a cute single-stemmed 4-in. plant, spreads by underground stems to fill a space 4 ft. × 4 ft. in your garden, devouring everything in its path. Certain species, such as *Valeriana officinalis*, become invasive because of prolific reseeding. Timely deadheading can help prevent reseeding, but if this has been missed just once, populations can quickly get out of control. A great amount of time is often required to keep invasive species managed either by lifting seedlings or by digging out pieces of the expanding clump. Unless you enjoy that kind of thing, use invasive species with caution.

MAKING PLANTS "FIT"

Having considered the site and the types of plants you want to incorporate in the perennial garden, you now need to look at the arrangement and spacing of the plants. Proper spacing of perennials can be hard to determine even for the experienced designer. Even when you think you have it all just right, one plant grows larger than anticipated and another stays small, so at one time or another something is too close and something else a bit too far away. This is just the way of nature. Knowing the ultimate width of any perennials you want to use in your design is crucial to planning. One recommendation is to plant perennials in drifts or groups using odd numbers, preferably with at least three of a kind of a single species. (Planting in groups of odd numbers is based on the concept of "Unity of Three," as visually the eye will tend to draw a line between or divide even-numbered groupings of plants.) For genera like *Monarda*, however, using many plants together may mean you and your family moving out of your home to give your beebalm the space it will need. Even the lovely lady's mantle (*Alchemilla mollis*) can alarm the new gardener when its tiny two leaves turn into a 2-ft.-wide clump within a few years—normally a single plant repeated in several spots along a border is more pleasing than a group of three plants that would cover a 6 ft. × 6 ft. area (see Plate 67).

I always keep the ultimate size of a plant in mind when designing, but I also space plants rather close to reduce weed competition and to produce the lush, full style I prefer within a short period of time. Closer spacing can require more maintenance in the long term in the form of pruning or transplanting (which I find more appealing than weeding) because plants may need to be trimmed to stay in their own space, or they may eventually need to be thinned or moved to maintain proper proportions—but results usually make it worth the effort.

It is hard to give specifics on spacing because of the many variables, such as initial plant size, regional differences, soil conditions, and so on. As a general guideline, small plants (under 1 ft. tall) or plants at the front of the border should be spaced 8 to 12 in. apart. Intermediate-sized plants (1 to 2½ ft. tall) are best spaced 15 to 24 in. apart. Spacing of 15 in. seems to work best for the majority of perennials, including *Coreopsis*, *Salvia*, *Veronica*, and so forth. I usually start the plants off in 1-quart containers (4¼-in.-pots). When starting with gallon sizes I space similar species at 18 in. Larger growing plants such as *Baptisia*, *Monarda*, ornamental grasses, and others I space 2 to 3 ft. apart. With *Baptisia* and *Monarda* I use single plants, giving them 2 or 3 ft. of space, and then repeat them elsewhere in the border if appropriate.

When designing you need to know the square footage of area your drift will cover. (I normally design on quarter-inch graph paper, with the scale ¼ in. = 1 ft, and then I can count the number of squares per drift to determine the square footage.) Once the square footage of area is determined you can calculate the number of plants needed for that area by multiplying the area by the number of plants per square foot—that is, number of plants needed = square footage of area to be covered × number of plants per square foot. The following chart shows the number of plants per square foot for a given spacing.

SPACING	# OF PLANTS PER SQ. FT.
12 in.	1.0
15 in.	0.64
18 in.	0.45
24 in.	0.25
36 in.	0.11

For example: to space plants 18 in. apart in an area of 7 sq. ft. would require 3 plants (7 sq. ft. of area × 0.45 plants per sq. ft. = 3 plants).

Now that you have taken the time to design an award-winning garden, take the time to properly prepare the soil, plant the perennials, and maintain the garden by reading the rest of the story presented in the following chapters. Good luck!

CHAPTER 2

Bed Preparation: Insurance for Success

WHILE factors such as garden size, design, light exposure, and plant hardiness are undeniably important in preparing your garden for perennials, time spent properly preparing the planting bed is equally vital to the continuing health of your plants and is the key to reducing future maintenance. A perennial growing in a healthy, nutritious soil will require less fertilizer and it will be less stressed, thereby improving its ability to fend off attacks from disease and pests. Of course, some perennials can be temperamental and require coddling. Even if we do everything right and follow all the rules, we still lose them.

Research has indicated that about eighty percent of all plant problems are related to poor soil (Patterson et al. 1980). It is a waste of time, money, and valuable natural resources to try to "Band-Aid" an ailing plant by using a variety of chemical fertilizers and/or pesticides. Usually the problem could have been avoided initially by incorporating the proper amounts of organic matter and other soil amendments to provide additional nutrients and to alter the properties of the soil, which increases the availability of air and water to the plant.

Perennials can double or even triple in size in the first season if the beds in which they are growing are correctly prepared with sufficient organic matter (see Plates 16–20). Unfortunately this critical step in the garden/landscape building process is often overlooked and given a lower priority than other tasks. Creating good soil is hard work, to be sure, and it will not win any popularity contests when challenged against the joy of selecting which plants to use, or colors to combine, or all the other glamorous aspects of creating a garden. If you are an industry professional, you may need to take the time to educate your clients on the importance of investing in proper soil preparation. The most critical time to have good soil is while the plants are establishing themselves.

If possible, beds are best prepared in the autumn so that the new bed goes through the freeze-thaw cycles of winter to create a more structured, friable soil. I don't have this luxury in my business because we are so busy and people usually want as much done as possible when we are installing a garden in the autumn. One of my preferred approaches is to prepare the beds and plant the woody plants in autumn, come back the following spring to lightly re-till the bed, if needed, and then plant the perennials.

In this chapter I am going to discuss soil (not dirt) requirements for perennial gardens in general. As always, we must remember the axiom "right plant for right place." Some perennials will tolerate poor clay soils, while others thrive in dry sandy soils (see Appendix C, lists 1–3). The preparation process starts by determining the existing soil conditions. But, as I hope to make clear, we gardeners can improve on existing conditions to enable us to grow a much wider palette of plants, including many that may not be ideal for the original soil type.

Native plants are not to be overlooked in the selection process, as many outstanding species can tolerate a wide variety of less-than-ideal soil conditions. Yet, even for most of the natives, some bed preparation is beneficial if not vital to establishment.

KEY STEPS TO BED PREPARATION

A few basic steps should be followed to ensure successful bed preparation. Let's look at some key elements: (1) testing the soil; (2) eliminating perennial weeds; (3) making sure the soil drains well, yet is able to hold water and nutrients; (4) providing sufficient organic matter in the soil; (5) adding supplemental fertilizer if the soil does not have ample phosphorus—a key nutrient for perennial plant establishment.

Testing the Soil

Testing of the soil is a step all too often ignored. I have become a firm believer in testing soil having worked with a variety of different sites for clients. It is the only way to effectively determine what soil conditions you are starting with. Experts say that in the United States alone there are approximately 15,000 different soil types. Soil should be tested to determine soil type (Is the soil a clay, a sand, silt, loam, or a combination of these?), pH (level of acidity or alkalinity), organic matter content, and available phosphate and potash.

You can test the soil yourself using soil testing kits, or send it to soil testing labs, or to your county cooperative extension agency. These services can run various tests on your existing soil as well as on your chosen soil amendment, and they will make recommendations. It is also helpful to perform soil tests after the beds have been modified so that you can see the results.

The Perennial Plant Association (PPA) provides the following standards for perennial garden soils (these figures are the *minimum* for an amended soil): pH of 5.5–6.5, organic matter content of 5% (by weight), 50 pounds per acre (25 parts per million) available phosphate, and 120 pounds per acre (60 parts per million) available potash. I generally work with soils that are high in clay and low in organic matter (1–3%), which I find analogous to working with concrete. Most of us are working with problematic, disturbed urban soils, hence the importance of amending the soils properly.

Soil pH

I find that perennials tend to be rather flexible when it comes to soil pH. In central Ohio the pH is neutral to alkaline, about pH 7–7.8. (A pH of 7 is neutral; anything higher is alkaline and anything lower indicates acidity.) I never attempt to lower the pH to accommodate acid-loving perennials or to raise it for alkaline lovers. I have good success with both types as long as the other requirements are met—most critically, sufficient moisture in summer and good drainage in winter. Only if you are doing everything else right and yet are still having trouble growing acid- or alkaline-loving plants should you consider altering the soil pH to succeed with any particular plant. Lime can be used to increase soil pH and sulfur to decrease pH; the type and quantity needed to increase or decrease soil pH will be determined by your soil type. Refer to your soil test for pH recommendations.

A few perennials that prefer slightly acidic soil include *Iris ensata*, *Kirengeshoma palmata*, and *Asclepias tuberosa*; *Asclepias tuberosa* can have problems if the pH is above 6.5. *Dianthus*, *Gypsophila paniculata*, and *Lavandula* as well as most silver-foliaged plants are examples of perennials that prefer alkaline soil.

Eliminating Perennial Weeds

Get rid of perennial weeds *before* you plant a garden full of desirable perennials— it will certainly make your life more enjoyable. Eradicating weeds is the one instance in which I will resort to the use of chemicals. When working with grassed areas that are to be turned into gardens or existing gardens full of weeds and undesirable plants, I apply glyphosate (Round-up; another option might be Finale) to new planting areas. Glyphosate is a nonselective, nonresidual herbicide that is systemic in its action (meaning it must come in contact with the shoots of the plant and then travels to its roots), so it is best applied when the plants are actively growing and when temperatures are above 50°F. I usually apply glyphosate in early April in Ohio for spring installations. I outline the shape of the new bed using a garden hose or a heavy-duty electric extension cord (which is lighter weight and more flexible than hose), and then spray within the outlined area to get the correct shape (Plate 25). After waiting about 14 days to be certain all perennial weeds are killed, I go into the area and rototill directly through the dead vegetation, if it is not too heavy. (Seven days is the typical manufacturer's recommendation if the weeds are annuals and/or grasses.) Sometimes a good number of aggressive weeds are not destroyed by the first spraying and so it is necessary to come back for several additional sprayings to ensure that they have been killed. This step is not one you want to rush, or else you will be fighting with those weeds for the rest of your life or the life of the garden.

If you do not want to use chemicals, you can cover the bed area with several layers of moistened newspaper and mulch or other lightblocking material such as black plastic. Then wait, perhaps up to 6 months depending on the conditions, for the weeds to be destroyed.

Well-Draining Soil

More perennials are killed by wet overwintering conditions than by actual cold winter temperatures. This is why well-draining soil is essential for perennials. Part of the research for my master's degree focused on the cold hardiness of herbaceous perennials. Most of the species I studied were able to tolerate low temperatures when everything else was constant, but these same species did not survive in the field studies when exposed to excess moisture and/or fluctuating soil temperatures. Perennials can simply rot during the winter if the soil is not properly drained, and this is often mistakenly attributed to cold temperatures, labeling them "not hardy." Yes, they are not hardy—but to excessive moisture.

Perhaps you are one of the chosen few who has that perfect soil for perennials—a fertile loam that is well draining but also retains adequate moisture. If so, I am envious of you and wish you happy gardening! But most of us are not so blessed. My own soil and most of the soil I work with for clients is very poorly drained. Soil texture (clay, silt, sand, loam) can be an indication of what kind of soil drainage you have. Sandy soils are sometimes too well drained, requiring constant watering. On the other hand, if puddles tend to stick around for more than half a day following a rain, or if your soil is constantly soggy, you can be sure that you have a drainage problem (and probably lots of clay). Most of you probably know your soil type and are not happy with it. (If you're not sure of your soil type, you can run a drainage test, as described below.) In any event, let's discuss how to improve the drainage of your clay soil or to increase the moisture retention of your sandy soil.

To ensure a well-draining soil, avoid low-lying areas. Add organic matter to the beds at the rate of approximately one-third by volume, or 4 in. per 12 in. of soil—this will also improve moisture and nutrient retention in sandy soils. (I will discuss organic matter in greater depth later in the chapter, as it is so vital for all soils.) Creating a slightly raised bed will increase the gravitational pull of water down through the bed.

Drainage tiles may be needed in some cases to improve drainage, but this should be considered only after you have considered all other factors. I have seen isolated instances where the compaction of the subsoil during construction of the home was so extensive that no matter what bed preparation was done, drainage tiles were still necessary to improve drainage. Tiles can be expensive and will often clog if not properly installed, so they are best used only as a last resort.

After preparing the beds you can check whether you have achieved proper drainage by performing a percolation test. Dig a 12-in.-diameter hole the depth of the amended area. Fill with water and let drain. Fill with water again. This water should drain in less than one hour. If it does not, drainage needs to be improved either with further soil preparation or with tiles.

Organic Matter

If you remember only one thing from this discussion of soil preparation for perennials, I hope it will be the importance of adding organic matter to the beds in sufficient amounts and to sufficient depths. Organic matter improves the physical, chemical, and biological properties of the soil. Research has shown that the application of organic matter can increase plant growth by anywhere from 20 to 100% while maintaining higher than average survival rates. This has not only been shown in landscape settings but has been verified in field research (Smith and Treaster 1990). The main focus in preparing soils for perennials should be improving soil structure. In clay soils organic matter creates structure and increases air space. In sandy soils it increases moisture and nutrient retention, reducing leaching. Organic matter also increases the availability of all necessary nutrients and it increases the microbial and earthworm populations, which truly create a living, or biologically active, soil. Research throughout the United States has shown that most composts, if applied properly and at recommended rates, can reduce the incidence of many soil-borne diseases. This is due to the ability of composts to support beneficial microbes that suppress disease-carrying microbes. Finally, high levels of organic matter in the soil can reduce compaction and erosion and can buffer against toxic substances present in some soils.

The type of organic matter to use depends on soil type, local availability, economics, practicality of application, and personal preference. It is important to know the nutrient content of the organic matter. Any organic amendments should be tested before use. If you obtain compost from a soil company, the company should provide information on the nutrient content, pH, percentage organic matter, soluble salts, and heavy metal content (if applicable). If they don't offer this information, I urge you to request a test to be run, because not all soil amendments are the same. Soil companies also will usually provide recommended application rates for their product; it is advisable to follow them. The higher the organic matter content of the material, the higher its soil conditioning properties. For composts with a high nutrient content, over-application of the product can injure or kill the plants. Work with your compost supplier to find the best product and to help determine the proper rate.

Keep in mind, too, that warm temperatures and microbial activity are responsible for the release of nutrients, so in cool weather a small application of a quick-release complete fertilizer may be needed at planting. Incorporating fertilizer at bed preparation is discussed at greater length later in the chapter.

Organic amendments should be free of weeds, insects, diseases, and foreign material. I had the unfortunate experience of buying a compost that was full of weed seeds on one of my jobs. When the seeds began to sprout, well after planting, correcting the problem entailed having the weeds analyzed first to find out if they were annual or perennial (a key concern in this brand-new and large perennial planting), then trying to have the company stand behind its product while satisfying the client at the same time. Definitely something to avoid if at all possible—know your source.

As I mentioned earlier, you can mix some of the soil amendment with your existing soil (at the proper proportions) and have the mixture tested by a soil testing lab for very specific, and accurate, recommendations.

Types of Soil Amendments

There are many different types of organic soil amendments from which to choose. Again, what you choose will depend greatly on what is locally available. I will share with you what is generally available in my area for landscapers and gardeners. I will also indicate the approximate nutrient analyses of these particular amendments. Remember, always test your own! I will not discuss the raw ingredients for various composts—e.g. leaves, grass clippings, sawdust, raw manure, hay, etc.—as these materials should be composted first before being added to the perennial garden. Adding uncomposted material can rob nitrogen from the soil and starve your plants for a year or more.

Leaf humus. Supplies a wide range of essential plant nutrients. One leaf humus product that is available to me is about 38–43% organic and has pH 7.7, with a nutrient analysis of 1.0-0.4-0.5, referring to the percentage nitrogen, phosphorus, and potassium (N-P-K) by weight. Keep in mind that oak leaves are acidic and maple leaves are more alkaline, so the incorporation of either in your humus will affect the pH of the material.

Canadian sphagnum peat moss. Very low nutrient providing (less than 1% N); acidic, pH about 4. Canadian sphagnum peat moss is excellent for improving aeration of clay soils to increase drainage, and it improves the ability of sandy soils to hold water and nutrients. It is sterile and weed free. When used in combination with compost it helps reduce compaction that can sometimes occur when compost is used alone. Depending on the climate, peat can take several years to break down in the soil, as compared to composts, which can be partially broken down within months, and manures, which break down in several weeks. Canadian sphagnum peat moss, which grows at fifty times the rate at which it is harvested, has proven to be a sustainable resource. Its use is environmentally sound.

Sphagnum peat moss should not be confused with the dark black peat (muck soil) often sold and used like topsoil. Dark black peat is so far along in its decomposition that it does little to improve the structure of the soil. You want the bales of sphagnum peat, not the bags of muck peat.

Composted biosolids. The fancy "cocktail party" name for composted municipal sewage sludge. Composted biosolids can improve the physical structure of soil by increasing drainage, aeration, and moisture retention. It also recharges soil with microbial life. Sewage sludge is composted with different bulking agents, so again there will be differences in products from different sources. The one I use is composted with hardwood chips; others might be bulked with sawdust or other bulking materials. The pH is slightly above neutral, averaging pH 7.3–7.6, and the organic content is 56–72%. It contains a well-balanced macro- and micronutrient content (1.0–1.5% N, 0.4–2.0% P, 0.2–0.4% K) in organic forms, so the nutrients are released slowly over time and thus with no concern for burn, assuming the material has been applied at the recommended rates. Within the first year after application approximately 25% of the nitrogen is released, 10% in the second and third years, and 5% in the fourth and fifth years; during the first year approximately 30% of the phosphorus and 70% of the potassium are available (Tyler 1996). Because compost is high in phosphorus, supplemental phosphorus fertilizer might not be needed at bed preparation, depending on the quantity of composted biosolids used and the quantity of phosphorus present in native soil. Composted biosolids also supply good levels of calcium, magnesium, zinc, iron, and copper.

Because of the varying composition of composts from different sources, I want to re-emphasize the importance of requesting tests for nutrient content, pH level, and levels of soluble salts. Heavy metals, fecal pathogens, and parasites must be strictly controlled at all composting locations; detailed studies have shown that these factors do not pose a concern under existing regulations. Your supplier can provide you with information on these as well as on nutrient content, percent organic matter, and recommended application rates. Again, follow these recommended rates, because over-application of compost can lead to many other problems.

Research by Dr. Elton Smith of The Ohio State University shows a 29% increase in dry weight of perennials when grown in soils amended with composted biosolids (Smith and Treaster 1991). Research at the University of Florida shows a reduced occurrence of soil-borne diseases in beans and tomatoes grown in soil amended with composted biosolids. Composted biosolids have also been shown to help suppress disease in turf.

We as gardeners, landscape and horticulture professionals, and general stewards of the land have a commitment to our environment to utilize these alternatives for waste recycling.

Mushroom compost. A byproduct from mushroom production is another good amendment for improving soil properties. One available to me is a combination of steam-sterilized horse manure, sphagnum peat moss, brewer's grain, lime, and gypsum. It contains about 60% organic matter and has a pH of 7.8–8.2. High in nutrients, mushroom compost has a N-P-K content of 1.5-0.75-1.5, and it also supplies calcium. This is just one recipe, and not a common one at that. As always, request an analysis of the available product, including soluble salts, which can be high, and information about how it is processed. Not all products are the same.

Bark composts. Low-nutrient providing, often used to improve the structure of soils. Bark compost material composed of large, coarse particles up to $2\frac{1}{2}$ in. in size will help loosen heavy clay soils. Finer particles help bind sandy soils. Make sure it is composted, or you will need to add supplemental nitrogen. Research by Dr. Harry Hoitink at The Ohio State University has shown that hardwood bark compost can naturally suppress root rots, *Fusarium* wilts, and some nematode infections (Hoitink et al. 1995). The soil must be well draining in order for disease suppression to be effective.

Composted manure. A valuable source of major nutrients, trace elements, and large populations of bacteria—the bacteria can help convert organic material into humus. It's imperative that the manure has been composted to temperatures high enough to kill weed seeds, or major problems will arise. And all manure is not created equal, with chicken, horse, cow, swine, and sheep all offering varying levels of nutrients. Conditioning properties will depend on the animal source and on the bedding material used. Horse manure with straw bedding, which is high in fiber, helps hold clay particles apart. Users of cow manure swear by it, claiming that the nutrients are more readily available to the plants than in other manures.

Compost. This catch-all category includes homemade composts or commercial composts from mixed yard wastes. Composts of yard wastes are critical not only to our gardens but to our world. We are all aware of the environmental problem of solid waste. Anytime we deadhead, prune, rake leaves, or collect and bag grass clippings and throw them away, we contribute to this terrible problem. I was astounded to find that the U.S. Environmental Protection Agency estimates from 1993 show that 80% of the compostable yard waste generated (26.3 million tons) is occupying our landfills. Several states have enacted legislation banning yard waste from landfills. The time is here—composting is a must. All gardeners and industry professionals must support this action by composting and by utilizing commercially available composts of yard wastes. Many soil companies and city landfills will take yard waste at no charge and transport it to composting facilities for processing. You can contact your local EPA office or cooperative extension office for composting guidelines.

Composts offer all the benefits mentioned for organic matter in general: wonderful soil conditioning, nutrient and microbial enriching, and disease suppression. As with all soil amendments, knowing what a particular compost is made of and how it was composted is essential. What are its levels of nutrients? (The N-P-K nutrient analysis can range anywhere from less than 0.5-0.5-0.5 to 4-4-4.) Nutrient imbalances can exist in composts; for example, low levels of nitrogen are found in composts made from sources high in carbon, such as woody materials or leaves. But there can be significant differences in organic matter content with different types of compost, and one cannot truly know the benefits or shortcomings of a given compost without test results, finding out the same criticals as with the other amendments—organic matter content, nutrient content and availability, pH, and source. Remember that the organic matter content of compost affects its soil conditioning abilities. These variables also can affect the recommended rates of application of the material.

Topsoil. Many people think bringing in some topsoil and dumping it on the garden-to-be is the solution to providing "good" soil for their plants. It is not. There is no practical definition of topsoil and there are no government or trade standards that a topsoil provider must meet. Technically speaking, topsoil is the first 2 in. of the ground. This 2 in. may be fertile soil or it may not, depending on the location. Topsoil can be low in organic matter and nutrients. If used by itself, topsoil may do little if anything to improve the soil. Sometimes it can take ten yards of topsoil to equal the benefits in one yard of a composted material. Topsoil also can have the further disadvantage of containing weed seeds and herbicide or pesticide residues if it was scraped off farm fields. It is important to know your supplier and to ask for an analysis of the topsoil you buy.

Topsoil with a high organic matter content can be useful in blends with other organic materials where it serves as a stabilizer in otherwise light soil mixes. Other times it can be used independently as the base soil in raised planters to be "topped off" with a 6- to 8-in. layer of a good organic soil blend.

Gypsum. Gypsum, or calcium sulfate, is a commonly used soil conditioner for clay soils. It helps improve the structure of only certain types of clay soils found in the western United States. It does little or nothing to improve soils in the Midwest or East. It can aid in the removal of salt (sodium chloride) from soils.

Sand. Another questionable soil amendment depending on your soil texture. Without delving into the soil triangle from old agronomy class days, I'll try to explain. If you have a soil that is already fairly high in sand, incorporating additional sand in the soil can improve it by moving your existing soil into another textural class—say, that of a sandy loam. But if you are working with a soil low in sand, such as a clay or clay-loam soil, adding a little bit of sand will make matters worse. In this texture of soil 6 to 8 in. (30% or more by volume) of a *very coarse* sand would be needed to improve your soil. Most people are not willing to add that much sand to their soils.

Aggregates. Other coarse soil-amendment products are occasionally used in perennial gardens to improve the aeration of heavy clay soils. Perlite, grower's grit (crushed limestone used in the agricultural industry as chicken feed), ceramics, fired-clay materials such as crushed brick, and fine gravels are a few such soil amendments that are available.

Variety seems to be the spice of an amended soil's life. Due to the variety of plants we use with a variety of different needs, using a mixture of different organic amendments is most beneficial. You can see from the preceding discussion that each amendment has a little something special of its own to offer. Mixing different soil amendments gives us a bit of the best of all of them.

Fertilizer at Bed Preparation

The fertilizer added at bed preparation should be based on soil tests and on the nutrient level of the organic matter amendment. If the organic matter is high enough in the required elements, additional fertilizer at bed preparation might not be needed—another good reason to have your mixture of soil and amendments tested. Phosphorus is the key nutrient in perennial garden establishment, due in part to its role in root establishment and flowering. Phosphorus levels can be high in some organic amendments. Care should be taken to not get too high a phosphorus level, which makes other elements such as zinc and iron unavailable. (You're usually safe if using an organic amendment like composted biosolids, which are high in phosphorus but also high in zinc, iron, and magnesium so they are not tied up due to high phosphorus.) Because nutrients in organic matter are slow release and depend on moisture and warmth for release by microbial activity, fertilizer can be beneficial in cool-weather installations to ensure a good start even if the organic matter contains sufficient quantities of nutrients. Fertilizer must be worked into the soil because phosphorus is immobile in the soil. I prefer to till fertilizer into the beds.

In general, the fertilizer recommended for bed preparation is 2 lb superphosphate (0-20-0) and 2 lb 5-10-5 per 100 sq. ft. of bed. If you use a fertilizer with a rate other than 5-10-5, calculate amounts so that you add one pound of nitrogen per 1000 sq. ft. of bed space. (Since the N-P-K analysis refers to percent by weight, 2 lb of 5-10-5 fertilizer contains 0.1 lb of nitrogen, which is appropriate for 100 sq. ft.)

Many fertilizers that are used in organic gardening can be used for bed preparation. I won't get into a detailed discussion here of the various types, but I will mention a few with which I have experimented. Cottonseed meal supplies nitrogen and is also acidifying in its action. Soft phosphate or rock phosphate (in acidic soils) supplies phosphorus as well as 23 micronutrients and won't burn roots. Green sand, which is marine potash, supplies 5 to 6 micronutrients and acts as a catalyst to release the nitrogen in the cottonseed meal. Application rates for these materials should be based on a soil test, with consideration for the type of organic soil amendments used, and on recommendations from your local county extension office.

BED PREPARATION TECHNIQUES

Once you determine your soil type and what materials need to be added, it is time to prepare the bed for planting. As stated earlier, adding 4 in. of organic matter per 12 in. depth of soil is ideal. It is important to work the organic matter into the beds as deeply as is practically possible. The plants will root more deeply, thus improving their tolerance to drought and to cold and fluctuating temperatures. Organic matter also breaks down more slowly when incorporated into the soil, so the benefits are longer lasting than if it were just spread on top of the soil.

Double digging is often recommended for preparing a new perennial bed. If you haven't heard of this back-breaking technique, count your blessings. It involves removing 12 in. of soil, amending the subsoil with organic matter to an additional 6 in. deep, amending the removed topsoil, and then returning the amended topsoil to the bed. Double digging is said to be wonderful for the soil; I'm not so sure of the consequences to the digger. I can't think of its practical application for almost any circumstance, and I can't understand how this historical English bed preparation technique has gained so much popularity in modern references. Actually, I never witnessed double digging while I was working in England and Europe for 2 years. Everyone should try it once—at least that's what I used to tell my Ohio State University horticulture students. In the perennials lab I would have the students help me double dig beds in the university's arboretum. I'm sure it prompted a few to change majors. And in fact, I never noticed any differences in the plants' performance in those beds as compared to the ones that were rototilled.

I usually don't go the ideal 12 in. deep when preparing beds. I am able to work down 8 to 9 in. with a rototiller, which for practical purposes is what I do with my business. Only in the rare cases where we are renovating a perennial bed, and the beds had been worked and amended in previous years by the client, have we been able to till 12 in. deep. I have had great success with tilling to these shallower depths and still adding 4 in. of organic amendments, which also serves to provide slightly raised beds. Going only 8 or 9 in. deep means organic matter is being added at approximately 50% by volume.

Adding the soil amendments is the most labor-intensive part of installation. First we till the existing soil, then we start adding our different amendments one at a time, re-tilling and blending these in with the existing soil. We make several runs over the beds, working to greater depths and blending each time until it is workable and ready for planting. The amendments are raked and leveled on the beds, with a final leveling with rakes when all the tilling is done. By the time the whole process is complete, it's like planting in chocolate pudding—truly a treat.

Wheelbarrows are usually sufficient for transporting the soil amendments to the beds. Construction equipment (such as Bobcats) is required only with very large amounts of organic amendments or when there are long distances to travel. Heavy equipment like Bobcats can create compaction in the garden.

Care must be taken to not create a cleavage point where the good soil meets the poor existing subsoil, or a hardpan (a hardened or cemented soil layer) can develop. I generally do not experience this problem, but in cases where the tiller can't penetrate the existing soil, sometimes the subsoil must first be worked up by hand using shovels and forks. Then you can get through it with the tillers. I have heard of cases where companies come in with a back hoe to loosen the existing compacted subsoil, then the soil is worked in by hand and with tillers to incorporate soil amendments and ensure organic matter to a greater depth in the soil. Sometimes the existing soil is removed completely from the site and new soil and organic matter is brought in. Very seldom do I have to do this even in our poor clay soils. If this method is used, it is still important to make sure there is not a point at which the new soil meets with a hard layer of poor compacted subsoil.

The soil should be dry before you try to work it, but not too dry, as either too wet or too dry conditions can damage the soil structure. Scheduling installations around the weather is always a challenge in the spring and autumn seasons. I won't work in the beds if they are too wet from a previous day's rain. Not only does it further damage the structure of the soil, but it also increases labor time. If the bed is just slightly too wet, adding sphagnum peat moss first will help absorb some excess moisture and will make the beds workable. It is also important to stay off of the beds as much as possible after preparation, especially if the soil is moist, to avoid compaction. Walk around the outside of the beds or stay on the designated maintenance/access paths, if possible.

The soil is said to have sufficient organic matter when you can work it with your hands. An abundance of earthworms is also a sign that the organic matter content is good. Our amended beds generally test out to approximately 16–18% organic matter, improved from the original 2–3% of the native soil. Remember, the PPA recommendation is a minimum of 5% organic matter. Most authorities say 6–8% is good for increased perennial plant growth. I have had great success with this higher amount of organic matter for both plant establishment and growth in later years. I find that it is about 4 to 5 years before I need to start adding more organic matter to the soil. But a word of caution: if you get above 20% organic matter, you are really working with what is considered more of a container mix, and your watering practices need to be monitored. You could be back to an excessively moist soil due to the excess organic matter.

Some horticultural references suggest adding as much compost as you can get your hands on. This is unfounded advice—too much of a good thing is still too much. Too much organic matter can cause soil to become spongy. Also, excess quantities of certain composts can lead to increased disease and insect problems, and even death of the plants. From a business and economical view, the law of diminishing returns comes into play as well.

Calculating Amounts of Needed Amendments

Adding the proper 4 in. of organic matter (30% by volume) requires a little of what I call "perennial gardener's math." It's no use to look at an area and guesstimate how much organic matter to use—after 20 years of working in the industry I wouldn't trust myself to do it. Proper calculation helps ensure accuracy and takes little time. On landscape installations, where efficiency is profit, the proper amount of material must be ordered from your supplier. In most circumstances you are not able to walk over to a compost pile and get more organic matter when you need it.

To accurately calculate the amount of organic matter required you will need to know the square footage of your bed. Square footage is determined by multiplying length by width. If you have an irregularly shaped bed, it is helpful to sketch it out on some type of grid paper (as discussed in Chapter 1) so you can add up the grids to get your square footage. Following is an example of how I calculate the soil amendment needed for a 100-sq.-ft. (10 ft. × 10 ft.) bed. In this example I am incorporating 2 in. (or 0.166 ft.) of compost and 2 in. of sphagnum peat moss to get my 4 in. of needed amendments.

2 in. (0.166 ft.) of compost per 100 sq. ft. of bed =
0.166 ft. × 100 sq. ft. = 16 cubic feet

Then, to calculate the amount of compost needed in cubic-yard units, divide by 27 cubic feet (1 cu. yd.):

16 cu. ft. ÷ 27 cu. ft. = 0.6 cubic yards

In this case I would go ahead and bump up my estimate and bring in one cubic yard of compost.

2 in. (0.166 ft.) of sphagnum peat moss per 100 sq. ft. of bed =
0.166 ft. × 100 sq. ft. = 16 cu. ft.

Then divide by 4 cu. ft. to determine the number of 4-cu.-ft. bales of peat needed to cover the 16-cu.-ft. area:

16 cu. ft. ÷ 4 cu. ft. = four 4-cu.-ft. bales

The total cubic footage can also be divided by 6 cu. ft. because a 4-cu.-ft. bale of peat moss is compressed and can actually cover 6 to 8 cu. ft. Depending on how poor the soil is, I make my calculations based on 6-cu.-ft. coverage, so in this example I would use 2½ or 3 bales of peat.

You can see that an area as small as 100 sq. ft. requires quite a bit of soil amendment—one cubic yard of compost and a minimum of two-and-a-half to three 4-cu.-ft. bales of Canadian sphagnum peat moss. An eyeball estimate for such an area probably would come up short of the actual organic matter needs, leaving the gardener wondering why the perennials didn't flourish despite the amendments to the new bed.

If you are amending several beds at one time and working with many yards of soil, keeping track of the number of wheelbarrow loads of soil that have been added is helpful for ensuring that the appropriate amount is incorporated in each bed. Approximately 4½ *heaping* 6-cu.-ft.-capacity wheelbarrows make one cubic yard.

After adding the calculated amount of needed amendments, I then use gardener's intuition, observing, feeling, working, and smelling the soil to determine if the beds are ready for planting. More organic matter may still be needed before the soil has the correct texture. In most situations, however, with the proper initial soil calculations, the gardens are ready to go.

Soil "Recipe" for Success

Different people swear by many different soil "recipes." I will share the formula that I have used with great success in my own business, Horticultural Classics & Consultations. The perennials double or triple in size in their first year using these amendments and techniques. Hopefully the photographs of our jobs in this book speak for themselves. (Keep in mind, however, that my technique might not be appropriate for you, as soil conditions vary.)

Horticultural Classics & Consultations "Secret Recipe"
compost blend: 2 in.
sphagnum peat moss: 2 in.
8-32-16 fertilizer: 1¼ lb per 100 sq. ft.

Our compost blend is a combination of one-third leaf humus, one-third composted biosolids, and one-third soil. The soil portion contains a small percentage of composted yard waste and has a 5% organic matter content. The 8-32-16 nutrient analysis for the fertilizer (wheat starter fertilizer) is based on soil tests that were done on beds after preparing them without adding any fertilizer to determine if there were deficiencies. I do believe that no matter how scientific and calculated we get with our soils, there is still something "magical" happening over which we have no control. I have been very happy with the results of our soil preparation techniques, but I am always looking at new methods and materials that may be better from the horticultural or economic perspective. I have tried many different soil amendments and am happiest with the above combination. I encourage you to experiment and find out what works best for you. After all, much of the fun of gardening is experimentation.

I hope this chapter has given you a better awareness of the importance of proper soil preparation—otherwise I haven't accomplished my goal. To summarize the steps of this fundamental element in perennial garden success:

- Test the soil.
- Outline the area with a garden hose and spray with a nonselective, non-residual herbicide such as Round-up. Wait 14 days. Repeat the application if not all perennial weeds are killed.
- Add 4 in. of organic matter (a variety of organic matter is best and it's best to have it tested to determine the nutrient analysis and organic matter content) and till it into the existing soil to a depth of 8 to 12 in. Creating slightly raised beds, perhaps outlined in stone, is often the best approach.
- Add phosphorus and a complete fertilizer if nutrients are not present in sufficient quantities in the added organic matter, and till into the bed.
- Plant, being careful to avoid compaction of the newly prepared bed (see Chapter 3).
- Wait for outstanding results. (Plates 25–32)

Planting and Establishment

PLANTING

NOW that you have devoted time and money in preparing your site and creating fabulous soil for your perennials, you'll want to plant them properly. Many different variables need to be considered, such as plant size, time of year, and planting depths, in addition to the appropriate mulch, watering practices, fertilizer, and weed control.

Plant Size

Once you have decided which types of plants you want to grow, you need to select the appropriate sizes for your garden area. You can choose from a variety of sizes of perennials. The most common are one-quart (sometimes called 4 in., or properly 4¼ in.) and one- and two-gallon sizes, and bareroot. With a well-prepared soil and rapid growth of the perennials in the first season, starting with larger size plants usually is not necessary (Plates 16–17). I use predominantly one-quart sizes. For ornamental grasses I like to use two-gallon containers; it takes forever for a one-quart *Miscanthus*, for instance, to attain the scale and impact in the landscape that I am looking for, although it may be appropriate for other gardeners' needs. Out of desperation in those limited cases where the larger size of a grass wasn't available, I have used three or more smaller plants grouped together. I don't like to make a habit of it and have only done this with grasses and *Buddleia*. Smaller growing genera of grasses, such as *Carex*, *Festuca*, and *Luzula*, usually come in one-quart or one-gallon containers. Perennials like *Astilbe*, *Hosta*, *Dicentra* cultivars, and various ferns are most often available in the larger size pots, including three-quart sizes. For autumn installations I use one-gallon sizes, with the belief that the larger plant with a more extensive root system has a better chance of establishing and is less likely to heave (pop out of the ground) with fluctuating soil temperatures in winter. Iris, peony, and poppy are often sold as bareroot plants.

Keep in mind that a new perennial garden planted with quart-size plants is going to appear small immediately after installation. If you are in the horticulture or landscaping industry, it is good practice to show your clients photographs of previous jobs taken right after planting and then of what the same gardens looked like three months later, and so on. It will be more comforting for them than trying to visualize in their heads how a lush perennial garden will develop from such small plants.

Timing

In central Ohio—which is plagued with wet, cold soil in the spring, hot and dry summers, often early frost in the autumn, and fluctuating winter temperatures without reliable snow cover—timing of planting can be a challenge. The best time for spring planting in this area is mid-April through May. With my business, we're usually still installing jobs into June and early July, and of course my own gardens don't see much planting until then, but the later we go into the summer, the harder it is for the plants to establish. The best time for autumn planting is from late August to early October. Ideally planting should be finished by October first, but we sometimes go until the 15th. I must admit that I prefer spring planting to autumn planting, although I do both. More plants seem to be available in the spring, and with the cool and moist conditions the plants establish quickly and are sufficiently well rooted before winter. With our unpredictable Ohio autumns and winters I have at times had trouble with plants not overwintering well from autumn plantings. Plants notorious for frost heaving, such as *Heuchera*, and tender ones such as *Anemone* ×*hybrida* and *Kniphofia* must be spring planted. In late October and early November I prepare beds and plant woody plants, and then come back in the spring to plant perennials. Pamela Harper and Fred McGourty, in their book *Perennials: How to Select, Grow and Enjoy* (1985), indicate planting times favored by growers in different areas of the country: Northeast Coast (Boston to Philadelphia): April to May, September to mid-November; New England (inland): April to May, September; Mid-Atlantic Coast: October to November; Southeast: February to early April, October to November; Plains States: April to May, September to mid-October; Central (eastern slope of Rocky Mountains): April to May; Pacific Northwest (coastal): March, September to October; California: February to April, October to November; Southwest: February to April.

Laying Out the Plants

Before planting, it is important to lay out, or place, the plants, arranging them on the site according to your design (Plate 41). That way, any on-site adjustments can be made by simply shifting the pots around. On limited occasions a plant or two will have to be lifted, moved, and replanted, although no one likes this, including the plant.

If you have a long border, start with a few key plants placed as anchors along the border, particularly the large-growing species such as great coneflower (*Rudbeckia maxima*), grasses, or maybe a shrub rose. Then start setting plants out at one end and work your way down. If you are working with a crew, they can be planting behind you. It is wise to run a 100-ft. tape measure along the edge of the bed to keep a check on where you are in the design. I measure the actual spacing between plants using a metal tape measure to follow the scale created during the planning stages (discussed in Chapter 1). It is time-consuming but is the only way I have found to do the job accurately on large, complex designs with a wide variety of species. I do the same in my own gardens when I'm putting in a new bed or adding several plants to an existing garden. Even after years of practice I still have the fear of getting to the end of the bed and running out of space or plants—and it has happened!

When working with several beds on a property I try to stay ahead of the crew by placing one or two of the beds while the crew finishes preparing the soil in the others. This way no one is standing around with nothing to do while I lay out the garden. It's also efficient to have another knowledgeable plant person on board who can help gather the plants and hand them to you as you are placing them in the bed.

As previously mentioned, try to stay off of the newly prepared beds as much as possible to minimize soil compaction. Walk around the outside of the beds or stay on the designated maintenance/access paths when planting and mulching. I often lay small pieces of plywood down and stand on these when planting in large areas that are not accessible from outside the bed, or when the soil is moist.

Planting Depth

Containerized perennials should be planted at the same depth at which they were growing in the pot. Plants placed too high can dry out, and if too low they are more subject to collar rot. *Dicentra*, *Iris*, and *Paeonia* have overwintering buds that sit on or near the soil surface; if planted too deeply, these perennials not only might not flower, but they can also rot. Particular care must be taken with peonies to not plant with buds more than 2 in. below the soil in cooler climates (see discussion of *Paeonia* in Section Three for more details). Bareroot plants ideally should be soaked in a bucket of warm water for 30 to 60 minutes prior to planting. Also, any dry containerized perennials should be watered before planting.

Further Notes on Planting

The soil between newly planted perennials should be leveled before mulching. A small shrub rake is most effective for this. I leave only one plant label per group of plants in the ground, which keeps the new planting from looking like a "mouse cemetery" with little white labels sticking up from the ground. In addition the labels will not be pulled out by the rake or will not pop out with fluctuating temperatures. I also leave a label next to each very small plant, such as late-emerging *Platycodon*, *Eupatorium*, or *Amsonia*, so that these plants do not get covered with mulch.

I prefer to use a trowel for most planting, although with the one-gallon and larger perennials the transplant spades, sometimes called poacher spades, are a hot commodity. This is a narrow, lightweight small spade (weighing only about 4 lb and measuring 39½ in. long). It is great for these larger size plants, and some of my crew like to use it for quart-size ones as well. If any plants are root bound, I make three cuts in the root ball with hand pruners before planting (Figure 3-1)

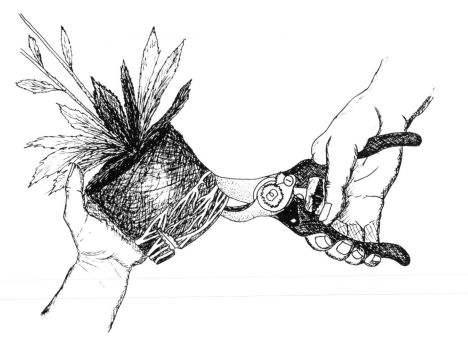

Figure 3-1. If a containerized plant is root bound, make three cuts into the rootball to help promote branching of the roots into the newly prepared soil.

to promote adventitious roots that branch into the newly prepared soil. Plants can be firmed into the soil by pressing on them with your hands; larger grasses and perennials can be firmed in with your foot. Again, nothing dramatic is needed here, and be careful that a well-meaning crew member isn't stomping the perennials to death.

If a plant looks like it has become leggy in the container, cut it back by one-third to one-half at planting to help create a fuller, healthier plant. *Artemisia absinthium* 'Lambrook Silver', for one, often needs this treatment.

When planting new perennials into an existing garden where the entire bed has not been prepared, be sure to dig a sufficient-size hole, at least two times the size of the rootball. This helps prevent the plant's roots from growing into soil that has not been properly prepared while the new plant is establishing. Incorporate organic matter into the hole and the backfill during planting.

Amateur and professional gardeners alike have a tendency to accumulate used plastic pots and flats at an overwhelming rate. A huge section of my barn is usually occupied by stacks of them. I have found nurseries that will take them, some specifying certain sizes or shapes. I urge you to do the same rather than throwing them out.

Transplanting

When transplanting perennials it is best to water the plant the night before you plan to move it. Dig the hole as near to the size as you think you'll need, making any necessary adjustments immediately before planting. Take as much soil with the plant as possible. Add organic matter to the new hole and backfill. Firm the backfill in as you go, water when the root ball is covered, and then continue to fill the hole. Transplanting ideally should be done in early spring as new growth is emerging or in early to mid-September. It's best after flowering, and plants should be cut back by one-half to two-thirds before transplanting if in a mature state. Transplanting can be done even when the plants are in flower, but they must be handled with extra care. Plants such as *Astilbe, Coreopsis, Geum,* and *Phlox* can handle transplanting while in flower. Larger plants as well as certain genera such as *Dictamnus* (which is difficult to move even under ideal conditions) or *Papaver* will have more trouble at such nonconventional times. Transplanting on a cloudy or overcast day with low wind is best. Plants may need to be shaded for a couple of days if transplanting is done during a period of high temperature or if the plant is in a mature state. See the Encyclopedia of Perennials in Section Three for transplanting requirements or limitations for particular plants.

MULCHING

We have become a society of over mulchers, feeling compelled to go out every spring and mulch whether it's needed or not. Mulching makes the garden look neat and tidy, but we are suffocating our plants by piling the mulch up, especially on shallow-rooted woody plants like azalea and rhododendron, as well as potentially contributing to rot of our perennials.

A variety of different materials are available that can be used for mulching, but a light fine-texture material is most suitable for perennials (Plate 43). I use a pine bark that is actually sold as a soil conditioner. It is similar to but slightly smaller than pine bark mini-chips and is dark, looking like the soil itself. Pine bark is easy to apply and to work with later for any additional planting. It can be worked directly into the soil. If I am applying a top-dressing of compost, I do not use additional bark or other mulching products.

In the spring it is best to wait until the soil warms before mulching. No more than 2 in. of mulch should be applied, and it is most critical to keep the mulch away from the crowns of the perennials, as mulching over the crown will cause rot. I like to mulch the beds with 2 in. of material after planting, when the perennials are establishing. After that I use it with discretion, keeping the doses between 1 and 2 in., a sufficient amount to help control weeds, reduce moisture evaporation and temperature fluctuations, and protect against erosion and soil compaction. For perennials I find that reducing winter temperature fluctuations in the soil is a primary benefit of mulching. Not only is frost heaving harmful to the plants, but research indicates that fluctuating temperatures also can cause certain physiological changes in herbaceous species that can weaken the plants and lead to death.

I rarely apply extra mulch for the winter. I only use perennials that can take our winters without this extra maintenance chore. Besides, I enjoy my perennial garden in the winter and don't like the idea of mounds of mulch or evergreens laying about. The exception would be for perennials transplanted or divided in autumn, which need 3 to 4 in. of mulch applied over their crowns after the ground has frozen. If you choose to grow marginally hardy perennials you will also need to follow this practice. In addition, certain subshrubs will burn if there is not persistent snow cover. They can be protected with evergreen boughs, specifically old Christmas trees, cut into manageable pieces. Be sure they are light and open, such as pines. Rodents can also be a problem under the covers.

Mulch is generally sold in 2- and 3-cu.-ft.-size bags; it is also available in bulk in 1-cu.-yd. increments. To calculate the total number of 3-cu.-ft. bags of mulch needed to apply 2 in. of material to an area, divide the total square footage of the planting bed by 18 sq. ft. To calculate the number of 2-cu.-ft. bags needed, divide the square footage by 12 sq. ft. If using bulk material, one cubic yard of material will cover 162 sq. ft.

WATERING

Proper watering of the newly planted perennial bed is vital to establishment of the plants. It is a good idea to check the new bed every other day for the first month after planting, not only to help guard against plants drying out, but also to allow you to get in touch with your new garden. Plants should be watered well, by hand, immediately after planting and mulching. With hand watering, water can be directed under the foliage right on the root ball where it is needed. I like to use a water wand because it makes it easy to reach into the plants and apply the right amount of water. A water wand is a long plastic extension with a nozzle on the end that can be attached to the end of a hose to deliver a fine spray of water.

The rule of one inch of water per week holds true while the plants are establishing. Use a rain gauge to determine how much water is being applied. Cans set up in various areas can determine coverage if a sprinkler is being used for watering. When perennials are just establishing, shallower and more frequent watering is needed because the plants are not yet rooted very deeply. As the plants become more established, after the first month, less frequent, deeper waterings are required to encourage the perennials to root more deeply and increase their drought resistance. Watering in the morning helps reduce incidence of disease and water lost through evaporation. Keep a close watch on watering in the first year to ensure that plants are not over or under watered. In subsequent years plants can become acclimated to drier conditions with less frequent watering. In my own gardens, although I will coddle newly planted perennials, watering well until established, I irrigate established plants only when I think they can't possibly stand another dry day. This is sometimes after weeks with minimal rainfall. Sure, some plants will succumb to drought, but most tolerate these conditions. There is no need to waste a valuable resource such as water, particularly when large quantities of water is not necessary for a beautiful perennial garden. Don't try to keep a moisture hog, such as *Ligularia*, alive in an extremely dry site at the expense of excess watering. I have been able to grow *Ligularia* in soil that remains moderately moist by lining the planting hole with a plastic bag to create a bathtub effect, which holds more moisture around the plant and reduces the need for large amounts of supplemental watering. The plants still usually will wilt midday on hot days, but they recover nicely by evening.

A garden, particularly a new garden, should be watered into autumn as long as it is dry but not frozen. Just as perennials need well-draining soil for proper overwintering, they have a better chance of survival if they don't go into the winter in a dry condition.

If you are using an automatic irrigation system, make certain that the timer is set for more frequent shallower waterings when the plants are establishing, and then, as the plants establish, that it is adjusted for deeper, less frequent waterings. This is often a problem with automatic systems, as contractors set the timers as they do for turf, which is not appropriate for perennials. Drip irrigation systems have the great advantage that they are more efficient at moisture conservation, but the disadvantage is that problems in the irrigation system can go undetected because you can't see them. Watch plants with subirrigation closely for signs of line failure, be it a leak or clog. Make sure that the irrigation system has a rain gauge so that if sufficient rain has fallen your irrigation will shut off. Troubles with irrigation can be a big problem with perennial plantings during establishment and in subsequent years if not closely monitored. Whatever irrigation system you choose, if you are not setting it up yourself it is a good idea to meet with the irrigation contractor to review the garden design, with its varied cross section, *before* the system is designed and installed. If using above-ground systems, make certain that taller plants are not blocking the spray from adjacent shorter plants.

FERTILIZING

Most perennials do not require large amounts of fertilizing; some, in fact, may resent such treatment, responding by producing excessive vegetative or leggy rank growth, minimal or no flowers, and possibly stunted root systems due to the highly soluble salts in the fertilizer. Silver-foliaged plants are particularly sensitive to overly rich conditions.

If soil is prepared properly from the start with nutrient-providing organic matter, supplemental fertilizing or top-dressing might not be necessary for several years after planting. Rod Tyler, soil scientist and author of *Winning the Organics Game* (1996), states that a soil amended at bed preparation with 20% well-aged, quality compost, with an analysis of 1% nitrogen, will be sufficient to support most annual, perennial, tree, and shrub growth for at least the first year without any additional fertilizer. Tyler goes on to demonstrate that the nitrogen availability from such a compost usually is 25% for the first year, 10% for the second and third years, and declining to 5% in the fourth and fifth years. This means that, if one inch of compost is used at bed preparation, 4 lb of nitrogen per 1000 sq. ft. will be available in the first year. This is remarkable since the general recommendation for perennials, as stated in Chapter 2, is 1 lb of nitrogen per 1000 sq. ft. Tyler cautions that organic nitrogen is dependent upon warm temperatures and microbial activity for release. In cool conditions a small amount of quick-release fertilizer at planting will ensure adequate nutrients until the nitrogen is released in the compost with the coming of warm temperatures.

Beyond the insight into soil preparation that Tyler's research provides, it also suggests by extension that the majority of plants would benefit from a 1- to 2-in. top-dressing of compost about once every 3 years, when the nitrogen availability from the compost begins to decline to about 10%. The recommendation often found in reference books to top-dress a garden annually with 3 to 4 in. of compost may be more than is necessary in many cases. You should keep in mind, though, that slightly higher amounts of compost might be needed in the South than in the North because the humus in the soil tends to break down more quickly in the heat.

Top-dressing with compost appears to be the best method for providing sufficient nutrients for perennials, and I rarely use fertilizer in my own gardens. Most of my perennial beds went 5 years with no additional nutrients and showed no visible signs of the need for it. A bed fertilized with a general-purpose granular fertilizer after 3 years showed no noticeable difference with the beds that were not. After 5 years, when some plants started to show decline (and this was in part due to the need for division of some of them), I tested the soil and found that the organic matter content had fallen to 6% (from approximately 16% after bed preparation). I top-dressed with 2 in. of compost (a blend of composted biosolids and leaf compost), and this had a noticeable effect on the plants, providing more robust growth and better flowering. Tyler's recommendation for 1 to 2 in. of compost as a top-dressing every 3 years was based on a garden that started with 8% organic matter. Since my beds begin with about 16% organic matter (which I am more comfortable with than 8% organic matter), it seems that they can go for 4 or 5 years before top-dressing is needed.

For a garden initially prepared with less than 20% compost and which started with an organic matter content of less than 5%, fertilizers can be helpful for providing some immediate nutrients while the organics are building up in the soil and are slowly becoming available to the plants. In such a garden, in temperate soils, three consecutive yearly one-inch applications of compost may be made to build up the organic matter in the soil. Take care to scratch or incorporate the compost lightly into the soil. The soil should be tested before the fourth-year application. Once the soil reaches an organic content of approximately 8%, compost application can be spaced to about once every 3 years.

Current research to validate that perennials growing in a rich organic soil need additional fertilizer is obscure, if there is any such research at all. As shown earlier, my personal experience hasn't revealed any great need for it. Yet, for insurance in my clients' gardens, I use a light application of a general-purpose, quick-release fertilizer in the spring following the first year. The belief here is that if any additional nutrients are needed it will be in the spring when the plants are going into rapid growth and the organic nutrients in the soil may not be available due to cool weather conditions. Sprinkle the fertilizer around the base of the plants, avoiding the new growth to prevent burning. Watering in the fertilizer or applying it when the soil is moist also reduces the chance of burn. Moist soil is generally not a problem in central Ohio at the end of March or early April, which is usually when I am applying fertilizer. I top-dress with 2 in. of compost in the fourth or fifth year after the initial planting, along with any divisions and renovations that may be needed.

Fertilizer needs and rates of application ideally should be based on soil tests, but tests are not always practical on an annual basis. I base my calculations of fertilizer needs on the general recommendation for perennials, which is 1 lb of nitrogen per 1000 sq. ft. The quantity of fertilizer should be based on this rate rather than on the recommendations on the fertilizer bag, because the latter rates can be too high for most perennials.

The granular fertilizer I use has an analysis of 12-12-12 or 5-10-5. So to calculate, for example, the amount of 5-10-5 fertilizer needed per 100 sq. ft. of area, based on 1 lb of nitrogen per 1000 sq. ft., start with the fact that one-tenth of the total, or 0.1, will be needed for 100 sq. ft. (Remember, too, that since the numbers for the fertilizer refer to percentage of N, P, and K by weight, a 5-10-5 fertilizer has 5% N, or 0.05.)

0.1 lb N per 100 sq. ft. ÷ 0.05 N = 2 lb fert. per 100 sq. ft.

Next, convert pounds to cups (c) for easy measuring. For the general-size pelleted material that I use, 1 lb of fertilizer equals 1½ cups. (You should test and weigh your own material because different fertilizers will have differences in granular size and bulk density.) So the 2 lb of fertilizer needed for a 100-sq.-ft. area translates to 3 c of fertilizer per 100 sq. ft.

If using the 12-12-12 fertilizer, 0.83 lb of fertilizer is needed per 1000 sq. ft. (That is, five-twelfths of 2 lb is 0.83 lb.) I round up to 1 lb per 100 sq. ft. when using 12-12-12.

I have also started to use organic fertilizers, including cottonseed meal (6% nitrogen, 2–3% phosphorus, 2% potassium), colloidal phosphate (0% nitrogen, 18–22% phosphorus, 0% potassium, 27% calcium, 1.7% iron, plus silicas and 14 other trace minerals), and greensand (0% nitrogen, 1% phosphorus, 5–7% potassium, 50% silica, 18–23% iron oxide, and 22 trace minerals) as well as Earth-rite (a composted soil conditioner containing animal, mineral, and sea products that can be applied as a top-dressing) as substitutes for the chemical fertilizers.

Perennials such as delphinium, peony, chrysanthemum, daisy, phlox, astilbe, and repeat-blooming daylilies are heavy feeders and may need a spring application of fertilizer as well as a summer application with a water-soluble fertilizer, even in soils high in organic matter. Delphiniums, for example, produce pale green new growth after being cut back, and this is a sign that fertilizing is needed. Repeat-blooming daylilies, such as *Hemerocallis* 'Happy Returns', especially benefit from foliar feeding when first in bud. A water-soluble chemical (Peters' 20-20-20 or something similar) or organic fertilizer (such as fish emulsion or a seaweed-based product) can be chosen for foliar feeding. Foliar feeding results in a quicker uptake of nutrients. It should be performed early in the morning on an overcast day to prevent burning.

Again I must stress that proper initial preparation of your beds with organic matter can save on time and maintenance later. This point is clearly displayed when it comes to fertilizing perennials. If the soil is rich and the growing conditions are good, supplemental fertilizer is not necessary for most perennials. Top-dressing with 1 to 2 in. of a high-quality aged compost every 3 years is the best approach to providing nutrients to most perennials, except in the case of heavy feeders that may need supplemental fertilizing. The minimal use of fertilizers in perennial gardens is also environmentally friendly.

WEED CONTROL

Ensuring that a bed is free of perennial weeds *before* planting is the first critical step toward weed control. If you are going to skip this detail, surrender now!

Close spacing of perennials is of benefit not only to the commercial grower selling many plants, but also to the home gardener because it helps eliminate weed competition. The biggest battle with weeds will be fought in the early spring, when weeds have sufficient light and room to grow since the perennials are still small. In the spring it can be difficult for even the savvy gardener to distinguish between a weed and a desirable perennial: "if in doubt, don't pull it out." A bit later in the plant's growth you will be able to make the clear call. Try to keep up on the weeds, or a relatively easy, methodical task can turn into a procrastinator's nightmare.

Identifying the beast as annual, biennial, or perennial and its growth habit as stoloniferous, rhizomatous, or clump forming is necessary for developing the proper battle plan. Pre-emergent herbicides such as DCPA (Dacthal) or trifluraline (Preen) are sometimes used on perennial plantings for control of annual weed seeds. The problem with these herbicides is that they are species-specific with regard to which perennials they are safe to use on. In diverse plantings there is the risk of injury.

Careful application of glyphosate (Round-up) using a paintbrush can be effective on perennial weeds. I also know of gardeners who prefer a technique that involves wearing a cotton glove over a plastic glove, dipping the cotton glove in the herbicide, and then wiping the growing tips of weeds with the glove.

Most of the time I simply weed by hand. I like to use what's referred to as a Japanese weeding knife, which works really well on even the deepest rooted weeds. (And no one else will mess with you when you're using it either.) I stay away from the use of chemicals.

Avoid seed set on the weeds as much as possible. One year I had a fantastic, specimen, 6-ft. bull thistle (*Cirsium vulgare*) flowering in my garden that made quite a show at an open garden tour. Visitors looked at it questioningly, afraid to ask whether it was another unusual plant of some sort, although it looked strikingly familiar. Could it be a type of *Acanthus*, or *Cynura?* I deadheaded the early flowers before seed set so that I could enjoy the flowers (and this little game) before removing the entire weed plant from the garden. Not something I would recommend on a regular basis, but look at the choices pruning provides.

CHAPTER 4

Pests and Diseases of Perennials

USUALLY few major pest and disease problems will be encountered in perennial gardens if time has been put into the proper selection of insect- and disease-resistant species, as well as into locating plants in the proper sites for optimal growth. There should be no reason to grow plants that require serious chemical controls since so many outstanding perennials are free of pests or are unlikely to be seriously damaged. Battling pests with the use of controls that aren't truly necessary is only a waste of time and contributes to the destruction of our environment. We need to be tolerant of a few holes or spots on leaves, or even in some years the destruction of the whole plant. Remember, herbaceous perennials will often send up new foliage later in the season even if totally defoliated early on or if pruned down as a result of serious damage. They will at least be back the following year to give it another try. Give a plant a couple of seasons—they may be affected with ailments some years, while in others they sail through cleanly, usually depending on weather conditions. If all our efforts at proper plant selection, sound cultural practices, patience, and the use of environmentally sound control methods have failed, then I think it's time to ask the afflicted plant to leave the garden!

A stress-free plant is less susceptible to disease and insects than one growing in a stressful environment. Proper soil and proper water management are key to reducing stress on perennials. Keeping the garden free of debris is also helpful. Some gardeners believe that yellow foliage attracts insects and so believe that deadleafing is vital to avoid welcoming trouble (although I have not found this to be the case). Many insects and diseases overwinter on decaying foliage of certain perennials, so infected foliage should be removed from the garden in the autumn —do not compost these materials if your pile does not reach temperatures high enough to ensure that the pests are killed. Avoiding overhead irrigation can help reduce the chance of disease and its spread. The spacing of perennials in the garden can affect certain species' susceptibility to pests. Having a diverse number of species in the garden is important because many pests and diseases are species-specific, and so your whole garden or a big part of it won't be wiped out if you include species that are not prone to the pest in question. Using varied species in the garden is also important for beneficial insects. You can encourage beneficials in your gardens by planting perennials that produce a lot of pollen or nectar. This includes members of the daisy family (Asteraceae), veronica, and butterfly weed (*Asclepias tuberosa*).

The first step in pest control is identifying the pest and determining if it is truly a problem. Too often the insecticide or fungicide is quickly grabbed and sprayed on the plant without a clue as to the real problem. Spotting or yellowing of leaves, for instance, can simply be a physiological problem, without a pest anywhere in sight. I have had perennials such as silver brocade beach wormwood (*Artemisia stelleriana* 'Silver Brocade') and copper fennel (*Foeniculum vulgare* 'Purpureum') completely eaten by what appeared to be just some caterpillar. It turned out to be butterfly larva (Plates 44–45). Fennel is preferred by the anise swallowtail and the black swallowtail. Many other perennials are favored larva food: *Anaphalis* and *Antennaria* are favorites of the painted lady, and *Ruta* of monarchs. This demonstrates the importance of proper identification of the "pest" in question. The plants look horrid, but who cares? They are serving, at this stage, a far more important function than just looking good. After all, we want butterflies in the garden. Perennials usually recover from any such damage either that same year with fresh basal growth or the following season. They may go through the same cycle every year, but this might be just as important a function as being ornamental. When you see orange beetles on your *Echinacea* and *Heliopsis*, don't spray them with the fear that the beetles are going to destroy your perennials—let these beneficial soldier beetles do their part in helping combat pests.

If you find that you have a problem you can't ignore or tolerate, you need to decide what form of control measures to take. Manual or mechanical control with hands, feet, strong sprays of water, pruners, and traps should be the primary control. (Appendix C, list 7, provides a listing of perennials that can be pruned for control of pests and/or diseases.) This manual approach is normally the only one that I take in combating pests in my gardens and in my clients' gardens. Insecticidal soaps would be the strongest control worth considering in the perennial garden, and even these are necessary only in limited cases. Many of the pests discussed here can be controlled with insecticidal soaps if the gardener feels that it is finally necessary. A mask should be worn when spraying insecticidal soaps because they can irritate the lining of the lungs. Certain perennials, such as bleeding heart (*Dicentra*) and ferns such as the Japanese painted fern (*Athyrium niponicum* 'Pictum'), are sensitive to soap-based products. Test a small area first before spraying an entire plant or group of plants. Other chemical sprays and dusts, including naturally derived chemicals such as rotenone or pyrethrin-based products, are not necessary. Keep in mind that just because a product is naturally derived doesn't mean that it is not toxic to one degree or another, either to humans, fish, birds, pets, and beneficial insects.

When thinking about pests of the perennial garden it's worth remembering that phlox and mildew, hosta and slugs, bearded iris and borers, and columbine and leafminer are frequent companions. If you can't eradicate a problem completely, ask what can be done to reduce the problem, or consider how you can alter your attitude to accept some of it.

Powdery Mildew

Powdery mildew can rob a plant of water and nutrients and cause leaf yellowing and even distortion of the plant, though usually only in extreme cases. Let's start by selecting resistant plants. I know of more than 20 mildew-resistant *Phlox*, in a variety of flower colors, heights, and bloom times, and I'm sure there are many more; a fair number of mildew-resistant beebalm (*Monarda didyma*) cultivars are also available. Some of these phlox and beebalm might not be totally free of disease, and again much depends on the weather conditions, but I think we can live with a light dusting or a spot or two—the plants definitely can. *Phlox* and *Monarda* both can be cut to the ground if mildew is a problem. They will usually put up fresh clean growth later in the season if provided with sufficient moisture and will not miss a stride the following year. When cutting down infected plants it's a good idea to disinfect your pruners by dipping them in a 10% bleach solution (1 part bleach/9 parts water) or at least wash them with soap and water after cutting to reduce the chance of continued spread.

Powdery mildew is a unique fungus in that its life cycle is not encouraged by free water but rather by high humidity and lack of air circulation, as well as temperature fluctuations, such as warm dry days and cool nights. Close spacing of plants can contribute to decreased air movement and so providing a bit more room for the plants and keeping them away from walls or thick hedges can help decrease problems. Thinning of mildew-prone perennials is often recommended to improve air circulation within the plant's structure, although with phlox I have not noticed any reliable difference between thinned plants and unthinned plants —both seem to get mildew equally well if the conditions are right. It seems that selecting resistant forms is the surest approach.

Other mildew-ridden perennials include *Pulmonaria* and *Chrysogonum*, which are often subject to attack in dry locations. Plants can be cut to the ground—sometimes new clean growth will be already evident under mildew-ridden foliage, but not always—and fresh clean leaves will emerge.

Rust

Rusts are rarely a problem with perennials. Improving air circulation around the plants and growing plants in lean, well-draining soil can help reduce the incidence of rust. If it does occur, the affected plant parts can be pruned off.

Slugs

A limited number of perennial genera are troubled by slugs—*Acanthus*, *Delphinium*, *Ligularia*, and *Hosta* come to mind. But since hostas are such a popular perennial in many gardens, slugs seem to be a rather prevalent problem.

Hostas with a thicker substance to their foliage and those for which the leaves do not come in contact with the ground are usually less prone to slug damage, although this will vary depending on location: how favorable are the conditions to slugs to begin with and how many of them are there? If a slug is hungry enough, I'm sure even the most discerning slug (if there are any) would eat the most thick-skinned hosta. (See the discussion of *Hosta* in Section Three for a listing of slug-resistant types.)

All the usual remedies can be used against slugs, including the beer bash (stale beer in shallow containers) and salt shaker approach, although these are not always practical from a contractor's point of view. I use diatomaceous earth (crushed sea diatoms) in clients' gardens for *Hosta* and *Ligularia* plants that suffer a good deal of damage. Apparently slugs don't like to crawl over the rough surface of the diatoms (such delicate creatures!), so a collar of sand or ashes around the plants may have similar effect. Diatomaceous earth is helpful in curbing the problem, not eliminating it completely, and it needs frequent replenishment. Van Wade, one of the premier hosta growers in the United States, has found that mulching with pine needles helps reduce slug numbers. Copper strips (sold as Snail-Barr) will give slugs a mild electric shock if they crawl over it.

Fortunately I do not have many problems with slugs in my personal gardens. This may be due to various factors: my gardens are generally on the dry side, and a bit of slug damage doesn't bother me. It may also be because I have a fair number of toads in my gardens, and toads are predacious of slugs. I do not use any metaldehyde-based baits because of their toxicity to cats, dogs, birds, and toads—all which live in the gardens. I have heard that delphinium and monkshood (*Aconitum*) have their own self-defense mechanism: after the first set of leaves are lost to the slugs, the plants send out a second set that are supposedly toxic to slugs. (Interestingly enough, both of these plants are poisonous to humans if ingested.)

Borers

When it comes to *Iris* and borers I feel the easiest solution is to avoid, or at least limit, the use of bearded iris. I never use them in clients' gardens, and the only ones I have in my own gardens were either given to me by my grandmother or by a friend or are reblooming forms that I wanted to test. I enjoy them enough when they are flowering, but I don't find *Iris* to be worth the trouble of the horrid leaves that follow. Of the reblooming forms, I have been happiest with one called *Iris* 'Perfume Counter', a purple-flowered cultivar on which the foliage holds up much longer than that of other forms that I have.

I feel the best alternative to bearded iris is Siberian iris (*Iris sibirica*). They add such great vertical form to the garden, and the flowers are gorgeous. The seedpods can be even more interesting than the flowers, contributing to the garden for the entire summer and winter. (Cut them in the spring for use in dried arrangements.) The foliage turns yellow in the autumn, providing ornamental benefits in that season. And best of all—no pests!!

Many people simply must have bearded iris, however, in which case a few tactics can be employed to fight the borer. If you can see it, crush the borer in the iris leaves. When the leaves are badly affected I cut them down to a few inches above the rhizome—it looks tacky, but better than the previous brown-spotted option. Cutting at an angle reduces the total "crew-cut" look. I also just pull out the brown, curled-up leaves at the base of the plants. It is important to cut down the leaves again, and remove any brown leaves at the base of the plant, in the autumn because the borer eggs overwinter on them. Do not compost infected iris leaves. Planting the rhizome high so that it is exposed to the sun helps reduce bacterial soft rot (*Erwinia carotovora*), which often sets in after the borers and in fact causes most of the trouble.

Leafminer

Leafminer can be handled simply by pruning off infested leaves or by cutting the entire plant to the ground when symptoms get severe. Do not compost leaves and be certain to clean-up debris in the autumn. Trying to prevent leafminers is a waste of effort since they don't cause long-term harm to the plants.

Japanese Beetles

The main pests that I have to contend with in my gardens are Japanese beetles, fourlined plant bugs, and grasshoppers. If you have small numbers of Japanese beetles, you can pick them off and put them in soapy water. But is it possible to have small numbers of Japanese beetles? I never have. I get masses of them in disgusting numbers. They are so taken by my rugosa roses (*Rosa rugosa*) and my porcelain vine (*Ampelopsis brevipedunculata* 'Elegans'), both of which they practically destroy each year, that they usually leave my perennials alone, except for *Kirengeshoma palmata*, *Lythrum*, and *Alcea rosea*. My son starts watching for the beetles in early June, and we both derive great pleasure from catching them, smashing them, or even more rewarding, putting them in one of his bug boxes, with plain water, and using them for fish bait in our pond. Bluegills and bass love them. Even the catfish go for them if they are hungry enough. We throw clumps of Japanese beetles into the water like chum to attract the fish. It's a bit scary how totally gratifying this bit of gardener's revenge can be, particularly baiting the hook! The only problem is that we are never able to keep up with the quantity that eventually descends on the gardens. I have started using traps placed about a hundred yards away from the gardens, and this has helped in reducing the numbers, but there is always some fish bait available even in September. If you live in a residential area you probably will only attract more beetles to your garden with traps, and you may need to persuade your neighbors to join in the trapping fun. The traps should be placed as far away from your beds as possible.

Fourlined Plant Bug

Fourlined plant bugs have only become a problem in my gardens in the last few years. They are something I had never even seen before this, and it was quite distressing to see the small, round, sunken tan spots on the leaves and sometimes stunted growth of my veronica, boltonia, even foxglove, and others that had always been pest-free up to that time (Plate 47). Fourlined plant bugs are particularly fond of members of the mint family (Lamiaceae). The nymphs are bright red and appear in May or June. The adults are greenish yellow and, as the name implies, have four black lines down the wings (Plate 48). There is only one generation of fourlined plant bugs per year. I control them by smashing nymphs and adults, when I can catch them. Sometimes plants seem to grow out of the damage. Other times, if the damage is too severe, I prune off the damaged sections. Some gardeners control nymphs with insecticidal soaps. The bugs lay their eggs in the stems of host perennials to overwinter, so it is important to cut these plants to the ground in the autumn and clean-up the debris. Do not compost the autumn debris.

Grasshoppers

Walking down my back garden path on a summer's day is like being in an Alfred Hitchcock movie, with scads of grasshoppers flying up at you. It truly adds another dimension to perennial gardening. On top of form, texture, color, movement, sound, and time, we have "bombardment," and I could certainly do without it. Grasshoppers seem to like to eat just about everything. They likely are prevalent only in country gardens.

I have had some success with a garlic-based product to fight the grasshoppers. It curbs them a bit, but I have a hard time keeping up with all the repeat applications this method requires. I start spraying in the first week of July and then seem to need to do it weekly from then on through August and into September. Most recommendations for controlling grasshoppers suggest also controlling or spraying adjacent weeds, which can be the original source of the problem, but when you have over 30 some acres of weeds around your gardens that's not a real practical approach.

Black Blister Beetles

This year I found, much to my horror, black beetles literally covering my Japanese anemones (*Anemone ×hybrida*) and ground clematis (*Clematis recta*). It was mid-July and they were doing a good job of completely decimating both species. I looked up the pests, only to discover that they were black blister beetles (Plate 46), which, without surprise to me, favor Japanese anemones and clematis as well as asters and dianthus. I also discovered that the larvae are in fact beneficial: they eat grasshopper eggs in the soil—amazing! So the dilemma was do I attempt a major control effort of the beetles, or do I use them as a natural defense against my grasshoppers and let them eat my anemones and clematis, which are the only plants they harmed? Obviously the black blister beetles were here for a reason, and it felt wrong to me to mess with the intended natural balance. I did knock off as many as I could, with a booted foot, and smashed them. Do not handle the adults with your bare hands; the blister beetles get their name from a nasty chemical they spray, called cantharidin, which causes severe skin inflammation and blisters. You can also use chemical-resistant gloves to knock the beetles off into a bucket containing a solution of soap and water.

Interestingly, *Clematis recta* plants that had been cut to the ground earlier in July (to control their sprawling habit), before the appearance of the beetles, missed the damage of the beetles' attack. From now on I will prune clematis to the ground before the beetles attack. Any beetles that remain when the new growth emerges are easily knocked off and smashed. In fact, pruned plants went on to bloom again sporadically in September.

For the anemone you should prune to the ground the bare, brown, leafless stems that remain after the beetles have eaten all the leaves. New growth will emerge nicely, though my plants failed to flower. In future years, if the blister beetle numbers increase and spread to other species of perennials, I may need to resort to different tactics. But for now I want to see if the black blister beetles have any noticeable effect on my grasshopper population.

Aphids, Spidermites, and More ("Oh my!")

Aphids, spidermites, and spittlebugs are sucking insects that sometimes affect perennials, although these pests generally don't do much damage to the plants. *Heliopsis*, for one, is often loaded with aphids without any sign of harm, at least not until early September when most flowering is finished and the plants are beginning to decline a bit anyway. If aphid damage becomes evident after flowering, the entire plant can be cut to the ground. Aphids, spidermites, and spittlebugs can be washed off with a strong spray of water.

Thrips can damage flower buds or distort petals and stunt growth on perennials such as daylilies (*Hemerocallis*). Affected plant parts should be pruned off and destroyed. This might mean shearing down the troubled daylily, but it will develop new growth in a number of weeks, depending on the moisture it receives.

Disease Problems

Stem and root rots can occur in certain perennial species where soil conditions are too moist. Damaged plants should be removed, and soil drainage improved. Perennials troubled with different leaf spots should have the affected parts pruned off if they are a problem.

Peonies in particular can have a host of problems. They look tatty and start to decline with the heat of August weather. This is because new eyes, or dormant growth buds, start to form at this time, taking the strength from the foliar portion of the plant. Klehm Nursery, famous American peony growers, recommend that gardeners not prune the plants until after the first of September in zones 3, 4, and upper zone 5, until the end of September in the rest of zone 5, and until after early October in zones 6, 7, or below. Resist pruning back even if the plants look ugly so that they can continue to photosynthesize, which will usually mean healthier plants the following year.

The red peonies, as well as the more fragrant forms, are always more susceptible to disease. Klehm Nursery explains that this is due to the fact that the red peonies produce more carbohydrates (evident by sticky sugars on the buds). Botrytis, an airborne disease, sticks to these buds more easily. *Paeonia tenuifolia* 'Flore Plena' (double fernleaf peony), which is red, is very susceptible to disease, so it is recommended that this form be deadheaded immediately after flowering to prevent the entry of disease from the mushy dead flower into the soft stem. Soil should also be kept well drained. If peonies are infected with disease, prune off infected parts and remove any debris from the base of the plants. All foliage and debris from around the plants must be removed each autumn and destroyed, not composted, to remove the possible sources of the *Botrytis* and *Phytophthora*.

Other Pests

Rabbits, raccoons, squirrels, chipmunks, and deer all add to the already challenging world of perennial gardening. Most of us have problems with at least one if not several of these "beasts."

My best defense mechanism against most such garden intruders are my cats, who live exclusively in the gardens and woods of our property. My dog also contributes to the defense of the gardens. These pets can do their own damage of course, but they have great benefits against the small rodent-type pests. I have had little problem even with rabbits, thanks to the cats, which is incredible considering our home's country setting. I have suggested that clients acquire cats if the rabbit damage is serious. If a cat isn't the answer, I have gone to fencing the border with chicken wire and leaving it up all season (Plate 49). The fencing isn't visible from a distance once the perennials fill in, and it beats trying to use repellents against the rabbits, which wash off with the rains and need to be applied frequently to the emerging new growth of perennials, particularly pruned perennials. Composted sewage sludge used in soil preparation is said to help deter rabbits as well as voles.

Chipmunks and squirrels do their damage by digging around the roots of perennials, particularly over the winter. The roots are then exposed to freezing temperatures, which can be the cause of the plant's demise.

I have trouble with raccoons. Whenever I plant new perennials in the gardens, that very night (I'm sure they're watching me with binoculars from the trees) the raccoons dig up the plants and leave them laying on top of the soil. I have found that sprinkling black pepper on the soil around newly planted perennials usually prevents the damage. I buy pepper in the industrial size and in rather large quantities (the grocery clerks aren't sure what kind of cook I am!). I have also successfully used powdered garlic when I've run out of pepper. I know of other gardeners who rely on black pepper and/or garlic to control moles, rabbits, ground hogs, and squirrels. Pepper and garlic powder need to be reapplied to newly planted areas after a rain. A home remedy that is said to control most pests as well as insects recently caught my eye in *Avant Gardener*. It consists of three cups of hot peppers and two cloves of garlic mixed with two cups of water in a blender for about two minutes. Allow the mixture to steep for 24 hours, strain, add one tablespoon soap powder as a sticking agent, and dilute with two gallons of water. An important thing to keep in mind with any "home brew" is that none of these items is registered for use as pesticides on plants. Toxic reactions may occur with certain species. Care should always be exercised with the use of any product.

Getting back to dogs in the garden for a minute, I am blessed with a golden retriever who is an exceptional listener. When she was young she learned quickly the importance of the command "no gardens," and so even if her frisbee lands in the gardens she waits on the outside until the launcher of the bum throw comes and fetches it out for her. Many breeds of dogs are not so cooperative, however. For many, digging is preferred over frisbees. Or simply lying on a prized perennial will suffice. In such cases I have had clients use either chicken wire around the border, if it is small enough, or yellow tape tied from stake to stake around the garden, which keeps the dogs out but also makes the garden look like it is constantly under construction. The surest approach is the use of an invisible electronic fence around the gardens.

Deer deserve a book of their own, and several are available. If you have problems with deer, I'm sure any of the above so-called pests seem like a piece of cake comparatively. Combining a variety of control measures, from cultural to mechanical, is the best approach to keeping deer away. Several different deer repellents are available, and Deer Away, made from rotten egg solids, seems to be the most effective one currently on the market. You should alternate repellents so that the deer don't get accustomed to them. And of course the repellents need to be applied frequently to rapidly growing perennials.

Milorganite, Milwaukee's composted municipal sludge, is sold as an organic fertilizer and has been shown to help keep deer away. Its effect is lessened in the autumn when the odor is less pronounced.

A new deer fencing, made of 7½-ft.-high black plastic mesh, is practically invisible and lasts 10 years. It is also fairly inexpensive. Obviously, the entire area must be completely enclosed in order for the fencing to be effective. Some gardeners use a 4-ft. chicken wire "mulch" around plantings, and others place Vexar, a dark bird netting, over plants while in bud or use it as a mulch.

Growing plants on the lean side, trying to avoid lush succulent growth, and growing a variety of plants may help in deer prevention. Deer usually avoid pubescent, aromatic, spiny, or toxic plants. In Appendix C, list 8, I have provided a list of plants that are resistant to deer, but this should be used as a guideline only. Damage from deer depends on many factors, including the size of the deer population, the amount of space available to them, other available food sources, weather conditions, and time of year. Certain plants may never be eaten in one garden and the favorite treat of deer in another.

One hopes that perennial gardens are full of people and friendly creatures. It is our duty as gardeners to minimize damage from pests by selecting resistant plants, practicing sound cultural habits, accurately identifying any problems, and then handling it with some tolerance and manual controls before resorting to any form of chemical control that might have an effect on the friendly visitors.

CHAPTER 5

Staking

STAKING is not my idea of fun. No matter what kinds of stakes or technique I use, it's still a chore I could do without. One way to skirt around staking is to select tall plants that are self- supporting, but this isn't always a solution because what is free standing in one situation might not be in another. This can be due to richer or moister soil, heavier winds or rains, more shade, the fact that division is needed, or sometimes I'd swear it's simply contrariness on the plant's part! Another way to get around staking is to use shorter growing cultivars. Planting close so that neighbors can help hold up the falling individual is a choice method for light airy perennials, although heavier tumbling plants will simply pull their companions down with them. Sometimes plants need to be lifted up off smaller neighbors or else the smaller counterpart might remain completely hidden, or it can rot from the lack of light and the high moisture under the canopy. Pinching or cutting back is one of the most effective ways to avoid staking. Unfortunately, even with all these alternatives, staking isn't always avoidable. (See Appendix C, list 9, for perennials that require staking.)

So, if staking needs to be done, do it early, after the first flush of growth but before full growth. The stems need to be sturdy, and flower buds should not be formed yet. Stakes placed early are easily hidden by maturing foliage. Avoid waiting until it is too late, when the plants have already toppled over and the stems have started to be affected by polarity.

Staking should be done as naturally as possible, without adulterating the normal habit of the plant. Follow the natural line of the stem. Use natural materials such as branches whenever feasible, and for ties use jute or string that blends well and is biodegradable (plastic-coated twist ties are not!). Examine the plant closely. Perhaps only the center of the plant is falling open. In that case only the sagging section of the plant, not the entire thing, needs to be staked. Don't tie the stem so tightly that it looks restricted. Let stems have a bit of slack to allow some movement.

Single stakes such as bamboo or steel bamboo-look-a-likes are most effective for plants with spiked flowers (a group of flowers on a single upright stem) or with single heavy flowers. Tie the jute or string around the stem first and then around the stake, or make a twist in the tie, so that the plant is not in contact with the stake (Figure 5-1). Sometimes the stem will need to be tied in several locations along the stake. The stakes ideally should end approximately 6 in. lower than the flowers or about three-fourths the mature height of the plant. The exception would be large-flowered plants with weak stems, in which case the flowers simply snap at a spot above the stake, infuriating the gardener. Weak-stemmed perennials, including the large-flowered Pacific hybrid delphiniums, need to be staked all the way to the tip of the flower to prevent this—I'd rather grow *Delphinium* ×*belladonna* 'Bellamosum', a reliable smaller plant with smaller and airier flowers that doesn't need support all the way up the stems.

Hoops or rings are useful for full bushy plants such as peonies. The hoops should stand at half the mature height of the plant. The plant should be allowed to mature and spread out above the hoop naturally.

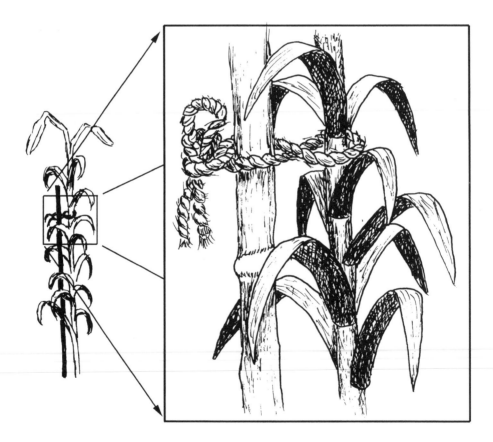

Figure 5-1. Single-stake method. Note the twist in the tie to keep the plant from coming in contact with the stake.

Plate 1. The rewards from maintaining a perennial garden are worth the effort, as shown here in the author's garden in June (and throughout the season in Plates 2–8).

Plate 2. This area of the author's gardens is a busy place in June, for enjoyment as well as for maintenance.

Plate 3. July is a peak bloom time in this area of the author's gardens. Here drifts of lower maintenance plants like *Coreopsis verticillata* 'Moonbeam' harmonize with the higher maintenance *Monarda didyma* 'Cambridge Scarlet'.

Plate 4. An outstanding combination in July of *Liatris spicata* 'Kobold',
Heliopsis helianthoides 'Summer Sun', *Crocosmia* 'Lucifer', *Delphinium*
×*belladonna* 'Bellamosum', and *Hemerocallis* 'Hyperion'. (Author's garden)

Plate 5. Within this garden certain plants, including *Delphinium* 'Magic Fountains', require more
time to maintain—such plants should be selected only if the gardener is willing to do the work to
help them grow. (Author's garden)

Plate 6. Proper maintenance can keep the garden looking good into the heat of August. (Author's garden)

Plate 7. Autumn can be a beautiful time of year in the perennial garden if the plants are properly cared for throughout the season. (Author's garden)

Plate 8. Autumn in the author's garden.

Plate 9. A "before" photo showing the existing conditions for a proposed garden site.

Plate 10. The same garden 2 years after installation. (Author's design, Columbus, Ohio)

Plate 11. Close-up of a small island bed at the entry to the home, showing *Coreopsis verticillata* 'Moonbeam' combined with *Rosa* 'Sea Foam', *Phlox maculata* 'Alpha', and a weeping purple-leaved beech. (Author's design, Columbus, Ohio)

Plate 12 & 13. An English-style double border, being watered-in after planting (*above*), and brimming with full perennial plants later that season (*below*). Each bed is 6 ft. wide, and they are separated by a 4-ft.-wide grass path. (Author's and homeowner's design, Worthington, Ohio)

Plate 14. A small border garden of perennials and annuals at planting.

Plate 15. The border 6 weeks later, featuring *Stachys byzantina* 'Helene von Stein', *Nierembergia* 'Mont Blanc', *Iris sibirica* 'Caesar's Brother', and *Verbena bonariensis*. (Author's design, Worthington, Ohio)

Plate 16 & 17. This garden was planted using mostly small quart-size (4¼ in.) perennials (*above*, just after installation), but with the correct soil used at planting, the growth on perennials is so great within just 3 months' time (*below*) that it usually isn't necessary to plant larger size containers. (Author's design, Upper Arlington, Ohio)

Plate 18 & 19. A cutting garden at planting (*above*) and 3 months later (*below*). The perennials have doubled or tripled in size due to the proper preparation of the soil with sufficient organic matter. (Author's design, Upper Arlington, Ohio)

Plate 20. A closer look into the garden reveals healthy, robust perennials that developed in the same season of planting. Included here are *Sedum* 'Autumn Joy', *Aster novae-angliae* 'Purple Dome', and *Centranthus ruber*.

Plate 21. This shady small garden (18 ft. × 24 ft.) didn't look like it had much promise at first notice.

Plate 22. Within a couple of years, however, this little space developed into a peaceful retreat. This was achieved by incorporating a broad palette of plant material in a mixed planting, planting in layers, using all the space, including vertical wall spaces for vines, and doing away with any lawn. (Author's and homeowner's design, Westerville, Ohio)

Plate 23. This small bed space (22 ft. × 14 ft.) in a retirement community didn't offer much cheer, even though the previous designer had considered "winter interest" and filled it with evergreens.

Plate 24. When transformed into a mixed planting full of color and changes with the seasons, this little garden became quite a conversation piece. A 2-ft.-wide path to facilitate maintenance helps break up the space, makes it appear larger, and offers visitors a chance to enter the garden and become a part of it. (Author's design, Columbus, Ohio)

Plate 25. The proposed garden is outlined with a garden hose and sprayed with the herbicide Round-up.

Plate 26. The bed is then amended with 4 in. of organic matter, creating a slightly raised bed. It is outlined with a low stone wall to help hold the soil.

Plate 27. The garden one year later. (Author's design, Pataskala, Ohio)

Plate 28. This proposed site for a perennial garden required several sprayings of Round-up to kill the weeds.

Plate 29. The garden was amended, and low stone walls were used to keep the soil from eroding down the slope.

Plate 30. The garden was developing nicely 1 month later.

Plates 31 & 32. After 2 months (*above*) the plants were already well established and off to a healthy start, and after 3 months (*below*) the rewards of the hard work from soil preparation were clearly evident. (Author's design, Westerville, Ohio)

Plate 33. In this garden with 30-ft. mature scotch pines (*Pinus sylvestris*), complex sun patterns meant that sunny spots were located adjacent to shady ones. As a result, sun-loving plants such as *Hemerocallis* 'Happy Returns' were planted next to the more shade-loving *Lobelia cardinalis* and *Thalictrum rochebrunianum*. Rounding out the scene are *Mazus reptans*, *Hakonechloa macra* 'Aureola', and *Hosta* 'Krossa Regal'. (Author's design, New Albany, Ohio)

Plate 34. A garden in a natural setting containing a mix of native and non-native herbaceous plants. Included in this design are natives such as wood poppy (*Stylophorum diphyllum*), maidenhair fern (*Adiantum pedatum*), and virginia bluebells (*Mertensia virginica*), plus cultivars of natives like fuller's white wood phlox (*Phlox divaricata* 'Fuller's White'), as well as non-natives such as various astilbe, hosta, and fringed bleeding heart (*Dicentra formosa* 'Luxuriant'). (Author's design, Galena, Ohio)

Plate 35. This large English-style border (backed by a low *Taxus* hedge) is approximately 116 ft. long and averages 16 ft. wide. Although it requires a good deal of maintenance, a garden of this size gives the designer room to work to create season-long interest, with repetition of colors and forms throughout. A 2-ft. catwalk runs along the back between the hedge and the perennials to facilitate maintenance. (Author's design, Royal American Links Golf Course, Galena, Ohio)

Plate 36. The beauty and diversity offered by this large garden with a variety of plant material is worth the effort. (Author's design, Royal American Links Golf Course, Galena, Ohio)

Plate 37. This small (14 ft. × 17 ft.) sunny front garden, located right next to a highly traveled sidewalk, requires close maintenance attention to keep plants reblooming and aesthetically pleasing all season for the many passersby. (Author's design, German Village, Ohio)

Plate 38. The mixed border at Inniswood Metro Gardens provides visitors with a wide array of plant material to learn about. Ornamental grasses such as elijah blue fescue (*Festuca glauca* 'Elijah Blue') and feather reed grass (*Calamagrostis* ×*acutiflora*) are combined with perennials such as autumn joy sedum (*Sedum* 'Autumn Joy') and moonbeam coreopsis (*Coreopsis verticillata* 'Moonbeam'), and annuals like victoria salvia (*Salvia farinacea* 'Victoria') and Italian white sunflowers (*Helianthus annuus* 'Italian White'). (Author's design, Westerville, Ohio)

Plate 39. Masses of perennials was the chosen style here because the garden is located a good distance from the home. Included here are *Rudbeckia fulgida* 'Goldsturm', *Artemisia* 'Powis Castle', and *Calamagrostis ×acutiflora*. (Author's design, Bexley, Ohio)

Plate 40. Larger groupings of perennials were used in this design to keep the planting in scale with the home and the size of the beds. Included here are *Hemerocallis* 'Happy Returns', *Salvia nemorosa* 'East Friesland', *Geranium sanguineum* 'New Hampshire Purple', and *Phlox maculata* 'Miss Lingard'. (Author's design, Westerville, Ohio)

Plate 41. Plants are placed according to the design and then planted.

Plate 42. The garden 3 months later. (Author's design, Sunbury, Ohio)

Plate 43. A fine, light-textured mulch is ideal for perennials.

Plate 44. If we want beauties like these visiting our gardens we need to pay the price of some damage by their larvae.

Plate 45. Larvae damage and "droppings" on *Artemisia stelleriana* 'Silver Brocade'.

Plate 46. Black blister beetle damage on *Clematis recta*.

Plate 47. *Digitalis grandiflora* damaged by four-lined plant bug in the nymph stage.

Plate 48. An adult fourlined plant bug. (Photo by Dr. Dave Sheltlar)

Plate 49. Chicken-wire fencing around an island bed of perennials can be used to keep rabbits at bay.

Plate 50. Lush foliage on perennials develops with pruning after flowering.

Plate 51. *Eupatorium maculatum* 'Gateway' pinched stem on the left, unpinched stem on the right.

Plate 52. The spontaneous purple and blue provided by seeding of alpine columbine (*Aquilegia alpina*) and Hungarian speedwell (*Veronica austriaca* subsp. *teucrium*) add greatly to this cottage garden. (Author's garden)

Plate 53. This chance seedling of *Rudbeckia fulgida* var. *speciosa* in the front path of the author's garden is a charming and welcome surprise.

Plate 54. Many perennials can be sheared and shaped after flowering, here showing *Baptisia australis*.

Plate 55. *Boltonia asteroides* 'Snowbank' pruned to create a layered effect, stepping up nicely to *Eupatorium maculatum* 'Gateway' behind it. (Author's garden)

Plate 57. *Sedum* 'Autumn Joy' pinched.

Plate 56. Smaller *Phlox* and *Lobelia* flowers produced from plants that were cut back for height control are a better scale for smaller arrangements.

Plate 59. Even more dramatic is the show that pinched autumn joy sedum plants provide in flower. (Photo courtesy of Boerner Botanical Gardens, Wisconsin)

Plate 58. Autumn joy sedum pinched and used as a low hedge is outstanding even without flowers. (Boerner Botanical Gardens, Wisconsin)

Plate 60. The author's mixed borders in winter.

Plate 61. The intricate deadheads of *Eupatorium maculatum* 'Gateway' are dazzling when covered with frost.

Plate 62. Evergreen perennials such as *Arum italicum* 'Marmoratum' contribute to the winter garden.

Plate 63. The evergreen *Dianthus deltoides* highlighted by snow in winter.

Plate 64. A weed whacker with a rigid plastic blade can help speed pruning.

Plates 65 & 66. Electric hedge shears do an efficient job of cutting down ornamental grasses in the spring.

Pea staking, or the use of fine twiggy branches, is effective with light airy plants such as *Clematis recta* (ground clematis) and *Gypsophila paniculata* (baby's breath) (Figure 5-2). It's a good idea to cut the branches when dormant to prevent them from rooting and sprouting in the garden while they are holding up your plants. Ideally the branches should be 6 in. shorter than the mature plant. I learned of this technique while working in England, and it's by far my favorite.

Linking stakes are available in many different sizes to fit a variety of plant sizes and shapes. They can be difficult to get into the ground at times, and then when you succeed, they may not be even, making it a challenge to link the stakes together. Yet I like them, especially for taller plants like Alaska shasta daisies (*Leucanthemum* ×*superbum* 'Alaska'). Linking stakes have the advantage that they can be inserted when the plant is a bit more mature.

Other staking devices that can be used with perennials include chicken wire held up with stakes, especially for thin-stemmed plants such as *Aster* or *Boltonia* (although neither of these genera require staking if pruned properly). The chicken wire cylinder should be shorter than the mature height of the plant and slightly narrower than the mature width. Tomato cages can be employed in a similar manner. Bamboo stakes connected by intricate crossing twine is a useful method for large perennials with numerous stems that require internal support. This

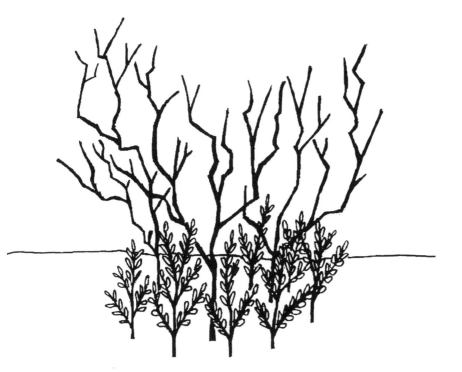

Figure 5-2. Pea staking.

technique can also be used effectively on perennials that were not staked and have fallen. If the stem tips have already started to bend, they may grow straight again if not too far gone, but in most cases it's best to pinch or cut them off; the stems will branch and fill in. Criss-crossing bamboo stakes is an effective way to hold up sections of low-growing plants such as *Nepeta* or *Geranium*.

If done properly, staking can help to greatly improve the appearance of many perennials. Don't let the plants fool you. One year my Alaska shasta daisies were looking stocky and upright, and I thought I was going to get away with not staking them. The gardens were to be photographed by a magazine, but that very night a major storm came through and knocked the plants silly. Needless to say, since then I have staked regardless of whether they looked like they were going to need it, because normally they do. Remember to remove the stakes after plants have been cut back. Empty stakes hovering over fresh new foliage is as obtrusive as any unstaked plant on its worst day.

CHAPTER 6

Division

APERENNIAL garden that has as its primary objective to be strictly "low maintenance" simply should not contain plants that require division annually or even every couple of years. No worries though, as there are plenty of perennials that don't require division for 3 to 5 years. And many can go 6 to 10 years or even longer without division. In fact, several perennials would rather not be bothered at all. (See Appendix C, lists 10–13, for guidelines on division requirements.) However, you should not let division requirements be too limiting a factor in your plant selection. It isn't as dramatic a procedure as it might appear at first. It can be very satisfying, having a rejuvenating effect on perennial and gardener alike.

There is plenty to do in the perennial garden without going around needlessly dividing perennials. The lists provided in Appendix C with time frames for division are guidelines only. The growing conditions often will affect whether a plant is going to need division sooner or later. Some invasive plants can be more or less aggressive depending on the soil, amount of moisture available, and so forth. The plants will send signs when division is in order: the flowers may get smaller; the clump may take on the appearance of a traffic jam, with the stems and branches getting all tangled up; the plant's may develop a hole in its center, taking on the form of a donut (Figure 6-1)—definitely not a fashion statement; the plant in general may have less vigor; it may flop more, requiring staking that it never needed in its prime; and it may need division to keep its spread in bounds. A perennial may also need division simply if the gardener decides they want more plants, or if their friends decide it for them.

The perennial division "gods" once proclaimed that spring-flowering plants should be divided in the autumn, and autumn-flowering plants divided in the spring. This gospel stuck, and you see it stated in most of the literature. I'm not about to overturn tradition! But you gain an entire season of growth if early spring-flowering plants are divided right after flowering in April or May. If you

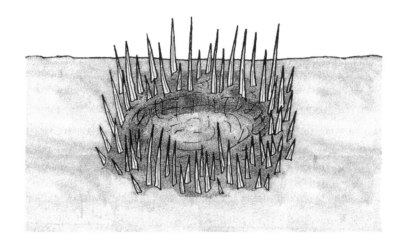

Figure 6-1. One sign that division is needed is when a hole or dead space develops in the center of the plant.

don't mind sacrificing flowers for that year, the plants can even be divided in very early spring before flowering. Spring division also gives more time for establishment before winter. The tale holds true that autumn-flowering plants should be divided in spring, and this includes most ornamental grasses. For these reasons I tend toward spring division for almost everything, whenever possible.

Plants not suitable for spring division include fleshy rooted perennials such as peony (*Paeonia*), oriental poppy (*Papaver orientale*), and Siberian iris (*Iris sibirica*), which are best divided in autumn. Siberian iris will tolerate spring division only with sufficient moisture. In the Midwest, September is a good month for autumn divisions. Divisions should be done about one month before killing frost.

Most plants will not divide well in summer; an exception would be bearded iris, which is dormant in the summer and traditionally is divided in August. The tough nuts like hosta and daylily and a few other rugged perennials will take summer division. A hosta may respond by flopping, but by the next season it will regain its normal habit. When dividing in the summer and autumn it is best to cut the plants back by one-half to two-thirds to reduce transpiration. Cutting the plants back before division also makes it easier to see where to divide, although many gardeners cut back the plants after division. With summer divisions extra care is needed to keep plants moist and shaded if hot and dry weather is expected.

Perennials with tough woody roots or taproots, such as *Aruncus*, *Asclepias*, *Cimicifuga*, and *Echinops*, should be divided in early spring before top growth emerges or very early in the autumn. This also applies to *Filipendula*, except for *Filipendula vulgaris*, which divides easily. These so-called difficult-to-divide genera don't always live up to their reputation. I have had fairly good luck with dividing young plants of *Echinops ritro* 'Taplow Blue' in early spring when growth was approximately 3 in. high. I have not been so lucky with older plants, though I know of gardeners who have.

Ideally spring divisions are made when the foliage is 2 to 3 in. high. In most cases the entire plant can be lifted from the ground using a spade or spading fork inserted into the ground about one foot away from the outside of the clump, depending on the species. Smaller growing perennials don't have as large a root system and so normally can be divided easily with a sharp nonserrated knife or sharp spade. If using a spade, work from the outside of the clump inward. Remember that the dead woody center is tough and often hard to pierce even with the strongest spade. Pulling apart clumps by hand is sufficient for genera with loose, spreading crowns and numerous shoots, such as *Aster*, *Monarda*, and *Stachys*. If you are doing small divisions, you may need to wash the soil off the roots to see what you are doing. To divide large thick clumps, especially for shasta daisy (*Leucanthemum* ×*superbum*), hosta, daylily (*Hemerocallis*), and border phlox (*Phlox paniculata*), the double-fork method is quick and easy (Figure 6-2). To divide clumps using this method, first lift the entire clump from the ground with a

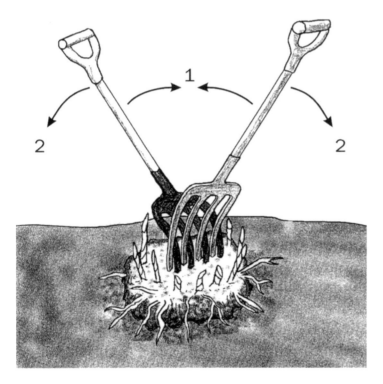

Figure 6-2. The double-fork method of division.

spade. Then insert one spading fork into the center of the clump, and insert a second fork parallel to the first, setting the forks back-to-back with the tines of the two forks intersecting. Pull the forks inward and then outward, and the clump will separate in two. You might have to repeat this process several times with a large clump. Once the large clump is broken up, a sharp nonserrated knife can be used for further divisions to obtain smaller pieces. Perennials such as peonies, which are fleshy rooted, do not divide well with the double-fork method and are best divided using a knife. *Astilbe* is also said to be a poor candidate for the double-fork method, but I successfully double-fork divided hundreds of them while working at a garden in Belgium (though it wasn't all that much fun!). Those astilbes must not have known better.

The number and size of divisions depends on your objectives. It is best to leave three to five healthy eyes (dormant growth buds) if you intend to rejuvenate the clump (Figure 6-3). Single eyes will give you the most divisions, but it will also give you small nonflowering plants that season. These small divisions are not recommended for the autumn.

If you simply want more plants from a perennial that doesn't need division, you can slice out sections of the plant early in the spring and it will fill in unnoticed. Groundcovers in particular or stoloniferous perennials that root freely at nodal joints can have these offshoots separated from the mother plant to de-

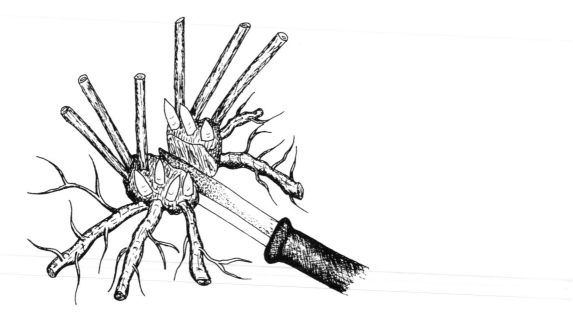

Figure 6-3. When making divisions you should leave at least 3 to 5 healthy eyes, such as on this peony (*Paeonia*) division.

crease spread and give you more plants. This same technique can be used for plants that form new plantlets off the mother crown, such as foxgloves (*Digitalis*) or violets (*Viola*). Lift the new rosette and separate it from the older plant with a knife. You can also take cuttings of certain perennials to obtain more plants if division is not desired or is too difficult.

Plants should be kept moist and shaded during division. Discard the old, nonviable center portion of the crown and cut off any dead or damaged growth or roots. Spread roots out evenly in the hole. Water well after planting, and watch the new divisions for the next several weeks. Small divisions may need protection from wind and sun for the first several days. Within a few weeks after establishment, plants may benefit from a light fertilizing. Fertilizing at planting can burn the plant roots if the fertilizer comes in contact with the roots, unless a weak inorganic solution or starter organic solution is used. The time when you are doing the divisions is also a good opportunity to incorporate organic matter into the hole before replanting, preferably a nutrient-providing amendment high in phosphorus. If the amendment is not high in phosphorus, you'll want to add some form of phosphorus to aid in establishment. Fall divisions should be mulched after the ground freezes.

Divided plants will reward you with an increase in vigor and flowering. Don't let this easy gardening technique intimidate you or limit your plant palette. Enjoy!

CHAPTER 7

Renovation of the Established Perennial Garden

FREQUENTLY I am called upon to help with an existing perennial garden; the call can come for a variety of reasons. The owners may have decided that they are tired of the existing planting. They may have planted the garden themselves, with little background knowledge, and it never quite measured up to their expectations, or the planting might have been pleasing at one time but is now overrun by aggressive weeds. Often the plant performance was less than optimal, either due to poor plant choices for the growing conditions, or more often than not, the real problem goes back to poor initial soil preparation. Usually the owners are attached to some of the plants in the garden but could do without others, opting for newer introductions with longer bloom times, more fragrance, or perhaps finer habits. They have moved and removed things, added and subtracted, but it still doesn't gel. What to do?

In such cases we opt to renovate the garden. You start with some of the existing plants, design in some new plants, and most importantly, amend the bed properly. It's a fun and at times daunting process, but one that is always worth the effort in the end.

The first step is to evaluate the site. How much sun does it really get? Have trees or shrubs matured in such a way that the sun patterns or moisture levels of the garden have changed since it was first planted? Has new construction changed any views?

Next, have the objectives or commitments of the owner changed? Is there now more or less time for maintenance? Are there new pets or new children? Perhaps interior redecorating, or taste, has changed the color focus of garden. This is a good opportunity to think things over clearly and thoroughly. The advantage in garden renovation projects is that you know what has and has not worked, and this can help greatly with decision making.

A primary concern in deciding which plants "make the cut" in the redesign is the prevalence of weeds. If stoloniferous weeds have really gotten into a plant, it may be best to get rid of the plant and just buy a new one, or something else, rather than risk reintroducing a fragment of weed that will take over the world even faster in your nice new organic soil. There is no sense in going to all the trouble of redoing a garden and then putting the weeds or aggressive perennials right back into it. And you are not doing your family or friends a favor by giving them such a plant either.

Aside from concerns of weediness, a plant may simply be a "dog" and not worth the effort to replant. Perhaps it was purchased in a weak moment, or was given to you by a well-meaning individual renovating his or her own perennial garden. It just might not fit into the new objectives for the garden.

In my business, I will visit the garden in the summer or early autumn when things are in active growth so that I can really see what is going on. (This is often to the dismay of the owner who has had to wait patiently since making his or her winter or early spring decision to "do something with the garden.") During this visit a list is made of everything in the garden, including approximate numbers or sizes of clumps and the condition and approximate location of the plants. Actual measurements help a lot, because when you are back at the drawing table months later, notes that say "a large clump of Siberian iris" or "a small clump of bergenia" lose all context and perspective. This preliminary visit is also the time to evaluate what plants should be considered for returning to the garden based on the owner's wishes and the plants' condition or worth. These notes will help during the redesign process, when it may be decided that additional plants also need to go. Even a plant that has been "cut from the draft" needs to be recorded for figuring labor and time involved in removing it from the garden, especially if the plant is to be spared for a friend.

After the initial note-taking visit to the site, I usually redesign the garden over the winter for renovation the following spring. Renovation can also be done in early autumn; particularly in areas with milder winters and in areas with very hot and dry summers, autumn may in fact be the preferred season. I am not comfortable with redoing an entire garden in the autumn, especially someone else's entire garden, not being sure of what the winter will bring. While redesigning you must decide how much of a plant is to be saved and where it can be used and where new plants can be integrated. This can be a bit challenging because you are not working with a clean canvas but rather are trying to save and use as many of the existing plants as possible, yet incorporating new ones as well.

Ideally the plants should be lifted from the garden in early spring when new growth is just emerging yet is high enough that you can see what is what. Lay a tarp down to protect the grass and place the plants on it. If the plants need to remain out of the ground for longer than a day before replanting—that is, if more work, such as weeding, needs to be done at a later time to prepare the bed for planting—I put them into flats and pots. Flats are good for small and shallow-rooted perennials, and pots are for large clumps of large-growing species. If any divisions are to be made, they should also be done at this time. The plants should be placed in the shade, kept watered, and sometimes need to be held there for up to two weeks. If replanting that same day, all plants are removed, divisions are made, and the beds prepared, planted, and mulched. Try to pick a cool and overcast day for garden renovation work.

If weeds or invasive perennials are a problem in the beds—and usually they are—the best approach is to remove the desired plants, and then spray the entire bed with Round-up (glyphosate) or other nonselective, nonresidual systemic herbicide. Any plants that aren't to be saved for reuse or recycling can be sprayed along with the weeds. Then wait two weeks and replant as above.

How long a garden renovation will take depends on several factors, such as number of plants to be saved, the age of the clumps to be moved, the condition of the existing soil, and the speed and efficiency of the people doing the work. I figure approximately one hour of labor for every 16 to 22 sq. ft. of bed.

Small sections of a large garden can be renovated individually so that the work is phased. It is risky to do the herbicide spraying in such a case, though, with "desirables" all around the renovated area.

Renovating a perennial garden, like renovating a room or a home, can be an involved project, but one that you'll be glad you ventured into when you sit back and enjoy the fantastic results.

CHAPTER 8

Introduction to Pruning

PRUNING is a term not normally associated with herbaceous plants, but when we deadhead spent flowers, pinch stems or buds, and cut back leggy plants we are actually pruning. It also might be referred to as grooming, shaping, shearing, or snipping. Whatever you like to call it, the benefits to our perennial gardens are countless. Pruning is my favorite thing to do in my gardens, far surpassing in my heart planting, dividing, staking, or any other element of gardening (weeding is not even in the race). I get excited writing, lecturing, even just talking about pruning perennials because I believe that it is critical to maintaining the beauty in the gardens we create.

In your personal gardens your mood, family and work schedules, and objectives will dictate if, when, or how often you're able to prune your plants. Sometimes I just don't have the time, or the desire, to get to all the pruning needed in my own gardens, and it shows. (That's when I tell visitors it's best to view the gardens from a distance.) Something as simple as reading to my son may have taken priority. I know that my gardens can wait for the day when I can catch up with them. Due to the nature and siting of my house and gardens, I don't have to worry about keeping up with the neighbors, or even about their chatter when things get a bit wild. If your garden style is more formal, or is in a more formal setting (and you care what your neighbors think), or if you garden for a public garden with scrutinizing visitors, you will need to keep up with the pruning more thoroughly. If you get discouraged when you see pretty pictures of gardens in books or lectures and you think yours doesn't stack up, remember that those gardens are photographed only on their "good hair" days.

Sometimes it bothers me to see my gardens unkempt, and if I have the time, I tear through them with shears and pruners flailing, trying to get everything looking just right—definitely a woman with a mission! At other times it doesn't bother me as much that things need to be pruned. Go with your mood, but always keep in mind that the time and hard work that you put into your gardens will help them to reach their full potential. A well-tended perennial garden shows. Too much neglect, for more than a year, will spell disaster.

In the landscape industry a company can't afford to be relaxed about pruning their clients' gardens. The company's reputation depends on the appearance of those gardens. Proper pruning will make the difference between a fair garden and a distinctive one.

More Than Meets the Eye

When I was first asked to write about pruning herbaceous plants, for the Brooklyn Botanic Garden Record Book (*Pruning Techniques* 1991), I thought it would be a straightforward topic. As I continued to work on the subject for another article for a magazine, and then began to lecture and to work on this book, I came to realize how very complex a topic it is due to the many variables involved.

Ironically, a great deal of pruning is based on common sense and comes naturally with experience working with the plants. Skill and art develops with practice. To me, part of the lure of pruning is working with your hands, as a sculptor might, shaping, forming, trimming. It can be a nurturing and gratifying (almost religious) experience. In my travels I have talked with gardeners from around the country, and it is always wonderful to watch how the best of them just look at a plant and naturally know how and when to prune it. This is part of the complexity of this topic, as the common-sense approach can be difficult to put into words with specifics. "Because you just do it" is not the best answer! This is not meant to intimidate the beginning gardener—just the opposite. Don't worry about hurting your plants by experimenting; you really can't do all that much harm. In most cases perennials are very forgiving.

I will share with you my personal experience as well as the experience of some of the best perennial gardeners in the United States. You will find that an individual perennial often can be pruned many different ways for similar results. There are also different ways it can be pruned for slightly different results. Certain tools or techniques may be preferred by some and not others. Use the information provided here as a guideline, then experiment, have fun, and learn as you go.

Why We Prune

What, how, and when to prune perennials varies from region to region, from year to year, and with the age of the plant. The condition of the plant, whether it is healthy or stressed, and the fertility of the soil will affect pruning requirements, as will weather conditions in a given year. Watch your plants closely: they usually will tell you by their appearance what kind of pruning is in order. If in doubt (and if I haven't given you the answer in the Encyclopedia of Perennials in Section Three), just watch the plant and experiment—leggy, tatty old growth and new fresh growth at the base of a plant are red flags summoning the pruners. Pruning also depends on the individual gardener's objectives. I have listed below some important objectives in pruning; they are discussed in detail in the chapters that follow.

Extend Bloom Period or Promote Repeat Bloom. Extending the bloom period or promoting repeat bloom is one of the most important reasons to prune perennials. Even though we all appreciate the many attributes of perennials, pretty flowers is probably the primary reason that most people grow them. Most perennials only flower for three weeks, some for an even a shorter period of time, so if something can be done to extend the flowering season, it will be a worthwhile endeavor. Deadheading, the removal of faded or spent—basically dead—flowers, is a rather morbid name for a technique that can give life to your garden through prolonged bloom or repeat bloom of certain species. In many, but not all, cases, if the bloom is not allowed to go to seed, the plant will continue to put out new blooms in an attempt to complete the life cycle. When we deadhead we force the plant to put its energy into new flower and shoot production, rather than into seed production.

Encourage Lush New Growth. Cutting plants back when old growth has become tatty can promote lush new growth from the base of the plant. This new growth contributes to the overall appearance of the garden, refreshing it and holding that spot in the overall design. Remember, foliage form, texture, and color contribute to the garden effect for a much longer period of time than do flowers (Plate 50).

Regenerate or Extend the Life of Plants. Pruning is not simply cosmetic. It may help satisfy the neat-nik impulses in some of us, but pruning can also increase the vigor and life expectancy of the plants, as well as improve their resistance to disease and harsh weather conditions. This is particularly true with woody perennials.

For a wide range of short-lived, usually biennial species, life span can be extended by several years if the plants are cut down immediately after flowering. As discussed above, biologically a plant's main goal is to produce seed, which will become the next generation. Unlimited seed production pulls strength from the plant and leads to death of these biennials. If the deadheads are removed before seeds start to set, the plants get confused, thus stimulating new shoot production and a further year of flowering. This can be an advantage or a disadvantage depending on your objectives. I often prefer seeding some species for a more natural, unplanned look. Pruning allows us these choices.

Some perennials can flower themselves to exhaustion and are then unable to form buds for the following year. To prevent this from occurring, the whole plant should be cut back to stimulate vegetative growth. This principle applies to a wide range of perennials. New growth produced from cutting back a plant early in the season is more vigorous and less stressed than the old dying foliage and is thus less likely to succumb to disease and weather damage.

Stagger Plant Heights or Bloom Times. For perennials growing in large groups, you can encourage the plants to mature to differing heights or to bloom at slightly different times by pinching or cutting back. This creates interesting gradations and extends the bloom time of a planting. You can delay flowering on a few stems of an individual plant to provide a longer bloom period at the expense of abundance.

Reduce Plant Height. Reducing plant height, and thus eliminating the need for staking, is an important pruning principle. The little bit of time it takes you to cut back or pinch perennials before they flower, creating more compact plants, will save you the headache and time of having to stake plants later.

Keep Plants in Own Space. I like full, lush (some may call it crammed) gardens with as little ground or mulch showing as possible and as diverse a palette of plants as possible. Such an approach requires some management of the planting to keep everyone in their own space. Sometimes this will mean the removal of one or several branches at the base of the plant or a few panicles off the top. Other times it means cutting the whole plant down to the ground, after its show is finished, to let its neighbor have room to shine. Intricate gardens with a high variety of plants often require this kind of policing. Mass plantings of only a couple of different species are far less likely to need the intervention.

Increase Flower Size or Numbers. Pinching a plant will often cause it to produce more, but smaller, flowers than it might normally produce without pinching. Removing, or disbudding, the side buds of a plant will produce one large flower on a long stem. If the terminal bud is removed, side shoots will produce many small flowers. Disbudding is most often practiced by growers of show chrysanthemums, peonies, and carnations and pinks. For certain plants the thinning of stems can produce larger flowers than those on unthinned plants.

Prevention or Control of Pests. Thinning stems on mildew-prone perennials can increase the air circulation around the plant and decrease the incidence of disease. The arrival of pests may also be discouraged by better air flow. If a perennial has been infected with a disease or insects, pruning off the damaged foliage and removing it from the garden can often be an effective method of control and prevention of further pest invasion. Preventing or minimizing pests and disease is discussed in greater detail in Chapter 4.

Enhance the Overall Appearance (Habit) of the Plant. Cutting a plant back before it flowers not only creates a more compact plant but can help shape the plant's habit. By cutting outer stems lower than inner stems you can create a more mounded plant and reduce unsightly legginess. Pinching or cutting back a perennial when it is first planted normally improves its habit. Physiologically, pinching or cutting back perennials simply breaks the apical dominance. The apical bud (or terminal bud) usually grows more vigorously than lateral or axillary buds due to the higher concentration of auxin produced in the apical bud. If the dominant growing tip is removed, the auxin/cytokinin (growth hormones) ratio is altered in the lateral buds, promoting their subsequent breaking and growth. Normally two branches will grow from each pinched stem, but sometimes more are produced (Plate 51). If a structured look is preferred in the garden, you can also shape plants after they bloom into neat rounded forms. Simply cutting off any deteriorating leaves, stems, or flowers can improve the overall appearance of a plant.

Remove Unsightly or Insignificant Flowers. Some perennials are worth keeping more for their foliage than for their flowers. The poor flowers may even detract from the beauty of the foliage, either in their appearance alone or by causing a decline in the health of the foliage. Such unwanted flowers should be removed from the plant before the buds open.

Clean-Up the Garden. Cutting plants to the ground in the autumn and spring is a significant part of cleaning up the garden, and most perennials are going to need it either before or after the winter. With certain species, cutting back before winter not only creates an orderly appearance in the garden, but is vital for removing debris that might otherwise harbor insects or disease over the winter. Species that pose no threat of harboring pests will provide winter interest for humans, and food and shelter for the birds, and these species can wait to be pruned in the spring.

There is also just the general clean-up needed throughout the season. This might involve the removal of a few dead leaves from a plant or of browning stems from a clump of fresh green ones. It could be the cleaning out of an area around the base of a plant to make room for its seeds to drop. There is tidying up to be done in the garden at almost any time of year, including in winter when a little time spent in the garden is a welcome change.

Bond With Your Plants. Pruning is a form of meditation for me. I find it very relaxing to go out into my gardens, sometimes just for some light snipping, other times getting into major shearing, depending on how I'm feeling. It connects me with my plants. I can see who's sending up new growth or flower buds or forming intriguing seedheads. In my country garden pruning connects me with nature, as the bees, hummingbirds, butterflies, chickadees, wrens, bluebirds, frogs, toads, and hawks carry on with their world around me. In my clients' gardens I feel like I know more what is going on after close inspection and caring for the gardens. This renewed sense of good health, that all is well in this sometimes crazy world, can't help but make you feel alive.

I'm sure that if I could prove this effect of pruning and gardening in general I could go on the road with a bestseller and a prescription for good health: along with eating sensibly and aerobic workouts, prune your perennials at least three times a week—for mental and physical well-being!

Benefits to the Landscape Industry. A well-pruned perennial garden obviously is going to look and perform better than one that is not well tended, even if pruning may not be identified as the improving factor to the untrained eye. If you are a landscape or garden contractor, I would suggest that you not install perennial gardens unless you or someone you trust plans on maintaining them. Your reputation rests on how the gardens look. A neglected perennial garden is not a picture for the portfolio. If the client chooses to do his or her own maintenance, you should provide specifications on the proper maintenance of the garden, especially the pruning requirements, species by species (perhaps a copy of this book would be helpful!). Follow up with several visits to answer any questions on-site with your clients, and be certain they understand the maintenance requirements. If your work looks good and your clients are happy, then you will be happy and rewarded with numerous referrals.

Types of Pruning

Pruning takes a variety of forms in varying regularity and at various times of year. Cutting back during the summer can be done before or after flowering, or both. Deadheading is a constant throughout the season. Pinching and thinning and disbudding are used less frequently but still must be part of the program. Deadleafing is frequently done in late summer and into autumn when plants are showing wear from the hot and dry weather. Pruning to prepare for winter and, more so, in the early spring are especially busy times. I will examine each of these topics in the following chapters.

Due to the complexity of the topic, it is difficult to make generalizations relating to all forms of pruning. For clarity I have tried to group the plants into categories, but remember that pruning perennials is very species-specific. You will want to refer to the Encyclopedia of Perennials in Section Three for pruning and maintenance information for specific plants.

Tools of the Perennial Plant Pruner

By-pass pruners, pruning scissors, and hand-held hedge shears are the primary tools needed for pruning perennials (Figure 8-1). The by-pass pruner is probably

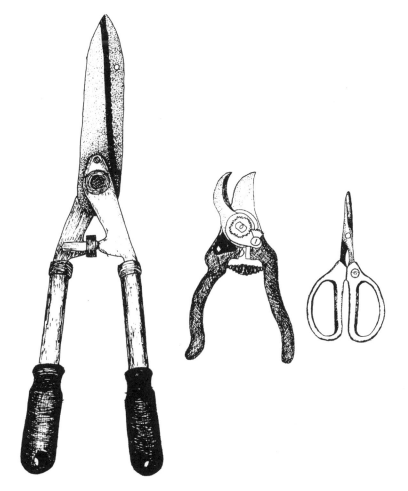

Figure 8-1. Tools of the perennial plant pruner (*left to right*): hedge shears, by-pass pruners, and pruning scissors.

the most commonly used tool for deadheading and cutting back. Avoid anvil-type pruners, which can crush stems. Hedge shears have become a favorite tool of mine for cutting back or shearing perennials either before or after flowering. Hedge shears can be used for shaping plants, and they are also effective for spring or autumn clean-up in the garden. Very sharp pruning scissors, which are sometimes sold as never-dull scissors, or bonsai/grape scissors are helpful and often essential when delicate deadheading of small flowerheads is needed. Pruning scissors are small and comfortable in smaller hands. (For an added bonus they come in attractive pastel colors!) They are very sharp and can cut a variety of things in the garden, from heavy branches to fingers—so be careful. When I first bought a pair of these, they were so popular that there would be a rush for them among my crew to see who could get them first. In some cases, particularly for large jobs or mass plantings, string trimmers can be used. And don't rule out the usefulness of a sharp thumbnail for snapping off dead flowers. Electric hedge shears work wonders on ornamental grasses in the early spring. I have never had to resort to a chain saw, although the temptation has been there on occasion when the gardens have gotten totally out of hand! Throughout the following chapters of Section Two and in the encyclopedia I will refer to the specific tool that I find works best for a given pruning job.

CHAPTER 9

Deadheading

"DON'T Be a Deadhead": this is the title of one of my more popular lectures about pruning perennials and preparing planting beds. When I was preparing this talk for a mixed audience of both professionals and homeowners I asked my husband to listen to it and give me his opinion, representing the very novice gardener. In his usual, patient way he waited until I was completely finished with the one-hour discussion, and then said, "you better tell them what a deadhead is."

Fortunately no one left the room during my first talk when they found out that I was discussing the removal of old or spent dead flowers and not old or spent rock 'n' rollers (although the latter does sound somewhat more intriguing). I have been called the "deadhead queen" by various colleagues because of my work with pruning—I'm not sure if there is any deeper meaning to this. . . .

Deadheading is beneficial to most herbaceous ornamental plants. Usually there is deadheading to be done from spring to killing frost. You'll enjoy the process more and are less likely to feel overwhelmed if you keep up with it. There are many reasons for deadheading. Primarily, deadheading can prolong the bloom period for plants on which the flowers open over a period of several weeks, or it can initiate a second flush of smaller, sometimes shorter and less numerous blooms on plants that have a single heavy bloom (see Appendix C, lists 14 and 15). It can improve the overall appearance of the plant, giving a fresh new look to an otherwise finished or even distracting item (see Appendix C, list 16). It can persuade biennials to behave like perennials. It can prevent self-seeding. I also like to remove deadheads or seedheads that weigh down the plant's foliage. Seed production can drain a plant's energy, and consequently, with certain perennials it can cause the foliage to deteriorate. Deadheading can promote vegetative and root growth rather than seed production and help retain the plant's healthy appearance.

The age of a plant greatly influences its deadheading needs. New plants give the gardener a grace period by requiring less frequent deadheading in their first year in the garden. The honeymoon, so to speak, is over after that first year, however, as deadheading hits full force the second season. Weather also greatly affects deadheading from season to season, with cool, moist weather extending the bloom life and sweltering heat and pelting rain decreasing it.

BASIC DEADHEADING METHODS

How to deadhead depends on the particular growth habit of the plant. The most common question I hear from people is "how far down do I prune?" Sometimes you need to remove individual dead flowers one at a time, or remove whole clusters of dead flowers, or cut off the entire flowering stalk or scape. Due to the fact that deadheading, as with other forms of pruning, is so species-specific, it is difficult to categorize or group plants into neat compartments. A key thing to look for when deadheading is the presence of new buds or new flowers. If they are present, deadhead to the new buds or flowers. In Appendix C, lists 17 and 18, I indicate those perennials that should be deadheaded to a lateral flower, bud, or leaf and those that should be deadheaded to the ground or to basal foliage. These lists are intended as general guidelines only, and a few of the plants could be in either list; consult the encyclopedia in Section Three for individual plant requirements. A review of some basic botany in Figure 9-1 may be helpful at this point.

Questions often arise about when to deadhead a plant that has a flower spike on which the flowers at the bottom of the spike open first, in which case the flowers at the bottom start to develop into seed while the flowers near the tip of the spike are still opening. (This flowering pattern is technically termed indeterminate.) If let go too long, often such a plant will produce rather long and gangly looking flower spikes, full of seed capsules and with two or so little flowers overwhelmed at the tip. This may be a personal preference, but it is best to not let things go this long. A general rule-of-thumb would be to deadhead when the seedpods outnumber the flowers or when the spike is about 70% finished with flowering.

Deadhead to a Lateral Flower, Bud, or Leaf

The majority of perennials require deadheading to a lateral flower, bud, or leaf. Plants of this type include popular perennials like shasta daisies, yarrow, salvia, and veronica (see Appendix C, list 17). Many of these perennials also require further cutting down to basal foliage after all flowering is finished (see Chapter 10, and Appendix C, list 27, for more information). To deadhead, prune off the dead flower stem to a new lateral flower or, if visible, to a lateral bud; if neither are apparent, cut the old flower off at the first lateral leaf (Figure 9-2).

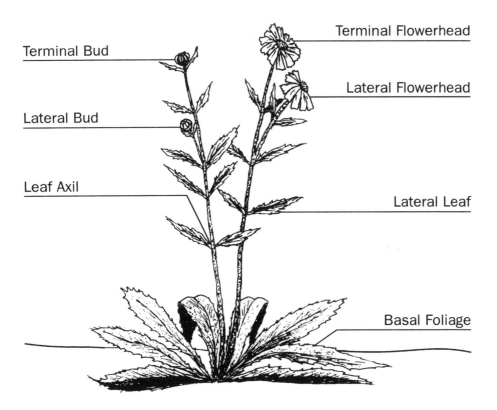

Figure 9-1. Basic botany for the perennial plant pruner, here showing the basic structures of shasta daisy (*Leucanthemum* ×*superbum*).

Many perennials can also be deadheaded by shearing, thus eliminating the tedious task of deadheading each individual old flower above a lateral leaf. Chapter 10 provides more information and illustrations on using this method. Also refer to Section Three for plants suitable for shearing.

Plants like balloon flower (*Platycodon grandiflorus*) and peachleaf bellflower (*Campanula persicifolia*) require careful deadheading of each individual flower along the stem. New buds are produced adjacent to the old flowers along the stem, and if the stem is cut back to the foliage before this flowering is completed, the bloom period will be greatly shortened (Figure 9-3).

Perennials such as *Aquilegia*, *Gypsophila paniculata*, *Hemerocallis*, and *Scabiosa columbaria* 'Butterfly Blue', which have branching flowering stems, also require careful attention to detail when being deadheaded. Deadheading for these plants involves cutting the old flower and its stem down to a lateral flowering stem or bud; then, when this next lateral stem or bud is done flowering, it is cut down to another lateral flowering stem, if present, or, if not, to the basal foliage (Figure 9-4). With daylilies (*Hemerocallis*), the individual deadheads—which be-

Figure 9-2. Deadheading for perennials with foliage on the flower stem, here showing *Heliopsis helianthoides*.

Figure 9-3. Deadheading for perennials with new buds adjacent to the old flowers, here showing *Campanula persicifolia*.

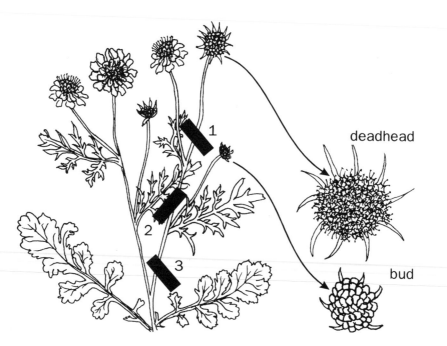

Figure 9-4. Deadheading for perennials with multibranched flowering stems, here showing *Scabiosa columbaria* 'Butterfly Blue'.

come wet, slimy, mummy-shaped dead flowers or, as I like to call them, "mush-mummies"—first should be pruned or snapped off using your fingers, taking care not to damage any of the new buds (see Plates 89–90). When no more new buds are visible in the bud cluster, the entire flowering stem should be cut off at the base (see Section Three for more details).

Deadhead to the Ground

Perennials with a single bare flower stem (sometimes with a few small insignificant leaves on the stem) should have their stem cut off close to the ground at the base of the plant when all flowering is finished (Figure 9-5). *Heuchera*, *Hosta*, and *Kniphofia* are examples of plants with this type of flowering (see Appendix C, list 18).

The renowned author, lecturer, and perennial gardener Elsa Bakalar taught me that some plants, like lady's mantle (*Alchemilla mollis*) and certain geraniums, which would normally be deadheaded to the ground or to basal foliage, can also be deadheaded by pulling the old flowering stems out of the plant, right to the root (Figure 9-6). This way, these otherwise wide-growing plants can be kept in bounds and even thinned in the process. Pulled stems often have roots on them that will take if replanted.

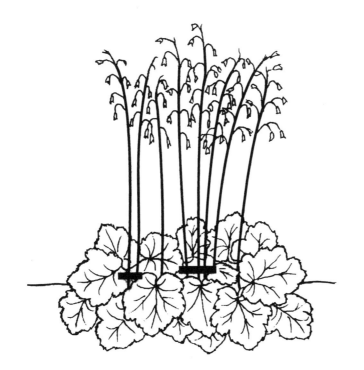

Figure 9-5. Deadheading for perennials with a single bare flower stem, perhaps with a few small leaves on the stem, here showing *Heuchera sanguinea*.

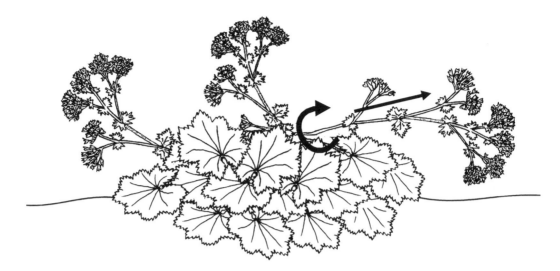

Figure 9-6. An alternative method of deadheading for wide-spreading mounded plants, here showing *Alchemilla mollis*. Twist and pull out the old flowering stem right down to the root.

TO SEED, OR NOT TO SEED . . .

The question of whether or not you should deadhead to prevent self-seeding depends primarily on your objectives for the garden and how you want to spend your time: deadheading or removing seedlings. (See Appendix C, list 19, for plants that reseed.) The weather can influence deadheading needs because it affects the amount of reseeding that occurs; wet springs, for example, can greatly enhance germination. Another consideration is whether the seeds will develop into the desirable plant. Species forms will grow true to type from seed, but cultivars may not and so allowing them to go to seed can be a pitfall. Sometimes this provides the gardener with pleasant surprises, but usually they are not so pleasant—these unpleasant progeny can take over the desirable cultivar, leaving you wondering what you started with. This is often the case with *Phlox paniculata* (see Plate 114).

Personally, I like some seeding in my gardens to promote that "unplanned" look (Plates 52–53). This approach can be promoted a bit too much, and I pay the price by spending a great deal of time removing unwanted plants. On the other hand, perennials such as columbine (*Aquilegia*) and rose campion (*Lychnis coronaria*) are rather short lived and readily perpetuate themselves if allowed to self-sow. Biennials such as sweet william (*Dianthus barbatus*), as well as some of my favorite annuals like Brazilian verbena (*Verbena bonariensis*) and nigella or love-in-a-mist (*Nigella damascena*), I treat as perennials because they self-sow reliably. The nigella stay close by the feet of their original parents. This is a point that also comes into play when deciding whether to allow plants to seed: do the seeds fall close to the parent—which won't mean too much work—or do they scatter everywhere—which can result in a great deal of work? You can be selective with your deadheading, particularly with prolific seeders, and remove all but a few deadheads to allow smaller numbers of seedlings in. This is a good approach but takes some forethought. If seeding is desired but the deadhead is unattractive, as in the case of a spiked flower like *Digitalis*, the spike can be shortened, thus still allowing for some seeding but without being so obtrusive. In some years you may not need any new seedlings, in which case the plants should be completely deadheaded. A predominately self-sown garden can be an economical approach for the budget-conscious gardener, although it does require intervention to keep it managed.

So, in certain instances, reseeding can actually be a reason for not deadheading, such as when it makes for a more diverse or more economical planting. Attractive seedheads is another big reason. Many plants, such as *Anemone pulsatilla*, *Asclepias tuberosa*, *Dictamnus albus*, *Sedum* 'Autumn Joy', and most of the ornamental grasses, extend their season of interest through the summer to the fall, perhaps even into winter, with their ornamental deadheads (see Appendix C, list 20). Care must be taken, however, to not allow too much seed formation; even if you choose to allow seedheads to form because they are attractive, physiological concerns for the plant remain. The seeds are a sink for the plant's energy and the rest of the plant may suffer. I found this to be true with Siberian iris. I got greedy one year and left all the deadheads on the plants until the following spring, at which time I cut them and used them for dried arrangements. The plants were drastically weakened, opened up in the center, and had a significant reduction in the number of flowers produced—all the signs that division is needed. The plants were only 2 years old, and Siberian iris usually doesn't require frequent division, so I figured that this condition was related to the number of seedheads allowed to mature. Now I remove about two-thirds of the seedheads and allow one-third to mature on the plants. This doesn't seem to drain them (see Plate 97).

Some plants are just so willing to please that they offer us rebloom as well as pretty seedheads. In certain cases you can have both at the same time if you deadhead a few flowering stems and leave others to ripen. In most cases, though, you will need to deadhead the entire plant, let it rebloom, and allow this secondary display to ripen for your ornamental seedheads.

Some perennials have unattractive deadheads that require frequent (daily is best) deadheading to look decent. Most modern daylilies (*Hemerocallis*), *Coreopsis lanceolata* (see Plate 73), *Hibiscus moscheutos*, and *Leucanthemum* ×*superbum*, to name a few, fall into this category. Plants of this nature are not good choices for the low-maintenance gardener. Older daylilies with smaller flowers, such as *Hemerocallis* 'Mdm. Bellum', are exceptions, as they drop their old flowers cleanly.

Perennials such as *Gaura*, *Linum*, and *Tradescantia* (whose flowers actually melt away) shed their petals discreetly, but they usually do this by the afternoon, thus leaving the evening devoid of their beauty—a let-down for the gardener who is away all day and can only enjoy the garden in the evenings after returning home. Other self-sufficient "petal droppers," including *Belamcanda*, *Coreopsis verticillata*, and *Lychnis coronaria*, hold their flowers for longer than one day (see Appendix C, list 21). It should be noted that although these plants neatly dispose of their dead flowers, they still are producing seedheads that produce seed, and so they may require deadheading either to prevent seeding or to help produce or prolong bloom. But at least they don't require daily attention like some of the others.

Astilbe, *Baptisia*, *Papaver orientale*, and others do not flower longer or repeat their bloom if deadheaded, so this extra work is not needed. It can also be beneficial to not deadhead perennials that flower late in the season, such as *Boltonia* or *Chrysopsis*, as their entire structure, including seedheads, can be left for winter interest. Perennials such as these that do not require deadheading are listed in Appendix C, list 22. This list also includes plants that normally do not reseed or they may have attractive seedheads, so if they are not deadheaded it isn't a problem.

Certain silver-leaved perennials, such as the artemisias, *Santolina chamaecyparissus*, and *Stachys byzantina*, have foliage that will deteriorate if the plants are allowed to go to seed. Deadheading allows the plant's energies to stay directed toward foliage production. These plants often are not blessed with particularly outstanding flowers anyway, and usually I remove the flower buds before they even open, keeping the plant in a strictly vegetative state.

Birds are another element to consider when deciding whether or not you are going to deadhead your perennials. Genera such as *Echinacea*, *Heliopsis*, and *Rudbeckia* are attractive to golden finch, and I have had flocks of golden finch in my gardens munching on these plants. *Echinacea* is a particularly favorite delicacy for the finches as well as for the juncos over the winter. The only problem is that *Echinacea* will seed in outrageous proportions all over the garden. I tried hanging bundles of cut stems from a tree, but the finches didn't seem to be as attracted to these as to the ones in the gardens, so I always leave a few drifts up for them in various spots. Hosta seeds are savored by chickadees. Watching the birds in the gardens in the summer and winter adds a special dimension to perennial gardening. (Appendix C, list 23, provides a listing of plants that attract birds.)

CHAPTER 10

Cutting Back

CUTTING back refers to pruning a plant to renew its appearance or encourage a new flush of growth and flowering, or to control its height or flowering time. In contrast to deadheading, which is the removal of a dead flower and its stem and perhaps a few leaves, cutting back generally means removing foliage, even a significant amount, as well as possibly removing flower buds or deadheads. This technique can regenerate or extend the life of certain perennials. It can be used to remove unwanted flower buds on plants grown exclusively for their foliar effect. Cutting back or shearing can also be helpful for keeping plants within their assigned space in the garden (see Appendix C, list 24).

Under certain circumstances it is necessary to cut perennials all the way down to the ground or to the foliage developing at the base of the plant. Plants that are to be cut to the ground need some coddling through such a traumatic experience. At the very least, keep them well watered. Aerating the soil with light forking or hoeing also seems to help. And sometimes a light top-dressing with compost or liquid fertilizer gives a needed boost. Growth often will be slow on plants that are cut back and left in poor dry conditions, and new growth might not occur until cooler conditions return later in the season. Plants that are highly stressed may be greatly weakened and in severe cases may not return. In southern regions or in areas with very hot summers, cutting plants back before the heat of August is advisable. If pruning later than the end of July, do not prune off as much or as far back on the stems as you might with earlier pruning.

Cutting plants to the ground can be an unnerving and traumatic experience for some gardeners as well. To ease the process, plants can be cut back in stages, if desired. For example, cut half the plant down to the ground and pull the other half over the wounds; wait for new growth and then cut the remaining part of the plant (Figure 10-1). In addition to assisting the gardener through this troubling procedure, pruning in this fashion means there will not be as large a hole in garden since the entire plant is not being pruned at one time.

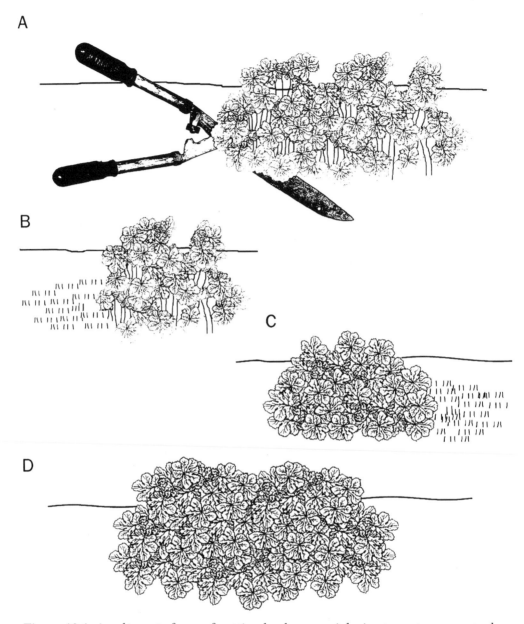

A

B

C

D

Figure 10-1. An alternate form of cutting back perennials, in stages to prevent a large hole in the garden or to assist a timid gardener through the "operation," here showing *Geranium platypetalum*.

The typical pruning tools can be used for cutting back (see Figure 8-1). Pruners work fine with small plantings, but on most jobs (including my own gardens) I resort to hedge shears. Grass shears or string trimmers for very large areas can also be used to help speedup this labor-intensive chore. Hedge shears and string trimmers don't cut as cleanly as pruners, but the plants help out by filling-in rapidly after pruning—usually within a week there will be new growth, and in

2 weeks you'll have a full lush plant again. A word of caution is in order when it comes to using hedge shears or string trimmers: be sure that the individual wielding the tool is trained in the way the pruning should be performed, both from the plant's point of view as well as from the operator's, otherwise unintended cuts may be encountered. Unless you have a lot of time to spare—and most people don't seem to these days—if using hand pruners simply grab a handful of stems and snip, rather than doing each individual stem one at a time.

I will discuss cutting back for maintenance and aesthetics, for height control, as a means of delaying or preventing flowering, and as a regenerative technique. Due to the complexity of this topic, I have placed plants into categories based on their flowering time: spring, summer, or autumn. As with most living things, plants don't always fit into neat categories, but it does help in simplifying this otherwise confusing information. The Encyclopedia of Perennials in Section Three provides detailed information on the best techniques for the specific plants.

Cutting Back for Maintenance and/or Aesthetics—Prune After Flowering

Perennials that are being cut back for purposes of maintenance or aesthetics should be pruned after flowering. Generally when plants are cut back after flowering the regrowth remains lower than the normal mature height of the plant, and if rebloom occurs the flowers often will be smaller in numbers and sometimes in size. In many cases, when pruning after flowering it is best to cut down to the start of new growth developing at the base of the plant, or the basal foliage. Personally, I am more comfortable pruning a perennial down to basal foliage, rather than pruning to the ground when no signs of life are evident. Regrowth usually is much faster and generally is ensured if pruning is done when basal foliage is present. When cutting plants to the ground do not cut flush to the soil but leave about 2 in. of stem, just in case new buds are present slightly above ground. They won't be damaged by too close a shearing if a few inches of stem remains.

Spring-Flowering Perennials

Many spring-blooming, low-growing rock garden or edging plants should be cut back or sheared by one-half after flowering (Figure 10-2). This severe pruning promotes attractive new growth and sometimes sporadic rebloom, and it prevents the plants from becoming straggly or woody or opening up in the center (melting out). Plants that benefit from this type of pruning include maiden pink (*Dianthus deltoides*) (see Plates 75–76), evergreen candytuft (*Iberis sempervirens*)

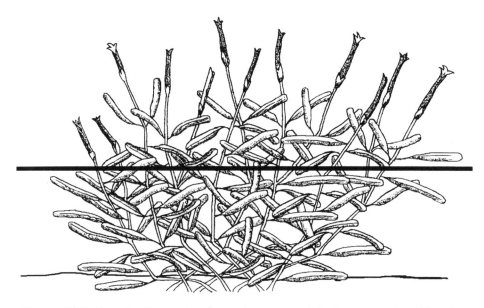

Figure 10-2. Pruning for spring-flowering perennials, here showing *Dianthus deltoides*.

(see Plates 92–95), and moss phlox (*Phlox subulata*). (See Appendix C, list 25, for a more complete listing of spring-flowering plants that benefit from cutting back after flowering.)

Although not a mat-forming perennial, Hungarian speedwell (*Veronica austriaca* subsp. *teucrium*) also benefits from a cut in half after flowering (see Plates 128–130). Catmint (*Nepeta*) may flower sporadically throughout the summer if cut back by one-third to one-half after the first spring bloom period. Plus, the plant's overall appearance is greatly enhanced by the pruning even if you don't get more blooms. If you miss the chance to cut back catmint in the spring and it starts to rebloom for you later in the summer, it will benefit from removal of the ratty foliage and dead flowers that will have fallen to the edges.

Some gardeners have good luck with cutting oriental poppy (*Papaver orientale*) to the ground immediately after flowering. New basal growth appears and remains to fill in the space through the summer, rather than leaving a void for much of the summer, which happens if plants are allowed to mature, die back, and then are cut down. I have pruned back poppies right after flowering for several years now but have not had good luck. In my garden the new growth doesn't appear until autumn, which is the same time that it appears when I don't cut the plants down right after flowering but allow them to die down naturally and then prune them. Besides, not cutting them down after flowering allows me to enjoy the ornamental seedheads that develop.

Summer-Flowering Perennials

Summer-flowering perennials differ from the spring-flowering types in the amount of cutting back that is required after flowering. (Appendix C, list 26, provides a list of plants to cut back after flowering for aesthetics in the summer and autumn.) Some plants look best if cut to the ground, or to new basal foliage, whereas others require a cut by one-half or one-third, and still others need 6 in. "left on top." Here individual needs come into play. As with other pruning techniques, the cutting-back requirements of perennials is greatly affected by the age of the plant, weather conditions, and soil conditions. First-year plants may be vigorous and may flower most of the summer without any cutting back, though in subsequent years they usually demand it. If the weather has been extremely hot and dry, as in southern regions, the plants are going to show more wear and will benefit from a trim to bring some fresh new growth to the garden.

The degree of cutting back is also specific to each species. Looking at a few plants from the genus *Geranium* gives us a good picture of just how individual the plants can be in their needs. *Geranium endressii* 'Wargrave Pink' looks unsightly in our hot summers if all the old stems are not cut back to the ground where new basal foliage is forming (see Plates 83–85); the closely related *Geranium* ×*oxonianum* 'Claridge Druce' and 'A. T. Johnson' need to be treated in a similar fashion. But *Geranium macrorrhizum* and *Geranium* ×*cantabrigiense* 'Biokovo' require nothing more than deadheading and maybe a touch of deadleafing.

Artemisia schmidtiana 'Nana' and *Thalictrum aquilegiifolium* are just a couple of other summer-flowering perennials that may benefit from being cut down to basal foliage after flowering. Grasses such as ribbon grass (*Phalaris arundinacea* var. *picta*) and variegated oat grass (*Arrhenatherum elatius* 'Variegatum') may develop brown leaf tips by late summer; the cure for this is shearing or mowing them to the ground to promote healthy new foliage. (See Appendix A for more extensive information about ornamental grasses.) Variegated bishop's weed (*Aegopodium podagraria* 'Variegatum') can be treated the same way. *Lamium*, which gets tatty in midsummer, can be cut down to new basal foliage, and the attractive new growth will last into early winter.

Plants such as *Amsonia tabernaemontana*, *Baptisia australis*, and *Euphorbia polychroma* get not only a cut but also a style when being pruned. These perennials may be formed into rounded shapes to add structure to a garden (see Plate 68). Hedge shears is the better tool to use for shaping perennials (Plate 54). Shaping plants in this way is commonly done in public gardens where a bit more formality is in order. The pruning done in public gardens can serve several purposes as cuttings are frequently taken for propagation, in addition to pruning for aesthetics or regeneration. This is something to keep in mind in the home garden as well.

Cutting Back to Basal Foliage After Deadheading

Many summer-flowering perennials benefit from two types of pruning to look their best. First they are deadheaded down to a lateral bud, flower, or leaf, which often means cutting them back by about one-third to one-half (see Chapter 9); then, as new basal foliage starts to develop and all lateral flowering (if any) is finished, the plants should be cut back to the newly emerged basal foliage (Figure 10-3). Sometimes you will get an additional bloom on plants pruned in this way, though the flowers tend to be smaller and fewer than in the initial two flowerings. Popular perennials such as shasta daisy, delphinium, and moonshine yarrow, as well as a slew of others, fit into this category (see Appendix C, list 27). Remember that after cutting plants down to basal foliage they'll appreciate your keeping them moist, aerating them, and perhaps top-dressing with organic matter, which would be nice but is not absolutely essential. In the case of heavy feeders like *Delphinium*, incorporating a top-dressing or a light water-soluble fertilizer after cutting back is especially helpful for healthy growth and rebloom. In one mild year I still had a bloom (albeit only one) on my *Delphinium* in December, which I proudly showed to some horticultural colleagues who were visiting for an early Christmas celebration (nothing like a little showing off!).

Figure 10-3. Pruning summer-flowering perennials by cutting back (deadheading) by one-third or one-half to a lateral bud, followed by cutting down to basal foliage, here showing *Achillea* 'Moonshine'.

As always, the age of the plant and weather conditions will greatly influence whether this type of pruning is needed. I have some old *Salvia nemorosa* 'East Friesland' plants that in most years do not produce many new flowers from lateral buds. Instead, after the initial bloom they open up in the center, begging to be cut back to new basal foliage, which in turn gives me some rebloom. Younger plants of the same cultivar produce nice lateral flowers, with deadheading, before needing to be cut down. Observing the plants and using a little common sense usually is your best guide as to what type of cut is in order.

Cutting Back for Height Control and To Stagger or Delay Bloom—Prune Before Flowering

For many summer- and autumn-flowering perennials cutting back before flowering can help limit the plant's height (see Appendix C, list 28). Especially in areas of high winds, controlling mature height may be needed to prevent plants from flopping or to eliminate the need for staking. This approach to pruning can also be used to layer a planting by creating interesting gradations in heights (Plate 55). Furthermore, overly fertile soil and too much shade for a sun-loving plant will produce leggy growth, and cutting back before flowering will often produce plants with a nicer, fuller habit as a result of increased branching. Many times, depending on the species, cutting back before flowering will produce smaller but more numerous flowers. When perennials are first planted they often benefit from cutting back for fuller first-year plants.

Bloom time in the garden can be staggered by selective pruning, and this can be used to the gardener's advantage in several ways. Simply pruning separate plants of the same species a week or so apart, or pruning only part of a group and leaving the rest unpruned, will stagger flowering by delaying bloom in the pruned individuals. Individual plants can also be pruned so that their flowering will coordinate better with a later blooming species. Staggering or delaying bloom extends the season of interest in a garden, particularly in a mass planting, and the technique is often used by public gardens for this purpose. Of particular note is Stonecrop Gardens in Cold Spring, New York, where different "moments" are created in the garden by pruning certain plants for special flower or color effects at specific times. I too have employed this technique when I have put together color combinations that I end up not liking. Though I may not want to move the plant because I like it where it's planted, I don't want it flowering at the same time as one of its neighbors, so I prune it back to flower later.

Individual plants will flower longer but not as profusely if a few stems are cut back to delay bloom. Many summer- and autumn-flowering plants can be delayed by cutting stems back by about 4 to 6 in. when the flower buds start to form. This can delay flowering by several weeks or more. If the chrysanthemum 'Clara Curtis' (*Dendranthema zawadskii* var. *latilobum*) is sheared while in bud, for example, flowering can be delayed by 1 to 2 months. With some perennials, cutting the plants back when the flowers are forming will result in no bud development and consequently no bloom (see Appendix C, list 29).

A delay in flowering can also be useful for the flower arranger who would like to have, perhaps, beebalm into August for arrangements. The smaller flowers that result from pruning before flowering are also often a better size for cut arrangements (Plate 56).

I have several clients who travel for several weeks or even a month during the summer. Often they will cut the majority of their garden down by about one-third or one-half, depending on the time and the plants, before they leave. They return to lush new growth and flowering on plants that otherwise would have flowered with no audience and would have looked finished and shabby upon the owners' return.

Although in many cases either pinching or cutting back can be used to achieve similar effects, I generally opt for cutting back rather than pinching. From a time standpoint, I prefer to cut something back once, rather than pinching and then having to come back and pinch again, and perhaps again, to create the desired effect. Certain perennials do seem to respond better to pinching than to cutting back, although from the physiological point they should be the same.

Most of my work concentrates on the effects of cutting plants back once before flowering. Perennials can be cut back at different times, or several times, for different effects, but in most cases pruning only one time makes sense from a maintenance standpoint. Pruning of plants before flowering (by one-half or two-thirds) is generally done in early to mid-June, because this is also the time when many spring-flowering species can be pruned after flowering. It gives the landscape contractor, for example, a time frame in which a large number of perennials can be pruned during one maintenance visit to a garden. Keep in mind that, again, this is an attempt to simplify a rather complex area of pruning. Pruning in early June will delay the flowering of many summer bloomers, but pruning earlier in the season may be preferable if no delay is desired. In warmer climates you may need to prune earlier due to faster growth earlier in the season, and you also may need to prune plants more heavily in such climates to effectively reduce their height. Due to the longer growing season in the South, late-flowering plants can be pruned later into the season to further delay flowering, while such pruning in cooler climates may result in plants that don't have a chance to flower before snowfall.

Timing of cutting back is an interesting area and one that is open to lots of fun and experimentation. The cut-off date to stop pruning perennials so that they will flower before cold weather, or so that they will or will not be delayed or by how much, is not known in most cases. General pruning dates are often given without sound experience, such as "don't prune after the fourth of July if you want flowers before frost." I have experimented with a variety of different pruning dates for different species, and the results are provided in Section Three of this book. With some plants, cutting back before flowering will decrease the floral display or the vigor of the plant or both. Some perennials, if cut back too often, or by too much, or too late in the season, may not flower nicely, or at all, or they may be stunted. Others may start flowering as soon as pruning stops no matter how late in the season, within reason. Why perennials respond differently is not completely understood. As is emphasized throughout the book, regional differences, age and vigor of the plant, weather conditions for the season, among other factors, can affect the results. Photoperiod (day length) and the obligatory cold period (vernalization) that many perennials require to induce flowering could also be responsible for differing results for different pruning techniques and different perennials.

An important thing to keep in mind is that often the more of a plant that is cut off or the closer it is pruned to its normal flowering date, the greater the delay in flowering. Also, the amount of delay is not directly related to the timing of the pruning. In other words, a plant cut back on the 30th day of the month will not necessarily have its flowering delayed 15 days longer than one cut back on the 15th day of the month. Keep in mind too the natural habit of the plant. Waiting until later to cut something back may result in a rather odd-looking shape to the plant. Plants that are cut back late may develop a tall single stem topped with a multibranched head, creating an awkward look to certain perennials (see Plates 124–125) reminiscent of the "standard" look often used for woody plants such as lilac or fuchsia.

Summer-Flowering Perennials

It is well-known that certain autumn-flowering perennials benefit from cutting back early in the season to reduce the need for staking, but it is not as well-known that this can be done with several different species of summer-flowering perennials as well. Summer-flowering phlox respond well to cutting back before flowering and can be treated in a variety of different ways to reduce height and delay flowering. *Phlox maculata* 'Alpha', for example, cut back by one-half when in bud in early June may flower at 18 in. rather than at 2½ ft., and about 2 weeks later than usual (see Plate 112). *Heliopsis* can also be pruned by one-half at the same time to flower at 2½ to 3½ ft., rather than at 5 ft., with about 1½ weeks' delay. Balloon flower (*Platycodon grandiflorus*) tends to flop, but pruning it back by one-half in early June can produce plants 1 to 2 ft. shorter than normal and with a 2- to 3-week delay in flowering.

Preventing flowering altogether, rather than just delaying it, by shearing or cutting off the flower buds may be desirable with certain perennials. I think of this pruning as a form of disbudding, although technically the term doesn't apply (disbudding traditionally refers to removing surplus buds to promote production of high-quality flowers or fruit)—but after all, it is removing the buds! This pruning technique is utilized when plants are grown mainly for foliar display or when the flowers are unsightly, distracting, or simply unwanted. Plants such as *Heuchera micrantha* 'Palace Purple' and *Penstemon digitalis* 'Husker's Red' are just a couple. I don't want the flowers of these plants to compete with the attractive foliage, so most of the time I cut off the buds as they set. When plants like *Teucrium* and others are grown for hedging purposes the flowers are not desired. Removing the flower buds is also effective in stopping the decline in vigor of many silver-foliaged plants, particularly silvermound artemisia (*Artemisia schmidtiana* 'Nana') or lavender cotton (*Santolina chamaecyparissus*), which decline after flowering. The flowers on these two plants are not especially attractive anyway, so why bother to keep them. Preventing flowering can mean several shearings if new buds develop after the initial pruning.

Autumn-Flowering Perennials

Many late-flowering plants benefit from being cut back before they bloom. As with the summer-flowering plants that benefit from cutting back for height control, the late bloomers treated in this way will have a fuller and more compact habit, less need for staking (if any is required), and staggered bloom time if desired.

Cutting back autumn-flowering plants for height control is normally done in mid- to late June in the Midwest, generally when the plants are 12 to 16 in. tall. Cutting back can be done later, depending on the usual variety of factors. Most of the time the plants should be cut back by one-half, but you can prune back by two-thirds or more depending on the plant and your objective. Pruning later may involve simply removing 4 to 6 in. from the tips of the plants.

Asters are among the first autumn-flowering plants that come to mind for cutting back, and they are one of several perennials for which pinching is the more commonly recommended technique but which respond just as well or better to cutting back. I find that cutting back these late-season beauties by one-half or two-thirds when the plants are 12 to 16 in. tall is more effective than pinching. The outer stems can be cut lower than the inner ones to create a more rounded habit and reduce the ugly legs usually associated with asters (Figure 10-4). Cutting back can eliminate the need for staking on most *Aster* cultivars, but some of the extremely tall ones may require it even with pruning, depending on the soil and weather conditions. Once cut back they usually flower at a sturdy 3 ft. or so. You can also select asters that won't require cutting back. One I prefer is the late-season (mid-October for us) *Aster tataricus* 'Jin Dai' (see Plate 72). It usually reaches only 4 ft. in height and doesn't need cutting back or staking. Lower growing forms can also be used, such as *Aster novae-angliae* 'Purple Dome', which reaches only 18 to 24 in. in height.

Sedum 'Autumn Joy' is often pinched for height control (see Chapter 11 for details), but it can also be cut back by one-half in the spring when plants are 8 in. tall (in the Midwest this is usually in the first week in June). Plants will have more but smaller flowers. Pruning also helps prevent flopping on plants growing in partial shade or very rich soils.

One usually associates chrysanthemums (*Dendranthema*) with pinching, but they can also be cut back effectively. I don't use many mums because of their lack of hardiness, but I have a few that I love that are tough as nails and quite attractive, and some do fine without any pinching or cutting back. I discuss these forms in more detail in the next chapter and in the encyclopedia.

When grown in the South *Eupatorium purpureum* can be cut back to 12 in. in early June and will flower at about 3 ft. in early August, compared to its typical 15-ft. or more mature height (see Plate 80). In the Midwest I pinch *Eupatorium maculatum* 'Gateway' for outstanding full plants with smaller flowers (see

Figure 10-4. Cutting back autumn-flowering perennials such as *Aster:* (*left*) cut back by one-half to two-thirds in early summer for height control; (*right*) plants can also be shaped, if desired.

Plate 81). A variety of techniques can be used on other natives to control their heights, and this is true of many perennials. Different gardeners have different techniques for the same plants, depending on their objectives or their situations. For instance, boneset (*Eupatorium perfoliatum*), great blue lobelia (*Lobelia siphilitica*), and ironweed (*Vernonia altissima*) can be cut back by one-half when 4 in. tall and then by one-half again when 16 in. tall. Or great blue lobelia can be pinched around the first of July, and ironweed can be cut to the ground when 2 ft. tall or cut back by 1 or 2 ft. when 4 ft. tall to stagger and delay flowering. A good example to demonstrate that pruning methods, as with many gardening techniques, are not set in stone.

Cutting Back to Regenerate or Extend the Life of Plants

A regenerative pruning cut can lead to a more vigorous plant and even a longer life in certain species. Richard Hansen and Friedrich Stahl, in their book *Perennials and Their Garden Habitats* (1993), write that certain short-lived perennials —*Centranthus ruber*, *Coreopsis grandiflora* 'Badengold', *Coreopsis lanceolata*, *Gaillardia* ×*grandiflora*, and *Leucanthemum maximum* among them—flower themselves to exhaustion and are consequently unable to form buds for the following year's shoots. To avoid this situation, Hansen and Stahl recommend that the whole plant be cut back to stimulate vegetative growth. In the Midwest, cutting back in late August or early September should allow enough time for growth to emerge before cold weather. This same principle could apply to a wide range of perennials. New growth produced from cutting a plant back is more vigorous and less stressed than the old dying foliage, and it is likely to be less prone to disease and weather damage.

Woody-stemmed perennials (or subshrubs) should be cut back to about 4 to 6 in. in the spring or early to midsummer if they have started to die back or grow leggy. Plants in this category include the heaths and heathers (*Erica*), sunroses (*Helianthemum*), St. Johnswort (*Hypericum calycinum*), lavender cotton (*Santolina chamaecyparissus*), germander (*Teucrium chamaedrys*), and thymes (*Thymus*). This also applies to lavender (*Lavandula*), which may need a hard cutting back in the spring every 2 to 3 years to hold a decent habit if the plant has become open and leggy. Many of these species tolerate cutting back so well that they can be used for low hedging.

The life of a whole range of short-lived, otherwise biennial species can be prolonged by several years if cut down immediately after flowering before seeds set; hollyhock (*Alcea rosea*), foxglove (*Digitalis purpurea*), and dame's rocket (*Hesperis matronalis*) fit into this category (see Appendix C, list 19). As mentioned under deadheading in Chapter 9, biologically a plant's primary goal is to produce seed to become the next generation. If this goal isn't accomplished, the plants put their energy into vegetative growth, thus extending the life of the existing plant.

Pruning Techniques for Peak-Season Long Performance

I like to look at spiderwort (*Tradescantia ×andersoniana*) as an example of a plant that benefits from several different pruning techniques to perform its best. When the plants are 12 in. tall (early May in the Midwest), cut them back by one-half to reduce legginess; after the first flowering, deadhead the plants, again cutting them back by about one-half (Figure 10-5). Be certain to prune above new lateral buds, if present. Be patient when deadheading spiderwort; the flowers melt away by afternoon, but many new buds still remain in the flower cluster, so make sure that the plant is finished flowering. After the second bloom from lateral buds, spiderwort plants may require cutting back by two-thirds or more for healthy new growth and possibly for another yet smaller show of flowers. Plants often need to be cut back by two-thirds or to the ground after the first flowering, skipping the deadheading step, depending on the growing conditions and the age of the plant. This is particularly true of older plants subjected to dry conditions, which look pretty tacky by midsummer. *Tradescantia* produces new growth and often will rebloom with sufficient moisture.

Figure 10-5. Pruning techniques for peak-season long performance, here showing *Tradescantia ×andersoniana*: (*left*) reduce height by one-half in early May; (*middle*) reduce height by one-half after first bloom by deadheading to lateral buds; (*right*) reduce height by two-thirds or more if necessary after all flowering is completed.

CHAPTER 11

Pinching, Disbudding, Thinning, and Deadleafing

PINCHING

PINCHING is one of the best known forms of pruning associated with perennials, and in particular associated with garden mums (*Dendranthema* ×*morifolium*). Anyone who considers themselves so much as a weekend gardener knows the supposed attributes and glories of pinching mums. But very few gardeners take full advantage of this valuable technique, which can enhance the habit and flowering effect of innumerable other perennials. Pinching is also a good alternative for the timid gardener who may be hesitant to do dramatic cutting back for height control. Pinching allows for experimentation, since you can pinch just a few stems on a plant, observe, and then decide what approach to take in subsequent years. If in doubt, you may not want to pinch an entire plant, although a bit of adventure is healthy. Always remember that perennials will come back next year in their original state—it's not like an apple (*Malus*) tree that may be marred for life with one improper pruning.

As with cutting back, pinching can be used to help keep plants in bounds, to prevent plants from growing tall and straggly, and to stagger the bloom period of an individual plant or a group of plants. Pinched perennials often produce more, but smaller, individual flowers than a plant that hasn't been pinched. You can shape a plant as well by pinching the outer stems shorter than the central stems. Flowers will be distributed more evenly over the entire plant with shaping, and plants will have leaves to the ground rather than having bare lower stems, which often require a facer plant to hide them. This problem is sometimes overlooked during the design process, so pinching can compensate for that oversight.

Although pinching and cutting back are often talked about interchangeably, the two practices differ in the amount of plant material that is removed and the tools that are used to remove it. Pinching usually involves removing only the growing tips and first set of leaves, or approximately $\frac{1}{2}$ to 1 in. (at the most 2 in.), of each shoot (Figure 11-1). Fingers work best for this task and are the most portable garden tools available. A sharp thumbnail is particularly handy, and I know some perennial producers who grow their thumbnails longer just for this purpose. Cutting back, on the other hand, involves removing more than 2 in. of growth, sometimes 4 in., 6 in., or even 1 ft. or more, and pruners are generally the best tool for this. Pinching involves less time initially, as it is fast work to go through a plant and pinch it. A plant may require a second or third pinching as well, so in the long run more time may be required when pruning a plant by pinching as compared to simply cutting a plant back by one-half once. As with other forms of pruning, pinching is best done by cutting the stem just above a node. Ideally the top bud should point outward; this prevents new stems from growing inward and creating an entangled, unproductive mess.

It is difficult to generalize as to the best time to do pinching. As with any form of pruning, when to pinch varies according to several factors, among them climatic conditions, seasonal weather, soil fertility, plant individuality, and the gar-

Figure 11-1. Pinching, here showing *Dendranthema*.

dener's objectives. Pinching usually is performed in May or early to mid-June in the Midwest; earlier if you are in California or the South and other warm climates. If you wish to retain normal bloom time, pinching must be done early in the season; early spring pinching will be necessary for late-spring-blooming plants. Any subsequent pinching should be done after two or three nodes' growth. If a delay in flowering is the objective, pinching close to bloom time will give the desired results. Pinching can be used to stagger bloom time: for example, pinch one-third of the plants in the bed well before normal blooming time; one week later pinch another third, and pinch the rest a week after that. Even pinching plants a few days apart will create an extended bloom season, though at the expense of a single abundant display. Pinching perennials when they are first planted often produces a more compact habit and better branching on first-year plants. With some perennials, long internodes are a sign that pinching will help improve growth habit. *Perovskia atriplicifolia*, for one, should be pinched when it is 12 in. tall to help control flopping. *Physostegia virginiana* should be pinched in early spring to control lankiness, whereas *Helianthus salicifolius* can be pinched in early July to create smaller plants for smaller spaces. More exact guidelines are given for individual plants in the Encyclopedia of Perennials in Section Three, including approximate height, time, and frequency of pinching, and Appendix C, list 30, indicates those perennials that respond to pinching.

Pinching is most commonly used on branching perennials. If we look closely at our plants, common sense tells us that it would be of no use to try to pinch an iris, for example, or a daylily, or crocosmia, or any other single-stemmed perennial. Pinching is of no benefit to plants growing from rhizomes, bulbs, or corms or to basal rosette-forming plants. *Heuchera* does not need its foliage pinched, and we all can figure out the consequence of pinching the flower stems. Pinching is not for the rhizomatous *Polygonatum* either. Some gardeners feel that plants with a spike or single large head of flowers are ruined if they are pinched because the big show will have been pinched off. The pinched plants may produce smaller lateral flower spikes, but not always. Some gardeners might find the smaller flower spikes to be an advantage. I like to pinch or cut back certain spiked plants, such as *Alcea rosea* and *Lobelia cardinalis*. Yes, the flower spikes are smaller, but they are more in scale with the smaller plant that is produced from pinching. In some cases, such as with *Digitalis* or *Verbascum*, pinching may simply result in no bloom. Plants that do not respond well to pinching are indicated in Appendix C, list 31.

As has been emphasized throughout this book, often several different pruning techniques can be used for the same plant. Many perennials can be either cut back or pinched depending on the desired results, timing, season, gardener's mood, and so forth. *Sedum* 'Autumn Joy', for example, can be cut in half when 8 in. tall or it can be pinched (Plates 57–59). I know several gardeners who prefer pinching autumn joy sedum because they claim that cut-back plants look too rough, or the stalks are tough and callused and thus break off easily. I have favored the results I have gotten from pinching, rather than cutting back, with perennials like shasta daisy (*Leucanthemum* ×*superbum*) and gateway joe-pye weed (*Eupatorium maculatum* 'Gateway'). *Boltonia asteroides* 'Snowbank', *Aster*, and *Artemisia* are just a few other examples of plants that can be either pinched or cut back, again depending on the intended result (and, again, refer to the encyclopedia for specifics).

I feel obliged when writing about pinching to cover mums in greater detail. Despite the fact that advice on pinching has been covered in every article ever written on mums, in every introductory horticulture or master gardener class, and passed along from every mum-growing-mum to mum-growing-daughter, hopefully a speck of something new will be provided in this rendition. With that I'll add that I don't pinch my mums anymore, but rather cut them back by one-half in early June. I also use what I consider "special mums," not your typical garden-center varieties. These special types are extremely hardy and some don't even need to be cut back. They look more natural to me than most either because of their single flowers or their overall habit and appearance (see Plate 74). *Dendranthema* 'Venus' is a nice single pink that becomes leggy unless cut back by one-half, which can create a full rounded plant to 2 to 3 ft. Two other hardy mums that I love are 'Viette's Apricot Glow' and 'Mei Kyo'. 'Viette's Apricot Glow' remains a compact 18 to 24 in. without pruning, and 'Mei Kyo' grows to about 2½ ft. but remains full and rounded with nice burgundy double blooms without cutting back or pinching.

Nevertheless, if pinching is the pruning method of choice, then spring-planted garden mums should be pinched for the first time a few weeks after planting. If the plants have buds on them when you buy them in the spring, pinch these off. If you have overwintered your mums, pinch when shoots are 4 to 6 in. long and then again 2 to 3 weeks later. The last pinch date depends on the climate and the type of mum being grown and the individual objectives. Generally pinching should be stopped in about mid-July in midwestern and northern gardens, whereas pinching may continue until late July or early August in warmer regions. Most mums benefit from three to four pinches for height control, except for the lower growing cushion types, which require only two pinchings. The number of times and how late in the year you pinch your mums is something you will want to play around with. You may find that by pinching a bit later you can delay flowering to a more suitable time for your needs. Keep in mind, however, that if you get "pinch happy" you may pinch away any chances of flowering before cold weather arrives. Mums need several weeks to set bud after the final pinch.

Pinching can be an important aid in maintaining perennial gardens, but it should be used with discretion. Avoid trying to create a garden full of rounded forms, all the same height, covered from head to toe in flowers, at the cost of plants with natural graceful habits and just the right amount of bloom.

THINNING

Thinning stems of perennials can help prevent disease, improve the overall appearance of the plant, produce sturdier stems, and in some cases, increase the size of flowers produced. Thinning allows more light and air into the plant and encourages better branching of the remaining stems. In addition to the removal of entire stems, thinning can mean removing flowers, leaves, or only certain branches, depending on the gardener's intentions.

Cut or pinch stems at ground level in the spring, when the plants are one-fourth to one-third their mature height. How many stems to thin depends on the type of plant and its size. In general, thinning one in three stems is sufficient. This can leave anywhere from 1 to 4 in. between the stems, depending on the species (Figure 11-2). Keep the stems fairly evenly spaced. Be sure to remove any weak or particularly thin stems as well. If in doubt as to how many stems to remove, remove more shoots, or else the thinning won't be effective and the time spent will be wasted.

Thinning is a useful tool to help the perennial gardener create the desired shapes or appearances in the garden. I use thinning throughout the season if a plant has become too full or dense for the effect that I hope to accomplish, and again this may mean thinning of flowers, leaves, or select branches and stems. When thinning in the summer, flowers, leaves, and select branches usually should not be cut to the ground—as entire stems should—but should stop at a lateral bud. An imbalance of weight in a garden may not be obvious on casual observation, but too much weight in the wrong spot will mar the overall appearance of the design. Scented oxeye (*Telekia speciosa*), for example, has very large coarse leaves, and if it isn't balanced properly with sufficient quantities of plants with finer textured leaves I will thin some leaves and maybe some stems to lighten it up a bit. If I have used a taller or slightly denser plant near the front of the perennial border to create a more diverse cross section to the garden, I sometimes will need to thin its flowers or foliage to allow you to see through it to the other plants. A plant's flowers may seem to outweigh the poor stems that are trying to support them, and in such a case the plant itself is out of balance. Thin some of these flowers. Use them in the home in floral arrangements and you will be happier all around. Purple-foliaged plants add depth to garden designs, but too much depth can create a somber feeling. Remedy this with thinning. Remember to step back and look at the plant as you are thinning so that you see what you are creating.

Thinning can serve a variety of functions for a variety of plants. *Aster, Delphinium, Monarda,* and *Phlox* are a few genera that may be less prone to mildew if their stems are thinned, although, as mentioned in Chapter 4, my experience has not shown much of a difference in the mildew on thinned phlox as compared to unthinned phlox. *Delphinium* and *Phlox* may also produce larger flowers if thinned by one-third. Other perennials such as bugleweed (*Ajuga reptans*), lady's mantle (*Alchemilla mollis*), bethlehem sage (*Pulmonaria saccharata*), lamb's ear (*Stachys byzantina*), and some hardy geraniums often benefit from a summer thinning to improve air circulation around the plant and prevent rot or mildew. I cut out some of the dense foliage on *Stachys byzantina* 'Helene von Stein' to open it up a bit when the humid weather comes, and this applies to other silver-

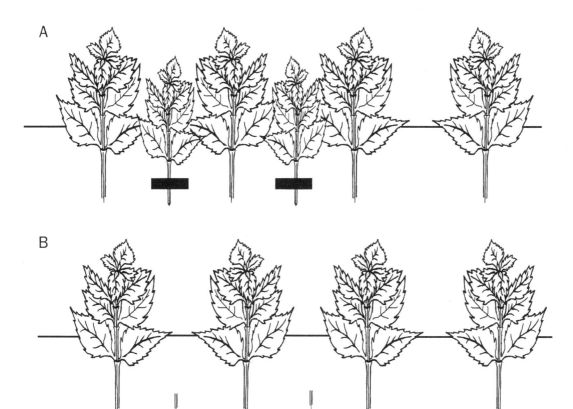

Figure 11-2. Thinning: before and after, here showing *Monarda didyma*.

foliaged plants as well. With *Alchemilla mollis*, *Geranium* ×*magnificum*, and *Pulmonaria* you can pull out some stems while you are deadheading to thin the plants and reduce the incidence of disease when water accumulates in the dense foliage. This can keep plants from getting too large as well.

DISBUDDING

Disbudding, the removal of flower buds, is a pruning technique that is usually associated with growing plants such as mums, carnations and pinks, dahlias, and peonies for floral shows or arranging. When disbudding for shows, side buds are removed so that the plant's terminal bud will produce a larger flower on a longer stem. Disbudding at least two pairs of the side buds is best; for even larger blooms, remove three pairs. Removing the terminal bud will cause the side buds to produce smaller but more numerous flowers. Disbudding the terminal bud can also eliminate the need for staking in the garden. Removing side buds along the spike of perennials such as *Lobelia* or *Delphinium* is not effective, but you can remove smaller side spikes from these plants and other spike-blooming plants such as *Aconitum* for a larger terminal spike. Whatever the method or intention of disbudding, buds should be removed before they get too large, otherwise unsightly scars will appear.

Flower buds may be removed from perennials for different reasons, including removing unsightly flowers or flowers that distract from the ornamental foliage of the plant. I often think of this as disbudding, because one is removing flower buds, but, as was previously discussed, technically it doesn't fit the usual horticultural description for disbudding.

DEADLEAFING

Charles Cresson, renowned horticulturist and author, popularized the term deadleafing. Appropriately enough, it refers to the removal of individual dead leaves. It is not cutting back stems. Deadleafing is the fine-tuning of the garden. The dead foliage has done its job. It's time to get rid of it and make room for any new foliage that may be ready to grow and contribute to the health of the plant. Deadleafing can mean removing yellowing and browning leaves for purely cosmetic purposes as well, as they are often distracting in the garden. A plant covered with one-third dead leaves looks like it's had it, but removing those leaves can give the plant a fresh look and improve the appearance of the garden. In this sense deadleafing is rejuvenating. Dead and dying leaves can also harbor insects and diseases.

Dead leaves sometimes are just the nature of the plant, no matter what the growing conditions. Other times, and most often, it is the result of some cultural condition. Dry or wet weather can cause leaves to yellow, scorch, or brown. Too much sun, heat, or humidity are other culprits. Placing the plant in the right conditions will minimize the problem. Of course, we have no control over droughts or monsoons, but if we stretch the growing conditions for the plant and increase its stress, we may have the added maintenance of deadleafing. Dying leaves on plants can also be a symptom of a larger problem that you may not be aware of, such as poor drainage, competition from a neighboring tree, or a break in an irrigation line. So think about the potential causes of dead foliage and what, if anything, can be done to correct the problem.

Pruning by deadleafing is done with many perennials, and in Appendix C, list 32, I've indicated the plants I most often need to deadleaf. My gardens don't have ideal growing conditions for *Primula*. The plants do well through the moist spring but start to fade with summer heat and drought. When summer comes I simply cut the yellow leaves from around the base of the rosette to create a fresh new look. I have *Fragaria* 'Pink Panda' plants that invariably develop brown leaves by midsummer. I grab handfuls of leaves out of the planting, not concerning myself if I pull out a few fresh leaves or even plantlets, as new ones will be fast to follow. My lady's mantles (*Alchemilla mollis*) always need old leaves cut off of them in late summer since they are sited in full sun. I have 25 of them repeating along the edges of two of my front gardens. I love my lady's mantles and wouldn't think of giving them up, so my choice is deadleafing. For years I pruned each leaf individually with hand pruners. I was about at the point of learning to like the plants with the dead leaves on them. Brown is a color too, I told myself. Then I fortunately discovered that hedge shears would do the job, and now I use the hedge shears to make quick work of this deadleafing task. New foliage waits below the old leaves to quickly fill in the space. I have seen this pruning of lady's mantle also referred to as shearing. Call it what you like, but you'll need to do it if they get too dry or receive too much sun.

A good deal of deadleafing is needed in the spring on evergreen plants such as *Asarum europaeum*, *Bergenia*, and *Helleborus* (also see Chapter 12). Their outer leaves deteriorate over the winter and removing them is all that is needed to start a new season. Elijah blue fescue (*Festuca glauca* 'Elijah Blue') is another plant that after most winters needs its dead leaves pulled out from within the clump in early spring (see Appendix A).

Pruning to Prepare for Winter and Pruning to Prepare for Spring

WINTER PREPARATION

IT used to be accepted practice to cut down most perennials in autumn. Strictly herbaceous gardens were left totally bare, a very depressing site, while mixed borders may have had the odd conifer, woody shrub, or rose bush left on its own to provide winter interest. Fortunately, as our appreciation for the winter forms and colors of perennials is heightened, as well as our awareness and sensitivity to the habits of birds and butterflies, we no longer mindlessly go out and cut everything back, leaving the garden naked of any signs of dormant plants.

Winter interest—contrary to what is preached by many well-meaning individuals, those who usually have limited knowledge of perennials—is not provided solely by junipers, yews, pachysandra, English ivy, or the odd mugo pine (with the requisite accompanying rock!). Certain conifers, particularly some of the dwarf forms, and broad-leaved evergreens do add a special dimension to mixed herbaceous borders, but many perennials contribute greatly to the winter garden as well. Such contributions are not only in the way of attractive seedheads, but form, structure, and foliage color are also notable qualities of perennials during the winter season. Perennials and grasses, with their often intricate seedheads and outstanding habits, hold snow, frost, and ice in a way special from other plants (Plates 60–61).

In addition to their ornamental qualities, perennials in the winter landscape are important resources for birds and butterflies. Butterflies such as the viceroy pupate in a sheltered spot for the winter, and other species of butterflies and moths lay eggs in the leaves of perennials for overwintering. If we cut down and compost these plants, we may be composting next year's generation of butterflies. A variety of birds frequent our feeding stations in the winter, and most of them also frequent the gardens. This includes finches (golden and house), red-breasted woodpeckers, juncos, chickadees, tufted tit mouse, cardinals, nuthatches, and sparrows (song and American tree). They visit to collect and eat seed from perennials such as *Echinacea*, *Heliopsis*, and *Rudbeckia*, or to use the perennials as cover and resting grounds, including fallen perennials. Some people bring cut branches into their garden areas for the birds. Don't think just because a perennial is going to fall that it should be removed from the winter scene. If the perennials weren't there, the birds would have fewer places to take refuge.

If you want some green in the winter, why not go for painted arum (*Arum italicum* 'Marmoratum'). In a protected site painted arum will give you an almost tropical look with its lance-shaped, silver-marked leaves (Plate 62). I love the gray provided by lavender (*Lavandula*), common sage (*Salvia officinalis*), and lamb's ear (*Stachys byzantina*) during the winter contrasted against the deep green of *Dianthus deltoides* (Plate 63) or evergreen candytuft (*Iberis sempervirens*). Pair *Helleborus foetidus*, with its glossy purple-tinted foliage and yellow-green flower buds that form in the autumn and hold through the winter, with the scarlet-streaked, gray-green foliage of *Geranium macrorrhizum* and the shiny green and silver foliage of *Asarum shuttleworthii*, and you have a combination worth venturing out to see on an otherwise stay-cuddled-in-the-house day. If the snow is too deep to allow you to enjoy these low-growing beauties, cross-country ski around a garden bearing grasses such as *Calamagrostis*, *Miscanthus*, and *Panicum* highlighted by seedheads of *Iris sibirica* and *Rudbeckia nitida* 'Herbstsonne' and the outline of *Buddleia*.

There are many low-growing evergreen perennials as well as tall perennials with evergreen or semi-evergreen basal foliage. Some plants will be evergreen in milder climates or in winters with early and persistent snowfall. They may look a bit forlorn in more severe situations after snow, wind, and subzero and fluctuating temperatures take their toll. Yet they have provided interest in late autumn and early winter, so they have earned their keep as far as I'm concerned. Perennials that have not evolved to be evergreen yet behave like evergreens due to milder conditions may be shorter lived.

One year at the end of January, after a snow melt, I counted approximately 50 different species of perennials that had green basal foliage or evergreen to semi-evergreen leaves, or leaves that simply remained green under a month-long snow cover. It looked like spring green, with spiderwort (*Tradescantia* ×anderso-

niana) shoots one inch or so high and beebalm (*Monarda didyma*) with four healthy leaves per shoot. The list of green plants also included *Geum, Stokesia, Veronica austriaca* subsp. *teucrium* 'Trehane' (which was an outstanding bright yellow), *Veronica alpina* 'Alba', and basal foliage on *Rudbeckia triloba*. The foliage of oriental poppy (*Papaver orientale*), which is usually left over the winter as a living mulch, was exceptionally green, looking as if it would send forth a flower bud at any moment. Following a month of sporadic snow cover and temperature extremes from −10 to 50°F, by late February many of these 50 species had become bedraggled, turning to mush. Some still looked good, however, including the poppies, *Penstemon digitalis*, *Phlox stolonifera*, and *Arabis procurrens*, with just a touch of bronzing on some of them.

With some plants, like *Pulmonaria*, you can't be sure what they're going to do. I have several different species and cultivars of *Pulmonaria*, and sometimes they hold up nicely into the winter and other years they are black by late autumn. On some plants just the outer leaves blacken and the inner foliage is nice. I still leave them unpruned or just prune the outer foliage and either cut them down over the winter or in the spring when needed.

Some perennials should not be cut down in the autumn because they can contribute aesthetically to the garden in winter. In other situations certain tender perennials can be left up for the winter to ensure overwintering. Marginally hardy perennials, such as monch aster (*Aster ×frikartii* 'Monch'), tender ferns, or mums, benefit from leaving the old foliage on the plants to provide insulation for the crowns during cold weather. I leave the old fronds on all ferns until spring, whether they are tender or not, and some ferns, like the christmas fern (*Polystichum acrostichoides*), are evergreen and hold up well through the winter regardless. An eye-opening research study out of Germany, conducted for Yoder Brothers in 1992, showed that mums that were not cut back in autumn resprouted substantially better and earlier in the spring than the plants that were pruned. Many of the cultivars tested had no overwintering losses if they were not sheared back in the fall, compared to 75–100% overwintering loss for those that were sheared. Wait until warm weather is ensured in the spring to prune mums down.

Another reason to not cut down certain perennials in autumn is demonstrated by *Ceratostigma plumbaginoides*. This species emerges late in the spring, sometimes as late as June in our area. I like to leave the old stems over the winter and into the spring until the plant emerges. This way, the old stems serve as an indicator that something is growing there, ensuring that the soil isn't disturbed or something else isn't planted in its space while it's taking its time awakening from the winter.

On the flip side of all these reasons to *not* prune in the autumn, there are many reasons why pruning is necessary before the coming of winter. One main reason to cut certain perennials back is that they can be the site of overwintering diseases or insects (see Chapter 4). Some notable examples include fourlined plant bug and mildew on *Monarda* and other members of the mint family, botrytis on peonies, and borers on bearded iris. Removing foliage and stems of these plants from the garden in the winter can help reduce maintenance problems for the following year. In addition, removing excessive debris such as fallen leaves and fallen deadheads decreases other potential sites for pests. I recommend raking large leaves of maples or sycamores out of the garden in autumn, as these can mat-down and hold water, contributing to the potential for crown rot on the perennials. Also, if large quantities of leaves litter the garden, most of it should be removed. It's not practical to get every leaf out—and what a bore it would be to try—but too many can be a problem.

In addition to pruning in autumn to minimize the incidence of pests and disease, there are aesthetic reasons to prune before the coming of winter. Some perennials simply do not contribute much to the winter garden; in fact, they may detract from it. In such cases I opt to cut the plants down. This might include veronicas or geraniums that have blackened and turned to mush, or a great coneflower (*Rudbeckia maxima*) that has fallen onto a frequented path. Certain ornamental grasses are better cut down before the winter because they either break down in the winter or lose their good color. *Arundo donax* and *Saccharum ravennae*, both large grasses, may fall over in late winter. *Imperata* loses its color and looks rather unsightly over the winter in most cases. If a grass is not reliably hardy, it should be left unpruned for the winter. (See Appendix A for more information on grasses.)

The pruning that is done during the growing season can dictate whether a plant needs pruning in the autumn for the winter. Many perennials that are cut back during the growing season remain as attractive low green mounds into the winter. For example, if *Centaurea montana* is pruned back in the summer and all that remains is fresh low basal foliage in the autumn, it doesn't need to be pruned again for the winter. On the other hand, if the plant was not cut back heavily during the season, the tall stems and leaves will blacken and require pruning back in late autumn. Also, if a perennial is deadheaded during the season, and so reseeding is not a concern, the rest of the plant may be able to remain for the winter. If the plant wasn't deadheaded, it may be best to cut the entire plant down before winter to avoid reseeding, rather than deadheading at this point.

Pruning to prepare for winter is a matter of personal choice. What some find attractive, others may find distracting. With certain clients or certain styles of gardens things need to be neat and tidy for the winter, and this involves more pruning in the fall. With others a more natural look is acceptable and a "fallen soldier" here or there over the winter can easily be removed in the spring with no harm done. In my personal gardens I leave more perennials up in the back gardens, which are more natural and less visited by guests in the winter months, than I do in my front entrance gardens—although these too are rather wild looking over the winter. I also like the option of leaving some things unpruned, and then if a plant declines by mid- or late winter I can go out and cut it down at that point. It gives me some gardening to look forward to during the winter when weather permits. Pruning selectively in the autumn or over the winter also helps ease the burden of spring clean-up. Your spring schedule may be an important factor in deciding what you leave during the winter.

In the encyclopedia I have indicated whether or not pruning is needed for the winter for the specific perennials. Appendix C, list 33, includes some of the plants that I don't prune for the winter. In this list it is assumed that the appropriate recommended pruning has been done during the season. You need to remember all the factors that come into play in determining whether a perennial should be pruned for the winter.

Perennials that are to be cut down for the winter should be cut down when they are dormant; usually this is after several killing frosts. For me this is generally early November when we are scheduling our autumn clean-up for clients, although in some years it has been late November. If perennials are cut down too early, when they are still actively growing, one concern is that they might put on new growth, use the carbohydrate reserves that were meant for the following season, be hit by a freeze, and not return the following year. Sometimes I will go ahead and cut down plants that are still very green or even flowering if I know that within a few days a freeze will come along and turn the plants to mush. If in doubt, you're better off leaving the plant up.

Plants should be cut back to within about 2 to 3 in. of the ground. Cutting back too close to the crown can cause certain plants to become damaged over the winter. On some perennials the overwintering buds are not beneath the soil, but rather are either level with, above, or only slightly below the soil, and so if you cut back too close you may be cutting into these buds. I once did this with some of my famous lady's mantles. I used a string trimmer and cut a few of them back too close. They were weak to emerge the following spring and parts of the crowns never regrew. I also know some gardeners in colder climates who leave about 6 in. of stems to help trap the snow and then cut back again in the spring.

Hedge shears are useful for most of the autumn clean-up. It's quick work to go through shearing the plants off at their bases, and then follow up with a garden fork to pick up large piles of debris. Hand pruners may be needed on some very tough stems, and I sometimes use a weed whacker with a rigid plastic blade for mass plantings. Workers must wear protective clothing and safety goggles when using this kind of equipment (Plate 64).

In a home garden, autumn pruning to prepare for the winter is a good time to have children involved. My son loves to help at this time of year, and I allow it because he can't really damage anything in the garden. No new plants are emerging that even small feet will crush, as in the spring, nor healthy ones growing next to ones to be pruned, as in the summer. My son holds the hedge shears with me, and he usually yells out something like "Ah Yah!," then he puts the "prisoners" in the "police car" (garden cart) and takes them to "jail" (compost bins).

EARLY SPRING PRUNING

Generally speaking, plants that are not pruned in the autumn need to be cut back, or possibly deadleafed, in the spring. Perennials like *Asarum*, *Bergenia*, *Helleborus*, and *Heuchera* need to have their dead leaves removed, particularly if they have been exposed to windburn or sunscald. *Epimedium* and *Helleborus* need to be cut back early in spring so that the new flowers and leaves are not masked by the previous season's tattered remains. Rotary mowers can be used on large plantings of *Epimedium*. The groundcover *Liriope spicata* also can be mown down in the spring. Moss phlox (*Phlox subulata*) may incur dead branches over the winter, or portions of the plant may die out, and these should be removed at this time. Evergreens may not need any additional pruning in the spring in some years, as their foliage stays fresh over the winter. *Phlox stolonifera*, *Dianthus gratianopolitanus*, and *Arabis procurrens* are just a few that usually fair well. Most often evergreen basal foliage doesn't need any additional pruning in the spring.

Certain subshrubs have their overwintering buds above ground, which classifies them botanically as woody plants but horticulturally they are classified with herbaceous perennials. They benefit from snow cover for protection and may experience tip die-back on the part of the plant above the snow line. Spring is the time to prune off those dead tips. This group includes heather (*Calluna vulgaris*), evergreen candytuft (*Iberis sempervirens*), lavender (*Lavandula*), germander (*Teucrium*), and thymes (*Thymus*). They may also need a hard cutting back in the spring if they start to grow leggy, as discussed in Chapter 10. Lavender normally only needs its dead tips cut off in late spring or early summer, once all the woody growth has had a chance to break. Often the beginning gardener will prune back lavender hard before winter, only to be disappointed that it doesn't return at all the following spring. Lavender may need a hard cutting back (down to 4 to 6 in.) in spring every 2 to 3 years to hold a decent habit if it has become open and leggy or if it's being used as a hedge. It can be cut back hard annually for hedging.

Another woody type, *Artemisia* 'Powis Castle', should not be cut back hard into old wood, or you may lose it. Butterfly bush (*Buddleia davidii*) is cut to the ground or to 6 to 12 in. in the spring. I usually cut it down to where I see new buds breaking, which generally is around 6 in. from the ground. The Viettes, of Andre Viette Farm and Nursery in Fishersville, Virginia, cut their *Buddleia* plants to 2 in. from the ground using a chain saw, due to the large numbers and sizes of their plants. Hand pruners are sufficient for my needs. Remember that *Buddleia* is really a woody perennial with a wanna-be herbaceous perennial complex. It usually is killed to the ground by cold weather. *Perovskia* can be cut to the ground to encourage sturdier plants; I prefer to cut mine down to live buds, which can be 6 in. or more above ground.

Electric hedge shears work best for ornamental grasses on large jobs (Plates 65–66). First tie the grasses together, which keeps excessive debris to a minimum, and then cut it down. It helps to have two people working together on this. Hand-held hedge shears do the trick on small quantities. A weed whacker with a rigid plastic blade can also be used. I've even heard of people using chain saws, but I've never needed such heavy machinery, even for very large grasses. Do wear gloves, as the grass blades can cut like razors. *Festuca glauca* 'Elijah Blue' normally only needs dead blades pulled from within the clump by hand. *Elymus glaucus* may behave similarly in mild winters. In severe winters I have had to cut elijah blue fescue back due to excessive tip burn on the blades.

I do most spring pruning in the early spring before new growth begins, usually sometime in late March or early April. Gardeners in milder climates may need to get an earlier start. You don't want a lot of new growth in the way while you are trying to clean-up the old stems and leaves. If some new growth is hit during spring clean-up, no harm done—perennials are very forgiving and will be quick to fill in, but if you cut it too late you may be altering the plant's ultimate height and even its flowering time on early blooming species.

Guide to Using
the Encyclopedia

THE pruning and maintenance information in this encyclopedia is based primarily on my personal experiences. I have actually performed the different pruning techniques for the various plants as well as done the follow-up "research," if you will, by tracking bloom dates, measuring plant heights and flowering size, and so forth. Many of the techniques that I have tried were suggested to me by gardeners from across the country, or were gathered from extensive research over the past eight years or so. My goal was to test the various techniques as well as try variations of my own—a very involved and complex process. My successes and failures are included with the plant entries. I have provided dates, plant heights, and other "vital statistics" whenever possible so that the information can be used as reference points. The perennials included in this encyclopedia, as well as other perennials, can be pruned in a variety of ways for similar or different results.

For the most part the pruning that was performed on plants before blooming (in an effort to create more compact plants that don't require staking, or to experiment with bloom times) was done in early to mid-June. I picked this time partly because it is also the time when a good deal of spring-flowering species are pruned after flowering, thus giving the maintenance contractor or the busy gardener one key time of the season to keep in mind for pruning a wide range of species. It is also an appropriate time based on the growth habits of many summer- and autumn-flowering perennials.

This is a pioneer project. Many questions about pruning perennials remain to be answered. Remember that what, how, and when to prune varies with weather conditions, regional variations, age of the plant, soil fertility, moisture availability, and the gardener's own objectives. The results of the pruning, such as amount of flower delay or time for regrowth, will also differ according to the above variables. Gardeners in the South or the far North may need to adjust the timing a bit on certain pruning. You may need to prune slightly heavier in the South due to the longer season and the effects of the heat on producing taller and leggier growth. In the North a lighter touch may be more effective for accomplishing the pruning goals in a shorter season. Although the information should be used only as a guide, with necessary adjustments according to individual needs and conditions, it is my hope that the information included with each plant offers gardeners precise guidelines for pruning, rather than vague recommendations that don't offer specific how-to's or results. Take these, experiment, learn, and grow.

The descriptions for each plant in the encyclopedia are fairly brief. My objective in writing this reference book was not to write another descriptive manual—such manuals have already been successfully written. The objective of this book is to provide new, and easily referenced, material specific to maintenance and pruning of perennials.

Height measurements that are given in parentheses under Size indicate the height of the foliage and is provided only if it is significantly different from the height of the plant in flower. Since many perennials are cut down or deadheaded down to this foliage, it is significant information to keep in mind while designing.

Cultivars and related plants are mentioned if they offer something unique, from a maintenance standpoint, as compared to the featured plant. In cases where a cultivar or variety is the perennial being featured, rather than the species form, more often than not it is because that is the form of the plant most commonly used in the industry. If you have difficulty locating information for a particular plant or cultivar, please consult the index, which may be able to direct you to the proper entry.

The chapters in the first two sections of this book will greatly aid the gardener in a more thorough understanding of the pruning and maintenance information provided in the encyclopedia. They provide insight not always included in the specific plant entries; I strongly recommend that you read and familiarize yourself with the information provided in the chapters. The numerous lists in the appendix can also serve as a quick reference on many of these maintenance requirements. For example, which plants need cutting back after flowering? Which ones should be divided every year, or every ten years, and so forth?

A–Z Encyclopedia of Perennials

Acanthus spinosus

Zone: 5–10
Common Name: spiny bear's breeches
Family: Acanthaceae
Description: spikes of mauve flowers; shiny
   thistlelike leaves
Size: 3–4 ft. (2–2½ ft.) high; 3 ft. wide
Exposure: partial shade
Flowering: June–July

PRUNING: Deadheads remain attractive for
several weeks after flowering is finished.
When they decline, cut to the ground. If
plants become tattered after flowering in
midsummer, they can be deadleafed or, if
severe, cut to the ground for complete
renewal of foliage. No additional flowering
will occur. Foliage often remains healthy
until late summer (early September), particularly if plants have received sufficient summer moisture, at which time the old declining foliage falls to the outside of the plant,
revealing fresh, newly emerging basal
growth. Hedge shears can be used to quickly
remove the old leaves. The new growth may
remain evergreen or at least semi-evergreen,
depending on the severity of the winter. Do
not cut back for the winter but cut off any
damaged leaves in the spring if needed. If
plants are grown for foliage alone, the flower
spikes can be easily pruned out when in
bud—plants will not flower if the buds are
removed.

OTHER MAINTENANCE: Although generally listed as hardy in zones 7–10, *Acanthus
spinosus* has proven reliably hardy in zone 5,
though not remaining as evergreen in bad
winters. Flowering is often reduced after
cold winters. Can be invasive in light soils,
and the spreading roots are difficult to
remove completely. Stays well contained in
clay soils and usually in dry soils. Benefits
from morning sun and will take more sun
and drier soils in cooler climates. Slug and
snail damage is often a problem. Well-draining soil is critical. Benefits from a winter
mulch in northern areas. Can be slow to
establish. Spring division every 4–5 years.

RELATED PLANTS: *Acanthus spinosus*
'Spinossisimus' is a much spinier form that
isn't fun to prune or weed around.

Achillea 'Coronation Gold'

Zone: 3–8
Common Name: coronation gold yarrow
Family: Asteraceae
Description: mustard-yellow flowerheads;
   fernlike scented gray-green foliage
Size: 2–3 ft. (1 ft.) high; 3 ft. wide
Exposure: full sun
Flowering: June–August

PRUNING: Deadhead to lateral buds, then
after lateral buds finish blooming, cut stems
down to basal foliage. Young plants usually

repeat bloom for a long period with dead-heading. Older clumps may not produce many lateral flowering stems; if this is the case, plants should be pruned down to basal foliage, skipping deadheading. Sporadic flowering may be produced from the basal foliage in some cases. Flowers are smaller in the second bloom phase. Yarrows bloom longer where summers are cool, only about half as long in hot regions. If foliage is infected with rust or other foliar diseases, deadleaf or prune off affected parts. Leave basal foliage over the winter as it holds up better than that on most forms. Cut out dead foliage in the spring if needed.

OTHER MAINTENANCE: Well-draining soil is the main element for survival. Usually trouble free if given full sun and well-draining soil; will tolerate dry soil. Normally does not need staking unless grown in excessively rich soil or too much shade. Divides easily in the spring or autumn, every 4–5 years. Relatively low-maintenance plant. One of the best yarrows for hot and humid conditions.

RELATED PLANTS: *Achillea filipendulina*, fernleaf yarrow, is one of the parents of *Achillea* 'Coronation Gold' (the other is *A. clypeolata*). It usually requires staking unless given full sun and dry soil.

Achillea filipendulina 'Altgold', 3-ft.-tall free standing, is a reblooming cultivar with deadheading.

Achillea filipendulina 'Credo' has large yellow flowers and strong stems that don't require staking.

Achillea filipendulina 'Gold Plate', 4½–5 ft. tall, usually requires staking.

Achillea filipendulina 'Parker's Variety', 3½ ft. tall, is very tough, drought tolerant, and free standing even with winds in the Midwest, but may need staking in areas with hot, humid summers. Produces abundant flowers for a long period with deadheading.

Achillea millefolium

Zone: 4–8
Common Name: common yarrow
Family: Asteraceae
Description: flat heads of red, white, or pink flowers; dark green ferny leaves
Size: 2–3 ft. high; 2 ft. wide
Exposure: full sun
Flowering: June–August

PRUNING: Young plants can be deadheaded to lateral buds for summer-long bloom. With age or when grown in conditions that promote leggy growth, such as very wet conditions or hot weather early in the season, plants may need to be cut back (hedge shears work well) by one-third to one-half after first bloom to prevent flopping, and then sheared again down to basal foliage as the second bloom phase is completed. Plants often send up sporadic small blooms from basal foliage. Deadheading prevents seeding. Cutting plants back by one-half or two-thirds before flowering in early June, or when about 18 in. tall, can produce shorter, stockier plants that are self-supporting early in the season, though they may still flop slightly by late season, depending on other growing conditions. Flowers are smaller but more numerous on cut-back plants and flowering may be slightly delayed. Cutting back after flower buds form may mean no bloom for the season. These aggressive yarrows often need pruning to keep them in their own space. Cut foliage as well as roots back, if necessary, to give neighboring perennials room. Leave basal foliage over the winter. Cut back any damaged sections in the spring if needed.

OTHER MAINTENANCE: Invasive habit, plants can spread 2–3 ft. in a season, and a good deal of maintenance is required to keep plants in bounds. Plants require staking if not cut back for height control. Division in spring or fall every couple of years keeps plants vigorous.

RELATED PLANTS: The Galaxy Hybrids (*Achillea millefolium* × *Achillea* 'Taygetea') offer a variety of outstanding colors, but the plants are short-lived in my experience and flop and spread like the species.

Achillea millefolium 'Fire King' is a long-blooming cultivar with deadheading that can go strong for 6 weeks and then sporadically for a total of 15 weeks. May need staking, but more self-supporting than others.

Achillea ×*kellereri* requires the old blossoms and one-third to one-half of the foliage to be cut after flowering.

Achillea ptarmica, sneezewort, is invasive and lanky and contracts mildew in hot, humid conditions.

Achillea 'Taygetea', 1½ ft. tall, flowers from May to hard frost with deadheading. Remove the flowers when they start to turn dingy.

Achillea 'Moonshine'

Zone: 3–8
Common Name: moonshine yarrow
Family: Asteraceae
Description: sulfur-yellow flowerheads; silver fernlike foliage
Size: 24 in. (12 in.) high; 18 in. wide
Exposure: full sun
Flowering: June–August

PRUNING: As the flowers fade, deadhead to lateral buds; when lateral flower stems finish blooming, cut down to basal foliage. Foliage remains attractive into winter. In early spring cut off any dead or old foliage, leave new growth at base. In areas with high heat and humidity, thinning plants can reduce moisture around crown and help prevent disease. Prune out diseased sections as needed; do not compost infected material.

OTHER MAINTENANCE: Requires well-draining soil to ensure perennial nature and to prevent melting out. Pythium and botrytis can be a problem in the South. Planting and mulching with coarse grit may aid survival in heavy soils. Avoid high-fertility soils and shade or plants will require staking. Not invasive like some other yarrows. Seems to weaken after a couple of years of strong flowering; at that point divide in the spring or autumn. Plants sustaining winter injury (from wet soils or fluctuating temperatures) may not flower the following season.

RELATED PLANTS: *Achillea* 'Anthea', 18–20 in. tall, has light yellow flowers and silver-green foliage. Seems to be a better selection than *Achillea* 'Moonshine' since it performs for longer periods of time without division and the growth habit is more upright, not requiring staking. It produces numerous secondary flowerheads that start to bloom just as the primary ones begin to fade. (Deadheading of the primary flowers keeps plants tidy, although the flowers are fairly attractive even after they have faded). Also, 'Anthea' is not prone to melting out in hot, humid climates as is moonshine yarrow.

Achillea ×*lewisii* 'King Edward' should be deadheaded to lateral buds to prolong bloom, then cut to new basal foliage when secondary flowering is completed. Well-draining soil is essential.

Aconitum napellus

Zone: 4–8
Common Name: monkshood
Family: Ranunculaceae
Description: blue-violet spikes of hooded flowers; deep green palmately divided foliage
Size: 3–4 ft. high; 1 ft. wide
Exposure: partial shade
Flowering: July–August

PRUNING: Most parts of the plant are toxic if ingested. When pruning or handling do not get juice from the plant into your mouth or in open wounds, and be certain to wash your hands immediately after cutting back plants.

Deadhead to lateral buds for a smaller second flowering. When secondary flowering is finished, cut down to new basal foliage if the old foliage declines, and fertilize if plants are pale. Sporadic small flowering may occur from the basal growth. Leave basal growth over the winter, and prune off in the spring. Plants can be cut back or pinched to control height, although this usually means removal of the large terminal spike. This will produce smaller but more numerous, and possibly later, flowers on sturdier plants. New plants can be cut back by one-half at planting for a better branching, slightly shorter first-year plant. Established plants can be cut back by one-half when 18 in. tall to increase fullness. Some gardeners cut plants back by 6 in. when plants are 2½ ft. tall and again by 6 in. when 3½ ft. tall. Staking may be necessary even with any of these pruning techniques used for height control, depending on conditions. If plants are not pruned for height control, side flower spikes can be pinched out to increase the size of the terminal spike if desired.

OTHER MAINTENANCE: Prefers a rich, high-organic, moist soil. Avoid hot locations and burning sun; water during dry periods. Won't tolerate tree root competition. Division can be done in early spring or fall, but plants are slow to establish, so best left undisturbed for many years. Requires staking.

RELATED PLANTS: *Aconitum ×cammarum* 'Bressingham Spire' is a 2½- to 3-ft.-tall selection by Alan Bloom that doesn't require staking. A good choice since pruning is not necessary.

Aconitum carmichaelii 'Arendsii' is a late-flowering monkshood that doesn't require staking, due to its strong stems, even though it reaches 3–4 ft. tall.

Aconitum henryi 'Spark's Variety' grows 4–5 ft. tall. Plants cut back by one-half when 15 in. tall, at planting, flowered at 3 ft., as compared to unpruned plants that flowered

at 4 ft. The flowers on pruned plants were slightly smaller and bloomed 14 days later. Pruned plants still require light support from surrounding perennials.

Aconitum septentrionale 'Ivorine' is a lovely cultivar with creamy flowers and upright growth to 2 ft., not requiring staking. Flowering usually starts in late May or early June. Tough to establish, but once it takes hold 'Ivorine' even seeds itself a bit if not deadheaded.

Adenophora liliifolia

Zone: 4–8
Common Name: lilyleaf ladybell
Family: Campanulaceae
Description: light blue bell-shaped flowers on tall spikes; basal leaves somewhat heart-shaped
Size: 18–24 in. (8 in.) high; 24 in. wide
Exposure: full sun to partial shade
Flowering: June–July

PRUNING: Deadhead plants to lateral buds to prolong bloom and prevent seeding. When all secondary flowering is finished, cut plants down to new basal foliage. Leave basal foliage over the winter, and clean-up in spring. If plants are grown in too much shade and flopping is a problem, they can be cut back or pinched in early May.

OTHER MAINTENANCE: Plants can be weedy in nature, spreading rapidly and/or seeding to take over a large area. Sections of the plant should be dug out annually to keep it in its intended space. This spreading nature was observed in clay soil—I can't imagine its run in sandy soils! Tolerates somewhat dry summers; requires well-draining soil. Roots are deep and fleshy and therefore difficult to divide. Long-lived plant. More useful for southern gardens than the bellflowers (*Campanula*), which it resembles, due to its heat tolerance.

RELATED PLANTS: *Adenophora confusa*, common ladybell, is taller (3½–4 ft.), has deeper blue flowers, and in my gardens is always flopping and rangy. I cut them back by one-half when they are 6–8 in. tall in May to obtain plants that are 2½ ft. tall, self-sup-porting, and sometimes slightly delayed in flowering. Deadheaded plants can flower into September. Cut down to basal foliage when finished blooming. Leave basal foliage for the winter. Not as heat tolerant as *A. liliifolia*.

Aegopodium podagraria 'Variegatum'

Zone: 4–8
Common Name: variegated bishop's weed
Family: Apiaceae
Description: variegated compound leaves; insignificant umbel flowers
Size: 8–10 in. high; spreading groundcover
Exposure: partial to full shade
Flowering: June

PRUNING: Plants become ragged by mid- to late summer, sometimes resulting from a leaf blight or from hot and humid weather, but whatever the reason, cut, shear, or mow to the ground for a flush of new growth. Foliage returns quickly after pruning. Shear flowers off to prevent self-sowing, or deadhead before seeds set. Prune out unvariegated shoots to prevent reversion of the plant back to its green relative.

OTHER MAINTENANCE: To say that this plant is invasive is an understatement. It spreads by underground stems and is best reserved for a bed that can be devoted solely to its existence as a groundcover. No prefer-ence as to soil type. Needs shade in warmer end of growing zone. Never plant in a peren-nial garden, or close to it, where it would have any chance of growing into a desirable planting. Definitely a high-maintenance per-ennial. Divide in spring or fall every 2–3 years. Truly a dog that should be avoided when there are so many other great perennials.

RELATED PLANTS: *Aegopodium podagraria*, bishop's weed, is green leaved and even more invasive than the cultivar.

Ajuga reptans

Zone: 4–9
Common Name: bugleweed
Family: Lamiaceae
Description: blue, white, or pink flowers; green, variegated, or purple leaves
Size: 6–9 in. (2 in.) high; 24 in. wide
Exposure: full sun or partial shade
Flowering: May–June

PRUNING: Deadheading prevents excessive seeding and improves the overall appearance of the plant. Hedge shears, or a weed whacker/string trimmer, can be used for large plantings. Plants usually can even toler-ate occasional, but not repeated, mowing. Cut back runners drastically whenever neces-sary to keep plant from spreading too far. Thinning of plants can reduce the incidence of crown rot; if plants are infected, prune out diseased sections. Plants are evergreen; do not prune for winter. Deadleafing may be re-quired to clean-up plants a bit in the spring or occasionally through the growing season.

OTHER MAINTENANCE: Invasive ground-cover, but fairly easily pulled to keep under control in gardens; avoid spread into turf areas. Unwanted seedlings are best removed when young. Crown rot is a significant prob-lem, particularly in southern gardens. Plant in areas with good air circulation and divide every 2–3 years to help reduce the problem. Tolerates poor soil.

RELATED PLANTS: Purple-leaved forms hold up best against both cold and heat, ex-cept for *Ajuga reptans* 'Catlin's Giant', which gets battered by zero-degree temperatures.

Ajuga reptans 'Burgundy Glow', a silver variegated form, is often killed completely down by cold.

Ajuga reptans 'Cristata' holds up very well, even in harsh winters.

Ajuga pyramidalis, upright bugleweed, is more upright than *A. reptans* and is slower spreading. Will seed strongly; deadhead to reduce the problem.

Alcea rosea

Zone: 3–8
Common Name: hollyhock
Family: Malvaceae
Description: single or double spiked flowers
    in a wide range of colors; large palmate
    and coarse leaves
Size: 3–8 ft. high; 3–4 ft. wide
Exposure: full sun to partial shade
Flowering: June–August

PRUNING: Biennial hollyhocks act perennial in nature if they are deadheaded and then cut down to new basal foliage as soon as all flowering is completed. Flowers from the bottom of the spike open first. Deadhead plants to lateral buds when the seed capsules (on the bottom half) outnumber the new flowers (on the tip). Plants frequently seed if not deadheaded; leave the seedheads if that is the desired way to perpetuate the plant in the garden. Deadleafing is needed to remove yellowing leaves, starting in June, and leaves damaged by Japanese beetles or rust. Destroy rust-infested leaves. Cut out all old flowering stems and old basal leaves to expose clean basal foliage in late summer when flowering is completed. The plants look so horrendous by this time that such pruning can be a welcome relief. The new foliage holds up well into the winter and may remain semi-evergreen under consistent snow cover or in mild winters. Remove any winter-damaged leaves in the spring. Tall-growing forms can be cut down once or twice before flowering to create later blooming, shorter plants that don't require staking. Flower spikes will be smaller but more in

scale with the shorter plants, and more useful for smaller flower arrangements (see *Alcea rosea* 'Old Farmyard', below).

OTHER MAINTENANCE: Hollyhock is definitely in the high-maintenance weight class. A choice plant of a variety of insects and diseases, and it's particularly demolished by Japanese beetles and rust. Staking is usually required unless plants are pruned or lower growing forms are selected. Rich moist soil and good drainage are essential.

RELATED PLANTS: *Alcea rosea* Chater's Series is a double perennial form.

Alcea rosea 'Old Farmyard' is a single, 6- to 8-ft.-tall perennial form. Plants may be cut back by one-half in about mid-May, or when 15–18 in. high, and then again when in tight bud around mid-June, or when 3 ft. tall-the last pruning is usually necessary because the plants may still be spindly. Pruning in this way will mean that plants flower at approximately 3½ ft. tall, rather than the typical 6–7 ft., and about 3 or 4 weeks later, starting around 20 July and continuing, although only lightly, into early October. Also, plants generally aren't as badly affected by Japanese beetles at this later date. Such pruning makes the plant usable in my front border, which adds to the cottage garden look, and it doesn't need to be relegated to a cutting garden once it is "reformed." A few branches can be left uncut at the second pruning in June to allow some flowers to bloom then and to provide color in the gardens and for cutting.

Alcea rugosa has pale yellow flowers and is resistant to rust. Doesn't fall over. Deadheading prolongs bloom into autumn. Grows 4 ft. tall.

Alchemilla mollis

Zone: 4–7
Common Name: lady's mantle
Family: Rosaceae
Description: chartreuse frothy flowerheads;

round, scalloped, soft, smoky yellow-green
leaves

Size: 15–18 in. (12 in.) high; 24 in. wide
Exposure: partial shade or sun
Flowering: June–August

PRUNING: Lady's mantle can be deadheaded
in a couple of different ways. The most common method is to cut the old flowering stem
down to the basal growth. The other approach
is to pull the old flowering stem out at the
base, which serves the additional purpose of
thinning the plant a bit, and if some root is
pulled out along with the stem it can be propagated (see Chapter 9 and Figure 9-6). Self-
seeding can be a problem in some gardens; if
this is the case, seedheads should be removed
before they mature. I don't have heavy seeding in my gardens, even with 20 or more
plants, and the few seedlings that I get are
welcome, so I prefer to leave the heads on
until they are brown, as I enjoy them at this
stage as well. Plants may send up sporadic
blooms later in the season if deadheaded.

Leaves will scorch if grown in too much
sun or in dry conditions. Deadleafing usually
is necessary. Leaves can be removed individually with pruners, or if scorch damage is
severe, foliage can be sheared, with hedge
shears, to a couple of inches from the base
early in the season, soon after flowering. Do
not shear too close to the crown, or plants
may be killed. Plants can also be deadleafed
lightly as needed early on, and then sheared
to the lush new basal foliage, which develops
under the old tatty leaves, in late summer. I
opt for this latter approach because I don't
like the hole that is created by shearing the
plant low early in the season. I have found
regrowth to be slow on plants sheared low
too early on, often delayed by a month or
more, particularly when the pruning is followed by hot and dry weather. The plants
seem to overwinter better if they are not cut
back in the autumn. Hedge shears make
quick work of clean-up of dead leaves in the

spring, but again it is important to avoid cutting close to the crown. Thinning the plants
as described above or by removing some of
the leaves can reduce moisture trapped in
the foliage, which can lead to disease problems, particularly in southern gardens.
Plants are wide spreading and some outer
leaves may need to be removed to keep
plants off of their neighbors.

OTHER MAINTENANCE: Plants prefer rich
moist soil in areas not exposed to hot afternoon sun. They will grow in sun or shade, but
require pruning as described above to keep
them looking decent. Divide in spring or fall
every 6–10 years. Lady's mantle is very effective when repeated along a border (Plate 67).

Amsonia tabernaemontana

Zone: 3–9
Common Name: willow amsonia
Family: Apocynaceae
Description: light blue star-shaped flowers;
    glossy slender leaves, nice yellow autumn
    color
Size: 2–3 ft. high; 3 ft. wide
Exposure: full sun to partial shade
Flowering: May–June

PRUNING: When grown in too much shade
or in overly rich soil, or where a more structured look is desired in the garden, *Amsonia*
will benefit from shearing back by one-third
to one-half and shaping after flowering.
Hedge shears do the trick. Cut outer branches
slightly lower than inner branches to shape
plants. Plants fill in nicely in 2–3 weeks at
about 1 ft. shorter than original size if cut
back by one-third. Pruned plants add a nice,
rounded shrublike structure to the garden as
compared to the flopping and open unpruned
counterpart (Plate 68). Look at the plant:
sometimes just a little cut off the top, such as
4–6 in. off the tips, is enough to remove the
weight and allow the plant to stand upright
again, particularly if the plant is in a fair

amount of sun. In some years, particularly those with moist springs, plants can seed by the hundreds, but fortunately seeds usually will drop directly at the base of the plant. Cutting plants back after flowering and removing seedpods at the same time will eliminate this concern. Plants can be cut down to 6–10 in. above the ground to improve growth habit, which may be needed especially in warmer climates or in areas of deep shade. Plants grown in full sun may not require cutting back, although deadheading may be necessary if seeding is a problem. Seedpods can be snapped off easily with a sharp thumbnail. Shorter growing forms should be selected if you want to avoid pruning. The plant takes a nice shrub form over the winter, but it may break down in heavy snows. Cut down in the spring. Some people may be highly sensitive to the milky sap produced by *Amsonia*, which can cause itching or burning upon contact. Protective clothing should be worn while pruning the plants.

OTHER MAINTENANCE: Easy-to-grow, hardy, low-maintenance plant. Tolerates both dry and wet soils for short periods, but generally prefers evenly moist conditions. Division is easy, in late spring or fall, but is not necessary for 6–10 years or longer. Requires staking if grown in shade and not pruned.

RELATED PLANTS: *Amsonia ciliata*, downy amsonia, is a fine-leaved, feathery form that opens up a bit after flowering. I shear 4–6 in. off the tops of plants grown in full sun and shape it for a wonderful habit.

Amsonia elliptica has wider, glossier leaves than *A. tabernaemontana*. Its nice form holds up fairly well as a rounded shrub in full sun with no pruning. Heavy seeder in moist years. Should be deadheaded before pods mature. When grown in shade, prune as for *A. tabernaemontana*.

Amsonia montana is a smaller version of *A. tabernaemontana* that holds its shape well without pruning.

Anaphalis triplinervis

Zone: 3–8
Common Name: three-veined everlasting
Family: Asteraceae
Description: white papery flowerheads; woolly three-veined leaves; zigzag stems
Size: 12–18 in. high; 12–15 in. wide
Exposure: full sun to partial shade
Flowering: August–October

PRUNING: Three-veined everlasting has long-lasting flowers and a long bloom period. Deadhead to lateral buds when flowers fade to keep plants looking fresh. Foliage declines if grown in too dry a soil, thus requiring deadleafing. If damage is severe, cut plants down to basal foliage when evident. Plants may also need pruning back due to damage from painted lady butterfly larvae.

OTHER MAINTENANCE: One of the few gray-foliaged plants that doesn't rot in moist soils or humid conditions; in fact, this species requires evenly moist soils, or the foliage will decline. Clumps increase at a moderate rate, but plants do not send out invasive stolons like other *Anaphalis*. Divide every 4–5 years in early spring. Do not prune for winter; cut back in early spring.

RELATED PLANTS: *Anaphalis triplinervis* 'Summer Snow' has whiter flowers than the species and is more compact (8–10 in.).

Anaphalis margaritacea is an invasive, higher maintenance plant, but it will take drier conditions than *A. triplinervis*. Native species appropriate for native setting.

Anchusa azurea

Zone: 3–8
Common Name: Italian bugloss
Family: Boraginaceae
Description: tiny bright blue flowers; large coarse leaves
Size: 4–6 ft. high; 2 ft. wide
Exposure: full sun to partial shade
Flowering: May–June

PRUNING: Deadhead plants to lateral buds to prevent excessive seeding and to prolong bloom. Foliage declines after bloom period. The plant's life expectancy can be prolonged by several years if cut back hard to the ground immediately after flowering; or, even better, cut back into the crown, going ½–¾ in. under the soil surface right to the roots. Do not prune again for the winter. Clean-up if needed in the spring.

OTHER MAINTENANCE: Plants require staking, particularly in high-fertility soil. Can be invasive in rich soil. Tolerates short periods of drought; rots in wet soils. Italian bugloss is a high-maintenance, short-lived perennial that deteriorates after the second year and must be divided. Plants do not respond well to autumn planting. Heavy seeders.

RELATED PLANTS: *Anchusa azurea* 'Dropmore' is floppy and requires staking.

Anchusa azurea 'Little John' grows 12–18 in., usually not needing staking.

Anchusa azurea 'Loddon Royalist', 3 ft. in height, may need staking, particularly in winds and storms.

Anemone ×hybrida

Zone: 4–8
Common Name: Japanese anemone
Family: Ranunculaceae
Description: white, pink, or rose flowers; trifoliate leaves
Size: 2–4 ft. (1¼–1½ ft.) high; 2 ft. wide
Exposure: full sun to partial shade
Flowering: September–October

PRUNING: Japanese anemone doesn't require deadheading to prolong bloom, but the old flowers tend to detract from the beauty of new buds and flowers. I usually deadhead once early in the bloom period, and then let the rest of the deadheads remain on the plants. The seedheads do not turn cottonlike, as do the flowers of many other members of the genus. Plants blacken and become quite unattractive with a hard frost, and are probably best cut down for the winter. Can be completely defoliated by black blister beetles in July (see Chapter 4 for details). The remaining bare stems of infected plants should be cut to the ground. New basal foliage quickly returns, but the plants most likely will not flower that season. Take care when pruning down stems after beetle damage to wear gloves and protective clothing, as a few beetles may still be on plants and can cause blisters on the skin upon contact. Japanese beetles also can do major damage to Japanese anemone leaves. I consider the damage from the Japanese beetles to be pruning for height control as my *Anemone ×hybrida* 'Queen Charlotte' flowered at 2½ ft., rather than its typical 3½ ft., with little delay in the flowering time as a result of Japanese beetle feeding in June. The overall vigor of the plant was reduced, however. I assume gardeners may be able to prune similarly by cutting back by one-half in early June when plants are 12 in. tall; my attempts at finding out the results of this have been hindered by black blister beetle damage on pruned plants.

OTHER MAINTENANCE: Plants prefer rich, well-draining organic soil. Often killed by wet overwintering conditions. Avoid periods of drought. Can be short-lived and requires mulching for the winter in northern gardens. Often slow to establish, but once Japanese anemone takes hold it can be invasive, requiring digging out to keep plants in their intended space and to control spread. I have grown them successfully in sun or shade, although morning sun is preferred to hot afternoon sun in hot locations. Divide every 10 years in the spring if needed to renew clump. Fall transplanting is fatal; spring planting is advised. Tall-growing cultivars (4–5 ft.) may need staking.

RELATED PLANTS: I have tried approximately 10 different cultivars of *Anemone*

×*hybrida* and I find the old standbys 'September Charm' (single pink) and 'Honorine Jobert' (single white) to be the longest lived and most tolerant to sun and drought once established. Both can be invasive.

Anemone tomentosa 'Robustissima' can be invasive but is well behaved in dry shade. Also afflicted by black blister beetles. More tolerant of temperature extremes than *Anemone* ×*hybrida*. Hardy to zone 3.

Angelica gigas

Zone: 4–8
Family: Apiaceae
Description: bold dissected foliage; 4- to 8-in.-wide burgundy flowerheads
Size: 3–6 ft. high; 2–3 ft. wide
Exposure: partial shade
Flowering: July–August

PRUNING: *Angelica gigas* is monocarpic, meaning it dies after setting seed, so the flowerheads should be cut off as soon as the flowers fade to prevent seed maturation. This extends the life of this normally biennial, or short-lived perennial, species. Deadhead to a lateral bud. If allowed to go to seed, it may produce offspring with great ambition if the conditions are favorable, but in my gardens only minimal offspring are produced (I wish there were more!). Flowers are attractive to beneficial insects. Deadleaf older yellowing leaves in late summer. All leaves drop off the stem after a frost, and unless the seedheads have been allowed to remain, the plant should be cut down at this time.

OTHER MAINTENANCE: Will grow in full sun but best performance is in locations with afternoon shade. Moist fertile soil enhances growth. May be affected by mites or leaf minor, but not of significant concern. It is a self-supporting giant that does not need staking.

RELATED PLANTS: *Angelica archangelica*, archangel, has the same pruning and maintenance requirements as *A. gigas*.

Anthemis tinctoria

Zone: 3–7
Common Name: golden marguerite
Family: Asteraceae
Description: golden-yellow flowerheads; fernlike foliage with woolly undersides; aromatic when touched
Size: 2–3 ft. high; 2 ft. wide
Exposure: full sun
Flowering: June–August

PRUNING: Plants can be cut back or pinched before flowering to help control flopping habit and to create fuller plants. One effective way to cut plants back is to prune off 6 in. in early to mid-May and then cut off another 6 in. in early June; this may delay flowering. After flowering but before seeds mature, deadhead to lateral buds for continued bloom. After secondary flowers fade, cut plants down to new basal foliage. A few sporadic blooms usually will be produced from basal growth. Unlimited seed production robs the plant of energy and can lead to death. Cutting plants back in late summer, usually late August or early September, allows more vigorous vegetative basal shoots to develop for overwintering, which may help prolong the life of the plant. The basal growth remains fairly evergreen; do not cut back further for the winter. Prune off any damaged growth in the spring. If allowed, plants will reseed to monstrous proportions, quickly filling a large area. Reseeding may be desirable in naturalized situations, and the seeds also attract golden finches.

OTHER MAINTENANCE: Tolerates hot, dry, and lean situations. Well-draining soil is critical to survival. Will require staking, particularly in rich soil, if not pruned to control height. Often short-lived. Divide every 2–3 years. Poor performance in regions warmer than zone 7.

RELATED PLANTS: *Anthemis tinctoria* 'Moonlight' has nice soft yellow flowers. Grows 2 ft. tall, often not requiring staking.

Aquilegia hybrids

Zone: 3–9
Common Name: long-spurred columbine
Family: Ranunculaceae
Description: wide range of colors and
    bicolored flowers; gray-green compound
    foliage
Size: 1–3 ft. (1 ft.) high; 1 ft. wide
Exposure: full sun to partial shade
Flowering: May–June

PRUNING: First deadhead to lateral flower
buds, then cut old flowering stems to the
ground when all flowering is finished to prevent seeding, which often results in undesirable strains. Deadheading can prolong
bloom, particularly on young plants. Deadleafing keeps plants in good condition, but if
severely affected by leaf miner or other pests,
plants can be cut to the ground. A fresh
mound of foliage will develop from the pruning. Do not be concerned if it takes several
weeks or longer for new foliage to emerge,
particularly under dry conditions. The clean
fresh mound of foliage can remain for the
winter. If plants have leaf miner or other
pests in the autumn, they should be cut
down for the winter; clean-up all debris from
around the plant. Destroy any and all pest-
infested leaves.

OTHER MAINTENANCE: Plants do best
with evenly moist, rich soil. Overly dry soil
will take its toll, as will overly wet soil, which
leads to crown rot. Avoid locations with hot
afternoon sun. Taller forms will need staking.
If columbine gets infested with borers, dig
out and destroy the entire plant. Plants can be
divided, with care, in the summer, although it
usually is not required. Columbine is short-
lived, normally persisting only 3–4 years.
Natural hybridization will occur between
species. Planting in different areas of the garden can reduce the cross-hybridization. Also,
planting among other perennials that will fill
in after the columbine is finished flowering
will help to hide ugly or cut-back foliage.

RELATED PLANTS: *Aquilegia* McKana
Hybrids are commonly available 30-in.-tall
plants, usually requiring staking.
    Aquilegia Biedermeier Strain are compact
12-in. cultivars. No staking needed.
    Aquilegia alpina, alpine columbine, is my
favorite species. Will seed, but not to nuisance level (see Plate 52). Grows 18–24 in.,
needs no staking, and is longer lived.
    Aquilegia canadensis, Canadian columbine,
reseeds heavily to colonize an area. Native,
easy to grow, less troubled by leaf miner.
    Aquilegia flabellata, fan columbine, is 8–12
in. high, requires no staking, and is longer
lived.
    Aquilegia vulgaris, granny's bonnet, is a
classic form often found in old gardens.

Arabis caucasica

Zone: 4–7
Common Name: rockcress
Family: Brassicaceae
Description: white fragrant flowers; gray-
    green pubescent leaves
Size: 12 in. high; 18 in. wide
Exposure: full sun
Flowering: April

PRUNING: Cut back or shear by one-half
after flowering to produce full plants, enhance subsequent year's performance, and
possibly cause sporadic summer flowers as
well as reduce seeding. Hedge shears work
well for this purpose, and plants can be
shaped at the same time. Plants that are not
pruned develop long bare stems with just a
few leaves on the ends and a sprawling habit.
Deadleafing is needed to remove yellow
lower leaves that often develop in the summer. Do not prune plants back for the winter,
but deadleaf as needed in the spring.

OTHER MAINTENANCE: Requires well-
draining soil, or it will be its demise. Melts
out in hot, humid weather. Short-lived.
Divide, after flowering, every 3 years.

RELATED PLANTS: *Arabis procurrens* is a better choice than *A. caucasica* for a number of reasons. It grows in poor dry soils as well as in richer soils, in sun or light shade. It has a dense crown of shiny green leaves that stays tight and doesn't need cutting back after flowering. Requires only deadheading. Deadleafing is not needed even if yellowing of leaves occurs, as tiny leaves fade away. Exhibits some autumn color and stays evergreen. The only downside are the flowers, which are slightly smaller and not as showy as those of *A. caucasica*.

Armeria maritima

Zone: 4–8
Common Name: sea pink
Family: Plumbaginaceae
Description: round, bright pink flowers on
    long stems; grasslike mounded foliage
Size: 12 in. (3 in.) high; 12 in. wide
Exposure: full sun
Flowering: May–June

PRUNING: Requires little pruning other than clipping off unsightly faded flowers and stalks down to basal foliage. Deadheading keeps young plants flowering through the summer and causes sporadic rebloom on older clumps. If no new buds are evident with the dead flowers, grab a handful of deadheads and prune off all at once, or use hedge shears to ease the labor in large plantings. Plants are evergreen. Do not prune for winter, but sections may need to be pruned off in the spring if there is winter damage.

OTHER MAINTENANCE: Performs best on poor and dry soils. Mats rot in the center in heavy clay, poorly drained, or overly rich soils, and plants are usually short-lived (3–5 years) under such conditions. Division is needed when cushions open up and decline, but division is often hard to do successfully, so it's best to replace plants at this time.

Artemisia abrotanum

Zone: 5–9
Common Name: southernwood
Family: Asteraceae
Description: gray-green, finely divided foli-
    age; non-ornamental yellow flowerheads
Size: 3–4 ft. high; 1½–2 ft. wide
Exposure: full sun
Flowering: July–August

PRUNING: Cut back tips by 6–8 in. in spring or early summer to prevent plants from getting rangy. If prone to very weedy growth, perhaps in rich soil, plants can be cut back even harder, taking them to within a foot of the ground. Avoid cutting into the old woody part of stems, which may result in death of the plant. Hedge shears are useful for shaping and cutting back plants. Removing the flowering stalks before the flowers open helps keep plants in good form. If allowed to flower, deadheading and shaping with shears can be done after flowering. Do not cut back hard after August as plants may not have time to regrow and harden before winter. Do not prune for winter.

OTHER MAINTENANCE: Best in well-draining or dry sites; wet soil or extreme humidity will cause the plant to open in the middle.

Artemisia absinthium 'Lambrook Silver'

Zone: 4–9
Common Name: lambrook silver artemisia
Family: Asteraceae
Description: gray, deeply divided foliage;
    yellow flowerheads
Size: 2 ft. high; 2 ft. wide
Exposure: full sun
Flowering: August–September

PRUNING: When half their mature height (normally in early June), plants can be pinched, or cut back by one-half, and shaped with hedge shears to reduce height and to prevent flopping later in the summer. I usually cut off the flowerheads as soon as I see them forming to better enjoy the silver foliage. A second trim may be necessary to keep plants looking good. Plants that are allowed to flower should be deadheaded to prevent seed set, otherwise foliage will deteriorate at the sake of seed production; deadheads also add a tarnished look to plants. Neglected plants may be killed if cut back too hard to old wood if no new buds are breaking. It's best to not prune hard after August as plants may not have time to harden for the winter. Lambrook silver artemisia is semi-evergreen, so do not prune for winter. When planting it is useful to cut back or pinch new plants for fuller, more compact first-year growth.

OTHER MAINTENANCE: Prefers poor, well-draining, even dry soil with an alkaline pH. It is an easy *Artemisia* to grow, and it doesn't spread invasively by underground runners like *Artemisia ludoviciana* 'Silver King' and others. Best artemisia for northern gardens if good winter drainage is assured.

RELATED PLANTS: *Artemisia stelleriana* 'Silver Brocade', silver brocade beach wormwood, requires excellent drainage for survival. Pinch plants to keep full and to prevent flowering. If allowed to bloom, deadhead before seed set. Cut back to control spread. Deadleafing of foliage at the base may be necessary. Do not prune for winter. I have had plants totally defoliated by larval feeding in summer (see Plate 45).

Artemisia lactiflora

Zone: 4–8
Common Name: white mugwort
Family: Asteraceae
Description: ornamental creamy white
    flowerheads; green divided leaves
Size: 4–6 ft. high; 3 ft. wide
Exposure: full sun or light shade
Flowering: August–September

PRUNING: Plants provided with sun and moist soils become surprisingly large (6 ft. tall) and require staking. Height and legginess can be controlled if thinned and pinched or cut back by 4 in., or even by one-half, depending on how unmanageable it tends to become, in late May or early June. Under dry conditions or poor soil, plants usually attain a manageable 3½- to 4-ft. height and require no pruning, thinning, or staking. In autumn, cut plants down to basal rosette, which remains fairly evergreen.

OTHER MAINTENANCE: Staking is required in conditions of moist, rich soil. Divide every 4–5 years. Long-lived.

Artemisia ludoviciana 'Silver King'

Zone: 3–8
Common Name: silver king artemisia
Family: Asteraceae
Description: woolly, gray, lance-shaped
    leaves; insignificant yellow flowerheads
Size: 2–3 ft. high; wide-spreading clump
Exposure: full sun
Flowering: August–September

PRUNING: If grown for foliar effect alone, plants should not be allowed to flower, which can lead to decline. Plants can be sheared back by one-half or two-thirds at the end of May or in early June to control flopping; they may benefit from another cut in half in mid-July. Plants can be selectively pruned to keep in shape. Plants that fall over in summer can be sheared back by one-third to one-half at that time and will return to good form. Although the height of silver king artemisia can be controlled, it is difficult to control the spread of this plant just with pruning, and it usually involves digging out the invasive roots. If grown for wreath making (which I feel is this plant's main attribute), pinching early in the season will keep plants fuller and will ensure flowering. Cut stems while in bud before flowers mature, in early to mid-

September in the Midwest, for best effect in wreaths.

OTHER MAINTENANCE: Plants are very invasive. As tempting as it is to grow this plant in the perennial border for the wonderful silver foliage, it isn't advisable. Best given a bed by itself where it can run and be used for cutting and yet will not take over the rest of the world. Some gardeners are experimenting with new commercially available barriers. Also, with its tendency to flop, it can do so in peace if given its own out-of-the-way space. Plants may rot in excessively moist soils or in regions with high humidity. If grown in the border, plants will require frequent (annual) lifting and dividing in the spring or autumn to control spread.

RELATED PLANTS: *Artemisia ludoviciana* 'Silver Queen' has foliage that is slightly less dissected. It is a fast spreader as well.

Artemisia ludoviciana 'Valerie Finnis', when sheared (with hedge shears) by one-half in early June, grew to 15 in. tall at maturity. Plants sheared by one-half in June and again in mid-July formed a nice 8- to 12-in.-high groundcover, compared to the flopping 3-ft.-high unpruned plants. Plants did not bloom under either pruning regimes. Some claim it is not invasive, although it is for me even in clay soil.

Artemisia 'Powis Castle'

Zone: 5–8
Common Name: powis castle artemisia
Family: Asteraceae
Description: finely cut silver foliage; insignificant flowerheads
Size: 2–3 ft. high; 3–4 ft. wide
Exposure: full sun
Flowering: August–September

PRUNING: Little quart-size plants can become 3-ft.-high and -wide specimens in the first season, which creates much excite-ment. Pinch before planting if leggy. Do not prune in the autumn, but in early spring plants can be cut back to control height and width. Make certain to not cut back too hard into the old wood, as this may kill the plant. Allow buds to start to break before pruning to provide a helpful reference point as to how far back to cut. Do not cut into wood that does not have live buds. Plants fill out quickly in a week or two after pruning. Hedge shears can be used during the summer to shape plants as needed and to keep them in their own space, as well as to remove flower buds before blooming, to help maintain the attractive appearance. If plants fall open in the summer, shearing back by one-third or one-half will return them to good form, and soon after they won't even look as though they had been pruned. Dead-leafing may be necessary if plants have received too much moisture.

OTHER MAINTENANCE: My biggest problem in the central Ohio area is lack of hardiness. Hardiness zones have not truly been determined for this relatively new plant. I have tried it in several different locations in clients' gardens and my own, only to have it live for one or even two years and then be killed over the winter. Planting in a protected site has allowed the longest life (3 years) in my experience. Division of this woody subshrub is difficult.

RELATED PLANTS: *Artemisia* 'Silverado'—not sure on the nomenclature of this plant, but I love it and use it anyway. Plants can be cut back by one-half at planting to promote fullness. Shearing back by one-half when just in bud, around early to mid-July, and then shearing off buds when they appear around the middle of August and again in the middle of September creates full, compact (8–10 in. rather than 18–20 in.), nonflowering plants that hold up well until the end of the season. The flowering stems are attractive, but if allowed to develop early in the season plants will not be as full as pruned specimens. The flowering also causes decline of the plant. Cut off deadheads to the base of the plant. In hot summers, plants that have been allowed to flower may need to be cut back all the way to fresh basal growth that develops in August. You could always try for the best of both worlds: prune in July and August for full plants, and allow some flowering in September. I use chicken grit in the hole as well as for a mulch when planting *Artemisia* 'Silverado' to reduce losses from wet soil.

Artemisia schmidtiana 'Nana'

Zone: 3–7
Common Name: silvermound artemisia
Family: Asteraceae
Description: finely cut silvery foliage; insignificant flowerheads
Size: 12–18 in. high; 15–18 in. wide
Exposure: full sun
Flowering: July–August

PRUNING: Clumps usually open up in the center by midsummer, which is a good time to cut the plant back to the new basal growth. If you are weak-at-heart about cutting back so drastically, you can do it in phases, as described in Chapter 10 (see Figure 10-1). Cutting back in phases is particularly helpful since silvermound artemisia usually is located right in the front of the border, where dramatic pruning is obvious. You can delay the plants from opening up by preventing flowering, either by shearing (plants can be shaped at this time as well) or pinching when flower buds are first evident. As with most silver-foliaged artemisia, silvermound artemisia's habit is best maintained if flowering is prevented entirely.

OTHER MAINTENANCE: Requires well-draining, low-fertility soil and good air circulation to prevent rotting; tends to rot in high humidity. High maintenance. I'm not sure how this plant ever gained so much popular-

ity—I suspect it is simply the fortune of being silver.

Arum italicum 'Marmoratum' ('Pictum')

Zone: 5–9
Common Name: painted arum
Family: Araceae
Description: spear-shaped, variegated deep green leaves; orange-red berries; jack-in-the-pulpit-type flowers
Size: 12–20 in. high; 18 in. wide
Exposure: partial to full shade
Flowering: May

PRUNING: Painted arum may require deadleafing when foliage dies down in summer to tidy up the area and allow the attractive fruit to be best displayed. Often this entails simply pulling leaves out gently by hand as they shrivel away. Do not deadhead, or you will lose one of the prime features of the plant: the ornamental fruit. When the fruit decline the stems usually become limp and are hidden by returning autumn foliage, so pruning of stems generally is not needed. Plants are evergreen or semi-evergreen, depending on the climate—do not cut back in the autumn. May need a bit of deadleafing in the spring so as to not detract from healthy foliage.

OTHER MAINTENANCE: Best in moist shady sites with soil high in organic matter. Tolerates drier soils when the leaves are dormant during the summer. Summer is also the best time to divide the plants, but this usually is not necessary for many years (6–10 years). Beautiful low-maintenance plant. Slow to take hold, but long-lived once established. Considered to be on the hardiness borderline in zone 5, often listed as zone 6–9, but has tolerated our Midwest winters, though it often dies down and comes back in the spring.

Aruncus dioicus

Zone: 3–7
Common Name: goat's beard
Family: Rosaceae
Description: plumelike creamy flowers;
    pinnately compound astilbe-like foliage
Size: 4–6 ft. high; 6 ft. wide
Exposure: partial shade
Flowering: June–July

PRUNING: The plants are dioecious (male
and female flowers borne on separate
plants), and although the male flowers are
more attractive in bloom, the female seedpods are more attractive for the winter—
what a dilemma! Nurseries do not distinguish between the two sexes anyway, so you
usually don't get a choice. The deadheads
may weigh down the foliage, which is an
obvious sign that deadheading would
improve the overall appearance of the plant.
Deadleafing may be required if scorching or
dry conditions are a problem. Self-seeding
may occur where male and female plants are
grown together, but it is seldom troublesome.

OTHER MAINTENANCE: Staking is not
needed, but heavy rain when the plant is in
flower will weigh the great plumes to the
ground. Best in moisture-retentive soil. Will
take full sun in cool summer climates. Tolerates tree root competition if soils are high in
moisture or in areas with heavy rainfall, although the competition will curb the plant's
size. Although rarely required (every 10 years
or more) and difficult to accomplish, division
is recommended in the spring. Tough roots.
Not for use in areas warmer than zone 6,
where performance is poor as a result of the
heat. It is slow growing in the first season or
two, but once it takes hold, stand back, as it
forms a large shrub. Allow plenty of space
when planting (at least 4 ft. diameter), since
the plant won't like being moved.

RELATED PLANTS: *Aruncus aethusifolius* is
a small 6- to 8-in. mound that should not be
deadheaded because the seedheads are ornamental over the summer and winter.

Asarum europaeum

Zone: 4–7
Common Name: European wild ginger
Family: Aristolochiaceae
Description: brown flowers hidden under
    shiny kidney-shaped leaves
Size: 6–8 in. high; 12–15 in. wide
Exposure: partial to full shade
Flowering: April–May

PRUNING: Minimal pruning is needed.
Plants are evergreen or semi-evergreen,
depending on the climate. Do not prune for
winter, but deadleaf as needed in the spring.

OTHER MAINTENANCE: Low-maintenance
plant. Prefers rich organic, moist but well-
draining, slightly acidic soil, although it has
performed well in more alkaline conditions
in my experience. Spreads slowly by rhizomes
and can be divided in the spring or early fall,
but division is rarely needed (6–10 years).
Avoid planting too deep. Dies out in zone 8.

RELATED PLANTS: *Asarum canadense*,
Canadian wild ginger, is a native deciduous
species that is more tolerant of alkaline conditions and heat and is more vigorous.

Asclepias tuberosa

Zone: 4–9
Common Name: butterfly weed
Family: Asclepiadaceae
Description: orange flowers; narrow foliage
Size: 2–3 ft. high; 2 ft. wide
Exposure: full sun
Flowering: June–August

PRUNING: Deadheading results in rebloom
about a month after initial flowering. Allowing some of the second bloom phase to
mature into the ornamental fruit prolongs
the season of interest. It is a heavy seeder.

The fruit should be removed before it splits and spills the seeds, if seeding is not desired. Do not prune for the winter, cut back in the spring.

OTHER MAINTENANCE: Butterfly weed is a native prairie plant that tolerates poor dry soil and is drought tolerant. Well-draining soil is essential, particularly in the winter. Prefers acid soil. Can be slow to establish but is long-lived once it takes hold. Late to emerge in the spring. Divide in the spring only when new growth starts. Division is difficult due to the taproot, but fortunately it's seldom needed. Mulching helps prevent frost heaving. Low-maintenance plant. Do not collect from the wild.

Aster ×frikartii 'Monch'

Zone: 5–8
Common Name: monch aster
Family: Asteraceae
Description: lavender-blue flowerheads; fine pubescence on leaves and stems
Size: 2–3 ft. high; 2–3 ft. wide
Exposure: full sun
Flowering: July–October

PRUNING: These plants seem to have a long bloom period even without deadheading. The new flower buds are born close to the old flowers, so if you choose to deadhead you must take care to remove each individual deadhead without damaging the new bud. Plants are often lanky; cutting back by one-half or more in late May or early June can improve the habit, and it may also delay flowering. Monch aster is a tender perennial. Several authorities recommend that it not be cut back for the winter in order to increase its survivability. Cut plants down in the spring after all danger of cold weather has passed.

OTHER MAINTENANCE: Needs winter protection in zone 5, and it will not survive wet overwintering conditions. Select a light mulch such as pine needles for protection to avoid crown rot. Provide light support, such as from pea stakes, if pruning is not performed.

RELATED PLANTS: *Aster ×frikartii* 'Wonder of Staffa' is even taller than 'Monch' and requires pruning for height control.

Aster novi-belgii

Zone: 4–8
Common Name: michaelmas daisy, New York aster
Family: Asteraceae
Description: lilac, purple, blue, red, white, or pink flowers, depending on cultivar; narrow, slightly pubescent leaves
Size: 1–4 ft. high; 1½–3 ft. wide
Exposure: full sun
Flowering: September–October

PRUNING: Deadhead or cut plants completely to the ground after flowering to prevent growth of seedlings, which do not develop true to cultivar type. Cutting plants to the ground can often come as a relief in the garden because foliage may blacken or deteriorate due to foliar diseases. Do not compost infected clippings.

Tall-growing forms of *Aster novi-belgii* respond well to pinching or cutting back to reduce height and eliminate the need for staking. Such pruning usually produces more flowers per plant as well. They can be treated like mums (*Dendranthema*) and pinched several times before mid- to late July. Pinching into late July usually will delay the flowering. A lower maintenance approach is to simply cut asters back once by one-half to two-thirds, depending on the ultimate size of the plant and the gardener's objectives, in early to mid-June. Plants can be anywhere from 12–24 in. in height at the time of pruning. Pruning again later can delay flowering, but the floral display may be slightly reduced. Asters cut back by one-half in mid-June and then cut back by one-half again in mid- to late July will flower 2 weeks later than plants pruned only once (the first of October rather than mid-September), and they flower at 18 in. tall rather than 3 ft. Plants cut back twice in this way were full and nicely formed, with what appeared to be just a minor reduction in the number of flowers. Another approach is to remove 4–6 in. off the tips of the plants in early August for about a 2-week delay but with less reduction in height (2 ft.). Removing 4 in. off the tips in early September, when the plants are in tight bud, may result in no flowering.

Plants can be shaped, by cutting the outer stems lower than inner ones, and thinned at the same time as they are initially cut back (Plates 69–70). Thinning is often recommended to improve the overall form of the plant and to increase the air circulation around the plant in the hope of reducing foliar diseases that often affect asters. Thin asters by about one-third or more, removing the weakest stems and leaving about 1 in. between stems. Personally, I have not seen much improvement in the plants' resistance to disease with thinning, but thinning does make room for branching of pruned or pinched stems. Shaping for lower outer branches can help hide the ugly legs that are often associated with asters. Deadleafing can also help keep plants attractive.

Some asters are attractive over the winter, but leaving the plants up can result in undesirable seeding. Be certain to cut down any diseased plants before winter and clean-up debris from the base of the plant.

OTHER MAINTENANCE: Plants prefer rich, high-organic, well-draining soil. Watering during periods of drought can reduce leaf decline. Good air circulation can help prevent foliar diseases. If aster wilt should occur, destroy the plants and the roots, as this is where the pathogen resides. Well-draining soil reduces the incidence of aster wilt. Asters benefit from being divided every year or two in the spring to keep them vigorous or to control their spread. Staking is required if plants are not pruned. Chicken wire held up by stakes is one effective method for staking asters.

RELATED PLANTS: Select dwarf cultivars if pruning and/or staking is not desired; even medium forms often need staking. Some notable dwarf forms of *Aster novi-belgii* include: 'Jenny', 12 in., red; 'Professor Kippenberg', 12–15 in., lavender-blue; and 'Snowball', 12 in., white.

Aster novae-angliae, New England aster, includes many tall cultivars, such as 'Alma Potschke' (Plates 69–70), and should be treated as for *A. novi-belgii*. *Aster novae-angliae* 'Purple Dome' is a good compact 18- to 24-in.-tall plant that doesn't require pruning for height control. Often listed as disease free, but this has not been my experience.

Aster oblongifolius var. *angustatus* 'Raydon's Favorite', Raydon's aster, is my favorite aster. I cut it back by one-half in mid-June, as with other asters, and it flowers at about 2 ft., rather than 3 ft., around early to mid-October (Plate 71). It is dense and full and has lavender flowers, flowering at a time when most of the rest of the garden is finished. Disease resistant. Divide every couple years to maintain vigor.

Aster tongolensis, east indies aster, a compact summer-flowering aster, does not need pruning for height control, but if deadheaded it may repeat flowering later in the season. The cultivar 'Wartburgstern' ('Wartburg Star') grows 18–24 in. with lavender-blue flowers.

Aster tataricus **'Jin Dai'**

Zone: 4–8
Common Name: jin dai tatarian aster
Family: Asteraceae
Description: lavender-blue flowerheads; large
    basal leaves up to 1 in. long

Size: 3–4 ft. (2 ft.) high; 3 ft. wide, spreading
Exposure: full sun
Flowering: October–November

PRUNING: *Aster tataricus* 'Jin Dai' is a self-supporting cultivar that normally doesn't require pruning for height control (Plate 72). It is a desirable plant because the only pruning that it requires is cutting back for clean-up in the spring. It can be pruned before flowering to layer the planting, if desired. Cutting plants back by one-half in mid-July produces 3-ft.-tall plants, rather than 4-ft. plants, but without any delay in bloom, which is good because these plants are very late to flower anyway, usually not until mid-October. Deadheading in the autumn is senseless, and the old flowering stems remain upright and strong through the winter. I have never had any seeding of the cultivar.

OTHER MAINTENANCE: 'Jin Dai' is an easy-to-grow aster. Clean foliage is free of pests and disease. Spreading underground stolons can be invasive. Divide in the spring every third or fourth year to control spread.

RELATED PLANTS: The straight species form of *Aster tataricus* may flower at 6 ft. in height. Cutting it back as described for the cultivar will also produce shorter plants. Lifting the stolons and pruning them off can control spread.

Asteromoea mongolica (Kalimeris mongolica)

Zone: 5–8
Common Name: double Japanese aster
Family: Asteraceae
Description: numerous small white flowers; small divided leaves
Size: 3–3½ ft. high; 2 ft. wide
Exposure: full sun to partial shade
Flowering: July–September

PRUNING: This perennial has a long bloom period even without deadheading. Old flowers simply dry up unobtrusively. Plants can be left up for winter interest and then cut down in early spring. They respond well to cutting back before flowering to reduce height, which can effectively layer the planting. Cutting back can also be used to slightly delay flowering on a few plants or on a few stems of an individual plant. Plants cut back by one-half in mid-June, when about 3 ft. tall, flowered at 2½ ft. rather than 3 ft.; they were also fuller than unpruned plants and flowering was delayed by about 1 week.

OTHER MAINTENANCE: Fairly low-maintenance plant except for its spreading root system, which can be easily controlled. This usually is necessary in the spring in about the plant's fourth year. Tolerant of a fair amount of shade. Adaptable, pest free, and normally no staking required.

RELATED PLANTS: *Asteromoea incisa* (*Kalimeris incisa*) grows 2 ft. tall and has single flowers with a shorter bloom period than the above species. Shear old flowering stems off to low mound of deep green foliage after flowering is completed in midsummer to clean-up the plant and for a possible light rebloom in the autumn.

Astilbe ×arendsii

Zone: 3–8
Common Name: astilbe
Family: Saxifragaceae
Description: white, pink, red, even peach flowers; green or bronzy ferny foliage
Size: 2–4 ft. high; 2 ft. wide
Exposure: shade
Flowering: June–July

PRUNING: Deadheading will not induce more bloom, and the dried seedheads extend the interest of astilbe through the season and even into winter. With certain cultivars or species of *Astilbe*, seeding can be a problem in some years, particularly if there is a moist spring. Once it is determined that seeding presents a problem, such plants can be dead-headed in the future. Deadleafing may be necessary to keep plants neat, particularly if subjected to dry conditions. If plants have totally "crisped" from prolonged drought, they can be cut to the ground for regrowth of fresh foliage later in the season with the return of cooler, moister conditions. Depending on the severity of the conditions, new growth may not return until the spring of the following season, if at all. Astilbe foliage can be subject to late-spring frost damage, particularly on *Astilbe* ×*arendsii* and *A. japonica* types; any such damage should be pruned off and plants will rebound nicely. Some gardeners remove the flowers of their astilbe when in full bud to delay bloom. I haven't had luck with this myself; when I remove the buds, the plants simply don't flower at all. Factors such as soil fertility and moisture level, as well as overall age or vigor of the plant and the particular species, most likely contribute to these different results. Do not cut back for winter, but prune in early spring. The old foliage may help protect the plant from winter damage in colder areas.

OTHER MAINTENANCE: Four key things to remember for best results with *Astilbe* plants are: (1) they are heavy feeders; (2) summer drought is their worst enemy-keep watered in July and August; (3) winter wetness is their next worst enemy; (4) and they should be divided every 3 years to maintain vigor. *Astilbe* needs high-nitrogen fertilization in the spring or autumn, either from composted manures or fertilizers or both. Dave Beattie, renowned astilbe grower, recommends using a general-purpose lawn fertilizer, such as a 20-10-10, in early October for best results. The overwintering structure of the plant increases in size in November, just before the last hard frost, and so an October application of fertilizer will help its development. Also, early flowering astilbe form buds in the autumn for next year's flowers. All late-flowering *A. chinensis* types, such as *A. chinensis* 'Pumila', are more tolerant of dry conditions; others should be kept moist during the summer. Astilbe plants will tolerate full sun if given plenty of moisture. In zones 3, 4, or 5, spring planting, or planting no later than 1 September, is advisable or else plants may heave, especially smaller growing forms such as *A. simplicifolia* 'William Buchanan'. If crowns rise above the soil, gently press in, and top-dress with organic matter. Divide in the early spring or midsummer before September.

Astrantia major

Zone: 4–7
Common Name: masterwort
Family: Apiaceae
Description: creamy white flowers with green or pink bracts; leaves palmately lobed
Size: 2–3 ft. (1½ ft.) high; 2 ft. wide
Exposure: partial shade
Flowering: June–July

PRUNING: Bracts are attractive for a long period. Deadheading can prolong bloom sporadically into September and prevent seeding, which under certain conditions can be prolific. Deadhead to lateral flower buds; when secondary bloom finishes, and before seeds mature, cut down flowering stems to basal foliage. Yellowing of the foliage may occur in summer, particularly in dry conditions; deadleaf, or if severe, cut back to new growth at base of plant. Leave this basal growth for the winter. Prune in the spring.

OTHER MAINTENANCE: Prefers moist, shady, high organic matter conditions. Can grow in sun if kept constantly moist. Spreads rapidly by runners under good conditions. Division in spring or fall every 4–5 years.

RELATED PLANTS: *Astrantia major* 'Rosea' normally does not seed itself.

Aubrieta deltoidea

Zone: 4–8
Common Name: false rockcress
Family: Brassicaceae
Description: small lilac to purple flowers;
    evergreen mat of tiny gray-green leaves
Size: 6 in. high; 24 in. wide
Exposure: full sun
Flowering: April–May

PRUNING: Plants can be sheared back by one-half and shaped in the late spring after flowering. Shearing prevents the plants from developing an open center, and it might encourage sporadic rebloom. Using hedge shears is fast and efficient, and plants will fill in quickly. This cutting back of the flowers and foliage before seeds mature accomplishes deadheading, thus preventing seeding, although false rockcress usually doesn't seed to heavy proportions. Plants may need to be cut back periodically from the outside to control their width. A second shearing in midsummer may be warranted if plants are not holding their compact form. *Aubrieta* is evergreen; do not prune for the winter. Sections of a plant that are damaged over the winter can be pruned off in the spring.

OTHER MAINTENANCE: Well-draining soil is essential to survival. Usually short-lived, especially the pink and red cultivars. I had some old purple-flowered forms growing on stone walls when I lived in England that were exceptional. A poor plant for southern gardens, particularly if not cut back after flowering. Divide in early spring or fall, perhaps every 1–3 years.

Aurinia saxatilis

Zone: 3–7
Common Name: basket-of-gold
Family: Brassicaceae
Description: bright yellow flowers; gray-
    green pubescent leaves
Size: 9–12 in. high; 18 in. wide

Exposure: full sun
Flowering: March–April

PRUNING: Plants seem to be longer lived if sheared back by one-third to one-half after flowering, before seeds mature; this also helps prevent the plants from opening up in the center. Plants can be shaped at the same time. Hedge shears work well for this purpose. Removing the deadheads prevents seeding, although seeding usually does not create an invasive problem. Deadheading each finished flowering stem individually as other stems are blooming keeps the plants neat and might prolong bloom a bit, but it is tedious work compared to removing the entire lot after all flowering is completed. Plants may require periodic deadleafing of rotten and tatty leaves during the summer months to keep them looking fresh. Do not cut back for the winter as this species is evergreen or semi-evergreen. In the spring, clean-up any damaged growth.

OTHER MAINTENANCE: Best in average, dry soil. Plants rot in wet soils, heat, and humidity. Overly rich soil contributes to sprawling habit. Division should be done in the fall, but plants resent being moved. Short-lived. Treated almost as an annual in the South and other warm climates where it can be planted in the fall, flower in the spring, and die in the summer. High maintenance.

Baptisia australis

Zone: 3–9
Common Name: blue wild indigo
Family: Fabaceae
Description: indigo-blue flowers on spikes;
    blue-green pea-like leaves
Size: 3–4 ft. high; 4 ft. wide
Exposure: full sun or partial shade
Flowering: June

PRUNING: Plants that are cut back by one-third and shaped after flowering form fresh rounded shrublike plants that hold up well for the rest of the season. This eliminates the flopping and opening up of plants that normally necessitates staking, particularly when they are grown in some shade. Cutting back also keeps plants in their intended space. Hedge shears work well for this task. Plants fill in nicely in about 3 weeks or so. As expected, plants cut back by one-half grow even smaller and narrower than those cut back by one-third, but in my opinion they are not as attractive and take longer to fill in to look decent. Shearing plants normally eliminates seedpods at the same time, although reseeding usually does not occur with *Baptisia*, and the seedpods, which turn black with maturity, are attractive and useful in dried arrangements. Removal of deadheads may not be desirable for this reason, although plants may flower more profusely the following season if they are deadheaded. Foliage blackens with heavy frost, and plants fall over by mid-January, or earlier depending on weather conditions. Still, I leave plants up for the winter. In a more formal setting it may be beneficial to cut *Baptisia* down after several killing frosts, or in January when falling occurs.

OTHER MAINTENANCE: Although slow to establish, *Baptisia* is tough, drought tolerant, and low maintenance once it takes hold. It takes low-fertility soils very well. Prefers acidic soil, although plants will tolerate higher pH conditions. Plants are slow growing and normally don't require division for 10 years or more, unless the expanding root system needs to be curbed. Although normally difficult to transplant, *Baptisia* can be moved successfully if given plenty of soil and the roots are undisturbed, especially when plants are still relatively small. Personally, I like to transplant in early spring, but it can also be done in late fall. Good plant for zone 8. If pruning is not desired but plants require staking, peony hoops placed over the plants in early spring offer an easy solution.

Begonia grandis var. evansiana

Zone: 6–9
Common Name: hardy begonia
Family: Begoniaceae
Description: small pink flowers in drooping clusters; light green succulent leaves with red veins
Size: 24–30 in. high; 18 in. wide
Exposure: partial or full shade
Flowering: July–October

PRUNING: Pinching encourages branching and keeps plants compact. Deadheading to lateral buds prolongs bloom, although hardy begonia has attractive pink seedpods that extend the interest of the plant. It is susceptible to stem rot, so when deadheading leave about 1 in. of flower stem on the plant. This will harden and fall off, thus avoiding fresh wounds on the main stem that can lead to infection. Dead leaves can also cause rot and should be removed. Do not prune off bulbils that form in the leaf axils of the plant; allow these to develop to encourage some seeding of this tender perennial, especially in northern areas, which will ensure constancy in the garden. Plants blacken with heavy frost. Cut down for the winter, and clean-up debris from the base of the plant.

OTHER MAINTENANCE: Hardy begonia prefers moist, high organic matter soil. Will take some sun in cooler regions. At its hardiness limit in zone 6, where cool winters are common, it needs a winter mulch. Plants are late to emerge (as late as mid-June in central Ohio); do not disturb growing area in early spring. Seldom needs division, generally every 6–10 years.

Belamcanda chinensis

Zone: 5–10
Common Name: blackberry lily
Family: Iridaceae
Description: orange star-shaped flowers; iris-like leaves

Size: 3–4 ft. high; 2 ft. wide
Exposure: full sun
Flowering: July–August

PRUNING: Old flowers literally roll up, and the seeds turn into attractive black berries. Plants will reseed, sometimes heavily under the right conditions, but allowing some seeding is recommended to ensure the presence of this often short-lived perennial in the garden. Removing some of the fruit before the seeds drop can reduce over-seeding, although seedlings are easily removed. If fruit is to be used for dried arrangements, cut before frost, as frost causes them to shrivel. The black berries add winter interest to the garden if allowed to remain. Remove any dead leaves and clean-up debris at the base of the plant through the summer and for the winter, especially where borers are a problem to reduce infestation. Do not compost.

OTHER MAINTENANCE: Successful over-wintering depends largely on well-draining soil. Plants are short-lived, particularly where summers are cool and moist. Tolerates colder winter temperatures in areas with long hot summers. Mulch in regions colder than zone 5, and avoid autumn planting to prevent frost heaving. Divide carefully in the spring or late summer, although it is easier to allow seedlings to replace the parent plant after a year or two. Plant may require staking in rich soils.

RELATED PLANTS: *Belamcanda chinensis* 'Freckle Face' is self-supporting and pest and disease free.

Belamcanda chinensis 'Hello Yellow' is a shorter yellow form. It grows to 12–15 in. and requires no staking. Has proven reliably hardy in central Ohio area.

Bergenia cordifolia

Zone: 3–8
Common Name: heartleaf bergenia
Family: Saxifragaceae

Description: pink flowers; shiny round evergreen leaves
Size: 12–18 in. high; 12 in. wide
Exposure: partial shade; full sun with moisture
Flowering: April–May

PRUNING: Deadhead to the ground to help maintain appearance. Plants remain semi-evergreen though are often damaged or bronzed over the winter. Do not cut back in the autumn; wait until early spring when faded leaves can be cut or pulled off the plant. Some deadleafing during dry summers, or if grown in too much sun, is usually needed to keep plants looking their best.

OTHER MAINTENANCE: Adaptable to a variety of soils, including some tolerance to drought conditions, but does not tolerate overly wet conditions. Prefers moist soils high in organic matter. Tolerates alkaline soil. Divide in the spring when clump opens up in the center, about every 4 years or longer. Rhizome may require top-dressing of compost if it is pushing up out of the soil. Flower buds are damaged in harsh winters. Relatively low-maintenance plant.

Boltonia asteroides 'Snowbank'

Zone: 4–9
Common Name: snowbank boltonia
Family: Asteraceae
Description: white daisy-like flowerheads; narrow leaves
Size: 3–5 ft. high; 3–4 ft. wide
Exposure: full sun to partial shade
Flowering: September–October

PRUNING: Plants normally don't require staking if grown in full sun and sheltered from winds, but if grown in more exposed areas, or in partial shade or overly rich soil, they have a tendency to fall over. Plants respond well to pruning before flowering, and it can be done in several different ways, depending on the final objective. Pruning of snowbank boltonia can be used to control height and/or to stagger bloom, or to layer individual plants or a large planting. Plants can be cut back by one-half to two-thirds in early June and the outer stems layered for fuller, self-supporting plants that grow shorter than unpruned plants with minimal or no delay in bloom. Alternatively, plants can be cut back by about one-third in mid-July, in which case they bloom at 2½ ft. tall, rather than 4 ft., and one week later than unpruned plants. It also creates an interesting layering effect (see Plate 55). If less dramatic height control is desired, plants can simply be pinched or have a few inches removed in early July. I never deadhead *Boltonia* because it flowers late in the season, until the frost takes it. Plants that are sturdy and self-supporting do not need to be cut back for the winter, but should be pruned down in early spring. If plants are floppy, cutting back before the winter may be desirable since more stems will fall with poor weather.

OTHER MAINTENANCE: Prefers well-draining, moist, organic soil, but will tolerate dry soil. Plants will be shorter if grown in prolonged dry conditions. Tolerates heat and humidity. Can spread rapidly in moist sandy soil and will even fill a large area (4 ft. × 4 ft.) in clay soil within about 5 years, but not invasively so in either condition. May require staking. Divide in the spring or fall every 4–5 years or as needed to control spread. Low-maintenance, problem-free plant.

RELATED PLANTS: *Boltonia asteroides* 'Pink Beauty' usually grows only about 3½ ft. tall, but it can be leggy and flop. Plants grown in partial shade and cut back by two-thirds in early June when 2½ ft. tall flowered at 2½ ft. but were still a bit floppy.

Brunnera macrophylla

Zone: 3–8
Common Name: Siberian bugloss
Family: Boraginaceae
Description: small, true blue flowers; coarse heart-shaped leaves
Size: 12–18 in. high; 20 in. wide
Exposure: partial to full shade
Flowering: April–May

PRUNING: Deadheading prevents reseeding, which can be abundant in moist locations but slim to none in dry sites. Most seeding occurs at the base of plant, and seedlings are easily removed or transplanted. Deadhead plants down to large basal foliage. Plants should also be deadleafed to remove foliage damaged by late-spring frosts, hot sun, or drought. Siberian bugloss can be cut back to the ground to stimulate lush new foliage if the old leaves start to decline severely in midsummer (mid-July in Ohio). Plants fill in nicely in about 3 weeks but will not return to full size that season. Keep plants moist after pruning. *Brunnera* foliage blackens with frost. Cutting back for the winter may be preferred.

OTHER MAINTENANCE: Plants prefer moist organic soil, and this is essential in southern areas. In northern gardens, however, plants will tolerate some dryness as long as they are shaded; they often respond by producing smaller leaves, and if the drought is prolonged they may go dormant. Leaves usually burn in hot sun, but will tolerate more sun in cool, moist climates. Division generally is not needed for 6–10 years or longer, but if necessary it should be done in the spring.

RELATED PLANTS: Several variegated forms of *Brunnera* are available, and they benefit from deadleafing or cutting back if the foliage deteriorates. Best growth is in shady, moist sites to prevent leaf scorching.

Plate 67. Lady's mantle (*Alchemilla mollis*) makes an excellent wide-mounded plant for repeating periodically along the edge of borders. (Author's garden)

Plate 68. *Amsonia* plants benefit from shearing back by one-third and shaping after flowering, here showing *Amsonia elliptica*. The plant on the left was sheared by one-third and shaped after flowering; plants on the right were not pruned and have a tendency to open up.

Plate 69. *Aster novae-angliae* 'Alma Potschke' shaped and thinned.

Plate 70. Regrowth on Alma Potschke New England aster 2 weeks after pruning.

Plate 71. This flowering Raydon's aster (*Aster oblongifolius* var. *angustatus* 'Raydon's Favorite') was cut back by one-half in mid-June.

Plate 72. *Aster tataricus* 'Jin Dai' is an outstanding aster that doesn't require pruning or staking.

Plate 73. *Coreopsis lanceolata* requires frequent deadheading to keep up its appearance.

Plate 74. Hardy chrysanthemum cultivars (*front to back*) *Dendranthema* 'Viette's Apricot Glow', 'Mei Kyo', and 'Venus', pictured here with dwarf fothergilla (*Fothergilla gardenii*) and virginia sweetspire (*Itea virginica*). (Author's garden)

Plate 75. Maiden pinks (*Dianthus deltoides* 'Brilliant') in full bloom.

Plate 76. Maiden pinks can be sheared with grass shears or hedge shears.

Plate 77. *Dianthus gratianopolitanus* 'Bath's Pink' being sheared and shaped after flowering.

Plate 78. A quick clean-up of the clippings from bath's pink dianthus using a shrub rake.

Plate 79. *Echinacea purpurea* 'Bright Star'. The shorter plants in the front were pruned in early July, and the taller plants in the back were left unpruned. This effectively layers the planting and delays flowering on the pruned plants, providing flowers later into the season.

Plate 80. This *Eupatorium maculatum* at Saul Nursery in Georgia was cut to 12 in. in early June. It flowered at about 3 ft., rather than the typical 15 ft. (Photo by Dr. Steven Still)

Plate 81. The outer stems of this gateway joe-pye weed (*Eupatorium maculatum* 'Gateway') were pinched while the inner stems were left unpruned to create a combination of large and small heads on fuller, layered plants.

Plate 82. Fennel (*Foeniculum*) can reseed to amazing proportions if not deadheaded.

Plate 83. *Geranium endressii* 'Wargrave Pink' in flower.

Plate 84. Prune sprawling stems of wargrave pink geranium that develop after the initial flowering.

Plate 85. Regrowth and rebloom emerges on *Geranium endressii* 'Wargrave Pink' within two weeks of pruning.

Plate 86. Unpruned *Helianthus salicifolius* reaches approximately 5 ft. in height.

Plate 87. The same sunflower plant the very next year grew to only 3 ft. with pinching.

Plate 88. *Heliopsis helianthoides* 'Summer Sun'. Plants in the front were pruned by one-half in early June. They matured to 3½ ft., rather than the typical 5 ft., and they started flowering about 2 weeks later than unpruned plants (pictured in the back of the planting).

Plate 89. The ugly deadheads or "mush-mummies" of daylilies (*Hemerocallis*) are not attractive additions to any garden and are best pruned off.

Plate 90. Snap the entire deadhead off daylilies with your fingers.

Plate 91. A comparison made late in the season of a daylily sheared to the ground (*right*) to a daylily left unsheared (*left*).

Plate 92. Evergreen candytuft (*Iberis sempervirens*) in full bloom.

Plate 93. Evergreen candytuft with deadheads.

Plate 94. Evergreen candytuft can be cut back by grabbing a handful of stems at a time.

Plate 95. Evergreen candytuft after being cut back.

Plate 96. Bearded iris flowers add brief beauty to this spring scene, only to be quickly followed by unattractive foliage.

Plate 97. Siberian iris (*Iris sibirica*) seedheads are an attractive addition to the garden, although leaving too many can rob the plant of energy.

Plate 98. Wait until new growth has broken from the old stems of lavender (*Lavandula*) before pruning out damaged sections.

Plate 99. Pinched Alaska shasta daisy (*Leucanthemum* ×*superbum* 'Alaska'), in the foreground, compared to those left unpinched, in the background.

Plate 100. *Liatris spicata* 'Kobold' showing the odd branching habit that can occur as a result of pruning.

Plate 101. *Lychnis coronaria* can be short-lived, and seedlings such as these ensure permanence of this perennial in the garden—much to the joy of the author's son, Zachary, who cherishes them for their bright color and soft leaves.

Plate 102. A plant of *Lythrum salicaria* 'Robert' that was sheared to the ground (*front*) compared to unsheared plants in the grouping (*back*).

Plate 103. Regrowth and flowering on *Althaea zebrina* after being cut down to 8 in. following the initial bloom period.

Plate 104. This transplanted patch of beebalm (*Monarda didyma*) was cut back in stages to create a layered effect and a sequence of bloom. The flowering part of this clump, in the back, was left unpruned, the middle part of the clump was pruned on the first of May, and the front part of the clump was pruned on the first of May and again in mid-May.

Plate 105. The front of this beebalm plant, which received the most pruning, flowered about 3 weeks later than the other sections, and the decline of the foliage in the front is also delayed as compared to the back section.

Plate 107. *Paeonia* 'Nice Gal' is beautiful in bloom and doesn't require staking.

Plate 106. *Nepeta sibirica* 'Souvenir d'Andre Chaudron' responds well to pruning before flowering to create fuller, more compact plants. The plant on the left was unpruned, and the plant on the right was cut back by one-half in early June when 2 ft. tall.

Plate 109. *Paeonia* 'Festiva Maxima', photographed at the same time as 'Nice Gal' in the previous photo, exhibits the unsightly foliage decline of many peonies.

Plate 108. The foliage of nice gal peony holds up well through the season compared to many other peonies, such as 'Festiva Maxima' (Plate 109).

Plate 110. Alpha phlox (*Phlox maculata* 'Alpha') in full bloom.

Plate 111. Alpha phlox being deadheaded to a lateral bud to extend the bloom period.

Plate 112. Alpha phlox responds well to pruning for height control and to delay flowering. Shown here is a pruned plant in the foreground with an unpruned plant in the background.

Plate 113. Cutting 4 in. off the tips of *Phlox maculata* 'Rosalind' when in bud can result in this odd flowering effect.

Plate 114. Seedling variability in *Phlox paniculata*.

Plate 115. A shorter, fuller, later flowering flamingo phlox (*Phlox paniculata* 'Flamingo') resulted from cutting plants back by one-half in mid-June.

Plate 116. Balloon flower (*Platycodon grandiflorus*) responds well to cutting back before flowering to reduce height and eliminate the need for staking. These pruned plants matured to 18 in., compared to the normal height of 2 to 3 ft.

Plate 117. The appearance of *Pulmonaria* plants can be greatly improved by removing old flowering stems. The old stems have fallen to the outside of this clump of *Pulmonaria longifolia* 'E. B. Anderson'.

Plate 118. The stems can be grabbed by the handful and pruned off to the ground.

Plate 119. Such deadheading leaves a fresh-looking clump of foliage that contributes to the garden for the rest of the season.

Plate 120. *Rudbeckia nitida* 'Herbstsonne' cut back by one-half in early June produces a shorter, 4¹/₂- to 5-ft.-tall plant such as this, which won't require staking even in a garden exposed to winds.

Plate 121. Cutting down *Salvia* to basal foliage after the initial bloom period results in attractive new growth, as shown here on *Salvia nemorosa* 'East Friesland' (with a seedling of alpine columbine joining it). Compare to foliage on plants not cut down, shown in Plate 122.

Plate 122. The shaggy growth on an east friesland salvia plant that was deadheaded through the season but not cut down.

Plate 123. *Sedum* 'Autumn Joy' being cut down in the spring. Note the light green nubs of new growth at the base of the plant.

Plate 124. Goldenrod (*Solidago*) pruned at the proper time (late May–early June) for height control creates an appealing plant.

Plate 125. Goldenrod pruned later in the season (mid-July) can develop an awkward habit.

Plate 126. Seeding of *Thymus* can be a benefit in the garden or landscape, particularly when it is used among stepping stones.

Plate 127. *Tricyrtis* pruned before flowering creates fuller, more heavily branched plants, as shown here comparing the stem of a pruned plant (*on the left*) with that of an unpruned plant (*right*).

Plate 128. *Veronica austriaca* subsp. *teucrium* 'Amethyst Blue' in full bloom.

Plate 129. Amethyst blue Hungarian speedwell sprawling unattractively after flowering without pruning.

Plate 130. Attractive mounded regrowth will develop on amethyst blue Hungarian speedwell within a few weeks of being sheared back.

Plate 131. *Veronica spicata* 'Blue Charm' pruned before flowering for height control and a slight delay in flowering, pictured in the foreground with an unpruned plant in the background.

Campanula carpatica

Zone: 3–8
Common Name: carpathian harebell
Family: Campanulaceae
Description: blue cup-shaped flowers;
    triangular leaves
Size: 6–12 in. (4–6 in.) high; 12 in. wide
Exposure: full sun or partial shade
Flowering: June–September

PRUNING: Young plants are little charmers
that provide a long bloom period with minimal pruning other than deadheading, which
will reduce seeding. Deadheading, and often
cutting back, is needed in later years to keep
plants attractive. Deadheading is a tedious
task due to the delicate nature of the plants.
Small sharp pruning scissors work well.
Depending on the conditions, plants may
require cutting back by about one-third or
more in midsummer for fresh growth and
possible rebloom. Plants can be cut back in
stages (see Chapter 10 and Figure 10-1). For
example, cut back one-third of the plant by
one-third, allowing the other sections to continue blooming. As the pruned section starts
to fill in, cut back another section of the
plant. This prevents a void in the garden and
keeps a part of the plant flowering most of
the season. If foliage is severely tattered, or if
plants open up in the center, plants will benefit from cutting to basal growth. Basal
growth should remain for the winter. Cut
back any dead foliage in the spring if needed.

OTHER MAINTENANCE: Plants aren't particularly long-lived, succumbing to heat, high
humidity, and dry or wet soils. Prefers a cool
soil, and summer mulch is useful, particularly in southern gardens. Division is required every 2 years and is best done in
the early spring or the late summer.

RELATED PLANTS: *Campanula carpatica*
'Blaue Clips' ('Blue Clips') and 'Weisse Clips'
('White Clips') are more desirable than the
species due to greater vigor.

Campanula poscharskyana, Serbian bellflower, is wonderful as a groundcover in dry
conditions and partial shade. If grown this
way, plants can be deadheaded once with
shears down to basal foliage when all flowering is finished. Foliage will remain semi-
evergreen to evergreen over the winter. Can
spread fairly quickly.

Campanula glomerata

Zone: 3–8
Common Name: clustered bellflower
Family: Campanulaceae
Description: purple or white flowers in clus-
    ters; heart-shaped to oval green leaves
Size: 18–24 in. high; 18 in. wide and
    spreading
Exposure: full sun
Flowering: June–July

PRUNING: Deadhead plants to lateral buds
to prolong bloom. As foliage starts to decline
and when all flowering is completed, plants
can be cut down to fresh basal foliage. Do
not prune for the winter. Clean-up as needed
in the spring.

OTHER MAINTENANCE: Plants prefer
evenly moist, alkaline soil. Can be somewhat
invasive in rich soils, though spread is minimal in poor soils. Performs better in partial
shade in hot climates. Often requires support
to keep upright. Divide in the spring or
autumn every 4–5 years or as needed to control spread.

RELATED PLANTS: *Campanula glomerata*
'Superba' has greater heat tolerance than the
species.

Campanula persicifolia

Zone: 3–7
Common Name: peachleaf bellflower
Family: Campanulaceae
Description: spikes of blue bell-shaped
    flowers; narrow leaves

Size: 2–3 ft. (²⁄₃ ft.) high; 2 ft. wide
Exposure: full sun or partial shade
Flowering: June–July

PRUNING: Most campanulas will flower longer with regular deadheading. When pruning the peachleaf bellflower it is important to not cut off the new buds that form along the same flowering stem as the previous flowers. This pruning can be tedious since each individual dead flower must be removed without damaging the yet-to-open new buds (see Figure 9-3). I like to use small sharp pruning scissors for this task. Deadheading reduces seeding, although some seeding should be permitted to ensure persistence of this rather short-lived perennial in the garden. When all flowering is finished the old flower stems should be cut down to basal foliage. Basal foliage persists for the winter and rarely needs clean-up in the spring. Pinching plants when the shoots are about 6 in. tall may eliminate the need for staking.

OTHER MAINTENANCE: Can naturalize by root spread and seeding, but not a nuisance. Not particularly long-lived, except in porous, sandy soils. Requires moist, well-draining soil for best growth, and afternoon shade in hot climates. Plants usually need staking, particularly in shadier spots. Divide every 3–4 years in the spring.

RELATED PLANTS: *Campanula lactiflora*, milky bellflower, can be deadheaded by cutting back by one-third after all flowering is completed, which often induces sparser rebloom in the autumn and also prevents self-seeding. Old flowering stems and foliage often decline after blooming; if this occurs, cut down to the new basal foliage that has developed. Most cultivars flop. Cutting off 4–5 in. before flowering in early May creates fuller plants. Cutting plants back in late June or early July in an attempt to delay flowering and control sprawling habit proved ineffec-

tive—it did produce compact, 1-ft.-tall upright plants, compared to the flopping 2½-ft.-tall unpruned plants, but they never flowered.

Campanula lactiflora 'Pouffe' is a dwarf, 10- to 18-in.-tall, self-supporting form.

Campanula latifolia, great bellflower, requires deadheading before seeds mature to prevent numerous seedlings. If you don't want to do the tedious task of deadheading each individual flower, wait until the deadheads out number the new flowers and cut the entire stem down to the basal foliage. For height control cut back as for *C. lactiflora*. Great bellflower can spread aggressively.

Campanula rotundifolia 'Olympica'

Zone: 2–7
Common Name: olympic scotch bluebell
Family: Campanulaceae
Description: tiny blue bell-shaped flowers; round leaves often disappear by the time flowering occurs
Size: 6–12 in. high; 12 in. wide
Exposure: full sun to partial shade
Flowering: June–September

PRUNING: Olympic scotch bluebell is long blooming even without deadheading, but deadheading prolongs bloom from spring to late summer on neater plants, and unless you're really quick to get them, seeding is usually ensured anyway, which in my area is essential to keep plants in the garden. It can seed to nuisance levels under ideal growing conditions, but I never have enough of this perennial to make me happy. Seedlings are easily removed if it becomes a problem. Deadheading can be an extremely tedious job due to the delicate nature of the flowering stems and the large number of them. It is easiest to use small sharp pruning scissors. In late summer plants should be cut down to the tiny basal foliage to remove tatty old growth and seedheads. Hedge shears can be used at this stage. Basal foliage remains evergreen over the winter.

OTHER MAINTENANCE: Very short-lived, usually only a couple of years. Good drainage is absolutely essential to survival. Alpine conditions are ideal. If you can keep plants for three or four years, division may be necessary to keep them under control.

Centaurea montana

Zone: 3–8
Common Name: mountain bluet
Family: Asteraceae
Description: fringed blue flowers; green
    leaves
Size: 1–2 ft. high; 1 ft. wide
Exposure: full sun or partial shade
Flowering: May–July

PRUNING: Depending on the conditions (or I think even the disposition of the plant), repeat bloom can be achieved simply by deadheading to lateral buds. Once all flowering is finished cut the old flowering stalks to the ground, leaving the fresh basal foliage. Plants are likely to rebloom in late summer. Older (or moody) plants, or plants growing in rich soil or overly shady conditions, usually become floppy, and weedy, after the first flowering. Cut entire plant back by two-thirds immediately after flowering for potential rebloom and a more compact habit. Deadheading or cutting back should be performed before seeds mature to prevent excessive seeding. If plants are cut back during the season, the low basal foliage can remain for the winter. Plants that were not cut back usually blacken and turn mushy with frost and are best cut down at this point.

OTHER MAINTENANCE: Best performance in poor, well-draining, alkaline soils. Tolerates some drought. Roots can spread rapidly to invasive proportions, particularly in cool northern gardens; not as hearty in the South.

Requires division every 2–3 years in the spring or fall.

Centranthus ruber

Zone: 5–8
Common Name: jupiter's beard
Family: Valerianaceae
Description: fragrant pink or reddish flowers
    in clusters; gray-green leaves
Size: 18–36 in. high; 24 in. wide
Exposure: full sun
Flowering: June–August

PRUNING: Deadhead to lateral buds as flowers are spent to encourage bloom from late spring to early summer and sporadically into August. Flowers longer in cool conditions. Plants are prolific seeders under favorable conditions; deadhead if seeding is not desired. Where plants bloom early and then stop in the heat of summer, or if plants fall after flowering, shearing by one-third to one-half after the first bloom often results in a second crop in August. This perennial is often short-lived, and it may be that plants deplete their energy reserves with so much flower production and then are unable to form buds for the next season's shoots. To prevent this from occurring, the whole plant can be cut back to 6–8 in. in late August or early September to stimulate vegetative growth, which may increase the plant's overwintering survival. Do not cut again for the winter; clean-up in the spring.

OTHER MAINTENANCE: Prefers infertile, well-draining, neutral to alkaline soil. Divide in the spring or fall every 1–3 years.

Cephalaria gigantea

Zone: 3–8
Common Name: tatarian cephalaria
Family: Dipsacaceae
Description: yellow pincushion flowers on
    tall wiry stems; compound leaves

Size: 5–7 ft. (3 ft.) high; 3–6 ft. wide
Exposure: full sun
Flowering: June–August

PRUNING: Flowering stems are branched, so deadhead to lateral new flowers. After all flowering is finished, cut flowering stems down to the ground. Deadleafing may also be necessary as plants are usually tatty by late summer or early autumn, particularly with dry conditions. If damage is major, cut plants down to about 1 ft. above the ground. They are not especially attractive at this stage, so it would be a good idea to include late-blooming plants as companions to help hide pruned plants. Plants don't appear to respond to cutting back or pinching before flowering to reduce height or delay bloom. Plants should be cut down for the winter. Leaves of cephalaria have tiny bristly hairs that can irritate the skin when pruning.

OTHER MAINTENANCE: Moisture is necessary to maintain health of the leaves. Sometimes requires staking. Divide every 2–3 years in the spring. Give plenty of space in the garden.

Cerastium tomentosum

Zone: 3–7
Common Name: snow-in-summer
Family: Caryophyllaceae
Description: small white flowers; mat-forming silver leaves
Size: 4–8 in. high; 18 in. wide
Exposure: full sun
Flowering: June

PRUNING: Plants should be sheared back by one-third to one-half and shaped after flowering to keep in good form and prevent open centers void of leaves. Hedge shears are the best tool for the task. The plant's typical "softness" will quickly return after shearing. Prune back whenever the plant gets out of bounds. Don't do any heavy shearing during

hot, dry conditions. Do not prune for the winter. Prune out any damaged sections in the spring as needed.

OTHER MAINTENANCE: Well-draining soil is essential for survival. Prefers infertile conditions. Often melts out in hot, humid weather. Spreads rapidly by underground roots. May require frequent division in spring or fall to keep in bounds; keep plenty of soil around the roots to ensure success. Often short-lived due to its tendency toward rotting.

RELATED PLANTS: *Cerastium tomentosum* 'Yo Yo' and 'Silver Carpet' are more compact than the species.

Cerastium tomentosum var. *columnae* is also more compact.

Ceratostigma plumbaginoides

Zone: 5–9
Common Name: plumbago
Family: Plumbaginaceae
Description: small blue flowers; small green leaves
Size: 8–12 in. high; 12–18 in. wide
Exposure: full sun to partial shade
Flowering: August–September

PRUNING: The only pruning that this plant requires is cutting dead stems to the ground once new growth is visible in the spring. Plants are late to emerge, sometimes not until early June in central Ohio, so leaving the bare stems and seedheads over the winter and into spring marks their spot in the garden and avoids chance of disturbance.

OTHER MAINTENANCE: Plants perform best with morning sun and afternoon shade. Well-draining soil is essential; tolerant of short periods of drought. Rhizomes can be invasive, making the plant suitable as a groundcover. In a mixed planting it will overtake low-growing perennials in its path, including *Coreopsis verticillata* 'Moonbeam'. Doesn't compete with tree roots. Usually considered a zone 6 plant, but it survives well in zone 5 with a light mulch or in a semi-protected area. Divide in spring as needed to keep in bounds.

Chelone lyonii

Zone: 3–8
Common Name: pink turtlehead
Family: Scrophulariaceae
Description: pink turtle-shaped flowers; thick green leaves
Size: 3 ft. high; 2 ft. wide
Exposure: full sun or partial shade
Flowering: August–September

PRUNING: Plants can be deadheaded if desired, but the seedheads are attractive and extend the interest of the plant so are best left on. Plants may flop, particularly if given too much shade. Plant height can be reduced by pinching in the early spring when plants are about 6 in. tall. For me, pinching in mid-June resulted in plants that never flowered. Do not cut back for the winter. Prune in early spring.

OTHER MAINTENANCE: Plants are moisture loving and will form nice stands if sufficient moisture is available. Plants grown under drier conditions will be shorter and less vigorous. Prefers high-organic soil and tolerates light shade. Divide every 4 years, if needed, in the spring or after flowering in autumn.

Chrysogonum virginianum

Zone: 5–9
Common Name: golden-star
Family: Asteraceae
Description: golden-yellow daisy-like flowerheads on prostrate stems
Size: 6–8 in. high; 12 in. wide
Exposure: partial to full shade
Flowering: May–June

PRUNING: Periodic cutting back of old flowering stems down to basal foliage will tidy up the plant and prolong the bloom, but it doesn't seem to be critical since sporadic flowering usually occurs into summer, before any major heat sets in, even without pruning. Flowering lasts longer in regions with cooler summers. Sporadic rebloom may occur again as the cool weather of autumn returns. Deadheading prevents seeding, but seedlings are easily removed and, especially in a woodland setting, may be welcome. Deadleafing is needed in the summer if plants dry out. Plants that get infected with mildew should be cut back to the base to prevent further infection. Remove and destroy pruned parts. Plants unaffected with mildew do not need pruning for the winter; clean-up in the spring if needed.

OTHER MAINTENANCE: Low-maintenance woodland or shade garden plant. Prefers moist, well-draining soil, but I have had good luck with golden-star in fairly dry shade locations, although rebloom is reduced. Plants may survive overwintering in zone 4 if given a winter mulch or consistent snow cover. Easily divided in late spring.

RELATED PLANTS: Cultivars of golden-star flower longer than the species. *Chrysogonum virginianum* 'Alan Bush' and 'Mark Viette' are long-blooming cultivars of choice.

Chrysopsis villosa (Heterotheca villosa)

Zone: 5–9
Common Name: hairy goldaster
Family: Asteraceae
Description: yellow daisy-like flowerheads; gray-green hairy leaves
Size: 3–5 ft. high; 4 ft. wide
Exposure: full sun
Flowering: August–September

PRUNING: Plants are full and nicely formed

if cut back by one-half in late spring to early summer (early to mid-June in Ohio) and can be nicely layered by cutting the outer stems slightly lower than the inside stems. If pruned again with the removal of about 6 in. off the tips in early August, when in tight bud, plants respond well by sending out 3 or 4 lateral flowering stems that start blooming about one week later than those of unpruned plants and thus bloom one week longer into the season. This effect can be achieved on individual plants by shearing a section or only the outside of the plant down by 6 in. If several plants are grown in a group, or in different areas of the garden, flowering can be delayed on some to extend the bloom season of hairy goldaster. Some gardeners experience a blackening of the plants with the coming of a frost, in which case the plants should be cut down at that point. I have had a different experience, however. I don't even deadhead the plants because I find the old flowers, which form pretty daisy-like brown dried seedheads, to be a nice feature of the plant, and they hold until the spring with no unattractive blackening of the plants. I cut plants down in the spring.

OTHER MAINTENANCE: Very drought tolerant. Provide good drainage, particularly in the winter. Give plants plenty of space to accommodate the wide habit. Divide every 4–5 years in the spring if needed.

RELATED PLANTS: *Chrysopsis villosa* 'Golden Sunshine' is a choice long-lived cultivar. It is clump forming.

Cimicifuga racemosa

Zone: 3–8
Common Name: bugbane
Family: Ranunculaceae
Description: white bottlebrush-shaped ill-scented flowers; ferny leaves
Size: 4–6 ft. (3 ft.) high; 2–4 ft. wide
Exposure: partial shade
Flowering: July

PRUNING: Allow seedheads to remain on bugbane for winter interest. Cut back in early spring. If plants receive too much sun or are allowed to dry out, scorching of the leaves may occur and deadleafing will be necessary to improve appearance.

OTHER MAINTENANCE: This woodland-edge native does best in fertile, moist, high-organic, acidic soil—with the emphasis on moist. Avoid hot afternoon sun. Individual flower spikes may need support. Division is difficult due to the thonglike roots, but it is rarely needed as clumps can remain undisturbed forever. If desired, divide carefully in the fall. Plants are slow growing.

RELATED PLANTS: *Cimicifuga simplex*, kamchatka bugbane, is autumn flowering and is sensitive to early frosts. More tolerant of basic soils.

Cimicifuga simplex 'White Pearl' (3 ft.) doesn't require staking.

Clematis heracleifolia var. *davidiana*

Zone: 3–9
Common Name: blue tube clematis
Family: Ranunculaceae
Description: blue flowers; coarse green leaves
Size: 3 ft. high; 4 ft. wide
Exposure: full sun to partial shade
Flowering: August–September

PRUNING: The variety *davidiana* is more herbaceous in nature than the species form of *Clematis heracleifolia*. Cut to the ground in early spring. Pinching plants when they are 12–15 in. tall can help control flopping. Deadleafing is needed to remove scorched leaves if plants dry out in the summer. Prune back as needed to keep blue tube clematis in its own space. Deadheads turn into cottony seedheads that are best allowed to remain.

OTHER MAINTENANCE: Requires support, and pea staking is the recommended method. Flourishes in moist, alkaline to slightly acidic soils, with high organic matter. Mulch to provide cool soil.

RELATED PLANTS: *Clematis heracleifolia*, tube clematis, is more woody in nature. Prune back hard in early spring to only a couple of nodes for more compact growth.

Clematis recta

Zone: 3–7
Common Name: ground clematis
Family: Ranunculaceae
Description: white fringed fragrant flowers; compound blue-green leaves
Size: 3–4 ft. high; 3 ft. wide
Exposure: full sun to partial shade
Flowering: May–June

PRUNING: Plants can be cut down after flowering for lush new growth and rebloom and as a means of minimizing black blister beetle damage. Shearing plants to the ground in early to mid-July or when the first beetles are sighted will avoid most of the feeding of the beetles. A few beetles may still be around as the new growth starts, and these can be knocked off with a booted foot or gloved hand and then stepped on; any damage by beetles at this point won't be significant. Be certain to wear gloves when pruning or staking, as a stray beetle may be hiding under the foliage and can cause blistering on your hands (see Chapter 4 for more details). Lush new growth will return in about a month after shearing, and plants will grow to nearly full size again and produce sporadic rebloom. Pea staking is required at this point, or plants can be left to crawl along the ground. Plants cut back by one-

third in early July received a good deal of beetle damage, but they put on new terminal growth after the beetles were gone. Still, plants didn't rebloom, had bare stems at their bases, and were never as attractive as plants sheared to the ground. Plants get mushy after a hard frost, and it may be desirable to cut them back at this time.

OTHER MAINTENANCE: Plants can be left to crawl, although pea staking lifts flowers up to a more visible height and restricts the space occupied by ground clematis in the garden. Stake in late April or early May before flowering starts. Fairly tolerant of dry conditions, but prefers moist, high-organic soil.

RELATED PLANTS: *Clematis recta* 'Purpurea' has purple stems and leaves that fade as they age, so cutting plants back after flowering, as described above, can send forth a new flush of purple foliage in August.

Coreopsis grandiflora

Zone: 4–9
Common Name: tickseed
Family: Asteraceae
Description: golden-yellow flowerheads; narrow green leaves on bushy plants
Size: 2–3 ft. ($^2/_3$–1 ft.) high; 1 ft. wide
Exposure: full sun
Flowering: June–August

PRUNING: Tickseed needs daily deadheading. Cut the entire flowering stalk to new lateral flower buds, if present, or to the basal foliage if no side flowering is evident. Deadheading keeps plants flowering and looking decent, prevents seeding, and reduces potential disease sites. Plants may need to be cut back in midsummer if they sprawl. *Coreopsis grandiflora* and its cultivars can flower themselves to exhaustion and thus will have trouble forming buds for the following year's growth. Cutting all the flowering stems down to the basal foliage at the end of August or in early September will stimulate new vegetative growth and may increase the plant's overwintering survival rate. Do not prune for the winter. Cut back as needed in the early spring before new growth begins.

OTHER MAINTENANCE: Requires well-draining soil for overwintering survival. Drought tolerant. Not long-lived; tends to be good for 2 or 3 seasons, and then needs division in the spring. Plants may flop; select lower growing cultivars.

RELATED PLANTS: *Coreopsis grandiflora* 'Early Sunrise' is the longest flowering cultivar and is more compact (to 18 in.). Prune as described above for the species.

Coreopsis grandiflora 'Goldfink' is more compact (9 in. high) and may need annual division to perform its best.

Coreopsis lanceolata, lanceleaf coreopsis, is similar to *C. grandiflora* and actually may be synonymous in the trade (Plate 73). Prune as above.

Coreopsis verticillata

Zone: 3–9
Common Name: threadleaf coreopsis
Family: Asteraceae
Description: yellow flowerheads; feathery green leaves
Size: 2–3 ft. high; 2 ft. wide
Exposure: full sun
Flowering: June–October

PRUNING: First-year plants may flower all summer long even without deadheading, but older plants require deadheading for best performance. They flower in early and midsummer and then sporadically, or they may rest totally in August and then rebloom in September and October. For a stronger and more attractive rebloom in autumn, plants can be sheared in August to remove deadheads, along with the few flowers that may be blooming at the time, using hedge shears or even a string trimmer for large plantings. Clean-up pruned branches by hand or with a small shrub rake. Deadheading also prevents reseeding. Plants with deadheads left on from the second bloom phase contribute to winter interest. Unless you want to avoid seeding, do not prune again until early spring. If seeding is a concern, cut down in autumn—string trimmers can be used at this time as well.

OTHER MAINTENANCE: Can spread invasively by underground stems, particularly in moist, sandy soils. Divide as needed every 2–3 years in spring or autumn. Long-lived. Requires well-draining soil, and is drought tolerant. Overly fertile soil leads to sprawling habit. Cultivars perform better than the species in areas warmer than zone 6 or 7.

RELATED PLANTS: Cultivars of *Coreopsis verticillata* should be pruned as described above for the species, although I have not witnessed reseeding of cultivars so I leave them for winter interest. It should be noted that first-year plantings usually don't need any deadheading to be attractive throughout the entire season.

Coreopsis verticillata 'Golden Showers' most likely needs staking.

Coreopsis verticillata 'Moonbeam' is an outstanding cultivar, but it lacks a bit in winter hardiness. Winter losses occur with unmulched plants in zone 5. Seems to prefer a bit more moisture than the species. Benefits from afternoon shade in warmer climates. Divide every 2–3 years to keep vigorous. I have never had self-seeding with this cultivar. Leave for winter interest.

Coreopsis verticillata 'Rosea' spreads very quickly to take over large areas, so it is not recommended for use in a mixed perennial border but rather on its own as a groundcover.

Coreopsis verticillata 'Zagreb' grows to 12 in. and requires no staking. Appears more cold hardy than 'Moonbeam'. Very drought tolerant.

Corydalis lutea

Zone: 5–7
Common Name: yellow corydalis
Family: Fumariaceae
Description: yellow tubular flowers; fernlike green leaves
Size: 12–15 in. high; 15–18 in. wide
Exposure: partial shade
Flowering: May–September

PRUNING: Deadheading seems to prolong bloom and reduces prolific seeding. Do be certain, though, to allow some seeding, or the species may be lost from the garden. Plants scorch or yellow if given too much sun or if allowed to dry out or, on the other hand, if it stays too wet. In any of these conditions, cut plants back to fresh basal foliage. Basal foliage does not need to be pruned for the winter and may remain semi-evergreen. If plants are not cut down to basal growth in the summer, prune down after several killing frosts for the winter if seeding is not desired.

OTHER MAINTENANCE: Even though no pests or diseases afflict this plant, yellow corydalis receives mixed reviews. Sometimes it is almost to weed status in the garden, reseeding with great ambition. I unfortunately have not had this experience. On the contrary, *Corydalis lutea* has been very short-lived in my own gardens and in clients' gardens, seeding only sparingly if at all. Plants are difficult to establish, but even if you make it past this phase, losses occur later or over the winter. Wet soils could be the main culprit. It prefers well-draining, even gravelly soils and slightly alkaline conditions. Likes to grow among rocks. Divide in the spring or autumn.

Crocosmia 'Lucifer'

Zone: 5–9
Common Name: lucifer crocosmia
Family: Iridaceae
Description: sword-shaped foliage; orange-red bloom
Size: 18–36 in. high; 12 in. wide
Exposure: full sun
Flowering: July–August

PRUNING: Deadleafing may be necessary in July or August in certain years due to spider mite damage. This may mean removing the dead leaves and leaving only the flowering stalk while still in bloom. The plant is self-cleaning and flowers simply drop off. I find the horizontal shape of the old bloom cluster and seed capsules to be attractive when first developing and so I leave these to extend interest. Then they often need to be cut down, along with any deteriorating foliage, by late summer.

OTHER MAINTENANCE: Hose off spider mites when they are first visible. Divide every 2–3 years in the autumn to keep vigorous, or separate offsets from the mother plant in the spring as growth starts. Prefers moist, well-draining, rich organic soil. Can be short-lived in zone 5; planting in a protected spot and mulching can improve overwintering success.

Delphinium ×*belladonna* 'Bellamosum'

Zone: 3–7
Common Name: bellamosa delphinium
Family: Ranunculaceae
Description: dark blue flowers on spikes; palmately divided leaves
Size: 3–4 ft. high; 18–24 ft. wide
Exposure: full sun to partial shade
Flowering: June–July

PRUNING: Deadhead to lateral flower buds,

if present; if lateral buds are not present, cut old flowering spike off at a lateral leaf. After all secondary flowering is completed and the old stems start to decline, cut back to newly developed basal foliage. Keep plants watered and well fed if new foliage is pale. Plants may send up sporadic, usually smaller and shorter, blooms later in the season. If disease is a problem, as is commonly the case in southern regions, plants can be thinned by one-third or so when about 6 in. tall, leaving at least 3–5 stems per mature clump. *Delphinium ×belladonna* 'Bellamosum' generally is not as prone to disease problems as is *D. elatum*, and thinning usually is not necessary in more northern areas. Disbudding or removing side flower spikes to encourage a larger terminal flower is not as applicable to this species as it is to *D. elatum* since a major appeal of bellamosa delphinium is its daintier flowers. Pinching ruins the plant's natural charm by removing the main terminal flowering spike, although smaller lateral flowers will still develop. Cutting plants back by one-half in early June, while in tight bud, in an attempt to delay flowering results in total removal of flowers and no development of new lateral buds for later bloom. Plants can be left over the winter and cut back in early spring, although removal of any staked flowering stalks before the winter is more aesthetically pleasing.

OTHER MAINTENANCE: This cultivar is the delphinium of choice in the Midwest because of its greater vigor, durability, and longer life as compared to *D. elatum*. It also produces more flowers, although in smaller spikes, and for a longer period. Problems with disease and reduced vigor are experienced more frequently in the summer heat of southern regions. Best in rich, high-organic, moist, well-draining soils. Prefers alkaline conditions. Staking usually needed. Divide carefully in the spring every 4–5 years, or possibly sooner in southern gardens if vigor declines.

RELATED PLANTS: *Delphinium grandiflorum* 'Blue Butterflies' grows 12–18 in. tall, with no staking needed. Dwarf forms may not respond well to pruning back after flowering. Do not cut back unless basal growth is evident and strong.

Delphinium elatum

Zone: 3–7
Common Name: delphinium
Family: Ranunculaceae
Description: blue, purple, or white flower spikes; palmately cut leaves
Size: 4–6 ft. high; 1–2 ft. wide
Exposure: full sun to partial shade
Flowering: June–July

PRUNING: Deadhead to lateral flower buds, if present; if not, cut off old flowering spike at a lateral leaf. After all secondary flowering is completed and the old stems start to decline, cut back to newly developed basal foliage. Plants will benefit from a top-dressing of compost and fertilizing with a quick-release soluble fertilizer at this time. Keep moist for sporadic smaller and shorter rebloom later in the season. When the young shoots are 6 in. tall, thin by approximately one-third, leaving at least 3–5 healthy stems per mature clump, to avoid over-crowding that increases susceptibility to disease. Removing lateral flowering spikes may increase the size of the terminal flower. Pinching to remove the large terminal spike spoils the main effect of the plant, although smaller side spikes will still bloom. Remove any flowering stalks for the winter, but leave basal foliage and cut back in the spring.

OTHER MAINTENANCE: The true "maintenance magnet." Not a beginner's plant, although it seems to be one of the first perennials people are drawn to, perhaps because of the glorious pictures that appear in so many British references. It does prosper better in England, due in part to the cool summers. This delphinium is prone to a host of diseases, which I won't even go into, and is a favorite food of slugs. Subject to crown rot in poorly drained soil. Short-lived. Dividing annually carefully in the spring may prolong life. Do not plant too deep. Requires staking. Heavy feeder so may need additional fertilizer in spring or summer. May be better treated as an annual.

RELATED PLANTS: Blackmore and Langdon Strains of delphinium tend to be more perennial if divided regularly.

Connecticut Yankee Series, including 'Blue Fountains', performs well in heat. Grows to 2 ft. tall. Has given the best performance of the cultivars in the Midwest.

Mid-Century Hybrids, such as 'Ivory Towers', 'Moody Blues', 'Rosy Future', and 'Ultra Violets', have stronger stems and are more resistant to powdery mildew.

Dendranthema ×*morifolium* (*Chrysanthemum* ×*morifolium*)

Zone: 5–9
Common Name: mum
Family: Asteraceae
Description: daisy-like flowerheads; lobed
  leaves
Size: 1–3 ft. high; 1–3 ft. wide
Exposure: full sun
Flowering: August–October

PRUNING: Mums and pruning go hand in hand. Cutting back or pinching before flowering will create more compact plants, often with more numerous though possibly smaller flowers. Pinching or cutting back may also delay flowering if done late in the summer. Naturally low-growing forms don't need pruning for height control, but it may be desirable to delay bloom, such as with early blooming cultivars.

As discussed in Chapter 9, pinching is often associated with mums, and vice versa.

The frequency and timing of pinching, whether employed for height control or to delay bloom, can be determined by experimenting according to your individual needs and expectations. Three or four pinchings is sufficient for controlling height on most mums, though lower growing types generally need only two pinchings. For mums that have overwintered, pinching can be initiated when the plants are about 6 in. tall (May) and then again every 2–3 weeks. New garden mums planted in the spring should be first pinched a few weeks after planting. The cut-off date for pinching depends on the climate and the type of mum, be it early or late season. Mums need several weeks to set buds after the final pinching. For early season mums (most garden-center varieties are early) and in gardens north of the Mason-Dixon line (colder than about zone 6), the usual recommendation is for pinching until about mid-July. For northern gardens, stopping in mid-July will assure bloom before heavy frost. In the Midwest, though, for even later bloom or for late-flowering cultivars, pinching into late July may mean flowers in October rather than September. In the South pinching can go as late as mid-August, particularly for late-blooming cultivars. Pinching or cutting back plants too late may reduce the floral display. (Results of cutting back mums in August in the Midwest are noted below.) Although pinching directly above lateral leaves makes for a neat initial appearance, removing 1 in. of stem with hedge shears simulates a pinch and accomplishes it much more efficiently. The plants fill in quickly, hiding any cuts.

One alternative to pinching, which I prefer, is to simply shear the plants once by one-half or two-thirds in early to mid-June. In the South a second shearing may be necessary for best results. Cutting plants back in this way may delay flowering. If staggered bloom on a large planting of mums is desired, an additional 4–6 in. can be removed from some plants later in the season (mid- to late July or to mid-August depending on your climate, as discussed above) to further delay part of the planting.

Mums usually are disbudded if grown for shows to produce a larger terminal flower. Disbud mums by removing all buds along the stem, except for the top largest bud. Remove buds when plants are in tight bud with no color showing.

How to prune mums for winter may be as important a question as when to pinch or cut back for height control. As discussed in Chapter 12, research in Germany, and confirmed in trials at Iowa State University, has shown that leaving the plants up for the winter greatly improves their overwintering survival rate. Do not cut down the plants until spring when all threat of cold weather has passed. Hedge shears, either hand held or electric, make for greater speed.

OTHER MAINTENANCE: Unless cold-hardy forms such as those listed below are selected, most mums are best treated as annuals. Ed Higgins, from the mum-producing firm of Yoder Brothers, provided some further tips for successful overwintering: avoid planting mums in areas subject to cold, drying winds; mums are heavy feeders but fertilizing should be stopped, especially in the North, by the end of July to discourage new growth late in the season; to promote roots that are well established by winter, keep the soil moist but not soggy through the autumn; avoid wet overwintering conditions; in northern areas, provide loose winter mulch after the ground freezes. Divide in the spring every year or two to maintain vigor.

RELATED PLANTS: The following *Dendranthema* cultivars have been reliably hardy in central Ohio, showing great vigor and requiring no additional feeding beyond good organic soil. These forms need no division for 4 or more years. (Plate 74)

Dendranthema 'Mei Kyo', 2 ft. tall, offers deep rose or burgundy small double flowers in late October. Pinching is not required as plants are naturally full and dense to the base. In fact, pinching or cutting back 'Mei Kyo' may delay the flowers too much in the North, since this is a late-blooming cultivar anyway. For trial purposes, I sheared plants by one-half in mid-June, and they started flowering in early November, rather than late October. They grew 15–18 in. tall, rather than 2 ft., and the floral display was a bit weaker than that on unpruned plants. Plants sheared by 4–6 in. on 15 August (these were not previously pruned) also flowered in early November, but the floral display was greatly reduced. These late-pruned plants experienced damage to the foliage tips from an early October frost, but the flowers were not harmed. A single plant can spread quickly, covering a 5 ft. × 5 ft. area in about 4 years. Division is seldom needed, but plants can be thinned by pulling out bunches of spent flowering stems, root and all, in the early spring.

Dendranthema 'Venus' has single soft pink flowers. Plants can be cut back by one-half to two-thirds in early to mid-June for 3-ft. compact growth and mid-October flowering. As a test to see if August pruning would be too late for flower formation in the Midwest I sheared plants again by about 4–6 in. on 5 August or 15 August. The plants flowered about one week later and at about 2 ft. high. Their habit was more desirable, their flowers delayed, and the floral display was only slightly reduced.

Dendranthema 'Viette's Apricot Glow' has single apricot flowers in mid-October. It is a compact 18- to 24-in. form that doesn't need any pruning to look spectacular.

Dendranthema zawadskii var. *latilobum* 'Clara Curtis' has pink flowers in mid- to late summer. May require pinching or cutting back to control height, particularly if the soil is rich. Pruning for height control is usually not required in clay soils. If later flowering is desired, plants can be sheared by 4–6 in. after the buds form to delay flowering by 1 or 2 months, depending on the weather conditions for the year. Sporadic bloom may occur in the autumn if plants are allowed to flower in the summer and are deadheaded or cut back to basal growth. Very floriferous; may actually bloom itself to death. Divide every 2–3 years to maintain vigor and control spread. Very cold hardy.

Dianthus ×allwoodii

Zone: 5–8
Common Name: allwood pink
Family: Caryophyllaceae
Description: pink or white fragrant flowers; gray-green leaves
Size: 8–18 in. high; 12 in. wide
Exposure: full sun
Flowering: June–July

PRUNING: Deadheading plants to lateral buds will keep them flowering for approximately 6–8 weeks, sometimes longer—this is the main pruning that is needed. The habit of the species and most of its cultivars is tufted, and I find that the allwood pinks do not respond to shearing after flowering like the mat- or cushion-forming *Dianthus* do. Such pruning results in weaker, thinner plants for this species. Plants have a tendency to get woody with age. They may be killed if cut back heavily into old wood, particularly if no new buds are breaking. Do not cut evergreen foliage back for the winter. Plants often need some foliage cleaned up in the spring from winter damage.

OTHER MAINTENANCE: Must have well-draining soil, and prefers alkaline conditions. Usually short-lived, particularly in areas with high humidity and clay soils. I like to plant with large amounts of grit and mulch with grit around the base of the plants. Keep heavy mulch away from the crowns. Give the plants space so as to increase air circulation.

RELATED PLANTS: *Dianthus plumarius*, a parent of *D.* ×*allwoodii*, is longer lived and offers many cultivars from which to choose. These plants are more cushion forming and will benefit from a shearing after flowering to keep them from opening in the center. Shear back by one-half or remove the old flower stems and at least one-third of the foliage. *Dianthus plumarius* may also benefit from a trim around the edges to reduce the size of the clump and to eliminate scraggly outer growth. Lift the foliage and trim off at the base of the bare outer stems underneath. Do not prune for the winter, but cut back if needed in the early spring.

Dianthus barbatus

Zone: 3–9
Common Name: sweet william
Family: Caryophyllaceae
Description: dense clusters of flowers atop green leaves
Size: 10–18 in. high; 12 in. wide
Exposure: full sun; tolerates partial shade
Flowering: May–June

PRUNING: Cut back by one-third to one-half immediately after flowering and before seed sets to get this biennial to act perennial. Another route is to let it go to seed and then enjoy the progeny. Sweet william self-sows so easily that it seems to be a perpetual in the garden. May contract leaf spot under conditions of high humidity, in which case deadleaf and destroy affected leaves. Do not prune for the winter, although plants usually need clean-up in the spring as some foliage gets damaged with severe weather.

OTHER MAINTENANCE: Plants require frequent division (every 2–3 years) to ensure a long life. Prefers alkaline soil and cool summers.

Dianthus deltoides

Zone: 4–9
Common Name: maiden pink
Family: Caryophyllaceae
Description: red, pink, or white flowers; mat-
    forming foliage
Size: 6–10 in. high; 24 in. wide
Exposure: full sun
Flowering: May–June

PRUNING: Cut back by one-half after flowering to keep plants from opening up in the
center. If done before seed set, cutting back
also will prevent reseeding. You can grab a
handful of stems and cut with pruners or
even old grass shears (Plate 76), or simply use
hedge shears for pruning. Pruned branches
are easily cleaned up with a shrub rake (see
Plate 78). You may get a sporadic flower or
two after shearing, although nothing of sig-
nificance. Maiden pinks can seed to a nuisance level and take over nonaggressive perennials. This can be used to an advantage if
planted between lightly traveled stepping
stones, in sun or partial shade, where the
seeding can create a moss-like effect. The
plants love the sandy and well-draining conditions that non-mortared stone walks provide. Also, plants may be short-lived, so some
seeding can be desirable to ensure constancy
in the garden. This species has nice evergreen
foliage that adds to the winter garden, so do
not cut back in the autumn (see Plate 63).

OTHER MAINTENANCE: Prefers well-draining, alkaline soil. Tolerates drought. Will
spread rapidly under ideal conditions, but is
often short-lived, rotting in high-moisture situations. Divide every 2–3 years in the spring.

Dianthus gratianopolitanus 'Bath's Pink'

Zone: 3–9
Common Name: bath's pink cheddar pink
Family: Caryophyllaceae
Description: pink flowers; blue-green leaves
Size: 12–15 in. (6 in.) high; 12–15 in. wide
Exposure: full sun
Flowering: June–July

PRUNING: Cut or shear off old flowering
stems and about one-third of the foliage after
flowering to enjoy the beautiful and reliable
blue-green foliage for the rest of the year.
Although deadheading each old flowering
stalk before seed sets will prolong bloom, it
is a tedious job, particularly on large plantings. I prefer to take what flowers I can get,
without the extra deadheading, and just
enjoy the foliage after one quick shearing.
Shearing plants with hedge shears and shaping by cleaning up any shaggy edges creates
especially nice results; plantings are easily
cleaned up of pruned branches with a shrub
rake (Plates 77–78). Plants fill in within a
week, forming a dense groundcover, and they
look great the rest of the season, including
into the winter. May require minimal clean-
up in the spring.

OTHER MAINTENANCE: Probably the best
low-maintenance pink. Good beginner plant.
Prefers a well-draining soil, but much more
tolerant of heavy soil as well as of heat and
humidity than other pinks and is much
longer lived. Doesn't require the frequent
division to keep plants vigorous.

RELATED PLANTS: *Dianthus carthusiano-
rum*, cluster-head dianthus, is 2 ft. tall with
deep pink flowers. Allow to seed, but not to
nuisance level, to ensure longevity in garden.
Cut back, after some seeding is allowed, to
grassy basal growth. May need some clean-
up in the spring.

   Dianthus gratianopolitanus 'Tiny Rubies', a
sweet low-growing pink with tiny flowers, is
one of my husband's favorite perennials—
goes to show that "real men like pinks." To
deadhead these numerous tiny stems of flowers I grab a handful at a time and cut. The
foliage usually is so low and ground hugging
that it is not cut during this procedure, just
the old flower stems. Again, flowering may

be prolonged with jumping on deadheading before seed has a chance to set.

Dicentra formosa 'Luxuriant'

Zone: 3–9
Common Name: fringed bleeding heart
Family: Fumariaceae
Description: cherry-red heart-shaped flowers; gray-green feathery leaves
Size: 15–18 in. high; 18 in. wide
Exposure: partial to full shade
Flowering: April–September

PRUNING: After all flowers fade on flower scape, deadhead down to basal foliage—this can prolong bloom into the autumn. Dead-leaf any browning or fading foliage to make room for new growth from the crown of the plant. Does not die-back in the summer like *Dicentra spectabilis*. Plants often flower late into the autumn; wait for several killing frosts before cutting down for the winter.

OTHER MAINTENANCE: Mixed performance of this plant puts it into the high-maintenance class as far as I'm concerned. Can be short-lived, at times never even establishing in the first year. At other times it does beautifully, with no apparent reason for the difference, although it is probably related to soil drainage. Not predictable. Requires rich, high-organic but well-draining soil, particularly over the winter. Will take some sun if provided sufficient moisture. Constant summer moisture will ensure a long bloom period. The overwintering buds of *Dicentra* are high on the crown, and if planted too deeply they can rot, further contributing to losses. Divide brittle roots carefully, only if needed, in the spring.

RELATED PLANTS: Cultivars may be *Dicentra eximia* or *D. formosa*, or hybrids of the two. Pruning requirements are the same for both species and for cultivars of either.

Dicentra formosa 'Alba', a white form, is often less vigorous than the pink forms.

Dicentra formosa 'Zestful' seems a bit more reliable than 'Luxuriant', but it doesn't flower as long.

Dicentra spectabilis, common bleeding heart, is an old-fashioned beauty that dies down after flowering. Foliage is more persistent if provided with consistent moisture and cool conditions, possibly holding into late summer in northern gardens. But normally die-back occurs in late spring or early summer, particularly if plants are allowed to dry out and if summer heat persists. Cut to the ground when foliage looks shabby. May self-sow readily, depending on the climate. Divide in late summer or early autumn when the foliage has died down.

Dictamnus albus

Zone: 3–9
Common Name: gas plant
Family: Rutaceae
Description: pink or white flower spikes; compound leaves
Size: 2–4 ft. high; 3 ft. wide
Exposure: full sun
Flowering: May–June

PRUNING: Flowers are self-cleaning. It is best to leave the seedheads, which form interesting star-shapes, to add interest in the garden through the summer and often into winter. Cut plants down in the spring. If any pruning is done when the plants are not dormant, care should be taken because the flowers and foliage can cause a dermatital reaction (skin irritation) in some individuals.

OTHER MAINTENANCE: Long-lived, tough plant that requires little care. Plant in fertile, humus-rich, preferably alkaline soil that does not get soggy, in sun or light shade. Plants take some time (2–3 years) to become established. Plants are very slow growing. Usually no staking is required. Division generally is not needed or recommended, as success rate is low.

Digitalis grandiflora

Zone: 3–8
Common Name: yellow foxglove
Family: Scrophulariaceae
Description: light yellow flower spikes; green
    leaves
Size: 2–3 ft. high; 1¼–1½ ft. wide
Exposure: full sun, partial shade, or heavy
    shade
Flowering: June–July

PRUNING: Benefits from two types of pruning to look its best. First deadhead to lateral buds. Then, as new basal foliage starts to develop and when all secondary flowering is finished, plants should be cut back to the basal foliage. Plants sometimes will rebloom, though usually the blooms are smaller and fewer than those of the initial flowering. Plants may seed under favorable conditions. Basal foliage looks good into the winter; cut back any dead leaves in early spring if needed. Pinching plants ruins the natural habit by removing the large terminal flower. Smaller lateral flowering stems will still develop on pruned plants.

OTHER MAINTENANCE: Easy-to-grow perennial foxglove. Long-lived. Does not require division for 5 or more years. Division can be done in the spring or autumn and can be accomplished simply by separating new plantlets from the mother crown.

RELATED PLANTS: *Digitalis grandiflora* 'Temple Bells' is shorter and has a decent rebloom with deadheading.

Digitalis lutea, straw foxglove, doesn't seem to rebloom as reliably after deadheading as *D. grandiflora*, although it looks better if old foliage is cut down to new basal growth in late summer when it starts to decline. Holds up through winter. Prune in spring if needed.

Digitalis 'Mertonensis' (*D.* ×*mertonensis*), strawberry foxglove, seeds itself freely; watch for seedlings in late summer. Not as long-lived as *D. grandiflora*. Divide every couple

of years to maintain vigor. This is a hybrid of *D. purpurea* and *D. grandiflora*.

Digitalis purpurea

Zone: 4–9
Common Name: common foxglove
Family: Scrophulariaceae
Description: pink, white, yellow, or rust-
    colored flowers in spikes; green leaves
Size: 2–5 ft. high; 2 ft. wide
Exposure: partial shade
Flowering: June–July

PRUNING: Deadhead to a lateral leaf or bud when about 70 percent of the flowering on the spike is finished; this avoids having a long, spindly, unattractive spike with numerous seed capsules at the bottom and a few stray flowers at the top. Cut back to basal rosettes immediately after all flowering is finished and before seed set to promote perennial nature of this biennial. Lifting the plants and replanting the new rosettes at this time will ensure vigor, otherwise the following year's flowers may be smaller in size. Plants can also be allowed to reseed before deadheading to ensure constancy in the garden. Common foxglove often looks tatty when going to seed, so cutting down most but not all flowering spikes will ensure some seeding, though not an overabundant amount, while keeping the plant a bit cleaner. The foliage may also get tatty by late summer if the plant is allowed to go to seed, in which case the foliage should be removed at this time.

OTHER MAINTENANCE: Performs best in well-draining yet moist soils high in organic matter, preferably with an acidic pH. Prone to a variety of diseases and to Japanese beetles, all of which contributes to foxglove's ratty late-summer appearance. Leaves and seeds are toxic if ingested.

RELATED PLANTS: *Digitalis purpurea* 'Foxy' blooms throughout the summer in its first year with constant deadheading. Only blooms early in the season in its second year. Best treated as an annual and replanted yearly.

Echinacea purpurea

Zone: 3–8
Common Name: purple coneflower
Family: Asteraceae
Description: pinkish purple daisy-like flowers with orange conelike center; coarse leaves
Size: 2–4 ft. high; 2 ft. wide
Exposure: full sun
Flowering: July–September

PRUNING: Plants seem to have a long bloom period even without deadheading, although deadheading makes the new flowers more prominent and keeps the plants looking fresh. I deadhead early in the bloom season and then curtail it in September, removing only the blackest heads and allowing the other seedheads to remain for the golden finch, who will feed heavily on the seedheads during September and October. Leaving the seedheads up for the winter provides food for many birds, including the juncos. But beware, leaving the seedheads also means excessive (an understatement) seedlings to contend with in the spring. They appear to have a 100% germination rate. I have started to compromise (since I'm running out of friends and family to whom I haven't already given flats of *Echinacea*), leaving only small numbers of seedheads for the winter. I enjoy the birds too much to remove them all, and the heads are so interesting when covered with snow. I know some gardeners who find the deadheads unattractive and opt to remove them for that reason.

Echinacea responds well to pruning before flowering as a means to delay bloom, providing fresh coneflowers into late September, even early October, for extended interest in the garden as well as for cut flowers at a time when unpruned plants are mostly faded and full of seedheads. Part of a drift of coneflowers can be treated this way, or coneflowers in different parts of the garden can be pruned for different peak flowering times. Two interesting approaches to pruning are described. Plants can be cut by one-half in early June or when they are about 2½ ft. tall. They will start to flower 2–3 weeks later than usual (mid- to late July), depending on the weather, and will bloom for 2–3 weeks longer than unpruned plants, going strong until late September. They may mature at about 1 ft. shorter than unpruned plants.

Another effective method to delay flowering is to cut off about 1 ft. of the plant while in bud in early July, or when it's about 3 ft. tall. The plants can look a bit rough at this point, but they will recover and flower nicely from mid-August until early October. They grow about 1 ft. shorter than unpruned plants (Plate 79).

It is interesting to note that, with either method, some basal shoots usually will be left below the level at which the plants are pruned. If this is the case, these unpruned shoots come up through the pruned plant and will flower about 1 week or so sooner than the pruned stems. Plant height is still reduced, as these stems naturally seem to grow to about the height of the pruned stems. Flowering is still extended with the pruned stems. Cutting plants to the ground in early June will delay flowering until mid-September, and on 2½-ft. plants, so all summer flowering is missed if plants are pruned to the ground.

The pruning advice applies to all the cultivars.

OTHER MAINTENANCE: Easy-to-grow perennial. Avoid high-fertility soil, which can lead to tall, leggy plants that require staking. Drought and heat resistant. Seldom needs division, but seedlings are best removed in the spring to control spread. Can attract beneficial soldier beetles in late August; be certain not to harm them.

Echinops ritro

Zone: 3–8
Common Name: globe thistle
Family: Asteraceae
Description: round blue flowerheads; rough spiny leaves
Size: 3–4 ft. high; 2–3 ft. wide
Exposure: full sun
Flowering: June–July

PRUNING: Globe thistle benefits from two types of pruning to look its best and to flower longest. First deadhead or cut back by one-third to one-half to lateral flower buds. Then, when new basal foliage starts to develop and all flowering is finished, plants should be cut back to basal foliage. Plants normally will rebloom from this basal growth, but usually the blooms are smaller, shorter, and less numerous than that of the initial flowering. Plants may seed occasionally if not deadheaded. Seedheads are attractive to the birds, so leaving a few deadheads from the last bloom phase may be a good compromise. Foliage may decline if not given afternoon shade in warm sunny gardens, in which case deadleafing will be necessary to keep plants attractive. Do not cut back for the winter; prune in the early spring.

OTHER MAINTENANCE: Very hardy, pest resistant, and drought tolerant once established. Well-draining soil is essential for survival. Does not need staking unless sited in overly rich soil. Can also spread strongly under such conditions. Division is not needed or recommended for many years and can prove difficult due to the thick, branching taproot. I have successfully divided young plants of globe thistle cultivars in early spring.

RELATED PLANTS: *Echinops ritro* 'Veitch's Blue' is particularly desirable because it's a good rebloomer.

Epimedium ×*rubrum*

Zone: 4–8
Common Name: red barrenwort
Family: Berberidaceae
Description: red flowers; heart-shaped leaves
Size: 8–12 in. high; 12 in. wide
Exposure: partial to full shade
Flowering: April–May

PRUNING: Plants usually are semi-evergreen (actually bronze) over the winter and become unsightly by very early spring. They should be cut down at this time so as to not detract from the early spring flowers. Some gardeners use rotary mowers in the autumn to clean-up large groundcover areas, which means missing out on the winter foliage but getting a jump on spring maintenance. This technique would also be useful for related species that have minimal winter interest. Deadheading may involve a little clipping here or there, but for the most part the maturing foliage hides old flowering stalks.

OTHER MAINTENANCE: Tough, long-lived, low-maintenance groundcover. Prefers moist, well-draining, high-organic soil, but great for dry shade once established. Will compete with tree roots. Moderate spreading. Division is seldom needed, but if desired, divide in the early spring before flowering or in the summer after the foliage has had a chance to mature.

RELATED PLANTS: *Epimedium alpinum*, alpine barrenwort, has foliage that dies back in the autumn. Along with *E. grandiflorum*, this is a parent species of *E.* ×*rubrum*.

Epimedium grandiflorum, longspur barrenwort, clumps increase slowly. Foliage starts to decline soon after the first frost and usually is completely gone by spring, thus not requiring cutting back. Somewhat difficult, but fully hardy.

Epimedium ×*versicolor* 'Sulphureum', bicolor barrenwort, is vigorously stoloniferous. One of the best for dry shade.

Epimedium ×*warleyense* spreads rapidly but not dense.

Epimedium ×*youngianum* 'Niveum', young's barrenwort, forms compact clumps that increase moderately fast.

Eryngium planum

Zone: 3–8
Common Name: flat sea holly
Family: Apiaceae
Description: flowers in small blue spiny
    bracts; almost leafless branching stems;
    heart-shaped unspined basal foliage
Size: 2–3 ft. high; 2–3 ft. wide
Exposure: full sun
Flowering: July–August

PRUNING: Individual flowers are ornamental for a long period of time. Deadheading doesn't seem to prolong bloom, but it makes the plant more attractive and reduces seeding. Deadheading can be tricky business due to the spiny nature of the plant. Trying to remove each flowerhead as it declines would drive even the worst neat-nik off his or her rocker. Waiting until most of the heads have declined on several of the flowering branches, and then going in to tidy up by removing whole branches, seems the most practical solution. Generally this needs to be done only once during the blooming season in early August. Then, in late August when most of the remaining flowering is finished and the unattractive brown heads develop, all flowering stems should be cut to the ground. Sometimes basal foliage will be present, other times it won't. With this regime some seeding will occur, but it's worth it compared to the tedious and painful process of deadheading each individual flower. Leave basal growth, which remains evergreen, for the winter.

OTHER MAINTENANCE: Normally self-supporting. Trouble free except for seeding. Does require well-draining soil; in fact, it thrives in dry, sandy soil. Tolerant of neglect during dry summers when you can't seem to make it out to the gardens with the sprinkler. Division is seldom necessary, and plants resent disturbance due to taproot.

RELATED PLANTS: *Eryngium alpinum*, alpine sea holly, is more desirable than *E. planum* but is seldom available in the trade; plants sold as this species may actually be *E. planum*.

Eupatorium maculatum 'Gateway'

Zone: 2–9
Common Name: gateway joe-pye weed
Family: Asteraceae
Description: rose-pink flowerheads; whorled
    leaves
Size: 5–6 ft. high; 3–4 ft. wide
Exposure: full sun
Flowering: July–September

PRUNING: Plants respond to several different pruning techniques before flowering either to reduce height, to create smaller flowers and fuller plants, or to stagger bloom. Reducing the height may not be an objective as the plants are lovely 5- to 6-ft.-tall self-supporting specimens with impressive large (7- to 8-in.-diameter) flowerheads. Slightly shorter, fuller plants may be useful in certain situations, however, such as to achieve proper proportions for combination with other shorter perennials. Pruning also produces slightly smaller flowerheads (5 in. in diameter), which can be more useful in flower arranging. Pruning may be desirable for plants grown in too much shade or overly rich soil, which produces larger plants with weaker, leaning stems.

My preferred technique is to pinch plants in early June when they are about 3 ft. tall. This causes 5 breaks to emerge from the one pinched stem, creating full plants with slightly smaller 5-in.-diameter flowers (see Plate 51). The plant's height normally is not noticeably reduced with this pruning, which I like, nor is the flowering time delayed significantly. A "have your cake and eat it too" situation can be attained by leaving several center stems unpinched to get the usual larger flowerheads on unbranched stems, and pinch the outer stems around it for some fuller growth and smaller heads (Plate 81).

Cutting back by 6 in. in early June produces shorter plants, by about 1–1½ ft., and flowers are slightly delayed, by about 1 week. Under certain situations the flowerheads may be reduced to about 4 in. × 2 in., which are not as ornamental as the flowers on pinched or unpruned plants. This technique also could be performed on only a few stems of the plant.

Some gardeners in warmer areas, whose plants reach 6–10 ft., have had success with cutting plants back by one-half when 2 ft. tall to obtain 4-ft.-tall flowering plants. I personally have not had success with this method, getting shorter plants (3 ft. tall compared to 6 ft.) that were weak and didn't flower. Variables such as climate, shade, competition, and age of plant may be responsible for the inconsistent results. Definitely a plant with which to play and experiment.

Deadheading is not necessary with gateway joe-pye weed since they have such a long bloom season without it. The flowers fade from early October to the first frost, and the fluffy seedheads that develop further extend their interest. Seeding is usually not a problem. The old stems and seedheads are attractive in the early winter garden (see Plate 61), but they tend to break under heavy snow and wind. Even when broken down they make good cover for the birds and so should be left if space is available. In a small garden where this habit isn't tolerable, cutting down in the autumn may be the pruning choice.

OTHER MAINTENANCE: Plants prefer moist locations; provide supplemental watering while establishing in the first year. Once established, plants are tough and tolerate short periods of drought. It takes 2–3 years for the plants to reach maturity. Division can be done in the spring but is only needed if plants get too big for their garden spot. Full sun is best to keep plants strongly upright.

RELATED PLANTS: *Eupatorium purpureum*, joe-pye weed, is a taller growing form, usually in the 7-ft. range or taller, depending on the climate and degree of light exposure. Plants can be pinched or even cut back heavily in early summer to reduce the mature height. In Georgia plants cut down to 12 in. in early June were compact and flowered at 3 ft. in early August, rather than the 15 ft. that it can attain in that region (Plate 80). Seeding may be a problem. Moisture is critical for best performance.

Eupatorium rugosum, white snakeroot, is a very heavy seeder that should be deadheaded. If the foliage declines, cut the whole plant down after flowering before seeds mature.

Euphorbia polychroma (*Euphorbia epithymoides*)

Zone: 4–8
Common Name: cushion spurge
Family: Euphorbiaceae
Description: yellow flowers in clustered inflorescences; green leaves
Size: 12–18 in. high; 18 in. wide
Exposure: full sun
Flowering: April–May

PRUNING: Plants can be sheared back by one-third and shaped after flowering but before seeds mature. Plants are heavy seeders, and shearing not only quickly takes care of deadheading but also helps produce a nicely shaped plant that is less likely to open up in the center. Hedge shears work well for this task. *Euphorbia* produces a sticky milky sap that can cause severe skin irritation in sensitive individuals. It is best to wear latex gloves when pruning these plants.

Plants can be left for the winter and cut back in the early spring. In southern areas plants may act almost like a subshrub, with buds breaking from old stems to create 3-ft.-wide plants. Plants allowed to develop this way in other parts of the country generally will not be as compact or as well formed, and pruning down to the base in the spring is likely to be more desirable.

OTHER MAINTENANCE: Requires well-draining soil, tolerates drought. May be susceptible to wilt in heat and humidity. Can be invasive in overly rich soil. Resents transplanting, and often doesn't require it for 10 years or more. If desired, divide thick fleshy roots, carefully, in the spring. Benefits from afternoon shade in southern gardens.

RELATED PLANTS: *Euphorbia griffithii*, griffith's spurge, can be pruned after flowering as described above for *E. polychroma*, or it may need to be cut back even harder (by two-thirds) to control flopping stems.

Euphorbia myrsinites, myrtle euphorbia, self-sows prolifically. Cut back flowering stems before the seeds disperse. Foliage remains an attractive blue-green through the winter if protected from afternoon sun and winds. Clean-up as needed in early spring.

Filipendula rubra 'Venusta'

Zone: 3–9
Common Name: queen-of-the-prairie
Family: Rosaceae
Description: fluffy deep rose flowers; compound leaves
Size: 4–6 ft. high; 4 ft. wide
Exposure: full sun
Flowering: July–August

PRUNING: Rebloom is minimal with deadheading, and the seedheads develop a rather interesting pinkish cast into the fall, so allowing spent flowers to remain on the plant is desirable. If foliage declines in late summer, cut the plants to the ground for a low fresh mound of leaves. Be certain to keep moist to

encourage regrowth, or it may not occur that season. Plants that were cut back by one-half in early June—when 2½ ft. tall and in tight bud—in an attempt to reduce height and delay flowering never bloomed. Queen-of-the-prairie usually does not respond to pinching either. Plants may fall over during the winter. If this is not welcome, cut back in the autumn; otherwise, leave for winter bird cover and then cut back in the early spring.

OTHER MAINTENANCE: Best summer-long performance is in moist, high-organic soil. Prefers cool climates. Tolerant of light shade. Usually requires light support, preferably by an obliging neighbor plant. The tough, thonglike root system is best left undisturbed for many years, unless you need to control spread, in which case divide in the autumn.

RELATED PLANTS: *Filipendula purpurea*, Japanese meadowsweet, has spent flowerheads that develop reddish tints, so plants don't need deadheading.

Filipendula vulgaris, dropwort meadowsweet, seeds abundantly, but seedlings are easily weeded out. In contrast to other *Filipendula*, this species transplants easily and is tolerant of drier soil.

Filipendula ulmaria

Zone: 3–9
Common Name: queen-of-the-meadow
Family: Rosaceae
Description: fluffy white flowers; compound leaves
Size: 4–6 ft. high; 3 ft. wide
Exposure: full sun to partial shade
Flowering: June–July

PRUNING: Removing deadheads may encourage some rebloom and will prevent abundant reseeding. If old foliage declines, cut the plant down for new basal growth development.

OTHER MAINTENANCE: Best in moist,

high-organic soils. Provide some shade in hot regions. Tough root systems do not require frequent division. Strong stems do not require staking. Prone to mildew in hot, dry, or stressed conditions.

RELATED PLANTS: *Filipendula ulmaria* 'Aurea' is valued for its golden foliage, which is more outstanding into the autumn if the plant is sheared back after flowering for new basal growth. Since flowering reduces the vigor of the foliage, a still-better option might be to prevent the plant from flowering altogether by shearing the flower buds off when they are just starting to form. This also prevents any chance of "mongrel" seedlings developing, which are green and vigorous growers that may overtake the golden parent.

Foeniculum vulgare 'Purpureum'

Zone: 4–9
Common Name: copper fennel
Family: Apiaceae
Description: feathery purple foliage; yellow-green umbel flowers
Size: 3–4 ft. high; 1½–2 ft. wide
Exposure: full sun
Flowering: July–August

PRUNING: Copper fennel is most often grown in the perennial garden for its ornamental foliage color and texture. Some gardeners remove the flowers while in bud to prevent flowering altogether so as to not detract from the foliar effect. Plants can also reseed heavily, and preventing the plants from flowering is a sure way to eliminate this problem. But fennel should really be permitted to flower, because the small flowers serve an important function in being the host for beneficial parasitic wasps. These wasps help control caterpillars, aphids, and other soft-bodied pests. Deadhead fennel after all flowering is finished and before seeds mature (Plate 82). Allowing a small amount of seeding can mean greater constancy of the plant

in the garden, as fennel are often short-lived. Fennel foliage can also serve an important function in the perennial garden in that it provides larval food for black and anise swallowtail butterflies. In some years this may mean total defoliation of fennel by late summer, in which case the bare stems should be cut to the ground at this time. The leaves hang limply from the stems if hit by a heavy freeze, so cutting down for the winter may be preferred to spring pruning.

Care should be taken when working with fennel because the plant's juices can cause a phyto-photo dermatitis in some individuals —this means that if the juice gets on the skin and is exposed to the sun a reaction will occur, creating dark purplish discoloration on the skin, which can develop into a blister or two, although usually not. (This does not resemble the irritation caused by poison ivy, as so many other plant dermatital reactions do.) The darkened areas can remain for several months and, if severe enough, can cause light scars. To avoid problems, you might work with the plants only on cloudy days or in the late evening when the sun is down, and wear long sleeves, long pants, and gloves.

OTHER MAINTENANCE: Requires well-draining soil. Fennel is tolerant of drought and heat. Fairly short-lived.

Fragaria 'Pink Panda'

Zone: 6
Common Name: pink panda strawberry
Family: Rosaceae
Description: pink flowers; sporadic tiny edible strawberries
Size: 6–12 in. high; spreading
Exposure: full sun to partial shade
Flowering: May–July

PRUNING: Plants require constant pruning to keep in bounds, especially when placed in the wrong location such as a perennial border. Best used as a groundcover on its own.

Requires deadleafing—a tedious task—if plants get dry in the summer, which causes scorching. Plants are semi-evergreen and require spring clean-up to remove foliage damaged from harsh winters. Do not prune for the winter.

OTHER MAINTENANCE: Can be extremely invasive when planted with other low-growing perennials, which strawberry will overtake. I had one plant spread over a 9 ft. × 9 ft. area in 4 years, weaving between and over everything in its path. The spread of this particular plant was stopped by one wet and cold winter, to the point where nothing remained. Well-draining soil is essential, particularly in the winter. Hardiness is unclear.

Gaillardia ×grandiflora

Zone: 3–10
Common Name: blanket flower
Family: Asteraceae
Description: daisy-like flowerheads in combinations of reds, yellows, and oranges; gray-green hairy leaves
Size: 2–3 ft. (1 ft.) high; 2 ft. wide
Exposure: full sun
Flowering: June–October

PRUNING: *Gaillardia* seems to flower continuously even without deadheading. This is a nice advantage, because if you don't deadhead you can enjoy the new flowers and the attractive spherical seedheads together, either in the garden or in arrangements. Self-seeding may occur, so deadhead if seeding is not desired. Some authorities feel that the tendency toward continuous bloom, although pleasing to the gardener, can work against the plant's chances of overwintering by directing its energy to flower production, rendering the plant unable to form buds for the following year's shoots. Cutting all flowering stems down to the basal foliage in late August or early September can stimulate vegetative growth before the coming of frost.

The plant may then form new basal buds and more vigorous shoots, which can improve the plant's chances of survival.

OTHER MAINTENANCE: Often short-lived, usually due to wet overwintering conditions rather than cold temperatures. Well-draining soil, particularly over the winter, is vital to survival. Drought, heat, and salt tolerant. Avoid overly rich soil. Tall-growing forms require staking. Divide in the early spring every 2–3 years to maintain vigor.

RELATED PLANTS: *Gaillardia ×grandiflora* 'Baby Cole' and 'Goblin' are dwarf forms not requiring staking.

Gaura lindheimeri

Zone: 5–9
Common Name: white gaura
Family: Onagraceae
Description: small white flowers above narrow leaves
Size: 3–5 ft. high; 3 ft. wide
Exposure: full sun
Flowering: June–October

PRUNING: Old flower petals simply drop off the plant, leaving tiny pinkish red tinted seed capsules on the spike. New flowers continue to open from the bottom of the flowering spike up to the top over a long period of time. Depending on the conditions and the age of the plants, flowering may continue for the entire summer and autumn even without deadheading. And because the stems are so fine and the seedheads so tiny, any finished spikes usually go unnoticed among the masses of blooming spikes. The whole appearance of the plant is so wispy, and the stems take on a nice scarlet tint in the autumn. The stems turn brown in midwinter and may fall under the weight of heavy snow. If plants are left up for the winter, reseeding may occur, usually near the base of the parent plants. Reseeding can ensure constancy of this often short-lived perennial in the garden. In some situations plants may appear to take a rest from flowering in midsummer; deadhead at this time, or shear in half, and rebloom normally will occur from late summer into autumn.

Gaura can be cut back or sheared before flowering for a nice effect to reduce the height of the plants and to produce fuller clumps with more flowering branches. The stems are so thin and weak on this perennial, however, that it seems no matter what height the plants end up flowering at they are still going to flop slightly or at least lean over a bit. Plants cut back in early June by one-half when 12–15 in. tall flower 1–2 weeks later than unpruned plants and they start flowering at 3 ft. and mature to 4 ft. (Flower stems on *Gaura* elongate through the bloom period.) Pruned plants will still lean on their neighbors, but not as much as the 5-ft.-tall unpruned plants. Cutting plants back by two-thirds may be more desirable to further reduce height.

Gaura responds in an interesting way to continued shearing and shaping. A couple of shearings can create full, deep green, 10- to 12-in. mounds. Flowering seems to be initiated as soon as pruning stops. Plants sheared by one-half in early June, and then again when in bud in mid-July and when in bud in mid-August, finally flowered in early October on 18-in. plants, elongating to 2-ft.-tall plants with a slight lean. The problem with this approach is that all the summer bloom is lost. Also, the amount of flowers seemed to be reduced. The shearing can be stopped in mid-July, after the second pruning, for flowering in mid- to late August on fuller, more compact plants than those that undertake only one shearing. This could be useful in preparation for a special September event in the garden, where smaller, fuller, fresh flowering specimens are in order.

Two shearings, or one heavier shearing, before bloom may be useful in southern gardens, where plants can become leggy with extended heat and humidity. Shearing can be repeated throughout the season, whenever buds are visible, to keep plants in a vegetative state, if desired.

OTHER MAINTENANCE: Adequate drainage is the primary requirement of this long-flowering, heat- and drought-tolerant perennial. Plants have a tendency to bend over, and this habit is even more pronounced in overly rich or wet soil. Use neighboring perennials for support. The stout taproot seldom needs division. Can be short-lived.

RELATED PLANTS: *Gaura lindheimeri* 'Corrie's Gold' is a variegated form that flowers in early summer and if cut back by one-half in late July will rebloom in September.

Gaura lindheimeri 'Whirling Butterflies' is a good cultivar to select because it is more compact than the species, reaching only 3–3½ ft. and with less bending. It is also self-sterile, so reseeding is not a concern.

Geranium endressii 'Wargrave Pink'

Zone: 4–8
Common Name: hardy geranium
Family: Geraniaceae
Description: pink flowers; palmately cut
   leaves
Size: 15–18 in. high; 18 in. wide
Exposure: partial shade
Flowering: May–June

PRUNING: Sprawling, straggly stems tend to develop after the initial flowering. Cut down to new growth at the base of the plant after flowering using hand pruners, or go for speed and use hedge shears. You may hit some of the new growth, but no harm done —the plants usually fill in with fresh mounds of foliage within 2 weeks. You may even get some sporadic rebloom for your efforts (Plates 83–85). For best regrowth, avoid prolonged drought after cutting back. Flowering may last longer in cool climates, and cutting back may not be necessary. Plants hold up well until late winter, at which point they often turn to mush. Cutting back in the autumn after several killing frosts may be desirable.

OTHER MAINTENANCE: Requires well-draining soil. Prefers moist soil in areas with hot summers, although fairly adaptable to short periods of dry conditions. Can tolerate more sun and drier soil in cooler climates. Seldom needs dividing. Divisions can be easily taken by reaching into the plant and separating a piece from the main crown in spring or autumn.

RELATED PLANTS: *Geranium* ×*oxonianum* 'Claridge Druce' and 'A. T. Johnson' are more vigorous and free flowering. Also better adapted to dry situations. Pruning as above, although in warmer climates plants may be semi-evergreen and hold up well for the winter.

Geranium ibericum 'Johnson's Blue' (*Geranium* 'Johnson's Blue')

Zone: 4–8
Common Name: johnson's blue geranium
Family: Geraniaceae
Description: blue flowers; palmately lobed leaves
Size: 18 in. high; 18 in. wide
Exposure: full sun or partial shade
Flowering: June–July

PRUNING: The performance of this plant varies. In some years the old flowering stems fall neatly to the outside of the clump, simply needing to be trimmed off, and the upright foliage in the middle holds for the rest of the season. This can be particularly true of young plants. Other years the entire plant may sprawl, requiring a cutting back to the ground to get it off of its neighbors. The habit may vary from plant to plant in the same planting, in the same year, at the same

age. Plants fall open badly in the winter and so are best cut back after frost in the autumn.

OTHER MAINTENANCE: Prefers well-draining, evenly moist soil. Divide every 4–5 years in the spring as needed. Pea staking can help hold plants up.

RELATED PLANTS: *Geranium himalayense* (*G. grandiflorum*), lilac geranium, performs best in cool, moist, well-draining locations. Develops a sprawling habit. Cut down to new basal foliage after flowering; no rebloom can be expected.

Geranium macrorrhizum

Zone: 3–8
Common Name: bigroot geranium
Family: Geraniaceae
Description: pink or white flowers; palmately lobed gray-green leaves, with scarlet autumn color
Size: 12–15 in. high; 18 in. wide
Exposure: partial to full shade
Flowering: May–June

PRUNING: Does not require cutting back like so many of its relatives. Deadheading is all that is needed to keep this geranium looking good, and this work is a treat to do, as brushing against the foliage causes it to emit its pungent scent. The foliage of this evergreen to semi-evergreen plant remains an attractive gray-green with tints of scarlet-red at the junction of stem and leaf through most of the winter. Do not prune back in the autumn, but in early spring simply cut off any dead foliage that developed from a harsh winter. Will readily self-seed if permitted, which along with the natural spreading habit of this plant can create a nice groundcover effect. If this effect is desired, do not deadhead until seeds have dropped. Plants are drought tolerant, but some leaves may yellow by late summer with prolonged periods of dry conditions. A quick deadleafing will return the plant to its fresh appearance. Beautiful autumn foliage color.

OTHER MAINTENANCE: Good low-maintenance geranium, very easy to grow. Drought and heat tolerant. Stoloniferous roots seldom need dividing. Can tolerate full sun in cooler climates.

RELATED PLANTS: *Geranium ×cantabrigiense* 'Biokovo' is a wonderful groundcover for dry shade that only requires deadheading to keep it looking good. Stays in a nice mound that turns scarlets and oranges in the autumn. Cut back any dead foliage in the spring if desired, but tatty old foliage is usually lost among new growth.

Geranium platypetalum

Zone: 3–8
Common Name: broad-petaled geranium
Family: Geraniaceae
Description: violet flowers on sticky stalks;
    rounded lobed hairy leaves
Size: 18–24 in. high; 18–24 in. wide
Exposure: full sun to partial shade
Flowering: June

PRUNING: A light trimming to remove dead flower stems that fall to the outside of the clump, and reshaping of growth, is all that is needed to keep this geranium going strong into the autumn, at which time it develops outstanding fall color. Prune old flower stems off at the ground. Deadheading and shaping can also be accomplished by pulling stems out of the plant, which not only serves to tidy up the plant, but it also opens the plant up a bit so it's not so dense, and it can keep the plant in bounds widthwise. Little rootlets may be found on the bottoms of excised branches, and these can be propagated. Broad-petaled geranium does not require the dramatic shearing to the ground that many of the other geraniums do. If foliage does decline slightly—although this is usually not the case—it is best to cut the

plant down in sections, perhaps one-third at a time, allowing regrowth of one pruned section before another is cut (see Figure 10-1). This is preferable to cutting the entire plant down at once, leaving a large hole in the garden. The plants are so wide that if cut in stages in this way they don't even look like anything has been cut off, and regrowth is very fast, reattaining the original height within two weeks. No rebloom will occur. Plants often hold foliage well into winter; if so, cut back in early spring before new leaves emerge.

OTHER MAINTENANCE: Easy-to-grow, low-maintenance perennial. Provide afternoon shade in hot climates. Seldom needs dividing.

RELATED PLANTS: *Geranium ×magnificum*, showy geranium, may require a little more trimming than its above parent, but this can be accomplished in the same manner—by pruning or by pulling entire old flowering stems out of the plant. If plants are leggy, cut down to basal foliage. Rebloom, if any, will be insignificant.

Geranium sanguineum

Zone: 3–8
Common Name: blood-red geranium
Family: Geraniaceae
Description: pink, magenta, or white flowers;
    cranelike seedheads; small lobed leaves
Size: 6–15 in. high; 24 in. wide
Exposure: full sun or partial shade
Flowering: May–September

PRUNING: I usually don't bother to go through the tedious process of deadheading the hundreds of little "cranes" that develop on this plant. I wait until most of the flowering, including sporadic rebloom, is finished and plants are looking rough, usually in late summer, and I cut the plant back (using hedge shears) to the fresh basal foliage, which turns crimson in the autumn. Plants do not need to be pruned down for the winter. The waxy leaves hold well until spring, at which point any dead leaves can be removed, although this usually is not even necessary as new growth quickly covers any dead foliage. Some reseeding occurs when deadheading is omitted. If deadheading is desired, rather than removing deadheads one by one with pruners, a less arduous approach is to shear them off along with about 4 in. of foliage after the main flowering is finished. Plants can be shaped at the same time if desired, which may be helpful to keep plants from encroaching into neighboring perennials' space. Sporadic rebloom appears to be the same on deadheaded and non-deadheaded plants.

OTHER MAINTENANCE: Very tough, long-lived, sun-loving geranium. Tolerant of many soil types, but requires good drainage and may spread excessively in overly rich soil. Tolerates drought. Usually doesn't require division. Side shoots can be removed, without lifting the plant, to help confine expanding clumps.

RELATED PLANTS: *Geranium sanguineum* 'New Hampshire Purple' and 'Elsbeth', although hard to tell apart from one another, are choice long-blooming cultivars. 'Elsbeth' appears to be more upright, whereas 'New Hampshire Purple' is wider spreading.

Geranium sanguineum 'Cedric Morris', a compact form (8 in.), has larger flowers that bloom about 2 weeks earlier and last longer than those of the species.

Geranium sanguineum 'Max Frei' has diminutive leaves and a more compact habit, growing 6 in. tall. May be a better choice where space is limited.

Geum hybrids (Geum coccineum × Geum quellyon)

Zone: 5–7
Common Name: geum
Family: Rosaceae
Description: yellow, orange, or scarlet flowers; fuzzy lobed basal leaves
Size: 18–24 in. high; 18 in. wide
Exposure: full sun
Flowering: May–June

PRUNING: Plants flower strongly in May and June and intermittently after that, sometimes until autumn, with deadheading. Flowering spikes are branched. Deadhead to lateral flowers, then when all flowering on the spike is finished cut it down to the foliage. If foliage declines after flowering, deadleaf or cut back once new basal growth is evident. Keep moist. Plants remain semi-evergreen into the winter; cut back as needed in the spring. Young or newly divided plants bloom stronger and longer than old plants.

OTHER MAINTENANCE: Short-lived plants. Research for my master's thesis showed geum to be not very cold hardy, nor tolerant of poorly drained conditions, particularly in the winter. Plants need a cool root run, and moisture in the summer. Performance is better in cooler climates; provide afternoon shade in hot regions. Annual division in the spring or late summer is required to maintain vigor.

Gypsophila paniculata

Zone: 3–9
Common Name: baby's breath
Family: Caryophyllaceae
Description: tiny white or pink flowers in large airy clusters; linear blue-gray leaves
Size: 2–3 ft. high; 3 ft. wide
Exposure: full sun
Flowering: June–August

PRUNING: Deadhead *Gypsophila* throughout the summer for more flower production and to keep it looking fresh. Deadhead to lateral flowers, and when all flowering is finished cut stems down to the rosette of foliage for rebloom in the autumn.

OTHER MAINTENANCE: Well-draining soil is essential to survival. Plants prefer alkaline conditions. More compact cultivars should be selected to eliminate or reduce the need for staking. Division is not recommended due to the thick roots of baby's breath. Short-lived.

RELATED PLANTS: *Gypsophila paniculata* 'Bristol Fairy', a 2-ft.-tall form, usually doesn't need staking.

Gypsophila paniculata 'Pink Fairy' grows to 18 in. and requires no staking.

Gypsophila paniculata 'Rosenschleier' ('Rosy Veil') is more tolerant of wet conditions, more vigorous, and longer lived than other taller cultivars. It grows to 18 in.

Gypsophila repens, creeping baby's breath, is hardier than *G. paniculata* and longer lived in heavy soil conditions.

Helenium autumnale

Zone: 3–8
Common Name: common sneezeweed
Family: Asteraceae
Description: red, yellow, or orange daisy-like
   flowerheads; narrow green leaves
Size: 3–5 ft. high; 3 ft. wide
Exposure: full sun
Flowering: July–October

PRUNING: The species and cultivars of common sneezeweed can be pruned in a variety of different ways to reduce height and possibly delay flowering. Pinching plants every couple of weeks, starting around mid-May and going until mid-June, will produce more compact plants with more flowers. Another method that offers similar results and possibly slightly delayed flowers is to simply cut plants back once by one-half or two-thirds in early to mid-June, layering the outer branches.

Some gardeners prefer to cut the plants back to about 12 in. in mid-July for bloom 6 weeks or so later on plants one-half the normal size, although a good deal of bloom time is lost with this technique. If such a drastic delay is not desired, a more practical alternative is to remove 4–6 in. off the tips of the plants when in tight bud, which will delay flowering by only a week or two. This technique is useful to delay flowering on a plant that was pruned earlier for height control. Other options for gardeners include removing the tips from a few stems on an individual plant to prolong the bloom of that plant, or removing the tips of a few plants in a large group to prolong the bloom of the planting. Deadheading also prolongs bloom.

Plants are usually spindly at planting and should be cut back by one-half at that time for shorter first-year plants.

Plants have dense foliage that can be prone to mildew late in the season. Plants should be cut back by one-half to two-thirds or even to basal growth, if present, after flowering to reduce occurrence of mildew or to remove infected foliage.

OTHER MAINTENANCE: Plants require sufficient moisture during the summer for best performance. They flounder in dry conditions and tolerate wet sites. Frequent division, every 2–3 years, often is needed to maintain vigor. Staking is required, even with many of the cultivars and hybrids, unless pruned. Tall, weaker growth is promoted by hot conditions.

Helianthemum nummularium

Zone: 5–7
Common Name: sunrose
Family: Cistaceae
Description: crepe paper-like flowers; gray-
   green narrow leaves
Size: 6–12 in. high; 12–18 in. wide
Exposure: full sun to partial shade
Flowering: May–June

PRUNING: In the early spring, before flower formation, plants may benefit from a light trim to create denser growth. Plants should be sheared by about one-third and shaped after flowering to maintain form. They may benefit from a heavy shearing every 2–3 years down to about 6 in., or lower for shorter forms, if they have gotten leggy. Heavy shearing will return the plant to a vigorous condition. All heavy pruning should be completed by mid- to late August so that these sub-shrubs can harden for winter. Plants are evergreen—do not prune for the winter.

OTHER MAINTENANCE: Good drainage is absolutely essential. Prefers rocky, dry, alkaline conditions with cool summers and mild winters. Avoid overly rich soil. Grit can be added to heavy soil at planting to improve water movement. Plants are shallow-rooted and should be mulched with evergreen boughs to reduce frost heaving and winter desiccation. Avoid planting or dividing in autumn. Divide every 4–5 years in the spring if needed.

RELATED PLANTS: The *Helianthemum* cultivars 'Ben Heckla' and 'Rose Queen' perform well in heat.

Helianthus salicifolius

Zone: 3–9
Common Name: willow-leaved sunflower
Family: Asteraceae
Description: golden-yellow daisy-like
    flowerheads; narrow leaves
Size: 5–6 ft. high; 3 ft. wide
Exposure: full sun
Flowering: late September–October

PRUNING: If plants are grown in full sun, stems are usually self-supporting. If given shade or overly rich soil, plants will be more open, taller, and weaker, requiring staking. Pinching or cutting back creates more compact growth. Plants grown in full sun that normally reach 4–5 ft. may grow to about 3 ft. when pinched in early July, and with no delay in flowering (Plates 86–87). Cutting plants back by one-half in mid-June also creates shorter plants with no delay in bloom. Shorter, fuller, more floriferous plants, whether grown in sun or shade, are a

welcome addition to the smaller garden. *Helianthus salicifolius* flowers so late in the season that deadheading to prolong bloom is not really practical, and the seedheads are attractive to humans and birds. I've never had reseeding of this species. Plants can be left up for the winter, although stems will break under the weight of snow and heavy winds. Cutting back after several frosts may be more desirable if a tidy winter appearance is the goal.

OTHER MAINTENANCE: Easy-to-grow plant. Seemingly tolerant of a wide range of situations, although it prefers moist, well-draining soil. Fairly drought tolerant once established. Wide spreading, so one plant creates an impressive site. Divide, if needed, in the spring every 4–5 years.

RELATED PLANTS: *Helianthus angustifolius*, swamp sunflower, is a taller growing sunflower with a more open habit, particularly in shady sites. Benefits from pruning as described above, although Allen Bush, the notorious nurseryman, reports that plants in his garden in North Carolina grow to 8–9 ft. even with cutting back by one-half in mid- to late June. This species might need a heavier hand with the pruners, or less southern hospitality! Requires abundant moisture, as the common name would indicate. Heavy feeder and seeder. Deadhead or cut down before seeds have a chance to mature. May be invasive in certain sites.

Heliopsis helianthoides 'Summer Sun'

Zone: 3–9
Common Name: summer sun heliopsis
Family: Asteraceae
Description: golden-yellow daisy-like flower-
    heads; green leaves
Size: 3–6 ft. high; 4 ft. wide
Exposure: full sun or partial shade
Flowering: June–September

PRUNING: Young plants bloom all summer long, almost nonstop, with minimal or no deadheading. With older plants, deadheading greatly increases the length of the bloom period. Deadheading also prevents seeding. Don't be too much of a neat-nik, however; leave some heads for the golden finches, who feed on them heavily in August but will frequent the plants as soon as seed is available. Some seeding can create a nice effect in the garden, as plants come fairly true to seed. Since *Heliopsis* can be short-lived, seeding may also be the only guarantee of longevity in the garden.

In certain years the entire plant may need to be cut down after flowering, around mid-September, if it has gotten tatty from sooty mold (remains of heavy aphid populations) or mildew or just wear from a long summer. Otherwise you can leave the plants up for further bird feeding. Selective cutting back of the worst stems or deadleafing of the worst leaves can also help keep the appearance presentable.

Plants respond well to cutting back before flowering to reduce the mature height and delay the bloom period. Three-foot-tall plants cut back by one-half in early June matured to 3½ ft., compared to the 5-ft. unpruned plants, and they started blooming 1½–2 weeks later and consequently flowered that much longer (Plate 88). Pruning in this way can be used to reduce the height of some individuals to create a nice layering effect for a planting, or to have different plants in different parts of the garden flowering at slightly different times. It provides flowers for arrangements over a longer period as well. *Heliopsis* probably could be pruned back even more for even shorter plants, or pruned slightly later, perhaps in mid- to late June, for an even greater delay.

OTHER MAINTENANCE: Fairly low-maintenance perennial once established. First-year plants sometimes struggle to take hold.

Prefers moist, organic soil but tolerates short periods of drought. Plants grown in rich conditions may need division every 2–3 years in the spring or fall to increase longevity; otherwise plants can usually go 5 years before division is needed. Red aphids usually attack the plants starting in May. They don't do much harm, unless a plant is badly infected, in which case the unsightly sooty mold that follows can literally cover the plant. Wash heavy aphid populations off with a strong spray of water. Beneficial soldier beetles may help control pest infestations.

Helleborus orientalis

Zone: 4–9
Common Name: lenten rose
Family: Ranunculaceae
Description: rose- or cream-speckled flowers;
    deep green palmate leaves
Size: 15–18 in. high; 15 in. wide
Exposure: partial to full shade
Flowering: March–April

PRUNING: Plants are evergreen, but the foliage can get battered by late winter. Prune off dead leaves at this time to make room for new growth and flowering. Some gardeners mow the old foliage off of large plantings of lenten rose for complete renewal. The flower sepals are attractive for a long time, even after their color has faded. *Helleborus* can reseed heavily, literally by the hundreds under certain conditions. Usually the seedlings are located at the base of the parent plant, and they will flower in about the third spring. This can create a nice effect in a natural setting, but it may not be desirable for every garden. Deadheading before seeds set can reduce the problem. *Helleborus* can be prone to disease in warm, wet, humid conditions; prune off and destroy affected parts.

OTHER MAINTENANCE: Prefers high-organic, moist, well-draining alkaline soil; will tolerate some dry conditions in the summer. Plants are slow to take hold but are long-lived and don't need to be disturbed once established-division is seldom, if ever, needed. If desired, divide in the spring. Plant in the spring to allow plants to establish before winter.

RELATED PLANTS: *Helleborus foetidus*, stinking hellebore, is the longest blooming hellebore, setting yellow-green buds in the autumn and opening in the spring. Foliage stays greener than most over the winter and sometimes takes on attractive purple tinting. When flowering stems decline, cut back to basal foliage for more vigorous new growth. Tolerates short periods of drought. Can be short-lived. Allowing some seeding can ensure permanence in the garden. On the hardiness borderline in zone 5, plants performed beautifully for 4 years and then were lost one hard winter.

Helleborus niger, christmas rose, prefers moister conditions than *H. orientalis* and is more difficult to establish after division. Best to leave undisturbed and avoid cultivation around its roots. Also slower spreading than lenten rose.

Hemerocallis

Zone: 3–9
Common Name: daylily
Family: Liliaceae
Description: trumpet-shaped flowers; straplike leaves
Size: 1–4 ft. (1–2 ft.) high; 1½ ft. wide
Exposure: full sun; partial shade for pastels
Flowering: June–October

PRUNING: The Greek term *hemerocallis* means "beautiful for a day," but it could also be understood to mean "not beautiful for more than a day." This being the case, daylilies are a deadheading nightmare. No matter how you refer to them—wet globs of tissue paper, slimy creatures, mush-mummies, or the like—daylily deadheads are ugly

(Plate 89). Many flowers are born per flower stem. Each flower can be snapped off the stem as it fades using the thumb and forefinger (Plate 90); be sure to get the entire flower and not just the petals, or the ovary will be left behind to develop into an unattractive seed capsule, which also detracts from the fresh flowers. Some purple-flowered forms, such as 'Plum Beauty' and 'Pleasant Lavender', can stain your hands like grape juice when you're deadheading them. When all flowering is finished on the flowering stem the entire stem should be cut back to the basal foliage. Deadheading not only keeps the plants looking good but is important for the repeat in repeat-blooming daylilies. Some daylilies with smaller blooms are more self-cleaning and don't require the stringent deadheading that the large flowering forms do (a few are mentioned below).

After all flowering and deadheading is finished, around mid-August, deadleafing begins. This involves grabbing clumps of dead leaves and pulling them out of the plant by hand. Trimming off yellow tips may also be helpful. If foliage decline is severe, and if a hole in the garden is tolerable (which in many cases is better than continual declining foliage), a more practical and time-saving approach may be to simply shear the whole plant down. The new foliage that emerges will be fresh and will hold through to frost (Plate 91). The plants either can be sheared to within a few inches of the ground or they can be cut down to new fresh leaves (6–8 in. above the ground) if the new foliage has already started to develop at the base of the plant. Hedge shears make quick work of shearing. Depending on the conditions, a plant sheared to the ground can take anywhere from a couple of weeks to a month for decent regrowth. The new mound of foliage will be shorter than the normal mature size of the plant. Be certain to keep the plants moist after shearing, or regrowth may not occur. Top-dressing with compost or an organic fertilizer may help ensure more vigorous regrowth. Cutting plants back can also serve as a method of controlling thrips, if the pests pose a problem.

Plants do not respond to pinching or cutting back when in bud in an attempt to delay flowering. If buds are removed, plants simply won't flower that season.

Daylilies can remain attractive into late autumn, and in mild areas some varieties may remain semi-evergreen. In these instances cutting plants back in the spring is preferable to cutting down for winter. In most cases, though, the foliage gets pretty tatty over the winter and should be cut back after several killing frosts. Sometimes the foliage can simply be pulled off by hand.

OTHER MAINTENANCE: Despite all the pruning requirements, daylilies are tough, long-lived, cold hardy, and tolerant of neglect. As with all perennials, daylilies prefer a high-organic, well-draining soil, but they are flexible, although they will rot if the soil is too poorly drained. Fairly drought tolerant. Daylilies are easily divided using the double-fork method (described in Chapter 6), and this can be done at anytime, although spring or autumn are best. Normally division is not needed for many years on older species, but the hybrids can get crowded and may require division every 4–5 years, even sooner for repeat-bloomers (see below). Partial shade is preferable for daylilies with pastel-colored flowers.

RELATED PLANTS: Repeat-blooming daylilies require frequent division, about every 2 years to keep them vigorous and blooming strongly, because it is the new rhizomes that produce the new flowers. They are also heavy feeders and should be given both a spring granular and summer liquid feeding. Deadheading is critical for good rebloom. Deadleafing is more desirable than cutting back after the first bloom, as future flowers might be cut off with the foliage. If the foliage looks poor after the first bloom phase, it is probably a sign that division is needed to rejuvenate the plants. Some repeat-blooming daylilies, besides the well-known 'Stella de Oro', include: 'Bitsy', 'Daily Bread', 'Fuzz Bunny', 'Happy Returns' (the flowers actually last 1½ days), 'Haunting Melody', 'Hazel Monette' (evergreen to semi-evergreen and hardy in the North with some rebloom), 'Jersey Spider', 'Winsome Lady', 'Yellow Lollipop' (rebloom and small flowers), and *Hemerocallis middendorffii*.

Some small-flowering daylilies include 'Boutonnier', 'Corky', 'Golden Chimes', 'Mdm. Bellum', and 'Toy Trumpets'.

Hesperis matronalis

Zone: 3–8
Common Name: dame's rocket
Family: Brassicaceae
Description: fragrant white or purple
    flowers; narrow serrated leaves
Size: 2–3 ft. high; 3 ft. wide
Exposure: full sun or partial shade
Flowering: May–June

PRUNING: Gardeners have a few pruning options with dame's rocket. The plants can be deadheaded before seed set, which may prolong bloom particularly if there is sufficient moisture; then plants can be cut down to the basal foliage after all flowering is finished, again before seed set, to cause this normally biennial plant to act more perennial in nature. The other option would be to allow seeding, which the plant may do somewhat heavily under certain conditions, to ensure constancy in the garden. Allowing the plant to go to seed is often more desirable because individual plants are usually short-lived. Cutting down the majority of old flowering stems before seed set but allowing a few to set seed will decrease the number of seedlings and keep the population more under control. If seeding is allowed, the parent plant usually will die.

OTHER MAINTENANCE: Prefers moist, high-organic, alkaline soil for best reseeding. Well-draining soil is essential, especially over the winter to ensure survival. Plants usually go dormant over the summer. I like to plant dame's rocket alongside or coming up through rugosa roses (*Rosa rugosa*) for a great combination, and then they will not be missed when pruned down or if they die down. Care should be taken to not plant close to natural areas where it may become invasive.

Heuchera micrantha 'Palace Purple'

Zone: 4–9
Common Name: palace purple coralbell
Family: Saxifragaceae
Description: greenish purple to reddish purple ivy-shaped leaves; tiny white flowers on spikes
Size: 15–18 in. (12 in.) high; 12–18 in. wide
Exposure: full sun to partial shade
Flowering: June–July

PRUNING: The flowers of purple palace coralbells get mixed reviews from gardeners. Some (and I'm one of them) feel that the flowers detract from the ornamental foliage and so remove the flowers in bud. Others find the flowers ornamental in their own right and let them do their thing. The foliage color will bleach or fade if grown with afternoon sun and leaves will scorch if allowed to dry out. Shearing off the old top growth in late summer or early autumn reveals colorful foliage below. Plants hold their color into winter to different degrees depending on the conditions for the year. Do not prune for the winter. Deadleaf or shear off any damaged leaves in early spring to make room for colorful new foliage.

OTHER MAINTENANCE: *Heuchera* usually will frost heave with fluctuating winter temperatures. Plant in the spring, in moist high-organic soil, to allow establishment before winter. Well-draining soil is also critical for overwintering success. Benefits from a winter mulch after the ground freezes. Gently press plants back into the soil in early spring if they heave over the winter. Division generally is needed every 3 years in the spring. Shade from afternoon sun in hot climates.

RELATED PLANTS: *Heuchera micrantha* 'Chocolate Ruffles' is my favorite, even over the numerous purple, "snow-splashed," crinkled and wrinkled forms, including 'Palace Purple'. Maybe having chocolate in the name has something to do with it, but its color and form hold up well without pruning and are distinct from the rest in my *Heuchera* book. I'm not sure if Dan Heims of Terra-Nova Nursery, the guru of *Heuchera* breeding, would agree, but it works for me.

Heuchera americana 'Garnet', American alumroot, is valued for its deep garnet winter foliage and bright garnet spring foliage.

×*Heucherella alba* 'Bridget Bloom', foamy bells, can have its bloom prolonged with deadheading.

Heuchera sanguinea

Zone: 3–8
Common Name: coralbell
Family: Saxifragaceae
Description: tiny red, pink, or white flowers; heart-shaped or rounded leaves
Size: 12–20 in. (8 in.) high; 12 in. wide
Exposure: full sun or partial shade
Flowering: May–July

PRUNING: Deadhead to prolong bloom. Old flowering stems can be trimmed off to the basal foliage using pruners, or they can be snapped off with a sharp thumbnail. Stems can even be simply pulled out of the plant when they have declined enough. Plants need deadleafing if they get too dry over the summer. Evergreen foliage usually holds well over the winter; deadleaf or shear off poor leaves, if needed, in the spring.

OTHER MAINTENANCE: Prefers rich, organic, alkaline, moist soil for best performance. Moist soil conditions helps to keep plants blooming. Well-draining soil is essential for overwintering. Fluctuating winter temperatures causes frost heaving. Plant in spring to establish before winter, and mulch after the ground freezes to moderate winter soil temperatures. Division often is needed every 3 years in the spring. Plants may get woody at the base, lifting the crowns up; top-dress with organic matter to keep crowns in contact with soil. Provide afternoon shade in hot regions, and avoid drought.

Hibiscus moscheutos

Zone: 4–9
Common Name: rose mallow
Family: Malvaceae
Description: large red, white, pink, or bicolored flowers; triangular leaves
Size: 3–8 ft. high; 5 ft. wide
Exposure: full sun or partial shade
Flowering: July to frost

PRUNING: Flowering is similar to that of daylilies in that individual flowers last only one day and then they eventually turn to mush and stick together. Deadheading before this stage keeps the plant's appearance up and may prolong bloom. Take care if deadheading in the evening when the flowers have just folded down as bees seem to enjoy resting in them at this time and may give the deadheader a stinging surprise. Seedheads are attractive and it may be desirable to leave them on the plant later in the season to extend the interest of the plant through the winter. Stems need to be cut down in the spring for new growth. Seeding may be a problem under wet conditions; deadhead regularly during the season and cut stems down for the winter if this is the case. Dead-leafing is needed during the summer if plants dry out.

Plants respond favorably to pruning before flowering in an effort to reduce height and create fuller plants. Some gardeners also do this in an attempt to avoid some early Japanese beetle damage, which can be so prominent on *Hibiscus*. Plants that normally flower at 4 ft. bloomed at 2½ ft. when cut back by one-half in early June when 16 in. tall. Flowering is usually delayed by about 1–2 weeks, depending on the conditions.

OTHER MAINTENANCE: Prefers rich moist soil. Good for wet sites. Although plants can grow tall, stems are strong and so staking is normally not needed. Plants are late to emerge in the spring; do not disturb area. Plants do not need division for many (10 or more) years. Division of woody crown is challenging and is best avoided. Heavy feeders; fertilize annually in the spring. Japanese beetles love *Hibiscus*.

Hosta

Zone: 3–8
Common Name: plantain-lily
Family: Liliaceae
Description: spikes of lavender, purple, or white flowers above green, blue-green, gold, yellow, or variegated leaves
Size: 2–3 in. to 3–4 ft. high; 3–4 in. to 5–6 ft. wide
Exposure: full or partial shade
Flowering: June–July (some forms September–October)

PRUNING: Deadheading of *Hosta* can often improve its appearance. Most hostas are not reblooming, but *Hosta nakaiana* forms are, particularly if deadheaded before seed set. Some hostas will set seed, which can supply food for birds, namely juncos and chickadees, over the winter. Most forms of *H. sieboldiana* and *H. sieboldii*, *H. tokudama*, and *H. ventricosa* usually form seed and are good choices for the bird-watching gardener. Of course, seeds can also mean reseeding. Reseeding may occur some years but not others, depending on the conditions. Plantlets are usually green and may or may not resemble the parent. They are easily pulled out, so they are not normally a nuisance. *Hosta ventricosa* will produce true progeny.

Disbudding, or removing all the flower buds when they appear on a plant, in an attempt to delay flowering will not consistently result in the plant forming new flower buds later. In most cases disbudding will prevent flowering altogether, or only sporadic later bloom will form. Pruning off of flower buds can serve the purpose, though, of creating fuller plants by directing the plant's energy toward vegetative rather than floral growth. This may be desirable for hostas on which the flowers are not very ornamental and take away from the appearance of the foliage or for plants grown solely for foliar effect.

Certain forms of hosta are susceptible to damage from late-spring frosts. If damaged leaves are pruned off and the plants kept moist, they usually will send up new fresh growth without missing a beat. It would be advisable, though, to cover small plants, particularly expensive or unusual ones, if a late frost is predicted, because they may have a hard time recovering from the damage. Dead-leafing may be necessary in the late summer, particularly if plants have gotten dry.

Leaving foliage on hostas over the winter can provide additional protection against cold temperatures. It can also provide cozy hangouts for slugs. The choice is up to the gardener. Hosta grower Van Wade, of Wade and Gatton Nurseries in Ohio, who has a "kajillion" hosta plants (what hosta grower doesn't!), cuts some of his plants down in the autumn and the rest in the spring to spread out the workload. Remember to leave seed-bearing hostas for bird feeding, if desired.

OTHER MAINTENANCE: Best performance is in moist, high-organic, well-draining soil, but these are adaptable plants. Hostas with a thicker and waxier substance to their leaves are often more tolerant of dry soils, but prolonged drought can mean the demise of most forms. Young plants should be mulched for the winter to prevent frost heaving. Van Wade recommends fresh white pine needles, which allow for good air circulation. Avoid mulching with heavy materials as they can lead to crown rot if not removed promptly in the spring.

Hostas generally prefer high-filtered shade with perhaps one-quarter to one-half of the day in morning sun. Hot afternoon sun, particularly in areas with hot summers, will scorch most hostas and should be avoided. Golds and blues prefer bright filtered shade, such as is provided by high overhead trees, for best coloring, but they tolerate heavier shade as well. Green forms such as *Hosta plantaginea* and *H. plantaginea* 'Aphrodite' as well as other fragrant or floriferous forms, although shade tolerant, benefit from morning sun for best flower production. Avoid very deep, dark shaded areas.

Division can be easily accomplished at almost any time of the year by the double-fork method (see Chapter 6) or even by just cutting a pie-shaped section out of the plant. Keep plants moist and shaded, and prune off at least one-third of the foliage if dividing during the warmer months or else plants may flop. Yet, in the spring when the new leaves are still curled is the preferable and most successful time for division. Division is often not needed for many years, perhaps never in some cases.

Slugs and hostas usually go hand-in-hand. It's risky to claim that certain forms are more resistant than others, because some slug will be waiting to prove you wrong. But here goes: hostas with heavier or thicker foliage are usually not as badly damaged, if at all. This may include *Hosta* 'Sum and Substance', *Hosta* 'Sagae' (*H. fluctuans* 'Variegated'), the *H. tokudama* and *H. sieboldiana* groups, and some "big blues," such as 'Big Daddy' and

'Blue Angel'. Also, forms on which the leaves don't come in contact with the soil, such as the vase-shaped *Hosta* 'Krossa Regal', are usually less prone to slugs. Diatomaceous earth is one form of slug control (see Chapter 4 for more suggestions on controls).

Hypericum calycinum
Zone: 5–9
Common Name: St. Johnswort
Family: Clusiaceae
Description: large yellow flowers; evergreen
  leaves
Size: 15–18 in. high; 24 in. wide
Exposure: full sun or partial shade
Flowering: June–August

PRUNING: Plants are evergreen to semi-evergreen, depending on the climate, although leaves are often battered by winter weather. Plants have a tendency to become straggly and twiggy if neglected. They benefit from a shearing down to 6–10 in. every year or two in the early spring to remove winter damage, improve density, and keep vigorous. Removing any crowded, weak, or dead branches at this time is also beneficial.

OTHER MAINTENANCE: A stoloniferous groundcover for dry, sunny or partially shaded locations. Flowering is reduced if the shade is too great. Plants can be invasive and may require sections to be dug out to maintain control every 2–3 years in the spring or autumn. Good for bank stabilization. Benefits from partial shade and moister conditions in southern gardens.

Iberis sempervirens
Zone: 3–9
Common Name: evergreen candytuft
Family: Brassicaceae
Description: white tufts of flowers cover
  entire plant; narrow evergreen leaves
Size: 6–12 in. high; 24 in. wide

Exposure: full sun
Flowering: April–May

PRUNING: Yearly, plants should be cut back by one-half after flowering to keep them full and compact. This can be easily accomplished with hedge shears or by grabbing a handful of stems at a time and cutting with hand pruners. Such pruning takes care of deadheading at the same time. Plants quickly fill in to form an evergreen mound that holds through the growing season and the winter (Plates 92–95). Some damage may occur in severe winters. Prune off damaged sections in the spring, if necessary.

OTHER MAINTENANCE: Well-draining soil is essential to survival, particularly over the winter. A good rock garden perennial. Avoid areas with high winds and strong afternoon sun in the winter if consistent snow cover is not reliable, as plants will quickly desiccate. Mulching with evergreen boughs can help alleviate the damage in such locations. Division is seldom necessary since plants form a subshrub growth habit. Stems may root as they come in contact with the soil; these can be separated from the parent plant and transplanted.

Iris hybrids, bearded
Zone: 3–10
Common Name: bearded iris
Family: Iridaceae
Description: bearded flowers in a variety of
  colors; swordlike flat leaves
Size: 2–4 ft. high; 2 ft. wide
Exposure: full sun
Flowering: June

PRUNING: Deadhead individual dead flowers, not the entire stalk, because new flower buds will open lower on the flower stalk. Old flowers turn to mush and require regular removal to keep plants attractive. When all flowering is finished, cut flower stalk off down to foliage. Leaves are often marred with different foliar diseases after flowering in late June. If plants aren't too badly affected, try selectively pulling off and trimming the worst leaves. If badly affected, which is usually the case, shear all foliage back to about 4–6 in. above the ground. Pull off any brown leaves that have shriveled and died down at the base of the plant. Sheared plants look as though they have had a crew cut. Individual leaves can be cut with hand pruners at different angles to create a slightly more natural look. This method is preferred by some gardeners, but it is more time consuming, and personally I feel that the plants are unattractive under either pruning regime. Nevertheless, the pruned foliage is preferable to the ugly unpruned foliage taking away from the beauty of neighboring perennials. Pruning tools should be disinfected before moving on to other perennials. Dump disease-infected foliage in a pile by itself where it can breakdown—do not compost. Regrowth, if any, can be slow, taking several weeks. The new foliage often is partially infested with disease again by late summer. Cut down all foliage in autumn after killing frosts and clean-up and remove all debris at the base of the plants. Borers can overwinter in old leaves and debris. Again, do not compost clippings.

OTHER MAINTENANCE: Bearded irises are truly a maintenance nightmare—Siberian iris (*Iris sibirica*) is the better alternative. Best planted in a cutting garden setting, or the like, away from the ornamental perennial border. Although large masses are dynamic when in bloom, the unsightly foliage that follows is not worth the initial pleasure. Foliar diseases, borers, and soft rot are all problems. Plant rhizomes high so that they are exposed to the sun in order to reduce the incidence of soft rot. Well-draining soil is also necessary to reduce rot. If rhizome is affected with soft rot, it should be dug out and discarded. Dark streaking in leaves is evidence of borers; prune off leaves and dig

out affected rhizome. Frequent division is needed to keep plants vigorous. Divide after flowering until August. Leave one fan per rhizome. Although most gardeners cut the foliage back when transplanting, some leave it on. The feeling is that the foliage aids in the establishment process, and in flowering for the following season, by providing more food to the rhizome. Taller forms over 30–36 in. usually require staking.

RELATED PLANTS: There are reblooming bearded irises that can repeat bloom anytime from late July until October or November. It's fun to see bearded irises with asters, mums, and pumpkins. Be certain to cut all old flowering stalks to the ground after the initial bloom period for a chance at rebloom. In my experience the foliage does not decline as quickly or as drastically on the reblooming beardeds as compared to other forms. Plants usually don't start to decline until early to mid-August. I simply pull off the poor foliage and trim the tips a bit, not cutting back heavily. Fresh new fans are usually evident under the old ones, and these are the sites of late summer to autumn flower production. Divide frequently to keep strong. Some reblooming forms include: 'Chaste White', 'Golden Encore', 'Immortality', 'Perfume Counter', and 'Royal Summer'. 'Perfume Counter', which I have been particularly enamored of, has purple flowers in June and then flowers again, to the amazement of every visitor, in October, although only lightly. Its foliage holds up much longer than that of others, sometimes by a month or more, often remaining clear into mid-August, at which time I simply pull off damaged leaves and snip off the yellow tips, leaving new interior leaves to be the site of bud production.

Iris sibirica
Zone: 3–9
Common Name: Siberian iris
Family: Iridaceae

Description: white, blue, or purple flowers; straplike leaves
Size: 2–4 ft. high; 2 ft. wide
Exposure: full sun or partial shade
Flowering: May–June

PRUNING: Deadheading doesn't prolong bloom of this beautiful plant, and the smaller deadheads don't distract from the plant like those of the large-flowering bearded iris. The season is extended with the magnificent seed capsules that develop (Plate 97). These hold through the winter and can be cut in the spring and used for dried arrangements. I remove about two-thirds of the old flowering stalks and leave the rest of the deadheads to enjoy. I have found that the plants experience reduced flowering and vigor the following season if all the seedheads are allowed to mature. Reseeding can occur if some pods are allowed to remain. Seedlings are easily removed, and friends love them. Siberian iris develops a nice golden autumn color as well, and the color holds into early winter. Wait until spring to cut the entire plant down.

OTHER MAINTENANCE: Good low-maintenance, multi-season plants. These sturdy irises usually are resistant to the borers and diseases that trouble bearded iris. They are adaptable to a variety of soils. Will tolerate partial shade but will flop if grown in too much shade. These fleshy rooted plants seldom need dividing and in fact resent it, taking a year or longer to fully recover. If you want divisions, it can be performed in the spring if sufficient moisture is provided, though autumn is often the best time to divide.

RELATED PLANTS: *Iris sibirica* 'My Love' is a rebloomer, in the Midwest, that should have all its old flowering stalks cut to the ground before seed set to encourage repeat bloom.

Kniphofia hybrids

Zone: 5–9
Common Name: red-hot poker
Family: Aloeaceae
Description: orange, red, or cream spikes; grasslike foliage
Size: 2–4 ft. (1¼–1½ ft.) high; 3 ft. wide
Exposure: full sun
Flowering: summer (specific time depends on the cultivar)

PRUNING: Diligent deadheading may prolong bloom. If earlier blooming forms are deadheaded, sporadic rebloom may occur later in the season (some reblooming cultivars are listed below). The old flower spike is unattractive anyway and should be removed by cutting it to the ground. The foliage may decline after flowering; if necessary, cut back by one-half to improve the appearance. Do not cut foliage back for the winter. Bundling up the leaves and tying them together over the center of the clump for the winter may help insulate the plant and prevent excess moisture accumulation in the crown, thus possibly improving survivability. Cut back in the spring when all threat of cold weather has passed, to about 3 in. from the ground, avoiding pruning too close to the crown.

OTHER MAINTENANCE: Plants are tender and short-lived due to lack of cold hardiness and death from wet overwintering conditions. Provide good drainage. Mulch around plants for the winter with a fine material such as pine needles to help moderate soil temperatures. Plant and divide in the spring for establishment before winter.

RELATED PLANTS: Some noted rebloomers include *Kniphofia* 'Alcazar', 'Earliest of All', 'Kingstone Flame', and 'Primrose Beauty'. 'Alcazar', 'Earliest of all', and 'Royal Standard' are reputed to be the hardiest cultivars.

Lamium maculatum

Zone: 3–8
Common Name: dead nettle
Family: Lamiaceae
Description: pink hooded flowers; green
    foliage with gray-green spot on midrib
Size: 8–12 in. high; 18–24 in. wide
Exposure: full to partial shade
Flowering: April–June

PRUNING: In midsummer (early July in the
Midwest) plants usually get tatty, especially
if grown in dry conditions. Cut or shear all
foliage and flowering stems back to fresh
basal leaves, which accomplishes deadheading in addition to refreshing the overall appearance. The new growth that develops
remains attractive through the winter. Plants
may not even require additional pruning in
the spring, as winter damage usually is minimal. In cooler northern climates plants may
remain compact without summer cutting
back. *Lamium* will reseed if the deadheads
are not removed, and cultivars may not grow
true to type.

OTHER MAINTENANCE: Vigorous grower,
but not invasive, by spreading roots. Good
groundcover for dry shade once established.
Prefers moist, well-draining conditions.
Divide if needed in spring or autumn.

RELATED PLANTS: Cultivars are preferred
over the species; prune as above.

Lamium maculatum 'Beacon Silver' has
silver leaves with green margins and lavender flowers.

Lamium maculatum 'Shell Pink' is light
pink. One of the longest blooming cultivars.

Lamium maculatum 'White Nancy' has
outstanding near-white foliage and white
flowers.

Lamium galeobdolon 'Variegatum', variegated yellow archangel, should be sheared
back to about 4–6 in. if plants get leggy, or
cut all the way down to new leaves at the

base of the plant if present. More aggressive
than *Lamium maculatum* forms. Should not
be used in the perennial border but as a
groundcover in dry shade.

Lamium galeobdolon 'Hermann's Pride' is
more clump forming and less aggressive
than 'Variegatum'.

Lavandula angustifolia

Zone: 5–9
Common Name: English lavender
Family: Lamiaceae
Description: purple flower spikes; narrow
    silvery fragrant leaves
Size: 12–24 in. high; 24 in. wide
Exposure: full sun
Flowering: June–July

PRUNING: Lavender can be deadheaded
after the first bloom period for a smaller
second bloom later in the summer. Individual old flowering stems can be removed one-
by-one or a handful at a time with pruners.
Hedge shears work best though, and the
plant can be shaped a bit at the same time.
The old stems from the second bloom phase
can be left on and then removed with spring
pruning, or if neatness is the priority they
can be cut off after flowering. The species
may reseed under certain conditions. Avoid
heavy pruning after late August so that
plants are able to harden before winter. Do
not prune plants for the winter. Winter-
damaged tips need to be sheared off annually. Wait to prune until new growth has
broken from the old stems in the spring,
sometimes as late as early June (Plate 98).
Plants can be shaped at this time as well.
Because lavender breaks from the old stems
it is really more a subshrub than a herbaceous
perennial. Many beginning gardeners lose
their lavender plants by cutting them completely down in the autumn or early spring
as they do to their herbaceous perennials.

Lavender has a tendency to grow straggly with age. Shear plants back heavily every 2–3 years in the spring to about 6–8 in. to maintain a more compact, vigorous plant. Do not cut low into old, nonviable wood. Neglected plants may develop thick woody stems with small bunches of foliage at the tips that topple to the ground. Plants left unpruned for many years usually cannot be restored to their former appearance. Lavender responds so well to shearing that it is often used as a low hedge. In such situations, shear and shape plants annually in the spring. Shaping may be needed again after the first bloom period.

OTHER MAINTENANCE: Plants require well-draining soil, especially to ensure survival over the winter. Losses can occur in severe winters without consistent snow cover. Heavy soils can exaggerate the problem by encouraging soft growth, which is more sensitive to winter injury. Alkaline conditions are preferable. Able to withstand dry conditions for extended periods once established. Susceptible to fourlined plant bug damage.

Leucanthemum ×superbum (Chrysanthemum ×superbum)

Zone: 5–9
Common Name: shasta daisy
Family: Asteraceae
Description: white daisy flowerheads; narrow toothed leaves
Size: 2–3 ft. high; 2 ft. wide
Exposure: full sun
Flowering: June–July

PRUNING: Deadheading can prolong bloom to amazing lengths, particularly on first-year plants, which often will flower from June until frost. Deadhead to lateral flower buds, and after all flowering from lateral buds is finished and new basal growth is developing, cut plants down to basal growth. Sporadic rebloom may occur, though the flowers are usually smaller in size and numbers. The nice, deep green basal growth looks great in the autumn garden and holds up well through winter. Shasta daisies are often short-lived. According to some authorities, one reason for the short life span may be that shasta daisies flower themselves to exhaustion. By cutting the plants down (as described above) in early September or before, vegetative growth is stimulated, and plants can form buds for next year's shoots, possibly extending the plant's life.

Taller forms can be pinched or cut back to produce shorter, more compact plants that don't require staking and flower slightly later. This pruning can also be used to layer a planting (or an individual plant), effectively hiding the bare stems of taller unpruned daisies.

OTHER MAINTENANCE: Shasta daisies need rich, moist but well-draining soil and frequent division (every 2–3 years) to maintain vigor. Division may be done with the double-fork method. Good winter drainage is essential for survival. Avoid prolonged drought. They are heavy feeders and benefit from a light spring fertilizer and possibly a liquid feed again in early summer. Good air circulation is helpful. Taller forms require staking—don't let them fool you. Sometimes they look like they're doing well, nice and upright, and then a good summer storm comes along and knocks them over on their sides. Staking at this point resembles an unmerciful lynching. I know, I've been fooled (as my experience described in Chapter 5 attests). Often short-lived, not reliably hardy in zone 5. Do not plant in the autumn.

RELATED PLANTS: *Leucanthemum ×superbum* 'Alaska' is an old-fashioned hardy form (to zone 4) that seems to hold up longer than most cultivars before division is needed (4–5 years). Alaska daisies pinched in late May flowered at 18–20 in. and 1 week later than the 3-ft.-tall unpruned plants (Plate 99). Plants cut back by about one-third at the same time had a similar bloom time and mature height as the pinched plants, but growth was not as full or vigorous as that on pinched plants. I'm not sure why there were such differences, but pinching seems to be the more desirable technique at this point. Requires staking if not pinched.

Leucanthemum ×superbum 'Becky' has an outstanding thick substance to its leaves and stems. It is a 3-ft.-tall, self-supporting form. Later flowering, normally from July to October with deadheading. Good heat tolerance for the South.

Leucanthemum ×superbum 'Silver Princess', a charming dwarf form (12 in.), is a flowering machine. Cutting down in September and annual division may help to keep it strong.

Leucanthemum ×superbum 'Switzerland' grows to about 30 in. and holds up well even in storms. Long bloom period.

Leucanthemum ×superbum 'T. E. Killen' has thick, sturdy stems at 24–30 in. and stands well.

Liatris spicata

Zone: 3–9
Common Name: spike gayfeather
Family: Asteraceae
Description: spikes of violet, purple, or white flowers; linear leaves
Size: 2–3 ft. (6–10 in.) high; 2 ft. wide
Exposure: full sun
Flowering: July–August

PRUNING: Deadheading often induces rebloom into August and September. The flowers open from the bottom of the spike to the top. Deadhead plants by cutting the entire spike down to the basal foliage when about 70% of the flowering is finished. Deadheading by cutting the spike midway may produce several smaller (6 in.) spikes, which can be useful for small flower arrangements. I find the seedheads, which turn fluffy and brown on red-tinted stems, to be interesting

in the autumn and winter, and so I usually elect to leave them up on shorter growing cultivars. They are also attractive to birds. Occasional seeding may occur.

Further testing should be done to determine the effects of cutting plants back before flowering for height reduction; results have been inconsistent to date. Branching of the flowering spike can occur, resulting in anywhere from 2 to 10 shorter branches from one cut stem; in other cases there was no branching and failure to flower. It appears that the taller the plant is when cut back, the more branches that break, possibly due to the greater number of breaking points on a taller stem. Plants cut back by one-half when 12 in. tall formed 2 branches; those cut back when 2½ ft. tall formed up to 10 branches (Plate 100). It is believed that the vigor of the plant may have a significant impact on the results of such pruning, with young strong plants responding more favorably.

OTHER MAINTENANCE: Well-draining soil, particularly over the winter, is critical to survival. Tolerant to drought. Plants may need division after the fourth or fifth year. Usually will require staking.

RELATED PLANTS: *Liatris spicata* 'Kobold' is an outstanding, more compact form (2–2½ ft.) of choice that doesn't require staking. Plants cut back by one-half in early June when 15 in. tall failed to flower.

Ligularia dentata

Zone: 4–8
Common Name: bigleaf ligularia
Family: Asteraceae
Description: yellow-orange daisy-like flowerheads; large rounded leathery leaves
Size: 3–4 ft. (3 ft.) high; 4 ft. wide
Exposure: full to partial shade
Flowering: July–September

PRUNING: Deadheading doesn't seem to do much to prolong the bloom of this perennial, but some gardeners may elect to remove the spent flowers so they don't detract from the attractive foliage. *Ligularia* often is grown solely for the lovely tropical feel provided by the foliage. Prune off flower buds if desired. Personally, I like the brown heads that develop, and it usually comes late in the season when brown is a more accepted part of the perennial garden. They also hold well for the better part of the winter and are attractive to the golden finches. The foliage often turns to mush, so I normally cut it off before winter. Deadleafing is necessary if plants dry out.

OTHER MAINTENANCE: Moist to wet conditions are necessary to keep the leaves from wilting in midday heat. Even in wet conditions, high summer temperatures can cause wilting. One of the few perennials that should be "bagged" to keep moisture around the roots. After digging the hole for the plant, line it with a plastic garbage bag, poke a couple of holes in the bottom of the bag, backfill with high-organic soil, and plant. This procedure improves the success rate with *Ligularia* even with short periods of dry conditions. Plants seldom require division; if desired, perform in the spring. Favored by slugs.

RELATED PLANTS: *Ligularia dentata* 'Dark Beauty' is an outstanding selection with new foliage that is darker purple than that of the species or other cultivars. Good heat tolerance.

Ligularia dentata 'Desdemona' has a purple lower leaf surface and stem. Good heat tolerance.

Ligularia stenocephala 'The Rocket' offers deadheads that are attractive to birds, but in some cases deadheads left on the plant may cause decline of the old foliage. If deadheads are removed, new purple-tinted leaves emerge and the old foliage holds nicely for the remainder of the season.

Limonium latifolium

Zone: 3–9
Common Name: sea lavender
Family: Plumbaginaceae
Description: clouds of tiny violet flowers above narrow, leathery basal leaves
Size: 24–30 in. (8 in.) high; 30 in. wide
Exposure: full sun
Flowering: July–August

PRUNING: Deadheading can prolong bloom, but plants have a long season of interest whether deadheaded or not. The highly branched flowering stems are just as attractive after the tiny flowers fall, and they are good for dried arrangements or, better still, left as a "dried arrangement" on the plant in the garden. They hold well into early winter but often snap off in heavy storms in later winter. The foliage is evergreen to semi-evergreen. Do not prune for the winter. Plants can be cleaned up in the spring, or new growth normally will fill in quickly to hide any old damaged foliage.

OTHER MAINTENANCE: Well-draining soil is essential to survival. Tolerant of drought and salt. Staking is usually not necessary except in heavy or overly rich soils. Resents division; allow clumps to remain undisturbed. Space plants at least 24 in. apart to allow for good air circulation and reduce the chance of crown and root rot.

Linaria purpurea

Zone: 5–9
Common Name: purple toadflax
Family: Scrophulariaceae
Description: purple or pink snapdragon-like flowers; narrow blue-green leaves
Size: 3 ft. high; 1¼–1½ ft. wide
Exposure: full sun to partial shade
Flowering: June–October

PRUNING: Deadheading can prolong bloom for most of the season. *Linaria* has a tendency to flop onto its neighbors. Although flopping is usually done gracefully, cutting plants back after flowering by about one-half to lateral flowering branches can help curb this habit. Pinching or cutting back plants in early May before flowering can also produce shorter, more compact plants with heavier branching but smaller and, in my opinion, less attractive flowers. If flowering stems decline, cut them down to new foliage that develops at the base of the plant. Toadflax can seed freely—allowing some seeding to occur is a good idea to ensure constancy of this short-lived perennial in the garden. Excess seedlings are easily removed.

OTHER MAINTENANCE: Plants prefer an infertile, fairly dry soil. Avoid wet conditions, particularly over the winter. Allow other plants to support flopping toadflax, or use light staking to help maintain the natural grace of the plant. Doesn't transplant well.

RELATED PLANTS: *Linaria purpurea* 'Canon Went' is a pink-flowered form. Seedlings usually come true if parent plant was not planted along with the straight species.

Linum perenne

Zone: 5–8
Common Name: perennial flax
Family: Linaceae
Description: sky-blue flowers; small narrow leaves
Size: 18–24 in. high; 12 in. wide
Exposure: full sun
Flowering: May–August

PRUNING: Each individual flower lasts only one day and the old flower petals drop neatly off the plant. Young plants may bloom for a long period without pruning. With age, plants usually get straggly by midsummer, in which case they can be sheared back at this time by one-half to two-thirds for production of new feathery growth and often a smaller rebloom. If plants open up again they may need another lighter (by one-third) shearing. Keep plants moist after pruning, particularly in hot regions, for better regeneration of foliage. Perennial flax may seed strongly; allowing some seeding can ensure permanence of this short-lived perennial in the garden. If seed is mature when plants are cut back, sprinkle some seeds onto the soil in the desired location to obtain seedlings for the following year.

Shearing plants before flowering by one-half in early May can help produce fuller plants. This is useful for newly planted *Linum* as well, which are often thin and spindly.

OTHER MAINTENANCE: Avoid poorly drained soil, which will shorten the life of flax. Prefers alkaline, dry soils. Avoid division of the coarse and sparse roots due to poor success. Short-lived.

Liriope spicata

Zone: 4–10
Common Name: creeping lilyturf
Family: Liliaceae
Description: small pale violet to white flowers; grasslike leaves; blue-black fruit
Size: 8–12 in. high groundcover
Exposure: full sun or shade
Flowering: August

PRUNING: Do not deadhead; the blue-black berry-like fruit that follow the flowers are attractive and can persist into early winter. Foliage is evergreen into midwinter and usually browned by early spring. Shear down or mow to the ground in spring for fresh new growth.

OTHER MAINTENANCE: This is a tough, low-maintenance, adaptable plant that can be used as a groundcover, as well as for erosion control in dry shady areas. Tolerates root competition from trees. Can be planted in the sun, but scorching of the foliage may occur, particularly in southern regions. Stoloniferous habit is too invasive for the perennial border—if planted in such a site creeping lilyturf will quickly turn into a high-maintenance perennial! Divide in the spring if needed.

Lobelia cardinalis

Zone: 3–9
Common Name: cardinal flower
Family: Campanulaceae
Description: bright red flower spikes; narrow foliage
Size: 3–4 ft. high; 2 ft. wide
Exposure: partial shade
Flowering: July–September

PRUNING: Deadheading can improve the overall appearance of the plant and may result in some sporadic rebloom. Do allow at least some of the flowering spikes to produce, and then drop, seed before deadheading to ensure seedlings of this short-lived perennial. Plants can also be pinched or cut back before flowering to produce more compact plants. Flowers of pruned plants usually will be more numerous but smaller and slightly delayed, depending on when the plants are pruned.

OTHER MAINTENANCE: Getting the plants through the winter is the trick. Leaving the stems on the plant for the winter, as in nature, may be beneficial for overwintering. Although native to wet sites, cardinal flower in a garden setting seems to do best in moist, high-organic soil that doesn't stay overly wet in the winter. Also benefits from a light mulch for the winter, although be careful because too much mulch can kill the plants. Remove mulch as soon as the soil warms in the spring to prevent losses. Self-sown seed-lings are the surest bet for longevity in the garden. Division can be accomplished by separating a side rosette from the parent plant in the early autumn. Dividing and moving the clump every 2–3 years can increase vigor.

RELATED PLANTS: *Lobelia siphilitica*, great blue lobelia, can be pruned as above, although some gardeners prefer to just pinch plants in early July. David Voyles of Wild-flower Farms gets good results with cutting back by one-half when 4 in. tall and again when 16 in. tall.

   Lobelia ×speciosa 'Queen Victoria' cut back by one-half in mid-June when 2 ft. tall flowered at approximately 2½ ft. in mid-August. Plants normally reach 4–5 ft. tall. The smaller flowers produced with pruning are nice for smaller cut flower arrangements (see Plate 56).

Lupinus hybrids

Zone: 4–6
Common Name: lupine
Family: Fabaceae
Description: spiked flowers in various colors; palmately compound leaves
Size: 3–4 ft. high; 1½–2 ft. wide
Exposure: full sun or partial shade
Flowering: June–July

PRUNING: Deadheading will prolong bloom and help prevent seeding. Seedlings are usually not true to type, but some interesting forms may be produced. After the initial flowering, usually sometime in mid- to late July, cut plants down to about 6 in. or down to the new basal leaves that have developed. Plants may produce sporadic rebloom. Cutting back is also an effective control against aphids, which often trouble lupines. Plants usually do not need to be cut back again until spring, when removing winter damage is necessary.

OTHER MAINTENANCE: A high-maintenance, short-lived perennial. Requires rich, high-organic, acidic, well-draining soil and cool summer temperatures for best performance. Provide afternoon shade in hot regions. Requires winter mulch in northern gardens. May require staking. Inoculating the roots with a legume inoculant before planting seems to improve performance. Divide by removing side shoots in the spring without lifting the whole plant. Yellow-flowered forms may be more tender.

Lychnis coronaria

Zone: 4–8
Common Name: rose campion
Family: Caryophyllaceae
Description: vivid magenta flowers; fuzzy
  gray stems and leaves
Size: 2–3 ft. high; 1½ ft. wide
Exposure: full sun
Flowering: June–July

PRUNING: Regular deadheading, every week or so through July and August, can prolong bloom by several weeks or more. Deadheading each small individual seedhead to a new lateral flower or bud is a tedious job. Snipping with sharp pruning scissors and just letting the deadheads drop to the ground appears to be the most efficient method. Deadheading before seed sets can prevent prolific reseeding. Plants are so narrow, though, that seedlings pop up along walks and between plants without much harm in large gardens, and they add a spontaneous charm. My son Zachary fell in love with this plant when he was two years old, and rose campion continues to be his favorite. He saved it from the compost pile, inspiring in me a whole new attitude toward the plant, and hence allowing innumerable seedlings to make a home in all our perennial gardens (Plate 101). Seeding ensures this short-lived plant's presence in the garden, and one approach to prevent overabundance is to allow only a few of the stems to seed, or leave up only some of the late flowers to set seed. But gardeners with limited space may still find them imposing.

Cutting the old flowering stems down to the fuzzy basal leaves before seed set, and thus preventing seeding, may prolong the life of the existing plant in the garden. These normally biennial plants may act more perennial in nature if treated in this way. Plants can be deadheaded and then cut down, or they can be cut down after the majority of the initial flowering is completed, skipping the arduous task of deadheading but also missing the prolonged bloom. If plants are cut down without deadheading, it is usually performed in late July. Plants may send up sporadic rebloom after being cut back, but not always.

Rose campion responds well to pinching or cutting back before flowering to reduce height and create more compact and attractive plants. Plants cut back by one-half when 15 in. tall in early June, while in bud, flowered at 2 ft. rather than 3 ft. and were strong even in partial shade. Flowering was delayed by 2–3 weeks. Plants pinched at 6 in. tall were also shorter and sturdier but with no flower delay.

Periodic deadleafing may be needed to clean-up plants if summer humidity and moisture are high. The gray basal foliage on the plants holds well into winter. Cutting off winter-damaged leaves in early spring is often necessary to improve the overall appearance of the plant.

OTHER MAINTENANCE: Well-draining soil, particularly over the winter, is key to preventing death from rotting. Clumps often open up in the center if the soil is too heavy. Frequent division is necessary to maintain vigor. A short-lived perennial.

Lythrum salicaria

Zone: 3–9
Common Name: purple loosestrife
Family: Lythraceae
Description: pink spiked flowers; narrow
  leaves
Size: 3–5 ft. high; 2–3 ft. wide
Exposure: full sun
Flowering: June–August

PRUNING: The straight species is a nuisance seeder into waterways and has been banned in several states. Although the cultivars are self-sterile, they may cross-pollinate with other cultivars or with wild forms. If *Lythrum salicaria* plants are to be grown at all, a cultivar should be selected and grown exclusively of other cultivars in the garden. Pruning to prevent seed set is essential. Plant away from natural waterways.

Plants should be deadheaded to prevent seed set, or sheared to the ground after flowering. Shearing after flowering not only ensures no reseeding, but it also encourages lush low plants behind which tall, later blooming perennials can be planted (Plate 102). Shearing to the ground is also helpful for plants on which the foliage is damaged by Japanese beetles or grasshoppers. Hedge shears can be used for both types of pruning. Young plants have a prolonged bloom if they are first deadheaded to lateral flower buds (with hand pruners) and then sheared. Plants sheared to the ground in late July or early August fill in nicely in about 2–3 weeks and normally hold longer into the autumn than unsheared plants. Keep plants moist after pruning. Rebloom may occur under certain conditions. Deadhead again when all reflowering is finished. Plants deadheaded in July and then cut down, due to tatty foliage, in mid-September did not regrow before winter.

Young, vigorously growing plants have been shown to respond well to pruning before flowering to delay bloom. Older, woodier plants may not have the same response—

seven-year-old plants cut back by one-half when in tight bud in early July failed to flower. Cutting older plants back earlier in the season, however, before bud set (mid-May), may produce desirable results.

The skeleton of *Lythrum* stems can be interesting over the winter, looking like a deciduous shrub because of its woody nature. Cut down in early spring before new growth begins.

OTHER MAINTENANCE: Good plants for wet soils. Avoid prolonged drought. Plants are tolerant of heat and humidity. Woody rootstock can be hard to divide; attempt in the spring every 5–6 years if flowering has declined.

Macleaya cordata

Zone: 3–8
Common Name: plume poppy
Family: Papaveraceae
Description: creamy plumes; large lobed
  leaves with gray undersides
Size: 6–10 ft. high; 6 ft. wide
Exposure: full sun
Flowering: July–August

PRUNING: Deadhead to lateral buds to prolong bloom and prevent abundant reseeding. Plants can be cut back by one-half in May for shorter, more compact growth. Cutting back later may delay flowering. Flowers tend to be smaller on pruned plants. New growth may be damaged by late frost, in which case it should be pruned off in the spring to make room for fresh foliage.

OTHER MAINTENANCE: Plants are high maintenance due to their extremely invasive root system. Avoid rich soil and shade, which can prompt even more aggressive behavior. Too invasive to be planted amongst other perennials. Best given a bed of its own to take over. Requires division in spring every 2–3 years to control spread. Staking not usually required.

Malva alcea 'Fastigiata'

Zone: 4–8
Common Name: upright hollyhock mallow
Family: Malvaceae
Description: pink hollyhock-like flowers;
    palmate deep green leaves
Size: 2–3 ft. high; 1½ ft. wide
Exposure: full sun to partial shade
Flowering: June–October

PRUNING: Deadheading plants can prolong bloom into mid-October. The brown capsules that develop after flowering detract from the plant anyway and are best removed. Deadhead to a lateral leaf after the entire cluster of flowers is finished blooming. The lateral leaves are the site of new bud formation. Deadheading prevents plants from reseeding to weedy proportions, but allowing a few capsules to mature and drop seed will ensure permanence of hollyhock mallow in the garden, as individual plants are often short-lived. Another approach that may be taken to try to prolong the life of the individual plant is to prevent seed set completely with deadheading, and then cutting down to fresh basal growth if the old flowering stems start to decline. Plants should also be cut down to basal foliage if they topple in late summer, or if the foliage is badly damaged by Japanese beetles or foliar diseases.

Plants respond well to pinching or cutting back to produce fuller plants. Pinching plants in early May can produce shorter but wider mounded plants. They will spread out a bit, reaching about 3 ft. in width and 1½ ft. in height. Pinching new plants at planting in the spring is advisable if shorter, wider plants is the desired result. If stems look weak, or if they open up, plants may benefit from an additional pinching or cutting back of the tips in early summer to get into form. Plants pinched in early May and then cut back by about 6 in. in mid-June were 2 ft. rather than 3 ft. wide and were sturdier than plants pinched only once in May. The species

form of hollyhock mallow (*Malva alcea*) also benefits from such treatment.

If plants flower into the autumn, cut back to low basal foliage after several frosts to reduce seeding over the winter.

OTHER MAINTENANCE: Short-lived, high-maintenance plants. Well-draining soil is necessary to ensure survival. Drought tolerant. Prefers alkaline pH, although adaptable. May require staking, particularly if given partial shade or if not pinched to control height. Requires frequent division, in the spring or autumn, to maintain vigor. Subject to Japanese beetles and a variety of other pests and diseases in southern regions, although it seems a bit more resistant in northern gardens.

RELATED PLANTS: *Althaea zebrina*—the nomenclature is unclear about this plant, but this is the name under which it is sold. Plants should be pinched in early spring as for upright hollyhock mallow to reduce flopping. Deadheading is critical to reduce prolific seeding, but it is a tedious job as new flowers are produced all along the stem close to where dead flowers are located. Sharp pruning scissors are needed. Better still, cut all old flowering stems down to about 8–10 in. after most of the initial flowering is finished but before seeds drop. Young or vigorously growing plants cut back in this way will regrow to approximately full size and will rebloom as in the first bloom period, flowering into mid-October (Plate 103). If you get lazy in this next bloom period and forget to deadhead, numerous seedlings in the spring will serve as a painful reminder.

Monarda didyma

Zone: 4–9
Common Name: beebalm
Family: Lamiaceae
Description: scarlet, violet, white, or pink
    flowers; squared stems

Size: 2–4 ft. high; 4 ft. wide
Exposure: full sun
Flowering: June–July

PRUNING: Deadheading can prolong bloom, particularly on young or vigorously growing plants. Older plants may not produce much rebloom, if any, with deadheading. Seeding may occur if plant aren't deadheaded, although in most cases this is minimal. Deadhead back to lateral flower buds. The plants may be infected with mildew after flowering is finished, and the foliage becomes unsightly. If this is the case, cut down to the new clean foliage developing at the base of the plants. The new foliage usually will stay low, about 6–8 in., for the rest of the season. Discard diseased foliage, and do not compost.

Cutting back once or twice before flowering encourages more compact growth and delayed flowering. Plants cut back by one-half in early May when approximately 12 in. tall flower about 1½–2 weeks later than unpruned plants and at 3 ft. rather than 3½ ft. If plants pruned in early May start to look spindly by mid-May, cutting them back again by about one-third can delay flowering by about 3 weeks and reduce the height to 2½ ft. (Plate 104). The number of flowers may be slightly less on plants pruned twice. This pruning can foster fresh flowers of beebalm into mid-August, rather than being finished at the end of July. Perhaps even more important is that the delay in flowering also means a delay in foliage decline. Since the foliage normally declines after flowering, plants that flower earlier also have tatty foliage earlier than plants that flower later (Plate 105). Thinning stems of beebalm can help reduce the incidence of powdery mildew (see Figure 11-2).

OTHER MAINTENANCE: Beebalms are wide-spreading plants due to rhizomes that can fill a 4 ft. × 4 ft. area. They are easily pulled out, but it is better to plant them singularly rather than in groups in most gardens. Highly prone to mildew. Select resis-tant cultivars for best performance (see below), although even these can develop some infection in years when the conditions are favorable for mildew. Provide good air circulation and avoid overly dry soil. Divide every 2–3 years to control spread and to keep plants strong. Division also prevents a hole from developing in the center of the clump.

RELATED PLANTS: The following *Monarda* cultivars are more resistant to or only slightly affected by powdery mildew: 'Blaustrumpf' ('Blue Stocking'), 'Colrain Red', 'Gardenview Scarlet', 'Marshall's Delight', 'Sunset', and 'Violet Queen'.

Nepeta ×faassenii 'Six Hills Giant'

Zone: 3–8
Common Name: six hills giant catmint
Family: Lamiaceae
Description: lavender-blue flowers; gray-green leaves
Size: 3 ft. high; 3 ft. wide
Exposure: full sun
Flowering: June–August

PRUNING: Deadheading doesn't seem to do much to prolong bloom on this catmint. Snipping off the old flowering stems can improve the appearance of the plant, though. Plants are sterile, so reseeding does not occur. Shearing down the foliage is not as critical with this catmint as with others, because this one doesn't decline to the degree that the others can. In my experience, plants may turn a bit yellowish in certain years and may open in the center with heavy rains, but normally not severely. It can be sheared and shaped after flowering, if desired, to keep it from falling over other perennials, or to induce lush new foliage. If sheared back by about two-thirds after flowering, plants stay more compact and the new growth holds the strong gray-green color. Often rebloom will occur, but not always, depending on the vigor of the plant and the conditions for the season. Plants look rough in the winter. Pruning after several killing frosts is advisable.

OTHER MAINTENANCE: Easy to grow. Requires average well-draining soil. Division is seldom required, but it can be performed in the spring.

Nepeta mussinii

Zone: 3–8
Common Name: Persian catmint
Family: Lamiaceae
Description: small lavender-blue flowers; gray-green leaves
Size: 18–24 in. high; 24 in. wide
Exposure: full sun
Flowering: June–July

PRUNING: As with the previous plant, deadheading doesn't do much to prolong bloom on this perennial. It is better to simply shear plants back by about two-thirds after flowering for lush new growth and sporadic rebloom. This shearing accomplishes deadheading and controls sprawling stems and declining foliage. Reseeding can occur, in large numbers in some cases, if plants aren't cut back before seed set. Not very attractive over the winter; cutting back after several killing frosts may be desirable.

OTHER MAINTENANCE: Easily grown in average well-draining soil. Some gardeners like to prop up the sprawling stems a bit. Seldom needs division, but it can be done in the spring if desired.

RELATED PLANTS: *Nepeta sibirica* 'Souvenir d'Andre Chaudron' can be cut back by one-half in early June, or when about 2 ft. tall (plants may be in tight bud), for fuller, more compact growth and a 3- to 4-week delay in flowering (Plate 106). Pruned plants flower into August, while unpruned plants are usually finished blooming in mid-July. Cutting plants back before early June will not produce such a delay in bloom. Deadhead plants to lateral flowering buds and then cut down to fresh new basal foliage after all flowering is completed.

Oenothera fruticosa subsp. glauca (Oenothera tetragona)

Zone: 3–7
Common Name: sundrop
Family: Onagraceae
Description: lemon-yellow flowers; narrow green leaves
Size: 2 ft. high; 1 ft. wide
Exposure: full sun
Flowering: May–June

PRUNING: Deadheads fall neatly from the plant. Plants can be sheared back by about one-third and shaped after flowering to create a nice form in the garden. If foliage should decline, cut plants down to low evergreen rosette. Do not prune again for the winter.

OTHER MAINTENANCE: Well-draining soil is essential to survival. Sundrop is tolerant of poor dry soil. Often short-lived. Divide in the spring or early autumn every 4–5 years.

RELATED PLANTS: *Oenothera speciosa* 'Rosea', rosy evening primrose, will have prolonged bloom for most of the summer if deadheaded. Stoloniferous rootstock can be invasive.

Onopordum nervosum (Onopordum acanthium)

Zone: 5–8
Common Name: scotch thistle
Family: Asteraceae
Description: pale purple thistlelike flowerheads; silvery thistlelike leaves
Size: 6–8 ft. high; 3–4 ft. wide
Exposure: full sun
Flowering: June–July

PRUNING: Most of the old flowers should be deadheaded since they detract from the new flowers and produce an overabundant amount of seedlings. Leave just a few dead-heads on the plants to mature and drop seed to ensure constancy of scotch thistle in the garden. It is a short-lived biennial and reseeding is the most reliable approach to prolonging the species's existence. After some seeding has occurred, cut plants down to basal foliage.

OTHER MAINTENANCE: Wet or poorly drained soil is fatal. Requires very dry, grav-elly, hot locations for best performance. Give plenty of space wherever it is planted.

Paeonia hybrids

Zone: 3–8
Common Name: peony
Family: Paeoniaceae
Description: pink, coral, white, or red
   flowers; coarse lobed dark green leaves
Size: 3 ft. high; 3 ft. wide
Exposure: full sun
Flowering: May–June

PRUNING: Deadheading peonies will not prolong bloom, but it will greatly enhance the appearance of the plant, since in most cases, particularly on double forms, the old flowers are so unattractive. Red-flowered peonies are particularly susceptible to dis-ease and should be deadheaded immediately as flowers fade to reduce the chance of dis-ease affecting the decaying flower and enter-ing the stem. The foliage on many forms becomes unsightly with the heat of August (Plate 109) as plants are starting to form eyes at that time and don't have much strength for the bush. It is best for the health of the plant to leave the foliage on the plant as long as possible, even if it's unattractive, so that the foliage can continue to perform photo-synthesis and provide food reserves. Peony experts recommend leaving foliage unpruned until after the first of September in zones 3, 4, and upper zone 5; leave until the end of September in the rest of zone 5. Gardeners in zones 6, 7, and warmer areas should try to leave the foliage until early October.

Peonies are subject to a host of diseases, particularly botrytis. Remove any infected leaves or buds. Plants that were not cut back in the late summer or autumn should be cut down for the winter to remove possible sources of infection for the following spring. Clean-up any debris from around the base of the plant. Anytime plants are cut down or dead leaves are removed, the clippings must be discarded—do not compost. (See Chapter 4 for more information on diseases.)

Peonies respond to disbudding. Removing the large terminal flower bud results in smal-ler flowers being produced by the plants. Often plants that are treated in this way will not require staking due to the decreased weight from the removal of the large termi-nal flower. Some gardeners elect to remove the smaller lateral flower buds to increase the size of the terminal flower.

OTHER MAINTENANCE: Deep, rich, well-draining, alkaline soil is preferred. Plant from September to October in the North and October to November in the South. Peonies planted in November should be mulched. Be sure to not plant the eyes more than about 2 in. below the soil surface in the North, or else flowering may not occur; planting at soil level is recommended for southern gardens. It usually takes 2–3 years for the plants to become completely established. Some other reasons peonies may fail to flower include too much shade, competition from tree roots, too much nitrogen, or late-spring frosts (or winter cold). Double forms need to be staked, and peony rings are best for this. Cool and wet spring weather can cause leggy growth, and thus staking may be necessary even on lower growing forms. Plants go for eons without division. If desired, divide peonies in late summer, leaving 3–5 eyes per division (see Figure 6-3). Mulch newly planted peonies to prevent frost heaving.

RELATED PLANTS: *Paeonia* cultivars such as 'Nice Gal' (Plates 107–108), 'Snow Swan', and 'Mister Ed' have foliage that usually holds up well through the season and may take on interesting autumn tones. 'Nice Gal', 'Vivid Rose', and the Bridal Series are examples of some lower growing forms that generally don't need staking. Consult a good peony book (such as *Peonies* by Allan Rogers, Timber Press, 1995) for more details. *Paeonia tenuifolia*, fernleaf peony, should be deadheaded immediately after flowering to reduce chance of disease. This applies both to the species and its many cultivars.

Papaver orientale

Zone: 3–7
Common Name: oriental poppy
Family: Papaveraceae
Description: large red, orange, pink, white, or salmon flowers; large coarse leaves
Size: 2–4 ft. high; 2 ft. wide
Exposure: full sun
Flowering: May–June

PRUNING: Poppies have outstanding seed capsules that extend the season of interest of this perennial, and deadheading doesn't do much to prolong bloom. Some gardeners have success with cutting the old foliage and flowering stems to the ground immediately after flowering to encourage new but smaller growth that remains to fill the space through the summer. Keep plants moist after cutting back. This pruning does not always work, however, and a hole may remain until the foliage returns in late summer. If not cut down immediately after flowering, the foliage declines over time, usually by the end of July, and should be cut down (or pulled off by hand) at this point. The new leaves that return in the late summer or autumn should

be left for the winter. The new foliage may serve as a living mulch and help insulate the crown from extreme temperature. The leaves often stay green through the winter and into spring, depending on the conditions. If the foliage does suffer winter injury, the new spring growth that follows quickly covers it.

OTHER MAINTENANCE: Well-draining soil is essential for survival. Mulch first-year plants. Plant or divide in August or September. Division generally is not needed for about 6 years or more. The plant's fleshy rooted taproot can make it a challenge to transplant. Oriental poppy is long-lived.

RELATED PLANTS: *Papaver nudicaule*, Iceland poppy, is a short-lived perennial that acts almost biennial in nature. Deadheading to prevent seed set and cutting down immediately after flowering may help to extend the life of individual plants.

Patrinia scabiosifolia

Zone: 4–9
Common Name: patrinia
Family: Valerianaceae
Description: clusters of tiny yellow flowers; pinnately divided leaves
Size: 3–6 ft. (1 ft.) high; 2 ft. wide
Exposure: full sun or partial shade
Flowering: August–September

PRUNING: Deadhead for prolonged bloom and to reduce abundant seeding. When flowering is finished, but before seed sets, cut stems down to basal foliage. Leave basal foliage for the winter.

OTHER MAINTENANCE: Provide rich, well-draining soil for best performance. I have had trouble establishing *Patrinia* after several attempts in my gardens and in clients' gardens—perhaps it has to do with the taproots. Plants are supposedly long-lived once established and seldom need division.

Penstemon barbatus

Zone: 3–8
Common Name: penstemon
Family: Scrophulariaceae
Description: tubular pink or scarlet flowers;
    low narrow leaves
Size: 2–3 ft. (²⁄₃ ft.) high; 1–1½ ft. wide
Exposure: full sun
Flowering: June–July

PRUNING: Deadhead to lateral flowers or
buds to prolong bloom. The overall appearance of the plant is enhanced by cutting back
old flowering stems to the basal foliage. The
low foliage remains evergreen over the winter and usually stays nice into spring. Pinching plants when they are 12–15 in. tall will
produce more compact, fuller growth.

OTHER MAINTENANCE: Survival depends
heavily on well-draining soil. Drought tolerant. May require mulching in winter for
extra protection. *Penstemon barbatus* is
short-lived, usually because of moisture
problems or a variety of foliar diseases.
Requires frequent division, about every 3
years in the spring.

RELATED PLANTS: *Penstemon digitalis*, foxglove penstemon, should be deadheaded to a
lateral leaf after flowering and then cut down
to new basal growth as old stems decline.
This species is longer lived and much hardier
than *P. barbatus*. It is also tolerant of wetter
soil conditions. The species of choice for the
lower maintenance garden.

   Penstemon digitalis 'Husker's Red' has
outstanding scarlet foliage. Cut down to new
basal growth if old foliage fades in late summer or autumn.

Perovskia atriplicifolia

Zone: 5–9
Common Name: Russian sage
Family: Lamiaceae
Description: spikes of lavender-blue flowers;
    fine gray leaves
Size: 3–4 ft. high; 3–4 ft. wide
Exposure: full sun
Flowering: July–September

PRUNING: In the Midwest plants flower for
a long time even without deadheading. In
southern gardens, where the plants may
flower earlier, deadheading may be beneficial
to produce rebloom. Susan Urshal, a gardener in Texas, likes to cut about two-thirds
of the stems by about two-thirds after flowering; the pruned stems send out new shoots
that will be reblooming by autumn.

   The straight species of Russian sage has a
tendency to flop or fall over a bit in most garden situations. Plants can be pinched or cut
back by one-half when they are about 12 in.
tall to obtain fuller plants.

   The silvery stems and seedheads of Russian sage provide nice winter interest. Generally plants are cut back to about 6 in. above
the ground annually in the spring, and new
buds break from these low woody stems.
Some gardeners prefer to cut plants all the
way to the ground, believing that the plants
are fuller if pruned in this fashion. Some
people don't have a choice, as plants may be
killed completely to the ground each winter.

   Perovskia may be harmed by late frosts,
although plants usually recover nicely. Trim
off damaged foliage if necessary to improve
the appearance of the plant.

OTHER MAINTENANCE: Drought-tolerant,
low-maintenance plants with a long bloom
period. Good for the beginning gardener. Well-
draining soil is critical for survival, particularly over the winter. Seldom needs division.

RELATED PLANTS: *Perovskia atriplicifolia*
'Longin' is more upright and narrower than
the species. Doesn't require pinching.

Phlox divaricata

Zone: 4–9
Common Name: woodland phlox
Family: Polemoniaceae

Description: light blue, white, or lavender
flowers; small green leaves
Size: 10–15 in. high; 12 in. wide
Exposure: partial to full shade
Flowering: May–June

PRUNING: Plants can reseed heavily to create a beautiful display in a naturalized or
woodland area. If reseeding is not desired,
deadhead before seed matures. One efficient
way to accomplish deadheading is to shear
off the old flowering stems, with hedge
shears, down to the low green foliage. If the
flowering stems are left on the plants for
reseeding, they usually become brown and
ugly by mid-July. Deadheading before this
time is best for keeping plants attractive.
Plants may be subject to powdery mildew in
hot and humid conditions. If affected, shear
down for lush new growth; do not compost
diseased material. Woodland phlox is evergreen and so should not be pruned for the
winter.

OTHER MAINTENANCE: Plants prefer
moist, humus-rich conditions. The foliage
will die down if allowed to dry out in the
summer or if given too much sun. Plants
are shallow rooted and should be planted
or divided in the spring to avoid the winter
frost heaving that can occur with autumn
planting.

RELATED PLANTS: *Phlox divaricata* 'Chatta-
hoochee' is a nice selection with more compact growth. The flowering stems of this cultivar are borne closer to the foliage than
those of the species. Deadhead and shape by
shearing off (with hedge shears) the old flower stems and about one-third to one-half of
the foliage. This pruning keeps the plants
bushy for the rest of the season. Foliage holds
up better in drought than that of the species.
Phlox divaricata 'Fuller's White' is heavier
blooming than the species and more tolerant
of sun.

Phlox maculata

Zone: 4–8
Common Name: early phlox
Family: Polemoniaceae
Description: white, pink, or rose clusters of
flowers; narrow shiny green leaves
Size: 2–3 ft. high; 3 ft. wide
Exposure: full sun
Flowering: June–July

PRUNING: Deadheading can greatly prolong
the bloom of early phlox, in some cases for
up to 2 months longer. Deadhead the main
flowering truss to above lateral buds. Plants
are self-sterile and will not self-sow, so deadheading to prevent mongrel seedlings is not a
concern. If the stems of the plants brown or
are affected with leaf spot, they should be
cut to the ground for regrowth and, if vigorous, rebloom may occur, although this is not
common. Keep moist and fertilize after cutting back for best performance.
    Pruning extends early phlox's season to
later in the summer and provides smaller
flowers, which are better for smaller cut-
flower arrangements. Plants can be pinched,
and they respond well to cutting back by one-
half and shaping at the end of May or in early
June before flowering to reduce the height
and delay the bloom. Plants in tight bud also
can be pruned by removing 6 in. or more to
obtain shorter plants and later bloom. Flowers are usually delayed by about 2 weeks but
can be delayed by up to 4 weeks with either
form of cutting back. If plants are stressed or
not strongly growing, pruning may further
reduce the flowering and quality of bloom.
See cultivars listed below for specifics.

OTHER MAINTENANCE: This species is a
good selection when it comes to *Phlox* because of its resistance to powdery mildew.
Plants are heavy feeders and need moist,
fertile, organic-rich soil for best performance. Division every couple of years will
maintain vigor.

RELATED PLANTS: *Phlox maculata* 'Alpha' cut back by one-half and shaped in early June produces outstanding plants that flower nicely at 1½ ft., rather than 2½ ft., and begin flowering 2 weeks later than unpruned plants, in mid-July rather than late June (Plates 110–112).

Phlox maculata 'Miss Lingard' plants cut back by one-half at the end of May flowered 3–4 weeks later than unpruned plants and at 2 ft. rather than 3 ft. The floral display of the pruned plants was not as effective as that of unpruned plants, but that was most likely due to the fact that the plants were stressed and in need of division to improve their vigor.

Phlox maculata 'Omega' is a white form with a pink eye that if deadheaded usually reblooms all white later in the summer.

Phlox maculata 'Rosalind' did not respond to pruning 4 in., rather than 6 in., off the tips of the plants when in tight bud in mid-June. Pruning off less of the stem must not have removed already formed lateral flower buds, which broke at the normal flowering time to create a rather bizarre effect (Plate 113).

Phlox paniculata

Zone: 4–8
Common Name: border phlox
Family: Polemoniaceae
Description: large flower clusters in white, pink, red, purple, or orange (to name a few); dull green leaves
Size: 2–4 ft. high; 2 ft. wide
Exposure: full sun
Flowering: July–September

PRUNING: Deadheading prolongs bloom on plants and prevents reseeding. Seedlings are not desirable because they are not true to type and often take over the more desirable parent plant (Plate 114). Thinning phlox by one-third or to 4–6 stems is often recommended to reduce the incidence of powdery mildew, but this is not always effective and in some years plants get mildew whether thinned or not. The gardener needs to decide whether it's worth the effort. Plants badly infected with powdery mildew should be cut to the ground, making sure to keep them moist and fertilized for regrowth. Do not compost clippings. All this being said, selecting mildew-resistant cultivars in the first place is really the best way to avoid the extra maintenance; see the listing of cultivars below.

Plants can be pinched or cut back and shaped to produce shorter plants and to delay flowering. Border phlox can be cut back by one-half in early to mid-June, or 6 in. or more can be cut off when the plants are in tight bud. Flowering normally will be delayed by 2 weeks with pruning, but it can be delayed by as much as 4 weeks. If plants are cut back earlier, say in mid-May, flowering may not be as greatly delayed. Pruning can be used to produce flowers later in the season on a few plants or on a few stems of an individual plant. Flower size is also reduced with pruning before flowering, which is nice for smaller cut arrangements. Stressed plants or plants in need of division may have weaker than normal flower production if pruned.

Be sure to prune down phlox for the winter if they are affected with mildew. Clean-up and destroy all debris around the plants to reduce the chances of infection the following spring.

OTHER MAINTENANCE: Border phlox are heavy feeders. They prefer moist, rich, high-organic soil. Avoid wet conditions. Give plants space, good air circulation, and avoid drought to help reduce incidence of mildew. Frequent division, every 3 years, in the spring helps to keep plants vigorous, and the double-fork method can be used. Discard the deteriorated center of divided plants and leave at least 3–4 shoots per division. Some cultivars may require staking.

RELATED PLANTS: The cultivars listed below are generally more resistant or at least less prone to mildew. The occurrence of disease may vary depending on the cultural and growing conditions for the season or on the weather, but at least the chances are better if these more resistant forms are selected over other more susceptible cultivars. Some resistant forms of *Phlox paniculata* include: 'Bright Eyes', 'David', 'Eva Cullum', 'Fesselballon', 'Flamingo', 'Franz Schubert', 'Katherine', 'Look Again', 'Orange Perfection', 'Pax' ('Peace'), 'Prime Minister', 'Sandra', 'Speed Limit 45', 'Sternhimmel', 'Tenor', and 'The King'.

Phlox paniculata 'David' cut back by one-half when in tight bud in mid-July started flowering in mid-August rather than late July. Plants were 2 ft. rather than 2½ ft. tall and the flowers were smaller.

Phlox paniculata 'Flamingo' had outstanding results when cut back by one-half in mid-June. Plants were 1½ ft. tall, rather than 2 ft., and flowered 2–3 weeks later than usual (Plate 115).

Phlox paniculata 'Franz Schubert' started flowering on 19 July rather than on 12 July when cut back by one-half, thinned, and shaped at the end of May. They flowered at 2 ft., about 6 in. shorter than normal. The pruned plants got a touch of mildew to the same degree as did unthinned plants.

Phlox paniculata 'Fujiyama', when cut back by one-half and shaped in early to mid-June, started to flower in mid-August, about 2 weeks later than normal, and at 3 ft. tall rather than the typical 4–4½ ft. Flowers were smaller. 'Fujiyama' is often noted as mildew resistant, although it is severely infected in my gardens.

Phlox paniculata 'Kathleen' had 6 in. pruned off when in tight bud at the beginning of July. It started flowering on 5 August, as compared to the 19 July flowering date of unpruned plants. The flowering plants were 2 ft. tall, rather than 2½ ft. tall, and the flowers were smaller.

Phlox paniculata 'Look Again' pinched on 11 June flowered in early August, 2–3 weeks later than normal. The flowerheads were 4 in. × 4 in. rather than 7 in. × 6 in., and the plants were 3 ft. tall rather than 3½ ft. tall.

Phlox paniculata 'Pax' ('Peace') pinched on 21 June flowered 3 weeks later than normal, on 5 August. There was only a slight reduction in height.

Phlox paniculata 'Speed Limit 45' when cut back by one-half at the end of May flowered at 3–3½ ft. tall, about 1 ft. shorter, with flowering delayed by two weeks, in late rather than mid-August.

Phlox stolonifera

Zone: 4–9
Common Name: creeping phlox
Family: Polemoniaceae
Description: purple, red, blue, or white
    flowers; small oval leaves
Size: 6–12 in. (2 in.) high; 12–15 in. wide
Exposure: partial to full shade
Flowering: April–May

PRUNING: Cut or shear deadheads down to creeping basal foliage to improve the overall appearance of the plant. Plants remain evergreen over the winter, so do not prune in the autumn. Although winter damage is not common, any branches that decline over the winter should be pruned off in early spring. Creeping phlox spreads by stolons, which can be pruned off to control spread if desired.

OTHER MAINTENANCE: Great low-maintenance perennial. Useful as a groundcover even in shady spots. Nice between stepping stones in a low-traffic path. Prefers moist, acidic, humus-rich soil, although plants are fairly adaptable. Avoid prolonged drought. Can take some sun in all but southern gardens. Not susceptible to mildew, as with other phlox. Divide, if needed, in the spring or summer after flowering.

Phlox subulata

Zone: 3–9
Common Name: moss phlox
Family: Polemoniaceae
Description: pink, magenta, red, white, lavender, or blue flowers; matlike foliage
Size: 3–6 in. high; 24 in. wide
Exposure: full sun
Flowering: April–May

PRUNING: After flowering is completed, shear plants back, with hedge shears, by one-half to prevent them from opening up in the center later in the season. Shearing before the seeds set also prevents reseeding of untrue types. Cut plants back if needed to control spread. Plants are evergreen; do not prune in the autumn, and clean-up any winter-damaged growth in the spring.

OTHER MAINTENANCE: Well-draining soil is key to survival. Moss phlox prefers slightly alkaline conditions. Division may be needed every 3 years to maintain vigor, and it should be done after flowering in the spring. Be certain to cut back foliage by one-half on new divisions.

Physostegia virginiana

Zone: 3–9
Common Name: obedient plant
Family: Lamiaceae
Description: pink or white tubular flowers; narrow green leaves
Size: 2–4 ft. high; 3 ft. wide
Exposure: full sun or partial shade
Flowering: August–October

PRUNING: Deadhead to a lateral flower bud or leaf to improve the overall appearance of the plant and possibly to prolong bloom. Pinch or cut back plants by one-half in the spring to prevent flopping, particularly in rich moist soils or shaded sites. Cut plants down to new basal growth if they develop a ratty appearance after flowering.

OTHER MAINTENANCE: Best growth occurs in full sun, although plants may still require staking. Prefers moist soil. A rather high-maintenance plant because it spreads aggressively, requiring frequent digging out of sections of the plant to keep it in bounds. Division every couple of years helps to maintain a decent plant. Best relegated to a naturalized garden where spreading and flopping growth habit is more acceptable.

RELATED PLANTS: *Physostegia virginiana* 'Summer Snow' may be less invasive but still requires frequent division.

Physostegia virginiana 'Vivid' is more compact and upright than the species, normally not requiring pruning, yet it's still a spreader.

Platycodon grandiflorus

Zone: 3–8
Common Name: balloon flower
Family: Campanulaceae
Description: blue, pink, or white "inflated" flowers that "pop" open with maturity; oval green leaves
Size: 2–3 ft. high; 2 ft. wide
Exposure: full sun
Flowering: July–September

PRUNING: Deadheading of balloon flower can greatly prolong bloom and keep the plants attractive. Each individual dead flower needs to be removed without damaging new buds, which are produced all along the flowering stem (as shown in Figure 9-3), and sharp pruning scissors work best for this task. Removing the entire flowering stem will remove future flowers. Snipping off the old flowers and simply letting them drop to the ground helps speed up this tedious deadheading. Minimal reseeding can occur, so you should deadhead before seeds mature if reseeding is not desired.

Balloon flower responds well to pinching or cutting back before flowering to control its flopping nature. Cutting plants back by one-half in late May to early June, or about one month before they flower, produces nicely branched, well-shaped, shorter plants with delayed flowering that will not require staking. Plants that normally mature at 2½–3½ ft. tall will mature at 1½–2 ft. tall with this pruning regime (Plate 116), and flowering can be delayed by 2–3 weeks. Plants cut back in mid- to late June may be delayed by as much as 4 weeks. After the foliage turns attractive colors in the autumn it blackens with several killing frosts. If you cut plants down at this time, leave about 6 in. of the old stems to mark the location of the plants since they are late to emerge in the spring. The old stems can be further pruned down once new growth is visible in the spring.

OTHER MAINTENANCE: Plants are slow to establish, but once they take hold they are long-lived and low maintenance. Provide high-organic, well-draining soil and a location where the plant won't be disturbed by cultivation around its roots. Can be difficult to transplant, and balloon flower doesn't need to be divided for 20 years or more. If division is desired, take plenty of soil, for deep roots, with the clump in the spring. Spring planting is required for best establishment. Plants are late to emerge in the spring, so be careful to not disturb the area. Usually requires staking, unless plants are pruned or shorter growing cultivars are selected. It's worth noting that popping the balloons does not damage the flowers—so enjoy!

RELATED PLANTS: *Platycodon grandiflorus* 'Mariesii' is a shorter form (1–2 ft.) that normally doesn't require staking.

Polemonium caeruleum

Zone: 3–7
Common Name: jacob's ladder
Family: Polemoniaceae
Description: small blue flowers on spikes; pinnately compound leaves

Size: 18–24 in. (10 in.) high; 18 in. wide
Exposure: partial shade
Flowering: June

PRUNING: Cutting plants down to lush basal foliage after all flowering is finished may produce some sporadic rebloom later in the summer. Stems decline by late summer anyway, so cutting them down early also keeps the plants looking fresh. Plants can be prolific seeders. If reseeding is not desired, cut plants down before seed has a chance to mature. Although long-lived in the North, plants can be short-lived in southern regions and so allowing some seeding may be the only way to ensure constancy of the plant in such warmer conditions. Leave the basal growth for the winter and cut off any damaged material if needed in the spring.

OTHER MAINTENANCE: Plants prefer rich, moist, humus soil. They will take some sun in cooler climates. Foliage scorches in very hot, sunny locations, requiring cutting back. Plants seldom need to be divided, but if desired perform in late summer.

Polygonatum odoratum 'Variegatum'

Zone: 3–9
Common Name: variegated solomon's seal
Family: Liliaceae
Description: white bell-shaped flowers; broad green and creamy white variegated leaves
Size: 2–3 ft. high; 2 ft. wide
Exposure: shade
Flowering: May–June

PRUNING: Deadheading is not required for this perennial, as the old flowers simply drop off the plant. Normally minimal, if any, fruit is produced on this cultivar of solomon's seal. The foliage holds up beautifully all season with no pruning. It turns an outstanding yellow in the autumn, and the leaves fall off the stems after several killing frosts. The stems usually loosen from the rhizome and fall over after killing frosts, and they are easily pulled off at this time as well. Do not tug on the stems as this will pull the rhizome out of the soil. Cut off the stem if it has not loosened itself for the winter.

OTHER MAINTENANCE: Wonderful low-maintenance perennial. Slow to establish—be patient with young plants—but long-lived once it takes hold. Prefers rich organic soil. Tolerant of drought and competition from tree roots once established. The slow-spreading rhizome roots seldom need division, but it can be done in the early spring. Leave several buds per division for best success with transplanting.

Pulmonaria saccharata

Zone: 3–8
Common Name: bethlehem sage
Family: Boraginaceae
Description: pink buds open to blue flowers; long and narrow silver-spotted leaves
Size: 9–15 in. high; 18 in. wide
Exposure: partial to full shade
Flowering: March–April

PRUNING: Old flowering stems of *Pulmonaria saccharata* have a tendency to fall to the outside of the plant after flowering, leaving a clump of basal leaves in the center. The old stems can be grabbed by the handful and pruned off at ground level, which also serves to thin the plants. Such pruning greatly enhances the plant's appearance and reduces the chance of seeding (Plates 117–119). If the foliage declines or if plants are infected with powdery mildew in midsummer, plants should be deadleafed or, if damage is severe, cut completely down to the ground. Do not compost diseased leaves. Keep plants moist after cutting down. Lush new growth will appear in about two weeks. *Pulmonaria* may remain semi-evergreen through winter, depending on the weather conditions, plant-

ing site, and the particular cultivar or species. Winter performance can differ with different cultivars in the same garden. If the foliage looks good going into the winter, you may want to leave the plants unpruned until spring. If this is the route taken, early spring pruning will be necessary to clean-up any damaged foliage before the early flowering begins.

OTHER MAINTENANCE: Plants do best with rich, high-organic, moist soil. Avoiding dry conditions can reduce the incidence of powdery mildew and leaf scorch. Plants do not need division for many years, and it's only necessary if the clump becomes crowded. Divide in late summer or early autumn, and keep moist, so that plants have a chance to establish before winter.

RELATED PLANTS: *Pulmonaria saccharata* 'Margery Fish' (*P. vallarsae* 'Margery Fish') exhibits greater mildew resistance than most.

Pulmonaria saccharata 'Mrs. Moon' may seed itself prolifically under wet and cool conditions.

Pulmonaria 'Roy Davidson' has foliage that seems to hold up well over the winter in most cases.

Pulsatilla vulgaris (Anemone pulsatilla)

Zone: 5–8
Common Name: pasque flower
Family: Ranunculaceae
Description: cupped purplish red flowers; silky hairs on foliage
Size: 12 in. high; 12 in. wide
Exposure: partial shade
Flowering: April–May

PRUNING: Leave deadheads on the plant because they mature into fantastic fluffy, multi-spined creatures resembling clematis seedheads. The leaves usually disappear in the summer after the seedheads emerge.

OTHER MAINTENANCE: Plants are short-lived unless provided with well-draining soil, particularly over the winter. Tolerates drought in cooler regions. Plants do not require division for many years; once plants are well established, divide carefully after flowering, if desired.

Ranunculus repens 'Pleniflorus' ('Flore Pleno')

Zone: 3–8
Common Name: double creeping buttercup
Family: Ranunculaceae
Description: double bright yellow flowers; three-parted leaves
Size: 18 in. high; spreading
Exposure: full sun to partial shade
Flowering: April–May

PRUNING: Plants should be deadheaded to prevent abundant seeding. Foliage may get tatty if the site is too dry. Shear off old foliage and keep plants moist to encourage new growth. Cut back or pinch expanding stolons to control spread.

OTHER MAINTENANCE: Double creeping buttercup can spread invasively by means of stolons. It is best planted in an informal area where the spreading habit is acceptable. Requires frequent division, in the spring or autumn, to keep in check. Prefers moist soils, which will only speed its expansion. Obviously high maintenance!

Rodgersia aesculifolia

Zone: 5–7
Common Name: fingerleaf rodgersia
Family: Saxifragaceae
Description: large clusters of white flowers; horsechestnut-like leaves
Size: 3–5 ft. (2–4 ft.) high; 4 ft. wide
Exposure: partial shade
Flowering: May–June

PRUNING: Deadhead flowers after they fade so as to better enjoy the outstanding foliage. Foliage is often damaged by late-spring frosts; prune off damaged leaves to make room for new growth. Leaves become scorched and tatty in late summer if not provided with sufficient moisture. In such cases, deadleaf to clean-up the plant, and be sure to increase the moisture provided to the plants in the future. Plants are not attractive over the winter and are best pruned down after killing frost.

OTHER MAINTENANCE: Requires moist, fertile, humus-rich soil for best growth. Although plants prefer constant moisture, they do not tolerate standing water. Protect from hot sun and strong winds. Avoid planting in frost pockets. Plants are slow growing and seldom need division, but it can be done in the autumn. With its impressive size, fingerleaf rodgersia can be grown as a single specimen.

Rudbeckia fulgida 'Goldsturm'

Zone: 3–9
Common Name: goldsturm black-eyed susan
Family: Asteraceae
Description: golden daisy-like flowers with black centers; broad coarse leaves
Size: 18–30 in. (12 in.) high; 24–30 in. wide
Exposure: full sun
Flowering: July–September

PRUNING: Plants have a long bloom period even without deadheading. Seedheads are attractive after the petals fall and are usually left on the plant for winter interest. They also provide good food for the birds in the autumn and winter. Plants may seed to almost weedy proportions in some situations, however, and if this is not desired some or all of the seedheads should be cut down. Stems may topple a bit over the winter as well. Pinching can produce more but smaller flowers on sturdier plants.

OTHER MAINTENANCE: Tough, long-blooming perennial. It is so widely used that it could be considered the "juniper" of the perennial world! Plants have a rhizomatous habit that can form fairly large colonies. Holes may develop in planting. Divide every 4 years to keep strong and to control spread. More frequent division may be needed in light soils where the spread can be fast. Not affected by powdery mildew and doesn't require staking.

RELATED PLANTS: *Rudbeckia fulgida* var. *speciosa* (*R. newmanii*), orange coneflower, can seed prolifically. Deadhead most of the seedheads to reduce the population if desired, but leave a few for the birds. Stems hold up well and basal foliage remains evergreen over the winter.

Rudbeckia maxima, great coneflower, has attractive seedheads that are favorites of the birds. Tall stems often break over the winter. Minimal seeding.

Rudbeckia triloba, three-lobed coneflower, is biennial in nature but usually lives more than 2 years. Very prolific seeder. Cutting most of the flowering stems down to basal foliage after flowering will prevent literally hundreds of offspring from developing, although you should allow some seeding to ensure permanence of the species in the garden. The stems that are allowed to remain will fall over in the winter but are still enjoyed by the birds. The basal foliage remains evergreen. Plants have a tendency to flop during flowering and may require staking. In a garden setting, pinching or cutting back may be desirable for sturdier growth. Plants pinched or cut back by about one-third when 2 ft. tall in early June flowered at about 4 ft., rather than 5 ft., with only a slight delay in bloom time. Cutting back further may be desirable to produce even shorter plants with a greater delay in bloom. Flower size is not noticeably reduced after pruning. A native plant, it is good in a naturalized area where free seeding and flopping are permissible.

Rudbeckia nitida 'Herbstsonne'

Zone: 4–10
Common Name: herbstsonne coneflower
Family: Asteraceae
Description: golden-yellow daisy-like flowerheads with drooping petals; bright green leaves
Size: 7 ft. (2½ ft.) high; 3 ft. wide
Exposure: full sun
Flowering: July–August

PRUNING: This coneflower has a long season of interest even without deadheading. Not a plant that could easily be deadheaded anyway by most but the tallest of gardeners without the aid of a step ladder. Attractive seedheads extend the season of interest and bring birds into the garden for feeding. Seeding is not usually a problem with this species.

Although often touted as having self-supporting stems (perhaps in more northerly gardens), plants in my garden topple over unless given light support. The wonderful height is one of the main reasons to grow this plant, but cutting back or pinching could be used for height control where shorter plants are desirable. Cutting back by one-half in early June when plants are 2 ft. tall can produce 4½- to 5-ft.-tall plants, rather than the typical 7-ft. height (Plate 120). Flowering may be delayed by a week or so. A few stems still may fall over at this height, but staking is not required. Cut any fallen stems down to the basal foliage before winter and leave the rest. Usually all stems will fall over sometime in the winter, but they are still enjoyed by the birds. If this untidy winter habit is not tolerable, cut all stems down late in the autumn, leaving the basal growth.

OTHER MAINTENANCE: Trouble-free plants except for light staking or pruning to handle massive height. Three or four sturdy stakes can be placed around the perimeter of the foliage in the early summer with twine tied from stake to stake as light support for any wayward stems. Divide every 4–5 years in the spring or early autumn.

RELATED PLANTS: *Rudbeckia nitida* 'Goldquelle' has large double flowers that need deadheading or else they look horrendous. Deadheading can also prolong bloom. May need staking in rich soil.

Ruta graveolens

Zone: 4–9
Common Name: common rue
Family: Rutaceae
Description: blue-green aromatic foliage; small yellow flowers
Size: 1–3 ft. high; 2 ft. wide
Exposure: full sun
Flowering: July–August

PRUNING: Common rue is actually a woody subshrub that may need to be sheared back to 6–8 in. in the early spring to maintain a full form. Do not do any hard pruning in late summer or plants may not harden in time for the winter. Plants can be grown exclusively for foliar effect, in which case the flowers are best sheared off when in bud. If flowering is permitted, shear off deadheads and shape plants before seed formation, or the foliage may yellow and decline due to energy expended toward seed production. Wear gloves and long sleeves when pruning rue, as some individuals may develop a skin irritation upon contact, which can be accelerated by hot, sunny weather.

OTHER MAINTENANCE: Well-draining soil is essential for survival. Tolerates heat and drought. Can be short-lived. Mulch in northern gardens for the winter. Seldom needs division.

RELATED PLANTS: *Ruta graveolens* 'Jackman's Blue' is a compact, 18- to 24-in.-tall form that doesn't seem to require as much pruning to maintain its form as compared to the species.
Ruta graveolens 'Variegata' new growth is forced by early spring pruning, which consequently enhances the variegation.

Salvia nemorosa

Zone: 3–8
Common Name: perennial salvia
Family: Lamiaceae
Description: violet-blue flowers; oblong green leaves
Size: 18–36 in. high; 24 in. wide
Exposure: full sun
Flowering: June–August

PRUNING: Deadheading of perennial salvia encourages a long bloom period. Deadhead to lateral buds. The reddish purple bracts that remain after flowering further extend the interest of the plant, and many gardeners opt to leave the bracts on the plants for a while before deadheading. Plants, particularly older ones, have a tendency to get leggy and open up as the season progresses. If the appearance declines, cut the plant down to newly developed fresh basal foliage. Later rebloom may sometimes occur, although the blooms are usually smaller and fewer in number than in the initial bloom phase. If plants are open and ratty after the initial flowering, it may be best to simply cut the plants down to basal growth, skipping the deadheading. Although this may leave a hole in the garden earlier in the season, fresh low foliage will return and is usually more appealing than the previous shaggy growth (Plates 121–122). Keep plants moist after cutting back to encourage stronger regrowth. If plants have not been previously cut back, remove top straggly growth for the winter, leaving the low basal growth.

OTHER MAINTENANCE: Provide well-draining soil for best performance. Drought-tolerant, tough plants. They have a tendency to flop if given too much shade or overly rich soil, or if division is needed. Any dividing should be done in the spring.

RELATED PLANTS: Select cultivars of *Salvia nemorosa* over the species form for more compact growth and longer bloom periods. 'East Friesland' ('Ostfriesland') and 'May Night' ('Mainacht') grow to 18 in. in height and 'Blue Hill' ('Blauhügel') reaches 20 in. These cultivars may be listed in the trade under *S.* ×*sylvestris*, of which *S. nemorosa* is a parent (and still other sources may consider these cultivars of *S.* ×*superba*).

Salvia azurea subsp. *pitcheri*, pitcher's salvia, is a 5-ft.-tall leggy plant for which pinching or cutting back is often recommended to control laxness. Plants cut back by one-half in early June when 15 in. tall reached 2–3 ft. in height, but the stems were still weak and very floppy.

Salvia verticillata 'Purple Rain' will have its bloom greatly prolonged with deadheading. Plants may require cutting back to basal growth after flowering to promote fresh growth and rebloom. Cut plants back if infected with powdery mildew.

Sanguisorba obtusa

Zone: 4–8
Common Name: Japanese burnet
Family: Rosaceae
Description: reddish pink fluffy flowers; gray-green divided leaves
Size: 3–4 ft. (2 ft.) high; 2–3 ft. wide
Exposure: full sun
Flowering: July–August

PRUNING: Deadhead after flowering to enjoy the attractive blue-green leaves. The outer foliage often declines by late summer, particularly with dry conditions; deadleaf or shear off down to fresh lower growth. Foliage crisps with autumn frost. Cut down for the winter, or leave up and prune back in the early spring.

OTHER MAINTENANCE: Not an overly exciting garden perennial, but the foliage effect is different. It is a tough, low-mainte-nance plant. Avoid dry conditions, or leaf scorching will occur. Can be subject to Japanese beetles. Divide every 4–5 years in the spring.

RELATED PLANTS: *Sanguisorba tenuifolia* 'Purpurea' should be deadheaded to prevent heavy seeding.

Santolina chamaecyparissus

Zone: 6–8
Common Name: lavender cotton
Family: Asteraceae
Description: bright yellow buttonlike flowerheads; tiny gray leaves
Size: 18 in. high; 18–24 in. wide
Exposure: full sun
Flowering: July–August

PRUNING: Plants should be sheared and shaped as needed in the spring. In most years shearing off the dead tips after the plant breaks bud is all that is necessary. A hard spring shearing to 6–8 in. every 2–3 years is usually beneficial to prevent the plants from becoming leggy. The flowers are enjoyed by some and considered a distraction from the foliage by others; those in the latter camp may choose to shear off the flower buds to prevent flowering. Plants also tend to lose their form if flowering is allowed. If buds are not removed before flowering, deadheads should be sheared off before seed formation, and plants can be shaped at the same time. Light shearing throughout the summer can help keep the plants in shape at the expense of flowering, and this is particularly useful if plants are being utilized as a low hedge. Plants may not tolerate hard shearing in the summer, particularly in hot regions. Also avoid any hard shearing after August so that plants have a chance to harden for the winter.

OTHER MAINTENANCE: Well-draining soil is essential to survival. Drought tolerant. May melt out in humid conditions. Winter mulching is beneficial in areas colder than zone 6.

RELATED PLANTS: *Santolina chamaecyparissus* var. *nana* is a 10-in. dwarf form that holds its shape better than the straight species.

Saponaria ocymoides

Zone: 3–7
Common Name: rock soapwort
Family: Caryophyllaceae
Description: small deep pink flowers; small oval leaves
Size: 5–10 in. high; 12 in. wide
Exposure: full sun
Flowering: May–June

PRUNING: Plants should be sheared back by one-half after flowering to keep them full and compact. Sporadic rebloom may occur. Shearing back before seed set prevents self-seeding, which can be troublesome in some gardens. Do not prune for the winter. Cleanup any winter damage in the spring as needed.

OTHER MAINTENANCE: Good drainage, particularly over the winter, is essential. Avoid overly rich soil, which promotes rank growth. Divide in the spring or autumn.

RELATED PLANTS: *Saponaria* ×*lempergii* 'Max Frei' flowers in midsummer. Cut back by one-half to two-thirds for sporadic autumn rebloom.

Scabiosa columbaria 'Butterfly Blue'

Zone: 3–7
Common Name: butterfly blue pincushion flower
Family: Dipsacaceae
Description: light blue flowers; green leaves
Size: 12 in. (6 in.) high; 12 in. wide
Exposure: full sun or light shade
Flowering: May–October

PRUNING: Deadheading prolongs bloom and keeps plants looking fresh. It can be a tedious job, as an established plant can produce hundreds of flowers in a season! And be careful, because it is easy to confuse the round bristly deadheads and the flat bristly new buds (see Figure 9-4). The flowering stems usually branch with two or normally more flowers per stem. Deadhead by cutting the old flower and its stem down to a new lateral flowering stem or bud, and when that lateral stem is finished flowering it should be cut down to another lateral flowering stem or bud, if present, or to the basal foliage. Sometimes the stems will not branch, in which case simply deadhead down to the basal foliage. First-year plants give the gardener a little honeymoon period by requiring only a couple of deadheading sessions to keep the plants going strong. In future years more frequent deadheading will be required. Also, with age, plants may tend to get slightly woody, developing a central leader, rather than staying in a nice herbaceous mound. Simply pinch back the woody central leader as it develops. Any severe pruning can kill the plant if no basal growth is breaking. Old flowering stems can be cut back before winter, but the basal foliage should not be cut back because it remains evergreen to semi-evergreen for most of the winter. Simply cut off any dead outer leaves in early spring before new growth begins.

OTHER MAINTENANCE: Without well-draining soil plants are usually short-lived, especially in heavy soils. High-organic, fertile soil is best, and plants prefer a neutral to alkaline pH. They like a cooler, more humid climate than is found in Ohio, but our summer heat hasn't seemed to ruffle them. Divide every 3–4 years, but only if the plants are crowded.

RELATED PLANTS: *Scabiosa caucasica*, pincushion flower, bears fewer flowers than the above species, but deadheading will help to prolong bloom through the summer.

Sedum 'Autumn Joy' ('Herbstfreude')

Zone: 3–10
Common Name: autumn joy sedum
Family: Crassulaceae
Description: pink (changing to rust) flowers in flat heads; fleshy green leaves
Size: 24 in. high; 18 in. wide
Exposure: full sun or partial shade
Flowering: August–September

PRUNING: *Sedum* 'Autumn Joy' should not be deadheaded, as it is among the most outstanding of perennials for winter interest. The spent flowers look amazing when coated with frost and snow. In the early spring they stand tall above light green nubs of new growth at the base of the plant, and it is best to cut them off at this time (Plate 123). The old flowering stems are often intact enough in the early spring to use in dried arrangements.

Plants may flop if grown in too much shade or in overly rich soil. They respond well to pinching or cutting back for height control. Smaller, more numerous flowers are produced and flowering may be delayed slightly. Plants can be cut back to 4 in. when they are about 8 in. tall, normally in early June. They could also be pinched at this time. Many gardeners prefer the results obtained from pinching as compared to cutting back, claiming that cutting back causes the plants to callus and break off in winter weather, whereas pinching does not (see Plates 57–59).

OTHER MAINTENANCE: Low-maintenance, undemanding perennial. Great for the beginning gardener. Normally pest free, but occasionally may be troubled by aphids. Provide well-draining soil and full sun for best performance. Drought tolerant. Division is not needed for many (6–10) years; it should be performed in the early spring when necessary.

RELATED PLANTS: *Sedum spurium*, two-row stonecrop, is best kept neat by cutting off the old flowering stems at the base.

Sedum telephium 'Atropurpureum' (*S. maximum* 'Atropurpureum'), great stonecrop, requires its tips pinched back to control sprawl and to keep it in a vegetative state.

Sedum 'Vera Jameson' can be pinched for fuller plants.

Sidalcea malviflora

Zone: 5–7
Common Name: checker-mallow
Family: Malvaceae
Description: pink flower spikes; round or lobed glossy green leaves
Size: 3–4 ft. high; 2 ft. wide
Exposure: full sun or partial shade
Flowering: June–August

PRUNING: Deadhead plants to lateral flowering spikes to keep them blooming into September and to prevent prolific seeding. Cut plants down to the ground if the stems should decline (usually due to hot and dry conditions), or when all flowering is finished. Some authorities feel that deadheading the plants regularly and cutting them down when all flowering is done will prolong the life of this often short-lived perennial. Keep plants moist after cutting down. If cut back in midsummer, low new growth and possible rebloom may occur. In especially hot summers, however, new growth may not develop until the return of cooler autumn weather, usually sometime in late September. If plants have not already been cut down, do so for the winter.

OTHER MAINTENANCE: Performs best in moist, cool climates. Foliage often declines with hot and humid weather and dry soil in summer. Keep plants moist during such conditions, but provide well-draining soil. Divide in the autumn after about the third year if needed; be careful when dividing, because of the taproot. May need support unless more compact cultivars are selected. Often short-lived.

RELATED PLANTS: *Sidalcea* 'Loveliness', 'Oberon', and 'Puck' are dwarf cultivars that reach 2–2½ ft. tall and normally do not require support.

Sisyrinchium angustifolium

Zone: 3–8
Common Name: blue-eyed grass
Family: Iridaceae
Description: tiny blue flowers with yellow
    throats; grasslike leaves
Size: 10–12 in. high; 8–12 in. wide
Exposure: full sun
Flowering: May–June

PRUNING: Deadheading individual old flowering stems doesn't seem to prolong bloom, and the flowers melt away nicely when finished. Shear plants back by one-half after all flowering is done and before seed set to keep foliage fresh and to prevent self-seeding. Do not prune again for the winter. Prune as needed in the spring.

OTHER MAINTENANCE: Plants require moist yet well-draining soil for best performance. May require frequent division (every 1–3 years) to maintain vigor; divide after flowering.

Solidago hybrids

Zone: 2–8
Common Name: goldenrod
Family: Asteraceae
Description: yellow plumes; green leaves
Size: 4–6 ft. high; 2 ft. wide
Exposure: full sun
Flowering: July–October

PRUNING: When goldenrods are grown in a border situation, rather than in a wild setting, they may benefit from the following pruning. Taller growing forms develop a better habit when cut back by one-half in early June, which reduces their height and creates more compact growth that doesn't require staking (Plates 124–125). Similar cutting back can also delay flowering on early bloomers. Another method that can be used with goldenrod is to pinch plants in May. Pinching will not reduce the plant's height as dramatically as will cutting back, but it creates more heavily branched growth, which may be desirable for shorter forms. Pinching in May usually delays the bloom of July-flowering forms into August, when flowering may be preferable. Early bloomers may get tatty by late summer and so can be cut down to the base if needed. Goldenrods often reseed; although plants can provide interest over the winter, cutting down the stems after flowering can prevent unwanted offspring.

OTHER MAINTENANCE: Tolerant of a variety of soil conditions, except extremes. Particularly drought tolerant. Avoid overly rich soil, which contributes to lanky growth. Goldenrods can be either clump formers or spreaders. Rapid-spreading rhizomes often require division or removal of the outside of the expanding clump to control spread. Clump-forming types may not need division until about their fourth year. *Solidago* should be divided in the spring or after flowering in the autumn.

RELATED PLANTS: Most *Solidago* hybrid cultivars are shorter growing than the native species. Some of the more notable such cultivars include: 'Cloth of Gold', 18–24 in. tall; 'Crown of Rays', 24 in., often starts flowering in July but can be delayed until August with pinching or cutting back; and 'Golden Fleece', a 15- to 18-in.-tall heavily branched and spreading form, flowers in late summer to autumn.

Solidago caesia, wreath goldenrod, is a woodland type that grows in partial shade and dry conditions. Avoid deep shade. It grows 1–3 ft. tall.

Solidago sempervirens, seaside goldenrod, tolerates poor, high-sodium, sandy soils. Grows 4–6 ft. tall and benefits from cutting back before flowering for height control.

Many hybrid cultivars, which most likely derive from *Solidago canadensis*, *S. sphacelata*, and *S. virgaurea*, can be rapid spreaders that require frequent control.

Stachys byzantina

Zone: 4–8
Common Name: lamb's ear
Family: Lamiaceae
Description: woolly, soft gray leaves; unattractive pink flowers on silvery spike
Size: 12–15 in. (8 in.) high; 18 in. wide
Exposure: full sun
Flowering: June–July

PRUNING: Deadheading keeps the plants attractive and reduces the decline of the foliage, which can occur for several reasons, including if the plant is allowed to go to seed. Removing the flowering spikes before they bloom may be desirable since the flowers are not especially significant and their appearance can detract from the outstanding silver foliage for which the plant is primarily grown. Plants may benefit from thinning in midsummer to open them up to more sunlight and better air circulation, thus reducing the chance for rot. Deadleafing of lamb's ear often is needed periodically throughout the summer to remove rotted or generally declined foliage. Leaves snap off easily with a sharp thumbnail. Cut back any large sections of the plant that may have rotted. Regrowth usually will occur in the autumn. Do not prune for the winter; cut off winter-damaged foliage in the early spring.

OTHER MAINTENANCE: Good drainage is the primary requirement for good growth. Foliar diseases and rot can occur in conditions of high moisture and humidity. Avoid overhead irrigation, and make sure foliage is dry going into the evening. Divide in the spring every 4–5 years to maintain vigor.

RELATED PLANTS: *Stachys byzantina* 'Helene von Stein' has dynamic large leaves that normally hold up well with minimal summer deadleafing in my garden. Thinning of some of the large leaves may be beneficial in southern gardens, although this cultivar appears to be more heat tolerant, as well as more winter hardy, than most forms. Deadhead, or prevent flowering altogether, to enjoy the fabulous foliage.

Stachys byzantina 'Silver Carpet' is a non-flowering form that saves the gardener the trouble of deadheading.

Stachys grandiflora (*S. macrantha*), big betony, is grown mainly for its attractive violet flower spikes. Deadheading usually doesn't prolong bloom, but it does improve the overall appearance of the plant and prevents reseeding. Plants benefit from cutting tatty foliage down to fresh basal foliage later in the summer. Foliage decline is likely to occur if plants are subjected to dry conditions. Plants can spread to form large colonies in rich moist soil, but spread is minimal in drier conditions. Flower quality and overall plant performance is improved if the plant is grown in partial shade in hot climates and provided with supplemental water.

Stokesia laevis

Zone: 5–9
Common Name: stokes' aster
Family: Asteraceae
Description: lavender-blue fringed daisy-like flowers; straplike green leaves
Size: 12–15 in. (8 in.) high; 15 in. wide
Exposure: full sun
Flowering: July–August

PRUNING: Deadheading can prolong bloom through the summer. Several flowers are born per flower stalk and they usually open from the top down. Deadhead old flowers down to new lateral flower buds, then cut the entire stalk off at the base when all the flowering is finished. Sporadic rebloom may occur. Deadheading often requires close inspection because the old buds and the new buds resemble each other after the petals fall off. The basal foliage remains evergreen into the winter. Cut off any dead foliage in the spring.

OTHER MAINTENANCE: Well-draining soil, particularly in the winter, is essential to survival of *Stokesia*. It is drought tolerant. May frost heave with fluctuating soil temperatures, so spring planting is recommended; avoid fall planting. Division in the spring is required about every 4 years to maintain vigor.

RELATED PLANTS: *Stokesia laevis* 'Alba' is a white form that is rather unattractive as the flowers fade. Deadhead regularly to keep up the appearance of the plant.

Stokesia laevis 'Blue Stone' has a longer bloom period than most. It may bloom for up to 12 weeks with deadheading.

Stokesia laevis 'Klaus Jelitto' was rated by many people as their favorite out of hundreds of perennials during an open tour of my gardens, probably due to the plant's large 4-in.-diameter sky blue flowers and glossy leathery leaves.

Stylophorum diphyllum

Zone: 4–9
Common Name: wood poppy
Family: Papaveraceae
Description: bright yellow poppylike flowers; lobed green leaves with silver undersides
Size: 18–24 in. high; 18 in. wide
Exposure: shade
Flowering: May–June

PRUNING: Plants self-seed nicely if not deadheaded, creating a naturalized effect in woodland plantings, and the drooping, silvery, poppylike seed capsules are attractive.

Deadhead if seeding is not desired. Foliage may yellow and completely deteriorate in hot, dry summers. Deadleafing helps to maintain a decent appearance for a bit longer; if foliage damage is severe, cut back to new basal growth if present. Keeping plants moist will also help the foliage hold longer. Sporadic rebloom may even occur. Plants usually completely die down in the autumn.

OTHER MAINTENANCE: Best performance of this native plant is obtained in high-organic, moist soils. Water during periods of drought to maintain foliage. Plants prefer to be left undisturbed. Divide in early spring or fall, taking care to not damage the thick, long roots.

RELATED PLANTS: *Stylophorum lasiocarpum* is an Asiatic relative of *S. diphyllum* that has larger, more deeply lobed leaves. It reputably has a longer bloom period in the spring and summer.

Tanacetum coccineum (Chrysanthemum coccineum)

Zone: 3–7
Common Name: painted daisy
Family: Asteraceae
Description: white, pink, lilac, or red daisy-like flowerheads; fernlike leaves
Size: 2–3 ft. high; 1 ft. wide
Exposure: full sun
Flowering: June–July

PRUNING: To prolong bloom, first deadhead plants to a lateral bud or leaf. Then, after all flowering is finished, cut or shear stems down to newly developed basal foliage. Sporadic rebloom may occur later in the season. Painted daisy often flops; pinching plants when they are about 6 in. tall can produce sturdier growth. Do not prune the basal foliage back any further for the winter, but trim plants as needed in the early spring.

OTHER MAINTENANCE: High maintenance. Sorry to say it, but this is a rather "doggy" perennial. Poor drainage, particularly over the winter, is the usual demise of this plant, and thus it is very short-lived on heavy clay soils. Provide afternoon shade in areas with hot summers. Supplemental irrigation during dry periods is beneficial. Subject to frost heaving, painted daisy benefits from a winter mulch. Spring planting is advisable. Requires frequent division, about every 2–3 years to maintain a decent plant. Staking is needed, or a gangly habit prevails. Really not worth all the trouble!

Tanacetum parthenium (*Chrysanthemum parthenium*)

Zone: 5–8
Common Name: feverfew
Family: Asteraceae
Description: white and yellow buttonlike
    flowers; fernlike scented leaves
Size: 1–3 ft. high; 2 ft. wide
Exposure: full sun to partial shade
Flowering: June–September

PRUNING: Deadhead or shear (with hedge shears) plants before too many seeds set, if at all possible, or you inevitably will have more feverfew than you could ever want. Feverfew is short-lived and is often considered biennial or even annual in nature, so allowing some seeding keeps plants in the gardens. Actually it's pretty hard not to have some seeding because it seems that even with the most diligent deadheading seeding occurs. Most cultivars come true from seed, and they are easily removed or transplanted if not in the perfect spot. Plants, particularly golden forms, may need to be sheared all the way down to new basal growth after flowering to maintain a strong appearance. Rebloom may occur. Low growth usually remains evergreen over the winter.

Plants can be pinched when they are about 6–8 in. tall and then again 2–3 weeks later. Or, easier yet, shear plants back by one-half when they are 12 in. tall or so. Flowering may be slightly delayed with pruning, and fuller, more compact plants are produced. Feverfew benefits from a light fertilizing when it is pinched or cut back.

OTHER MAINTENANCE: One of the few members of the daisy family that actually tolerates some shade. Give the plants good drainage in the winter to ensure survival. Dwarf forms often melt out in high humidity. Needs division every year or two in the spring to maintain vigor. (Although I really can't imagine dividing feverfew when there are so many seedlings!) For use in the informal garden where seeding is not considered invasive or weedy and is not a major maintenance issue.

RELATED PLANTS: *Tanacetum corymbosum* has neater, clean-cut foliage. It is a longer-lived species, although it is not readily available. Grows to 3 ft. tall.

Tanacetum vulgare, tansy, requires deadheading to prevent seeding. Plants spread invasively by underground roots, especially in fertile soil, requiring a good deal of maintenance to control.

Telekia speciosa (*Buphthalmum speciosum*)

Zone: 4–7
Common Name: scented oxeye
Family: Asteraceae
Description: yellow daisy-like flowerheads;
    large, coarse, heart-shaped leaves
Size: 4–5 ft. high; to 5 ft. wide
Exposure: full sun or partial shade
Flowering: June–August

PRUNING: The flowers, which attract a wonderful moth, are long-lasting, but they are produced rather sparsely for such a large plant. Cutting back, pinching, or removal of terminal flower buds in an effort to delay bloom or reduce height is not effective, and deadheading doesn't seem to do much to prolong bloom. The deadheads are unattractive, though, in their early stages (they become more attractive with age), so removal of a few of them, to lateral buds, will prevent the deadheads from detracting from the beauty of the new flowers. As the last flowers finish, leave the remaining deadheads for the golden finch to feed on in early August and September. Some of the large, coarse leaves may become tattered by midsummer, and removal by deadleafing improves the overall appeal of the plant. If damage is severe, often due to periods of prolonged drought, it is beneficial to cut all the old leaves and flowering stems down to the fresh foliage that has developed at the base. Plants blacken and turn to mush with frost; cut off foliage in late autumn but allow seedheads to remain for winter interest, if desired.

OTHER MAINTENANCE: Plants prefer moist soils, although they are tough and will tolerate alkaline, poor, even dry conditions for short periods. Plants expand to great proportions and so need to be given adequate space in the garden. Normally self-supporting, but a stem or two may bend over after a heavy rain or later in the flowering season. Scented oxeye does not require frequent division unless to control the spread.

RELATED PLANTS: *Buphthalmum salicifolium*, willowleaf oxeye, has shorter 1- to 2-ft.-tall stems, but they are weak and require support. Cutting back by one-half at planting or in late spring will often help to reduce the flopping problem, although it does not offer a complete cure. Deadheading will prolong bloom. Cut plants back after flowering to clean-up toppled stems.

Teucrium chamaedrys

Zone: 4–9
Common Name: germander
Family: Lamiaceae
Description: purple flowers; shiny evergreen leaves
Size: 12 in. high; 12–24 in. wide
Exposure: full sun
Flowering: June–July

PRUNING: Shear and shape plants in the early spring to about 6 in. from the ground if they grow leggy or woody or if they are being use for hedging. Shear off flower buds if bloom is not desired on hedge plants. Shearing off winter-damaged branch tips generally is needed annually in the spring, at least in the Midwest and colder areas, as germander invariably is injured over the winter. Plants can also be sheared by about one-third and shaped after flowering to promote fuller growth. Any heavy pruning should be done by late August to allow the plants to harden for the winter.

OTHER MAINTENANCE: Requires well-draining soil. Usually suffers winter burn in areas of high winds. Protect plants with evergreen boughs. Not really a reliable hedge plant in the Midwest, as winter damage is more the norm. Divide in the spring, if needed.

Thalictrum aquilegiifolium

Zone: 5–8
Common Name: meadow rue
Family: Ranunculaceae
Description: fluffy pink flowerheads; columbine-like leaves
Size: 2–3 ft. high; 2–3 ft. wide
Exposure: partial shade
Flowering: May–June

PRUNING: Plants often benefit from cutting down to the ground after flowering, when fresh new growth is emerging and old growth is declining, particularly in dry locations. In rich moist soil the foliage remains attractive all season long, and interesting seedheads develop that further add to the display. Meadow rue may seed itself if not deadheaded. If plants are not cut down after flowering, do so for the winter.

OTHER MAINTENANCE: Fairly low maintenance. Prefers rich moist soils. No staking required. Division generally is not needed for many years, but when it is it should be performed in the early spring or in the early autumn for establishment before winter. Pest free if given sufficient moisture.

RELATED PLANTS: There are a number of outstanding related species. Most of these are taller (3–5 ft.) and flower in the summer rather than the spring. They may benefit from pinching or cutting back when one-half their mature size, sometime in late May or early June, to reduce height and eliminate the need for staking. Foliage may decline after flowering, in which case the plants can be cut back partially or all the way down to basal growth if necessary. Some of the more notable relatives include *Thalictrum delavayi* 'Hewitt's Double', *T. flavum* subsp. *glaucum*, and *T. rochebrunianum*.

Thermopsis caroliniana

Zone: 3–8
Common Name: southern lupine
Family: Fabaceae
Description: yellow lupine-like flowers; palmately compound leaves
Size: 3–4 ft. high; 3 ft. wide
Exposure: full sun
Flowering: May–June

PRUNING: Interesting seedpods develop if the plants are not deadheaded. The foliage may decline by midsummer; cut the plants to the ground if this occurs.

OTHER MAINTENANCE: Southern lupine is often hard to establish due to its taproot, but once plants take hold they can survive with a good deal of neglect for many years. Tolerates low-fertility soil and drought. Avoid disturbing.

Thymus

Zone: 5–8
Common Name: thyme
Family: Lamiaceae
Description: small pink or purple flower spikes; tiny oblong scented leaves
Size: 3–12 in. high; 12–18 in. wide
Exposure: full sun
Flowering: June–July

PRUNING: Shearing off old flower stems on thymes before seed set will prevent reseeding, but allowing some seeding can be effective in the perennial garden (Plate 126). The tips of the plants are often damaged over the winter. Shear off dead branches to new growth in the early spring. Several distinct forms of thyme exist. Some are subshrubs and some are mat-forming ground covers. The larger, more upright-growing shrub forms may get leggy and woody with age. Shear down to about 6 in. above the ground and shape in the spring every 3 years or so to rejuvenate. Heavy pruning should be completed by late August so that plants have time to harden for the winter. Plants remain evergreen; do not prune for the winter.

OTHER MAINTENANCE: Well-draining soil is necessary to prevent rot. Tolerates low fertility and sandy, dry soil. Divide if plants die out in the center.

Tiarella cordifolia

Zone: 3–8
Common Name: foamflower
Family: Saxifragaceae
Description: white flower spikes; green heart-shaped leaves

Size: 12 in. (6 in.) high; 12–24 in. wide
Exposure: partial to full shade
Flowering: May–June

PRUNING: Deadheading improves the overall appearance of the plant and often produces sporadic rebloom later in the season. The foliage remains evergreen to semi-evergreen, so do not prune for the winter. Plants spread by stolons, and these are easily pulled up and cut off to prevent invasion.

OTHER MAINTENANCE: Requires humus-rich, acidic soil. Avoid sunny locations. Tolerates brief periods of drought. Stoloniferous habit is good for use as a groundcover and spread is easy to control. Divide in the spring as needed, or remove and replant runners at anytime.

RELATED PLANTS: *Tiarella wherryi*, wherry's foamflower, is a clump former. Shallow rooted. Plant in the spring for establishment before winter. Press back into the soil if frost heaving occurs.

Tradescantia ×andersoniana

Zone: 3–9
Common Name: spiderwort
Family: Commelinaceae
Description: purple, blue, white, or pink flowers; straplike leaves
Size: 18–24 in. high; 24 in. wide
Exposure: full sun or partial shade
Flowering: June–August

PRUNING: Plants usually are in flower for about 2 months or more, but individual flowers last for only half a day and then the petals neatly dissolve away. Normally all buds are closed by late afternoon (an important feature to keep in mind when designing an evening garden!). Once all flowering is finished in the cluster of buds deadhead down to new lateral flowers. Deadheading requires close inspection to be sure that all the flowers in the bud cluster have finished. Dead-

heading is particularly useful to prolong the bloom of young or vigorously growing plants, which may flower for the entire summer. Most often, though, the plant's foliage browns after the initial bloom, or it is infected with rust, normally by midsummer, and the plant will benefit from being cut back by two-thirds or to the ground (see Figure 10-5). New lush foliage emerges within about 3 weeks. The foliage remains low (6 in.) and plants often repeat bloom, although usually only sparsely. Keep plants moist for more vigorous regrowth. Plants that are stressed by drought, heat, or competition from other plants, or are in need of division, may not put on much, if any, new growth that season after pruning to the ground. Some plants in such conditions will put on a small amount of regrowth when the cool weather of autumn arrives. Cutting plants back or deadheading before seed sets will reduce reseeding, which can be prolific in certain cases.

Spiderwort has a tendency to flop and often requires staking. Cutting the plants back by one-half in early May or when they are about 12 in. tall can produce more compact plants. I have even cut plants back by about one-third later in May when they were in tight bud—I had forgotten to do it earlier in the month—and although the flowering was slightly reduced due to the removal of many of the terminal buds, the plant's habit was more pleasing.

If plants are cut to the ground in the summer, pruning again for the winter is usually not necessary except to remove any flowering stalks that may be present. The new low foliage often remains fairly green into the winter. Plants that are not cut back in the summer should be pruned after a killing frost, as the old flowering stems turn to mush.

OTHER MAINTENANCE: Good plant for moist areas. Better flowering occurs in sunny locations. Staking may be necessary unless plants are pruned or shorter growing cultivars are selected. Divide to keep vigorous or to control spread, in the early spring or autumn.

RELATED PLANTS: *Tradescantia ×andersoniana* 'Zwanenburg Blue' (deep blue), 'Snowcap' (white), and 'Pauline' (pink, and normally shorter growing at 15 in.) are just a few of my favorite cultivars.

Tricyrtis hirta

Zone: 4–8
Common Name: hairy toad lily
Family: Liliaceae
Description: starry lilac flowers heavily speckled purple; soft hairy oval leaves
Size: 2–3 ft. high; 2 ft. wide
Exposure: partial shade
Flowering: September–October

PRUNING: If the seeds have a chance to ripen before being hit by a frost (this is seldom the case in my Ohio gardens), young seedlings will appear at the base of the plant in the spring—*Tricyrtis hirta* does not seed aggressively all over the garden. If shorter, fuller plants are desired, toad lily responds well to cutting back by one-half in early June. Flowering may be slightly delayed with pruning. Plants turn to mush when hit by a heavy freeze. Cut down for the winter.

OTHER MAINTENANCE: Best performance is in rich, high-organic soil. Long-lived, easy to grow, and seldom needs division. Division should be done in the spring, if desired.

RELATED PLANTS: *Tricyrtis hirta* 'Miyazaki' is a self-seeding form.
  Tricyrtis formosana (*T. stolonifera*), formosa toad lily, spreads by stolons but not aggressively so. Cutting back by one-half in early June produces fuller plants that flower at 2 ft. rather than 3 ft. and with two breaks per stem (Plate 127).

Trollius ×cultorum

Zone: 3–7
Common Name: hybrid globeflower
Family: Ranunculaceae
Description: yellow or orange globelike flowers; dark green leaves
Size: 18–24 in. high; 24 in. wide
Exposure: partial shade
Flowering: June

PRUNING: The foliage on hybrid globeflower usually declines after all flowering is finished; cut the plants back at this time and keep them moist. Slight rebloom may occur in the autumn. Feeding the plants after cutting them back may help to encourage rebloom.

OTHER MAINTENANCE: Constantly moist, high-organic soils and cool climates foster best performance of this perennial. Not a good perennial for dry, hot regions. Supply supplemental irrigation during dry periods. Plants do not like to be disturbed, and division is not needed for many years. Divide in the spring only if essential, as plants are slow to establish afterwards.

Valeriana officinalis

Zone: 4
Common Name: common valerian
Family: Valerianaceae
Description: pink-tinged fragrant flowers; pinnately compound leaves
Size: 2–5 ft. high; 1–1½ ft. wide
Exposure: full sun or partial shade
Flowering: May–June

PRUNING: Plants have a tendency to seed themselves ad nauseam. Foliage gets tatty after flowering. The entire plant should be cut completely down to the ground after flowering, but before seed sets, for fresh new low growth. Plants do not need to be pruned again for the winter.

OTHER MAINTENANCE: Not really a plant for general use in the perennial garden. But even with all its faults, I still love valerian in my own gardens because nothing can beat its fragrance in the spring. I have only planted it for one client, in a cottage garden for fragrance, and I was politely asked to remove it and all of its offspring because the client thought it was too weedy. Oh well! It tolerates dry or wet conditions, partial shade, and alkaline soils.

Verbascum

Zone: 5–8
Common Name: mullein
Family: Scrophulariaceae
Description: yellow, rose, or white flower
    spikes; soft, often hairy, coarse leaves
Size: 3–6 ft. high; 1½–2 ft. wide
Exposure: full sun
Flowering: summer (varies with the species)

PRUNING: Most species of *Verbascum* are either short-lived perennials or biennials. Cutting the old flowering spikes down immediately after flowering may encourage plants to be more perennial in nature. It can also prevent the abundant seeding that often occurs with *Verbascum*, and pruning after flowering encourages some species to have a slight rebloom in the autumn. Allowing some seeding in the garden, though, may be the only way for the plants to persist.

OTHER MAINTENANCE: Plants need a lean, very well-draining soil for survival. Sandy or rocky soil is preferred. Drought tolerant. Death from "wet feet" is a common occurrence in heavy soils. Avoid high fertility, which can lead to lanky plants. Staking is usually required with the taller forms. Division is seldom necessary. Often attacked by spider mites.

RELATED PLANTS: *Verbascum chaixii*, chaix mullein, is a short-lived perennial.
    Verbascum olympicum, olympic mullein, and *V. phoeniceum*, purple mullein, survive

in zones 6–8 and are long-lived under the right conditions. *Verbascum olympicum* may rebloom in the autumn if deadheaded.

Vernonia noveboracensis

Zone: 5–9
Common Name: New York ironweed
Family: Asteraceae
Description: deep purple, flat-topped flower
    clusters; coarse green leaves
Size: 3–9 ft. high; 2 ft. wide
Exposure: full sun
Flowering: September–October

PRUNING: Deadheading plants before seed set can reduce prolific seeding, which may occur particularly in moist areas. First-year seedlings may be desirable, though, as they are interesting, usually short 12- to 14-in.-high plants with intense purple flowers and may be more attractive than the parent plant.
    When grown in rich moist soil plants can tower to 9 ft. tall, too large for many perennial gardens. Plants respond to a variety of pruning methods to reduce their height, to create fuller plants, to stagger bloom time, or to layer plantings. One such method is to cut the plants down to the ground when they reach 2 ft. tall. Another is to cut plants back by 1 or 2 ft. when they are 3–4 ft. tall. Plants cut back by 1 ft. won't have that great of a reduction in height, but they flower about one week later than unpruned plants. Plants cut back by 2 ft. may have about a 3-week delay in bloom and will flower nicely at 2–2½ ft. rather than 4–4½ ft.

OTHER MAINTENANCE: Interesting native plant that prefers moist, slightly acidic conditions. The moister the soil, the taller the plants may be. Pruning to reduce seeding and size may be desirable in most perennial gardens.

RELATED PLANTS: *Vernonia fasciculata* has a 4-ft. mature height and may be more manageable than *V. noveboracensis* for most garden settings.

Veronica austriaca subsp. teucrium (Veronica teucrium)

Zone: 3–8
Common Name: Hungarian speedwell
Family: Scrophulariaceae
Description: blue flower spikes; narrow toothed leaves
Size: 18 in. high; 24 in. wide
Exposure: full sun
Flowering: May–June

PRUNING: Plants have a tendency to sprawl and become weedy. Shear them back by one-half after flowering; hedge shears work well for this. A low mound develops in 2–3 weeks after shearing and the plants stay compact for the remainder of the season (Plates 128–130). No additional pruning is needed until the following spring. If plants are not sheared before seeds mature, reseeding can occur. Plants that are not cut back during the summer may develop long straggly growth that is unattractive over the winter, so if plants are not cut back in summer it is best to prune stems down to tiny basal growth in late autumn.

OTHER MAINTENANCE: Easy to grow. Provide good drainage. Pea staking can help support the plant during flowering. Divide in the spring or autumn if the plants get too big for their space. Excessive flopping may be a sign that division is in order.

Veronica spicata

Zone: 3–8
Common Name: spike speedwell
Family: Scrophulariaceae
Description: pink, blue, or white spike flowers; narrow toothed leaves
Size: 10–24 in. high; 12–24 in. wide
Exposure: full sun
Flowering: June–August

PRUNING: Deadheading will prolong bloom, and first-year plants often flower all summer if deadheaded. Deadhead plants by cutting them back to lateral buds or, if buds are not visible, to the first lateral leaves. Many forms, particularly the lower growing cultivars such as 'Red Fox' and 'Goodness Grows', should then be sheared down to the new basal foliage when all secondary flowering is finished. Hedge shears make quick work of this step. The low basal growth remains attractive for the rest of the season, and sporadic rebloom may occur. Some taller forms look best cut down to basal growth as well if their stems start to fall over or if they decline in late summer. Keep plants moist after cutting down.

Taller forms of *Veronica spicata*, such as 'Blue Charm' and 'Blue Peter', can be a bit floppy at times, particularly in overly moist or partially shaded sites; cutting these plants back before flowering produces nice results. 'Blue Charm', when cut back by about 6 in. in early June, flowered at 2–2½ ft., rather than 3–3½ ft., with about a one-week delay (Plate 131). 'Blue Peter' cut back by one-half in early June flowered at 1½ ft., about 1 ft. shorter than normal. If tall-growing forms are not cut down earlier in the season, tidy gardeners may opt for pruning plants down for the winter, as the plants are not especially attractive at that point.

OTHER MAINTENANCE: Provide well-draining soil, particularly over the winter. *Veronica* prefers fairly fertile soil. Staking may be required. My experience has shown that most cultivars and related species—including *V. spicata* 'Goodness Grows', *V. spicata* 'Icicle', and *Veronica* 'Sunny Border Blue'—require frequent division to maintain a strong plant, usually by about the second or third year.

RELATED PLANTS: *Veronica spicata* subsp. *incana*, woolly speedwell, is a gray-foliaged plant that must have good drainage for survival. Deadheading can prolong bloom. The foliage often gets tatty in midsummer; shear it down for quick regrowth. It is drought tolerant.

Veronica alpina 'Alba', white alpine speedwell, is long blooming with deadheading. Shear when all flowering is finished. The basal foliage remains evergreen through the winter in the Midwest and the South.

Veronicastrum virginicum

Zone: 3–8
Common Name: culver's root
Family: Scrophulariaceae
Description: white spike flowers; narrow green leaves
Size: 3–6 ft. high; 3–4 ft. wide
Exposure: full sun or partial shade
Flowering: August–September

PRUNING: Deadhead plants to lateral flower buds for a longer bloom period by one month or more. If the old foliage should brown, which often occurs after all flowering is finished, cut it down to new basal growth. Plants may flop in partial shade, but cutting them back by one-half in May or early June can result in more compact, self-supporting plants. Plants cut back by one-half in early May flowered at 18 in. tall rather than 3 ft.

OTHER MAINTENANCE: This native plant prefers moist, well-draining soil. Better growth in full sun. Staking will be necessary if plants are grown in too much shade or if they are not pruned prior to flowering. Performance may be improved with a summer feeding. Divide in the spring as needed. May be subject to fourlined plant bug damage.

Viola odorata

Zone: 5–8
Common Name: sweet violet
Family: Violaceae
Description: fragrant violet, rose, white, or blue flowers; deep green heart-shaped leaves
Size: 4–8 in. high; 12–15 in. wide
Exposure: partial shade
Flowering: April–May

PRUNING: Deadheading sweet violet can prolong bloom or cause repeat bloom later in the season, but it can be a tedious job. Use a sharp thumbnail to quickly snap off old flowers, or use sharp pruning scissors. Just let the old blooms drop to the ground, as trying to gather such small flowers could drive the gardener over the edge. Deadheading before seed sets can help reduce abundant seeding. I have used hedge shears to shear large areas after most of the bloom is finished to encourage fresh growth and a light repeat bloom later in the season. Plants spread by runners, often to weedy proportions. Prune runners back to keep plants in control. Shear back any rank growth in the autumn for better spring performance. Pinch plants before flowering if growth looks leggy.

OTHER MAINTENANCE: Sweet violet can become a high-maintenance "weed" due to seeding and invasive root system. Even if you have never planted violets they seem to appear out of nowhere. Very moist and fertile sites will enhance the plant's weedy nature. Lifting sections and removing them from the garden is needed often.

Ornamental Grasses

GENERAL MAINTENANCE

Most grasses prefer full sun, although some tolerate more shade (a list of shade-tolerant grasses is included below). Grasses benefit from a high-organic, well-prepared soil. It generally is best to plant them in the early spring or the early autumn to allow them to establish before either the heat of summer or the cold of winter. If planting in the summer or during periods of high temperatures, cutting the foliage back by about one-third will help reduce stress. Keep new plantings moist. Grasses are not heavy feeders, and overly rich or high-nitrogen soils can cause weak growth and increase the need for staking.

Grasses normally don't require division for about 5 to 7 years after planting. Division is best performed as the new growth emerges in the spring, although grasses will tolerate division at other times. Division can be difficult, often requiring the assistance of a good axe and saw. If growth progresses before division is accomplished, plants should be cut back by about one-third.

Pests are usually not a major problem for grasses. One pest that has become a concern on *Miscanthus* is mealybug. Mealybug is very difficult to control, and digging out and destroying infested plants is the most common recommendation. Do not compost removed plant material. Rust can occur under certain conditions in the spring; if rust develops, prune off infected leaves as soon as they appear. This may even involve shearing the plants to within a few inches of the ground.

PRUNING REQUIREMENTS

Although grasses generally do not require cutting back for the health of the plant, most will benefit from cutting back once a year, if for nothing else but the aesthetics of the garden. Grasses that are not cut back in the spring may be slower to start new growth, since the old foliage will impede the sun from hitting and warming the crown of the plant.

Most grasses should be cut back just before new growth begins in the spring; this is normally mid-March to early April in the Midwest or late February to early March in milder areas. *Calamagrostis* often breaks earlier than *Miscanthus* or *Pennisetum*, particularly during a mild spring, and may need to be cut back earlier. The grass will not be harmed if some of the new foliage that emerged in the spring is cut when you prune off the old foliage. Certain grasses may not need cutting back at all, only removal of any dead leaves by pulling them out by hand (such grasses are indicated in the list below). Putting aside the matter of outstanding winter interest, dormant foliage left standing on the plants often provides additional winter protection to the crown against cold and excess moisture to help prevent winter losses, as was discussed with overwintering perennials in general. Some gardeners choose to cut their grasses down in the autumn if the grasses tend to fall over or lose their color in winter, or if time is limited in the spring. (See below for a list of grasses that do not provide winter interest.) In some dry climates where dormant grasses may be a fire hazard, cutting them back is the law.

Most grasses should be cut down to within 3 to 4 in. of the ground. Certain grasses, particularly those that are inclined to be short-lived, resent close shearing and may not recover if cut down closer than 3 to 4 in. Tying the grass together with heavy twine before cutting it down can help tremendously with clean-up (see Plate 65). Once it is cut at the base, the bundle can be easily transported to the compost pile. It also helps if two people are working together. Wear gloves and long sleeves as well as safety goggles when cutting back, as the blades of the grass can be razor sharp. Hand pruners can be used on a small-scale planting, or hand-held hedge shears, electric hedge shears, weed-eaters with a blade, or even chain saws may be the tool of choice. As the size of the planting increases, so can the intensity of the tool used. I find electric hedge shears to be the most useful.

Deadheading may be necessary on spring-blooming grasses if the heads shatter or become unattractive later in the summer. Deadheading also reduces seeding on grasses so inclined (see list below). Some people feel that the flowers of certain grasses, such as blue fescue (*Festuca glauca*), only detract from the foliage, in which case the panicles can be removed before flowering occurs.

Grasses such as *Briza media* and *Elymus racemosus* 'Glaucus' (and others included in the list below) benefit from a shearing in the summer to produce a fresh crop of attractive foliage for later in the season. If the grass gets scorched during a dry period, warm-season species (such as *Miscanthus* and *Pennisetum*) can be cut to within several inches of the ground and cool-season grasses (such as *Calamagrostis* and *Festuca*) can be cut back by about one-third to promote a flush of new foliage. Be sure to provide sufficient moisture to cut-back grasses to ensure re-growth. According to John Greenlee, an expert on ornamental grasses and author of *The Encyclopedia of Ornamental Grasses*, spreading groundcover grasses such as *Carex glauca* may benefit from a shearing early in the season to force better tillering. He also said that gardeners in mild climates are experimenting with shearing warm-season grasses in July or August to form new growth for improved fall color, though often at the expense of flowering.

Some grasses, such as variegated forms of *Miscanthus*, have a tendency to flop and need staking (see list below). Cutting grasses down to 3 to 4 in. above the ground in June or July can reduce their height, eliminate the need for staking, and possibly put a large-growing grass more in scale with the rest of the planting. It may also cause a delay in flowering, depending on the species. Bob Saul of Saul Nursery in Georgia cuts variegated miscanthus down to 4 in. in early July when plants are 5 ft. tall. The results of such pruning are plants that mature at an upright 2½ to 3 ft. rather than a flopping 6 ft. In the Midwest I cut plants down to 18 in. in early July, and they grow 5 ft. within 2 weeks—obviously cutting down lower is in order. This is an area where more experimentation is needed.

The lists below group various grasses according to their pruning and maintenance requirements. Grasses should be cut back in the spring unless otherwise noted.

Minimal Spring Pruning

For the plants included here, spring clean-up may not be needed in some years, particularly when plants are young or if the winter was kind. Dead foliage should be pulled out by hand in the spring, or if winter damage is severe or if the dead foliage has accumulated, plants can be cut back.

Carex conica 'Marginata': Normally evergreen, but if dead tips develop the plants should be cut back to 2–3 in. above the crown.

Carex glauca: Semi-evergreen; if foliage looks tatty in spring, cut back to 2–3 in. above crown or shear to force tillering.

Festuca: Do not shear any closer than 3–4 in. from the crown. Can be cut in the autumn or spring; summer-pruned plants may not recover.

Helictotrichon: Semi-evergreen in cold climates. Usually requires minimal pruning.

Cut Back in Autumn or Winter

These plants have limited winter interest or color, or the stems break down, and are best pruned in the autumn or winter.

Arundo donax: Stems may flop over the winter; also loses a good deal of foliage.

Briza media: Foliage discolors with a hard frost, but old leaves may provide additional winter protection in cold climates.

Calamagrostis brachytricha: Attractive until late December.

Deschampsia: Foliage stays green until freezing temperatures.

Elymus (*Leymus*): Loses color; cut down to 4 in. from the ground in early December.

Glyceria maxima 'Variegata': Loses interest.

Imperata cylindrica 'Red Baron': Loses color.

Molinia caerulea subsp. *arundinacea* 'Skyracer': Stalks break off at the crown of the plant in rainy or snowy weather—self-cleans old foliage. Shorter growing *Molinia* may hold up better in the winter.

Pennisetum orientale: Loses winter interest in November, although I like to leave foliage up until spring to help overwinter marginally hardy *Pennisetum* in our area.

Saccharum ravennae (*Erianthus ravennae*): Attractive into January.

Spartina pectinata 'Aureomarginata': Loses interest in mid-January.

Spodiopogon sibiricus: Effective until hard frost.

Sporobolus: Holds until early December.

Cut Back in Summer

The plants listed here should be cut back in the summer to maintain fresh foliage.

Arrhenatherum: Mow or shear in late summer as foliage declines.

Briza media: Cut back to 3–4 in. above the ground at the end of June; the new foliage will stay nice until a hard frost.

Deschampsia: During hot summers, cut down to 12 in. in late August.

Elymus racemosus 'Glaucus' (*Leymus racemosus* 'Glaucus'): Can be sheared once or twice in the same season to produce new blue foliage for late-season interest.

Imperata cylindrica 'Red Baron': Cut off any reverted shoots immediately as they form—this is a very aggressive spreader.

Phalaris arundinaceae 'Feesey's Form': Rogue out any reverted shoots.

Phalaris arundinaceae var. *picta* ('Picta'): Mow or shear plants down as foliage declines in the late summer.

Deadhead To Reduce Seeding or Improve Appearance

Briza media

Calamagrostis brachytricha: Deadhead to reduce seeding.

Calamagrostis epigejos: Deadhead to reduce seeding.

Chasmanthium latifolium: Deadhead to reduce seeding.

Festuca: Flowers hold into August. Deadhead to reduce seeding. *Festuca* 'Solling' and *Festuca glauca* 'Elijah Blue' are sterile forms.

Hystrix: Flowers are effective into late August and then they shatter. Deadhead to reduce seeding. Plants are often short-lived; allowing some seeding can ensure constancy in the garden.

Koeleria glauca: Flowers lose effect by late July or early August.

Melica ciliata: Flowers deteriorate by late July.

Miscanthus sinensis: Heavy seeding is reported in southern regions. Care should be taken with *Miscanthus* grown in areas with an extended growing season or when using early flowering cultivars, which may seed later in the season.

Pennisetum alopecuroides: Seeds moderately in some situations. 'Hameln' does not seed; 'Moudry' is a prolific seeder.

Pennisetum orientale: Not normally an aggressive seeder.

Schizachyrium scoparium: May seed to nuisance level in a border setting.

Sorghastrum nutans: Seeding can be a problem if used in a border setting.

Attractive Foliage—Remove Flowers

The following grasses may benefit from having their flowers removed so as to not detract from the attractive foliage

Elymus racemosus 'Glaucus' (*Leymus racemosus* 'Glaucus')
Festuca
Helictotrichon

Invasive by Rhizomes

Elymus racemosus 'Glaucus' (*Leymus racemosus* 'Glaucus')
Glyceria maxima 'Variegata'
Miscanthus sacchariflorus: Less invasive on heavy clay soil.
Phalaris: 'Dwarf Garters' is slower spreading than most other forms.

Cut Back To Reduce Height

These grasses usually require staking and may benefit from cutting back before flowering to reduce their height.

Melica ciliata
Miscanthus sinensis 'Gracillimus', 'Silberfeder', 'Variegatus', 'Zebrinus'
Saccharum ravennae (*Erianthus ravennae*)
Spartina pectinata 'Aureomarginata'

Shade Tolerant

The following grasses are tolerant of full or partial shade. Grasses grown in too much shade will indicate such with a flopping habit.

Calamagrostis ×*acutiflora* 'Overdam': Requires shade from hot afternoon sun.
Calamagrostis brachytricha: Partial shade.
Carex: Excellent even in deep shade.
Chasmanthium latifolium: Partial shade.
Festuca: Partial shade.
Miscanthus giganteus (*Miscanthus* 'Giganteus'): Sun loving, but it tolerates partial shade.
Panicum virgatum: Sun loving but tolerates partial shade.
Phalaris: Browns in afternoon sun.
Sesleria autumnalis
Spodiopogon sibiricus

Perennial Garden Planting and Maintenance Schedule

IF you have a perennial garden there will always be something for you to do with your time. It may be a large physical undertaking, such as renovating the whole thing, or perhaps it's the small, simple mental pleasure of thinking about the garden and how beautiful it is, or was, or is going to be next year.

The information in this appendix provides a guideline to the seasonal tasks involved in managing a perennial garden, and it is meant to be just that—a guideline. Only by working with your garden will you gain a more thorough understanding of what needs to be done and when. I am quite a taskmaster, with a penchant for list writing. I think you will find it helpful to do the same. Walk around your garden and take notes on what needs to be done. Such notes can be used to organize a priority list with target times or dates for the various tasks—put the timeline on your calendar. In the spring, when things are beyond hectic in the garden, there's a pretty good chance you'll forget which plant you wanted to move and where, which one you intended to divide, or which one you wanted to remove from the garden

altogether. If you have the schedule and list that you started compiling the previous year, you will have one less thing to think about at the moment. This is particularly critical in the landscaping industry; with maintenance work to be done on many different gardens, it's almost impossible to remember what you wanted to do and when in each of them.

A word on garden journals. I'd like to be able to tell you that I keep one, one of those sweet journals with pretty drawings and inspirational phrases. I have made the best efforts in this direction but, to date, have failed. I do keep records in my weekly calendar so that I can see when I performed a certain task in my own or my clients' gardens. I keep notes, although brief, on specific maintenance tasks performed at each client's gardens on specific dates. For instance: "The *Tradescantia* and *Coreopsis* were cut back, the *Alchemilla* were deadleafed, we did general deadheading and weeding, and we staked the hillside aster that the dog stepped on at the Brown residence on 20 July. There were two of us there and it took 1½ hours." All these notes are helpful for planning in future years. It's a good idea to keep some kind of records, either in a book or on notebook pages (as I do, although they are usually covered with splashes of soil), in your personal garden files or, for professionals, in each client's file. Such notes have allowed me to compile the schedule contained in this appendix.

The garden planting and maintenance schedule that follows is a guideline for Midwest gardens; you will need to adjust it according to your regional conditions. Contact your local county extension agent for clarification on details specific to your growing area. Different annual weather conditions may affect the schedule as well. I have indicated here the ideal times for certain tasks. But, as we all know, you can't always get to things during the ideal time. It is best to adhere to these guidelines whenever possible, but keep in mind that perennials are very forgiving and are willing to bend on certain issues. Greater details on the how-to of each of the jobs can be found throughout the book, and especially in Sections One and Two. Specifics on individual plants are found in the Encyclopedia of Perennials in Section Three. In Appendix C I have compiled lists of plants by season to show when different species may require some form of maintenance (see lists 34–36). Appendix A provides pruning information and timing as it applies to ornamental grasses.

SPRING

There is usually so much to be done in the spring, it's not even funny. Fortunately, we've had the winter to regroup a bit, and in the spring our energy is high to get us through all the work. A busy spring is the time of year when some things may have to be put off until later when more time opens up—be willing to accept this and move on. Spring is the key time for clean-up, planting, transplanting, and dividing.

MARCH

The early part of March is usually still too cold and wet for any major activity. In milder years more can be done during the second half of the month, and this is when spring clean-up should get underway.

Planting
• Plant orders should be completed in the first week or two, if not already done; quantities may already be limited, particularly on the more unusual species.
• Ordering and purchasing tools and supplies should be done in early to mid-March. Clean and oil your tools if you didn't get to it in the autumn.
• March generally is too early for planting container-grown plants, as most are not yet available and the soil is normally too wet.
• Bareroot plants may be available in March and, if the beds are workable, can be planted at this time. They also can be potted into containers in March to allow them to get acclimated, and once they've had a chance to establish a bit they can be planted into the garden later—this is what I often do, particularly if plants arrive small.
• Take soil tests of future or existing beds. Be sure to test for organic matter content.

General Maintenance
• Remove any evergreen bough mulch, but keep handy in case of emergency cold weather. It's best to do this on a cloudy day to prevent burning of tender pale growth.
• Remove any other winter mulch from around the crowns of the perennials, but leave the mulch on the ground surrounding the plants for a couple weeks, or until early April (early May in colder areas). Again, mulch removal is best saved for a cloudy day.
• Press back into the ground any perennials that frost heaved over the winter.
• Fertilize gardens, end of March to early April.
• Top-dressing of beds can be done in late March and into April.

• Touch-up mulching can be done at the end of March.

Pruning

• In mild years, spring clean-up can begin in the last couple of weeks of March and continue into early April.

• Cut back plants that were left for winter interest. Watch for feather reed grass (*Calamagrostis* ×*acutiflora*) and other early emerging perennials such as *Pulmonaria* and *Epimedium*, which should be cut back before new growth has a chance to mature.

• Check evergreen plants for removal of dead leaves.

• Mow *Liriope*.

APRIL

April and May are usually the two busiest months in the perennial garden. I always remind myself to remain calm. This can be an unnerving time, to say the least, especially if you are in the industry. A good deal of planting, along with any spring maintenance that didn't get done in March, happens in April, provided the weather is cooperating.

Planting

• Renovation of perennial gardens should get underway in early April.

• Perennials can be divided and transplanted when growth is 3–4 in. high. If growth has gotten any larger, plants may benefit from cutting back by one-third to one-half.

• Divide woodland wildflowers after flowering. This applies only to plants in your gardens or on your own property—never collect from the wild.

• Add compost if transplanting or planting into an existing garden.

• A nonselective, nonresidual herbicide (such as Round-up) can be applied starting in about the second week of April when grass and weeds are actively growing.

• Installations and plantings usually begin around the third week of April.

• Be patient with late-emerging perennials such as *Begonia grandis*, *Ceratostigma plumbaginoides*, and *Platycodon grandiflorus*. Do not disturb or plant over them.

General Maintenance

• Fertilizing, top-dressing, and mulching that wasn't completed in March continues in April.

• April is a good time to aerate the soil with a fork or hoe; take care to not damage roots.

• All winter mulch should be removed by now in most gardens. In colder climates (perhaps zone 4 or colder) leave mulch until early May.

• Weeding begins with a bang, as the perennials haven't yet filled in enough to smother them out.

• Pea staking may need to be applied in the third or fourth week of April, particularly to fast-growing perennials like *Clematis recta* that undergo rapid growth at this time.

• Continue to fill bird feeders, as many birds migrate during late April into May and will reward you with a visit.

Pruning

• Early spring clean-up continues in April if not completed in March.

• Once warm weather is assured, prune down tender perennials such as mums (*Dendranthema*) and monch asters (*Aster* ×*frikartii* 'Monch').

• Pinching may be needed on perennials at planting.

MAY

Any planting that didn't get done in April should happen in May. I like to have the majority of the installations and planting for my business completed before the end of May, if possible, when the weather usually is still fairly cool. A good deal of pruning for height control also begins in May. Refer to the chapters on pruning in Section Two for details; consult the encyclopedia in Section Three for information on individual species and genera.

Planting

• Lots and lots of planting.

- In the home garden, for your records, take notes of locations of new plantings.
- Transplanting and division of summer- and autumn-flowering perennials can continue in May. Spring-flowering species can be divided after flowering.
- This is a good time to move or remove any unwanted perennial seedlings.
- Once everything has sprouted, take note of any empty spots for new plantings.

General Maintenance
- Top-dressing can continue early in the month if new growth isn't too large to interfere.
- Weeding continues; especially strong are the dandelions and thistle.
- Continue placement of pea stakes; hoops are needed on peonies.
- Mulch.
- Be on the lookout for the fourlined plant bug nymphs and crush them good.
- Slug control should be placed now.
- Aphids are active.
- Hang hummingbird feeders, as the birds are starting to dance in the columbine now.

Pruning
- Many summer-flowering perennials, including *Leucanthemum*, *Monarda*, *Phlox*, *Physostegia*, and *Tradescantia*, can be pinched or cut back for height control and possibly to stagger bloom.
- Thinning can be done now, especially for *Delphinium*.
- Lavenders and other subshrubs may still be breaking dormancy; see pruning options in Chapter 12.
- Spring-flowering perennials should be deadheaded or cut back or sheared after flowering.
- Do not deadhead biennials if seeding for the following year is desired.
- It is a good idea to pinch or cut back perennials by one-half at planting.
- Cutting back may be needed during divisions and transplanting.
- Prune off any growth damaged from late frosts. (In the Columbus, Ohio, area the last frost date is generally 20 May; one year a freeze on 12 May nipped the new growth on some perennials.)

SUMMER

Pruning, staking, and general maintenance are in order during the summer months. If you go away for an extended period in the summer, make sure there is someone around to water the gardens if needed, especially for a new planting. You may want to experiment with cutting back some or many of your summer-flowering plants before you leave for a long period so that you can enjoy their re-growth and flowering upon your return. You may also want to get weeds under control before you leave so that you don't have to face them when you return. Pruning in mid-summer is done to promote the autumn display. Take notes throughout the summer of plants to move or remove or divide or add, of new pruning techniques to try, of new colors to incorporate, and any other changes you may want to consider in planning for autumn and next year.

JUNE
Planting usually continues into and sometimes through June, but if the weather starts to get too hot by late June the perennials will have a more difficult time establishing. Also, plants that have been in containers all spring should be planted at this time. June is a big month for pruning, including cutting back, thinning, deadheading, and deadleafing.

Planting
- Try to finish all planting by mid-June, if possible.
- Transplanting and dividing can continue, but plants will need to be cut back and possibly shaded.
- *Dicentra spectabilis* can be transplanted now.

General Maintenance
• Be certain to keep new plantings well watered.
• Weed.
• Linking staking and single stakes should be placed in June.
• Prop up any stray branches off of neighboring plants, if needed.
• Watch for fourlined plant bug adults.
• Japanese beetles are the problem for the month.
• Baby grasshoppers are evident; apply garlic sprays now.

Pruning
• Continue to cut back spring-flowering plants, especially any that may be flopping, such as *Veronica austriaca* subsp. *teucrium* and its cultivars.
• Autumn-flowering plants should be pinched or cut back for height control as well as thinned and shaped.
• Numerous summer-flowering plants, including *Echinacea*, *Heliopsis*, *Phlox*, *Platycodon*, and *Veronica*, among others, can be cut back to extend flowering of plant groups or to create staggered or delayed flowering.
• Deadhead, Deadhead, Deadhead!!—to extend bloom of a variety of perennials and to reduce seeding of heavy seeders such as *Aquilegia*, *Iris sibirica*, and *Valeriana*.
• Prune or thin plants to keep them in their desired space. Make certain that any new perennials planted in an existing garden are not being overtaken or shaded by established neighbors widening with the warm weather.
• Deadleafing of spring-flowering perennials may be needed; the leaves of some summer bloomers, like daylilies (*Hemerocallis*), also may be starting to yellow.
• Shear down any declining foliage, if needed. Tall bearded iris may be a particular culprit, and columbine foliage may start to deteriorate later in the month.
• Cut back and shape *Amsonia* and *Baptisia* if desired toward the end of the month.

• Near the end of the month, certain hardy geraniums will need to be deadheaded or sheared back.
• Don't forget to cut flowers for fresh arrangements and for drying.

JULY
Early July is often the peak bloom time for traditional perennial borders. This can be an ideal time to take some great photos. Enjoy!

Planting
• Keep planting in July to a minimum, if possible.
• Transplant and divide with care.

General Maintenance
• Continue to keep new plantings moist, with deeper but less frequent waterings. For established plantings that have been dry for several weeks, watering may be in order now.
• Perennials that have been heavily pruned back also need to be kept moist.
• Weed.
• Heavy-feeding perennials or perennials that have been cut back for rebloom may benefit from fertilizing in July.
• Aerating may be needed in compacted areas.
• Staking may be needed for certain autumn bloomers.
• Watch for mites and black blister beetles and other pests.

Pruning
• Perennials that bloom a second time, including *Delphinium* and *Digitalis grandiflora* 'Temple Bells', should be cut back to basal foliage.
• Older plants of *Tradescantia* may need to be cut to the ground now.
• Most pinching or cutting back of autumn-blooming plants is completed in mid- to late July.
• Deadleaf plants that bloom in early summer, as needed.
• Deadhead more and more—perennials such as moonbeam coreopsis (*Coreopsis ver-*

ticillata 'Moonbeam') may need shearing now for a second bloom phase.
• Prune crowded or sprawling perennials to keep them in their space.
• Cut back any insect-ridden foliage, such as on columbine.
• Subshrubs that have gotten straggly may need hard pruning. *Lavandula* that is in good condition can simply be deadheaded in July to promote another flowering period in September.

AUGUST

Perennial gardens often take a bit of rest during the month of August. It is a busy month for cutting back "tired" plants that have finished blooming and deadleafing any scorched subjects.

Planting
• Any planting during August should be done with caution. Keep plantings moist and shaded.
• Bearded iris, oriental poppies, and peonies can be divided now.
• Design beds and order plants for autumn planting.

General Maintenance
• Weed.
• Don't forget to water the spring-planted gardens. Established gardens may also benefit from watering, as this is usually the key dry month.
• Aerating continues.
• Staking may be needed, particularly after storms.
• Do not apply fertilizer, so as to allow plants to harden better before the winter.
• Grasshoppers can be a problem this month.

Pruning
• Many plants require cutting back for aesthetics.
• Lots of deadleafing.
• Continue with deadheading.
• Prune plants to keep in desired space.

• Cut back finished, "tired" plants to make room for later bloomers.
• Asters and mums can be cut back by 4–6 in. to delay bloom, though at the expense of floral abundance.
• Cut back any insect- or disease-plagued foliage.
• Do not cut back subshrubs after late August, so that they can harden for the winter.
• Try cutting back short-lived species such as *Gaillardia* and *Centranthus* at the end of the month to stimulate vegetative growth.

AUTUMN

Planting starts again in autumn as the cooler weather approaches. Pruning is the major maintenance that continues in this season. It's enjoyable to be in the garden again—get your fill before winter sets in.

SEPTEMBER

September is the month to start getting back into planting. Enjoy all the summer-flowering perennials that are reblooming in September because you took the time to cut them back and/or deadhead them earlier in the season.

Planting
• Division and transplanting of spring- and summer-flowering perennials is accomplished with ease as the days start to cool down. Try to finish this by the end of the month so that plants can establish before winter.
• Move self-sown biennials as needed.
• Continue to order plants for autumn installations and planting.
• Bed preparation and planting can begin again.
• Peonies, poppies, and bearded iris (best planted by mid-September) are available for planting now.

General Maintenance
• Continue weeding.
• Keep new autumn plantings moist.
• Apply touch-up mulch if needed.

• Generally, no more fertilizer should be applied to the plants.

Pruning

• Deadhead late-summer and autumn bloomers such as *Echinacea* and *Heliopsis*.
• Cut back short-lived perennials in early September, if it was not done in late August.
• Continue to cut back faded summer-flowering perennials as needed.

OCTOBER

In the Midwest planting can continue until about 15 October; finish before then if possible.

Planting

• Finish planting in early October.
• Beds can be prepared for spring planting throughout the month.
• All divisions and transplanting should be finished by October.

General Maintenance

• Continue to keep new plantings watered if the weather is dry; established gardens may need water as well so that they can go into winter with sufficient moisture.
• Weeding is usually needed less by October.
• Rake leaves.
• Mulch tender plants once the ground is frozen.

Pruning

• 15 October is the approximate first frost date, at least in the Midwest. Some perennials may turn to mush at this time and should be pruned, if desired. Otherwise, wait for several killing frosts and prune in November.

NOVEMBER

November is the time for pruning to prepare for winter after several killing frosts.

Planting

• No more planting of herbaceous plants in the Midwest.
• Beds can be prepared for spring if the weather is permitting.

General Maintenance

• Top-dressing with organic matter, if not done in the spring, can be done after autumn clean-up.
• Be certain all water and irrigation systems are turned off and drain all hoses.
• Clean and oil tools after all clean-up is complete.
• Keep your pruners and a basket handy for work on a mild day.
• Recycle or return used pots, which have been accumulating all season, to accepting nurseries.
• Rake leaves. Mow or shred to speed composting.

Pruning

• Cut back perennials that are not desired over the winter or that harbor insects and disease.
• Deadhead some of the heavy seeders, but leave some for the birds.
• Do not prune evergreens, mums, tender perennials, or anything with attractive winter interest.

DECEMBER

Enjoy the holidays. Ask for gardening gifts. (Buy this book for all your friends!) Feed and watch the birds.

Planting

• Only in our dreams!

General Maintenance

• Mulch with old Christmas tree boughs once the ground has frozen.

Pruning

• On a mild day go out and prune some fallen plants to keep your mind clear.

JANUARY/FEBRUARY

Take vacations. Attend gardening conferences for inspiration. Design and plan for the new year using all your notes. Relax and regroup. Start ordering plants and seeds. Take some time on a mild day to go out and prune something to relieve your cabin fever. Watch the perennials when the snow melts to see what is happening. Keep track of temperatures, recording lows as well as temperature fluctuations, to help understand overwintering results. Press in perennials that may have frost heaved during times of thaw. Be sure your winter garden is what you have in mind; now is the time to note changes. Keep your bird feeder full. Remember that sunflower seed hulls can inhibit plant growth, and uneaten sunflower seeds and other bird seeds can sprout in gardens in the spring, creating a mess. Keep bird feeders out of the beds.

Lists of Perennials for Specific Pruning and Maintenance Requirements

These lists are to be used as guidelines only. As has been stressed throughout this book, a variety of factors, including climate, annual weather conditions, soil conditions, and even other cultural practices employed by the gardener, will affect a plant's performance. Refer to the Encyclopedia of Perennials in Section Three and the chapters of Sections One and Two for more information on individual plants and specifics on maintenance.

1. Perennials That Tolerate Wet Soil

Aegopodium podagraria 'Variegatum'
Aruncus dioicus
Chelone lyonii
Cimicifuga racemosa
Eupatorium maculatum 'Gateway'
Filipendula rubra 'Venusta'
Filipendula ulmaria
Helenium autumnale
Hibiscus moscheutos
Ligularia dentata
Lobelia cardinalis
Ranunculus repens 'Pleniflorus'
Rodgersia aesculifolia
Telekia speciosa
Tradescantia ×*andersoniana*
Trollius ×*cultorum*
Valeriana officinalis

2. Perennials That Tolerate Dry Soil Once Established

Achillea
Aegopodium podagraria 'Variegatum'
Anthemis tinctoria
Arabis caucasica
Armeria maritima
Artemisia
Asclepias tuberosa
Aurinia saxatilis
Baptisia australis
Bergenia cordifolia
Boltonia asteroides 'Snowbank'
Centaurea montana
Cerastium tomentosum
Ceratostigma plumbaginoides
Chrysopsis villosa
Coreopsis
Dianthus
Echinacea purpurea
Echinops ritro
Epimedium ×*rubrum*
Eryngium planum
Euphorbia polychroma
Foeniculum vulgare 'Purpureum'
Gaillarida ×*grandiflora*
Gaura lindheimeri
Geranium macrorrhizum
Geranium sanguineum
Helianthemum nummularium
Hypericum calycinum
Lamium maculatum
Lavandula angustifolia
Limonium latifolium
Linaria purpurea
Liriope spicata
Lychnis coronaria
Malva alcea 'Fastigiata'
Onopordum nervosum
Penstemon barbatus

2. Perennials That Tolerate Dry Soil Once Established, continued

Perovskia atriplicifolia
Ruta graveolens
Salvia nemorosa
Santolina chamaecyparissus
Solidago hybrids
Stachys byzantina
Stokesia laevis
Thermopsis caroliniana
Thymus
Verbascum

3. Clay Busters

The following list includes wild-flowers and native grasses recommended for clay soils. Reprinted with permission of Neil Diboll, Prairie Nursery, Westfield, Wisconsin.

Andropogon gerardi
Asclepias syriaca
Aster ericoides
Aster novae-angliae
Desmodium canadense
Echinacea pallida
Echinacea purpurea
Elymus canadensis
Eryngium yuccifolium
Helianthus ×laetiflorus
Heliopsis helianthoides
Liatris pycnostachya
Liatris spicata
Monarda fistulosa
Panicum virgatum
Parthenium integrifolium
Ratibida pinnata
Rudbeckia hirta
Silphium integrifolium
Silphium laciniatum
Silphium perfoliatum
Silphium terebinthinaceum
Solidago rigida
Sorghastrum nutans
Spartina pectinata
Vernonia fasciculata

4. Higher Maintenance Perennials

Achillea millefolium
Achillea 'Moonshine'
Adenophora liliifolia
Aegopodium podagraria 'Variegatum'
Ajuga reptans
Alcea rosea
Anchusa azurea
Anthemis tinctoria
Arabis caucasica
Artemisia ludoviciana 'Silver King'
Artemisia schmidtiana 'Nana'
Aster
Aurinia saxatilis
Campanula carpatica
Campanula persicifolia
Campanula rotundifolia 'Olympica'
Centaurea montana
Cerastium tomentosum
Coreopsis grandiflora
Delphinium elatum
Dendranthema ×morifolium
Dianthus ×allwoodii
Dianthus barbatus
Dicentra formosa 'Luxuriant'
Digitalis purpurea
Fragaria 'Pink Panda'
Gaillarida ×grandiflora
Geum hybrids
Helenium autumnale
Iris, bearded
Kniphofia hybrids
Leucanthemum ×superbum
Lupinus hybrids
Macleaya cordata
Malva alcea 'Fastigiata'
Monarda didyma
Physostegia virginiana
Ranunculus repens 'Pleniflorus'
Tanacetum coccineum
Tanacetum parthenium
Tradescantia ×andersoniana
Valeriana officinalis
Verbascum
Viola odorata

5. Lower Maintenance Perennials

Acanthus spinosus
Achillea 'Coronation Gold'
Amsonia tabernaemontana
Artemisia abrotanum
Artemisia lactiflora
Arum italicum 'Marmoratum'
Aruncus dioicus
Asarum europaeum
Asclepias tuberosa
Aster tataricus 'Jin Dai'
Asteromoea mongolica
Astrantia major
Baptisia australis
Bergenia cordifolia
Boltonia asteroides 'Snowbank'
Brunnera macrophylla
Ceratostigma plumbaginoides
Chelone lyonii
Chrysopsis villosa
Cimicifuga racemosa
Coreopsis verticillata
Dianthus gratianopolitanus 'Bath's Pink'
Dictamnus albus
Digitalis grandiflora
Echinops ritro
Epimedium ×rubrum
Eupatorium maculatum 'Gateway'
Filipendula rubra 'Venusta'
Filipendula ulmaria
Gaura lindheimeri
Geranium macrorrhizum
Geranium platypetalum
Geranium sanguineum
Helleborus orientalis
Hibiscus moscheutos
Iris sibirica
Liatris spicata
Ligularia dentata

Limonium latifolium
Liriope spicata
Perovskia atriplicifolia
Phlox divaricata
Phlox maculata
Phlox stolonifera
Platycodon grandiflorus
Polygonatum odoratum
    'Variegatum'
Pulmonaria
Pulsatilla vulgaris
Rodgersia aesculifolia
Rudbeckia fulgida 'Goldsturm'
Rudbeckia nitida 'Herbstsonne'
Salvia nemorosa
Sanguisorba obtusa
Saponaria ocymoides
Stylophorum diphyllum
Telekia speciosa
Thalictrum aquilegiifolium
Thermopsis caroliniana
Tiarella cordifolia
Tricyrtis hirta

6. Short-Lived Perennials

Achillea millefolium
Achillea 'Moonshine'
Alcea rosea
Anchusa azurea
Anemone ×hybrida
Anthemis tinctoria
Aquilegia hybrids
Arabis caucasica
Armeria maritima
Artemisia absinthium
    'Lambrook Silver'
Artemisia 'Powis Castle'
Aster ×frikartii 'Monch'
Aubrieta deltoidea
Aurinia saxatilis
Begonia grandis var. evansiana
Belamcanda chinensis
Campanula carpatica
Campanula persicifolia
Campanula rotundifolia
    'Olympica'

Centranthus ruber
Cerastium tomentosum
Coreopsis grandiflora
Corydalis lutea
Crocosmia 'Lucifer'
Delphinium elatum
Dendranthema ×morifolium
Dianthus ×allwoodii
Dianthus deltoides
Dicentra formosa 'Luxuriant'
Foeniculum vulgare
    'Purpureum'
Gaillarida ×grandiflora
Gaura lindheimeri
Geum hybrids
Gypsophila paniculata
Helianthemum nummularium
Kniphofia hybrids
Leucanthemum ×superbum
Linaria purpurea
Linum perenne
Lobelia cardinalis
Lupinus hybrids
Lychnis coronaria
Malva alcea 'Fastigiata'
Oenothera fruticosa subsp.
    glauca
Onopordum nervosum
Penstemon barbatus
Ruta graveolens
Scabiosa
Sidalcea malviflora
Tanacetum coccineum
Tanacetum parthenium
Teucrium chamaedrys
Verbascum

7. Perennials to Prune for
Pest and/or Disease Control

Achillea 'Coronation Gold'
Achillea 'Moonshine'
Aegopodium podagraria
    'Variegatum'
Ajuga reptans
Alcea rosea
Anaphalis triplinervis

Anemone ×hybrida
Aquilegia hybrids
Aster novi-belgii
Aurinia saxatilis
Belamcanda chinensis
Chrysogonum virginianum
Clematis recta
Coreopsis grandiflora
Crocosmia 'Lucifer'
Foeniculum vulgare
    'Purpureum'
Helenium autumnale
Heliopsis helianthoides
Helleborus orientalis
Hemerocallis
Hibiscus moscheutos
Iris, bearded
Lupinus hybrids
Malva alcea 'Fastigiata'
Monarda didyma
Paeonia hybrids
Phlox divaricata
Phlox maculata
Phlox paniculata
Pulmonaria saccharata
Stachys byzantina

8. Deer-Resistant Perennials

Adapted with permission from
the Cornell Cooperative Extension Service.

Achillea
Aconitum
Ajuga
Alchemilla mollis
Allium
Amsonia
Angelica
Aquilegia
Artemisia
Aruncus dioicus
Asclepias tuberosa
Aster
Astilbe
Aurinia saxatilis
Baptisia

8. Deer-Resistant Perennials,
continued

Bergenia
Boltonia
Buddleia davidii
Calluna
Campanula
Ceratostigma plumbaginoides
Chelone
Cimicifuga racemosa
Coreopsis
Dennstaedtia punctilobula
Dianthus
Dicentra eximia
Dictamnus albus
Digitalis
Echinacea purpurea
Echinops
Epimedium
Erica
Eryngium
Eupatorium
Euphorbia
Filipendula
Geranium macrorrhizum
Geum
Goniolimon tataricum
Gypsophila paniculata
Heuchera
Helleborus
Iberis sempervirens
Iris (occasionally eaten)
Kirengeshoma palmata
Lamium
Lavandula
Leucanthemum
Liatris
Lilium lancifolium
Linaria
Linum perenne
Lupinus
Lychnis coronaria
Lythrum
Macleaya cordata
Matteuccia struthiopteris
Monarda didyma

Myosotis scorpioides
Nepeta
Oenothera
Onoclea sensibilis
Onopordum acanthium
Origanum
Osmunda
Paeonia (occasionally eaten)
Papaver orientale
Penstemon
Perovskia atriplicifolia
Phalaris arundinacea var. *picta*
  (and most ornamental grasses)
Platycodon
Polemonium caeruleum
Polystichum acrostichoides
Primula
Pulmonaria
Ranunculus
Rodgersia
Rosmarinus officinalis
Rudbeckia
Salvia officinalis
Saponaria
Sedum 'Autumn Joy' (occasion-
  ally eaten: tall sedum are both-
  ered, low sedum are left alone)
Solidago
Stachys byzantina
Tanacetum
Thalictrum (occasionally eaten)
Thelypteris noveboracensis
Thymus
Tiarella
Tricyrtis
Verbascum
Veronica austriaca subsp.
  teucrium
Viola labridorica

9. Perennials That Require Staking

* = can be pruned to avoid the
need for staking

Achillea 'Moonshine'
*Aconitum napellus**

*Alcea rosea**
*Amsonia tabernaemontana**
Anchusa azurea
Aquilegia hybrids
*Artemisia lactiflora**
*Aster novi-belgii**
*Baptisia australis**
Belamcanda chinensis
Boltonia asteroides 'Snow-
  bank'*
Campanula glomerata
*Campanula persicifolia**
Cephalaria gigantea
*Chrysopsis villosa**
Cimicifuga racemosa
Delphinium ×*belladonna*
  'Bellamosum'
Delphinium elatum
Filipendula rubra 'Venusta'
Gaillarida ×*grandiflora*
*Gaura lindheimeri**
Geranium ibericum 'Johnson's
  Blue'
Gypsophila paniculata
*Helenium autumnale**
Iris, bearded
Leucanthemum ×*superbum**
Liatris spicata
Linaria purpurea
Lupinus hybrids
Malva alcea 'Fastigiata'*
Nepeta mussinii
Paeonia hybrids
*Platycodon grandiflorus**
Rudbeckia nitida
  'Herbstsonne'*
*Tanacetum coccineum**
Tradescantia ×*andersoniana**
*Veronica spicata**
*Veronicastrum virginicum**

10. Perennials That May Require Division Every 1–3 Years

Achillea millefolium
Achillea 'Moonshine'

Aegopodium podagraria
'Variegatum'

Ajuga reptans

Alcea rosea

Anchusa azurea

Anthemis tinctoria

Arabis caucasica

Artemisia ludoviciana 'Silver
King'

Aster ×frikartii 'Monch'

Aster novi-belgii

Astilbe ×arendsii

Belamcanda chinensis

Campanula carpatica

Campanula persicifolia

Centaurea montana

Centranthus ruber

Cephalaria gigantea

Cerastium tomentosum

Coreopsis grandiflora

Coreopsis verticillata

Crocosmia 'Lucifer'

Delphinium elatum

Dendranthema ×morifolium

Dianthus barbatus

Dianthus deltoides

Digitalis purpurea

Fragaria 'Pink Panda'

Gaillarida ×grandiflora

Geum hybrids

Helenium autumnale

Heuchera micrantha 'Palace
Purple'

Heuchera sanguinea

Hypericum calycinum

Iris, bearded

Leucanthemum ×superbum

Lobelia cardinalis

Lychnis coronaria

Macleaya cordata

Malva alcea 'Fastigiata'

Monarda didyma

Penstemon barbatus

Phlox maculata

Phlox paniculata

Phlox subulata

Physostegia virginiana

Ranunculus repens 'Pleniflorus'

Sidalcea malviflora

Sisyrinchium angustifolium

Tanacetum coccineum

Tanacetum parthenium

Veronica spicata

11. Perennials That May Require Division Every 4–5 Years

Acanthus spinosus

Achillea 'Coronation Gold'

Anaphalis triplinervis

Armeria maritima

Artemisia lactiflora

Aster tataricus 'Jin Dai'

Asteromoea mongolica

Astrantia major

Bergenia cordifolia

Boltonia asteroides 'Snowbank'

Campanula glomerata

Campanula rotundifolia
'Olympica'

Ceratostigma plumbaginoides

Chelone lyonii

Chrysogonum virginianum

Chrysopsis villosa

Delphinium ×belladonna
'Bellamosum'

Dianthus gratianopolitanus
'Bath's Pink'

Dicentra formosa 'Luxuriant'

Digitalis grandiflora

Eupatorium maculatum
'Gateway'

Geranium ibericum 'Johnson's
Blue'

Helianthemum nummularium

Helianthus salicifolius

Heliopsis helianthoides

Hemerocallis

Lamium maculatum

Liatris spicata

Oenothera fruticosa subsp.
glauca

Phlox stolonifera

Rudbeckia fulgida 'Goldsturm'

Rudbeckia nitida 'Herbstsonne'

Sanguisorba obtusa

Scabiosa columbaria 'Butterfly
Blue'

Solidago hybrids

Stachys byzantina

Stokesia laevis

Thymus

Tiarella cordifolia

Tradescantia ×andersoniana

Veronica austriaca subsp.
teucrium

Veronicastrum virginicum

12. Perennials That May Require Division Every 6–10 Years

* = resents disturbance

† = tough woody or thong-like
roots or taproot

Alchemilla mollis

*Amsonia tabernaemontana**

Arum italicum 'Marmoratum'

Asarum europaeum

Begonia grandis var. *evansiana*

Brunnera macrophylla

Echinacea purpurea

Echinops ritro†*

*Epimedium ×rubrum**

Filipendula rubra 'Venusta'†

Filipendula ulmaria†

Gaura lindheimeri

Geranium

*Iberis sempervirens**

Iris sibirica

Kniphofia hybrids

Ligularia dentata

*Limonium latifolium**

Nepeta

*Papaver orientale**

Patrinia scabiosifolia

Polygonatum odoratum
'Variegatum'

Pulmonaria saccharata

12. Perennials That May Require Division Every 6–10 Years, continued

Rodgersia aesculifolia
Ruta graveolens
Salvia nemorosa
Sedum 'Autumn Joy'
Telekia speciosa
Thalictrum aquilegiifolium
Tricyrtis hirta
*Trollius ×cultorum**
Verbascum

13. Perennials That May Require Division Every 10 Years or More

* = resents disturbance
† = tough woody or thong-like roots or taproot

*Aconitum napellus**
Adenophora liliifolia
*Anemone ×hybrida**
Aquilegia hybrids
Aruncus dioicus†*
Asclepias tuberosa†*
*Baptisia australis**
Cimicifuga racemosa†*
*Dictamnus albus**
Eryngium planum†*
Euphorbia polychroma
Gypsophila paniculata†*
Helleborus orientalis
Hibiscus moscheutos
Hosta
Paeonia hybrids
Perovskia atriplicifolia
Platycodon grandiflorus†*
Polemonium caeruleum
Pulsatilla vulgaris
Stylophorum diphyllum
*Thermopsis caroliniana**

14. Perennials To Deadhead To Prolong Bloom or for Rebloom

Achillea

Aconitum
Adenophora liliifolia
Alcea rosea
Anchusa azurea
Anthemis tinctoria
Aquilegia hybrids
Armeria maritima
Asclepias tuberosa
Aster ×frikartii 'Monch'
Astrantia major
Begonia grandis var. *evansiana*
Campanula
Centaurea montana
Centranthus ruber
Coreopsis
Corydalis lutea
Delphinium
Dianthus ×allwoodii
Dianthus gratianopolitanus 'Bath's Pink'
Dicentra formosa 'Luxuriant'
Digitalis
Echinacea purpurea
Echinops ritro
Filipendula ulmaria
Gaillarida ×grandiflora
Gaura lindheimeri
Geum hybrids
Gypsophila paniculata
Helenium autumnale
Heliopsis helianthoides
Hemerocallis
Hesperis matronalis
Heuchera sanguinea
Hibiscus moscheutos
Kniphofia hybrids
Lavandula
Leucanthemum ×superbum
Liatris spicata
Limonium latifolium
Linaria purpurea
Lupinus hybrids
Lychnis coronaria
Malva alcea 'Fastigiata'
Monarda didyma
Patrinia scabiosifolia

Penstemon barbatus
Phlox maculata
Phlox paniculata
Platycodon grandiflorus
Salvia nemorosa
Scabiosa
Sidalcea malviflora
Stokesia laevis
Tanacetum coccineum
Tiarella cordifolia
Tradescantia ×andersoniana
Veronica spicata
Veronicastrum virginicum
Viola odorata

15. Perennials That Do Not Rebloom with Deadheading

Acanthus spinosus
Amsonia tabernaemontana
Artemisia absinthium 'Lambrook Silver'
Artemisia lactiflora
Artemisia ludoviciana 'Silver King'
Artemisia schmidtiana 'Nana'
Arum italicum 'Marmoratum'
Aruncus dioicus
Astilbe ×arendsii
Bergenia cordifolia
Brunnera macrophylla
Cimicifuga racemosa
Crocosmia 'Lucifer'
Epimedium ×rubrum
Eupatorium maculatum 'Gateway'
Geranium platypetalum
Helianthus salicifolius
Iris sibirica
Ligularia dentata
Liriope spicata
Paeonia hybrids
Papaver orientale
Phlox divaricata
Stachys byzantina
Teucrium chamaedrys

16. Perennials To Deadhead To Improve the Overall Appearance of the Plant

Achillea
Alcea rosea
Alchemilla mollis
Anaphalis triplinervis
Anemone ×hybrida
Arabis caucasica
Armeria maritima
Artemisia abrotanum
Artemisia absinthium
  'Lambrook Silver'
Artemisia lactiflora
Artemisia ludoviciana 'Silver
  King'
Artemisia 'Powis Castle'
Artemisia schmidtiana 'Nana'
Aruncus dioicus
Aurinia saxatilis
Bergenia cordifolia
Campanula glomerata
Chrysogonum virginianum
Coreopsis grandiflora
Delphinium elatum
Dendranthema ×morifolium
Dianthus ×allwoodii
Dicentra formosa 'Luxuriant'
Echinacea purpurea
Echinops ritro
Geranium
Gypsophila paniculata
Helenium autumnale
Heliopsis helianthoides
Helleborus orientalis
Hemerocallis
Heuchera
Hibiscus moscheutos
Hosta
Iris, bearded
Kniphofia hybrids
Leucanthemum ×superbum
Malva alcea 'Fastigiata'
Nepeta ×faassenii 'Six Hills
  Giant'
Nepeta mussinii

Onopordum nervosum
Paeonia hybrids
Penstemon barbatus
Phlox maculata
Phlox paniculata
Phlox stolonifera
Phlox subulata
Physostegia virginiana
Polemonium caeruleum
Pulmonaria
Rodgersia aesculifolia
Ruta graveolens
Salvia nemorosa
Sanguisorba obtusa
Santolina chamaecyparissus
Scabiosa
Stachys byzantina
Tanacetum coccineum
Tanacetum parthenium
Teucrium chamaedrys
Tradescantia ×andersoniana
Verbascum
Veronica austriaca subsp.
  teucrium
Veronica spicata

17. Perennials To Deadhead to a Lateral Flower, Bud, or Leaf

Many of these perennials can also be deadheaded by shearing; refer to Section Three, Encyclopedia of Perennials, for details.

Achillea
Aconitum napellus
Adenophora liliifolia
Alcea rosea
Amsonia tabernaemontana
Anaphalis triplinervis
Anchusa azurea
Angelica gigas
Anthemis tinctoria
Aquilegia hybrids
Artemisia
Aruncus dioicus
Asclepias tuberosa

Aster
Astilbe ×arendsii
Astrantia major
Baptisia australis
Begonia grandis var. evansiana
Campanula
Centaurea montana
Centranthus ruber
Cephalaria gigantea
Chelone lyonii
Clematis recta
Coreopsis grandiflora
Coreopsis verticillata
Corydalis lutea
Delphinium
Dendranthema ×morifolium
Dianthus
Digitalis
Echinacea purpurea
Echinops ritro
Eryngium
Filipendula ulmaria
Foeniculum vulgare
  'Purpureum'
Gaillarida ×grandiflora
Gaura lindheimeri
Geranium sanguineum
Geum hybrids
Gypsophila paniculata
Helenium autumnale
Heliopsis helianthoides
Helleborus orientalis
Hemerocallis
Hesperis matronalis
Hibiscus moscheutos
Iris
Lavandula
Leucanthemum ×superbum
Ligularia dentata
Linaria purpurea
Lupinus hybrids
Lychnis coronaria
Macleaya cordata
Malva alcea 'Fastigiata'
Monarda didyma
Nepeta

**17. Perennials To Deadhead
to a Lateral Flower, Bud, or Leaf,
continued**

Onopordum nervosum
Paeonia hybrids
Phlox maculata
Phlox paniculata
Phlox subulata
Physostegia virginiana
Platycodon grandiflorus
Rodgersia aesculifolia
Ruta graveolens
Salvia nemorosa
Scabiosa
Sidalcea malviflora
Solidago hybrids
Stokesia laevis
Tanacetum coccineum
Tanacetum parthenium
Telekia speciosa
Teucrium chamaedrys
Thalictrum aquilegiifolium
Thymus
Tradescantia ×*andersoniana*
Veronica austriaca subsp.
  teucrium
Veronica spicata
Veronicastrum virginicum

**18. Perennials To Deadhead
to the Ground or to Basal
Foliage**

Acanthus spinosus
Ajuga reptans
Alchemilla mollis
Armeria maritima
Bergenia cordifolia
Brunnera macrophylla
Crocosmia 'Lucifer'
Dicentra formosa 'Luxuriant'
Epimedium ×*rubrum*
Geranium endressii 'Wargrave
  Pink'
Geranium ibericum 'Johnson's
  Blue'

Geranium macrorrhizum
Geranium platypetalum
Heuchera
Hosta
Kniphofia hybrids
Limonium latifolium
Liriope spicata
Phlox divaricata
Phlox stolonifera
Polemonium caeruleum
Pulmonaria saccharata
Ranunculus repens 'Pleniflorus'
Stachys byzantina
Tiarella cordifolia

19. Reseeding Plants
Deadhead before seeds mature if
seeding is not desired.

* = plants are often short-lived;
seeding may ensure permanence
in the garden
B = biennial plants; allow seeding
to foster new plants, or deadhead
to promote perennial nature of
existing plant

Achillea millefolium
Adenophora liliifolia
Aegopodium podagraria
  'Variegatum'
Ajuga reptans
*Alcea rosea**
Alchemilla mollis
Amsonia tabernaemontana
Anchusa azurea
*Angelica gigas**B
*Anthemis tinctoria**
Aquilegia hybrids
Arabis caucasica
Asclepias tuberosa
Aster novi-belgii
Astrantia major
Aubrieta deltoidea
Aurinia saxatilis
Begonia grandis var. *evansiana*
Belamcanda chinensis
Brunnera macrophylla

Campanula carpatica
Campanula persicifolia
Campanula rotundifolia
  'Olympica'
Centaurea montana
Centranthus ruber
Chrysogonum virginianum
Coreopsis grandiflora
Coreopsis verticillata
Corydalis lutea
*Dianthus barbatus**B
Dianthus deltoides
Digitalis grandiflora
*Digitalis purpurea**B
Echinacea purpurea
Echinops ritro
Eryngium planum
Euphorbia polychroma
Filipendula ulmaria
Foeniculum vulgare
  'Purpureum'
Gaillarida ×*grandiflora*
Gaura lindheimeri
Geranium macrorrhizum
Geranium sanguineum
Heliopsis helianthoides
Helleborus orientalis
Hesperis matronalis
Hibiscus moscheutos
Iris sibirica
Lamium maculatum
*Linaria purpurea**
*Linum perenne**
Lupinus hybrids
*Lychnis coronaria**
Lythrum salicaria (deadhead to
  prevent invasive quality)
Macleaya cordata
Malva alcea 'Fastigiata'*
Monarda didyma
*Onopordum nervosum**
Patrinia scabiosifolia
Phlox divaricata
Phlox paniculata
Phlox subulata

Platycodon grandiflorus
Polemonium caeruleum
Pulmonaria saccharata
Ranunculus repens 'Pleniflorus'
Rudbeckia fulgida 'Goldsturm'
*Sidalcea malviflora**
Solidago hybrids
Stylophorum diphyllum
Tanacetum parthenium
Thalictrum aquilegiifolium
Thymus
Tradescantia ×*andersoniana*
Tricyrtis hirta
Valeriana officinalis
*Verbascum**B
Vernonia noveboracensis
Viola odorata

20. Perennials with Attractive Seedheads

Arum italicum 'Marmoratum'
Asclepias tuberosa
Astilbe ×*arendsii*
Baptisia australis
Begonia grandis var. *evansiana*
Belamcanda chinensis
Ceratostigma plumbaginoides
Chelone lyonii
Chrysopsis villosa
Cimicifuga racemosa
Clematis heracleifolia
Clematis recta
Coreopsis verticillata
Crocosmia 'Lucifer'
Dictamnus albus
Echinacea purpurea
Eupatorium maculatum
  'Gateway'
Filipendula rubra 'Venusta'
Fragaria 'Pink Panda'
Gaillarida ×*grandiflora*
Helianthus salicifolius
Iris sibirica
Liatris spicata
Ligularia dentata

Limonium latifolium
Liriope spicata
Papaver orientale
Pulsatilla vulgaris
Rudbeckia fulgida 'Goldsturm'
Rudbeckia nitida 'Herbstsonne'
Sedum 'Autumn Joy'
Stylophorum diphyllum
Telekia speciosa
Thalictrum aquilegiifolium
Thermopsis caroliniana

21. Perennials with Self-Cleaning Flowers

Amsonia tabernaemontana
Aster ×*frikartii* 'Monch'
Asteromoea mongolica
Belamcanda chinensis
Ceratostigma plumbaginoides
Coreopsis verticillata
Crocosmia 'Lucifer'
Dictamnus albus
Fragaria 'Pink Panda'
Gaura lindheimeri
Limonium latifolium
Linum perenne
Lychnis coronaria
Phlox divaricata
Polygonatum odoratum
  'Variegatum'
Stylophorum diphyllum
Tanacetum parthenium
Tradescantia ×*andersoniana*

22. Perennials That Do Not Require Deadheading

This list includes plants that do not rebloom, that normally do not reseed or have minimal re-seeding, that have attractive seed-heads, or that have deadheads that contribute to a more attractive overall winter form.

Arum italicum 'Marmoratum'
Asarum europaeum
Aster tataricus 'Jin Dai'

Asteromoea mongolica
Astilbe ×*arendsii*
Baptisia australis
Boltonia asteroides 'Snowbank'
Ceratostigma plumbaginoides
Chelone lyonii
Chrysopsis villosa
Cimicifuga racemosa
Clematis heracleifolia
Clematis recta
Crocosmia 'Lucifer'
Dictamnus albus
Epimedium ×*rubrum*
Eupatorium maculatum
  'Gateway'
Filipendula rubra 'Venusta'
Fragaria 'Pink Panda'
Helianthus salicifolius
Hypericum calycinum
Liriope spicata
Papaver orientale
Perovskia atriplicifolia
Polygonatum odoratum
  'Variegatum'
Pulsatilla vulgaris
Rudbeckia nitida 'Herbstsonne'
Sedum 'Autumn Joy'
Thermopsis caroliniana

23. Perennials with Seedheads That Attract Song Birds

Anthemis tinctoria
Echinacea purpurea
Echinops ritro
Eupatorium maculatum
  'Gateway'
Helianthus salicifolius
Heliopsis helianthoides
Hosta
Liatris spicata
Ligularia dentata
Monarda didyma
Rudbeckia
Telekia speciosa

24. Perennials To Cut Back To Keep in Their Own Space

Achillea millefolium
Ajuga reptans
Alchemilla mollis
Arabis caucasica
Artemisia
Aster tataricus 'Jin Dai'
Aubrieta deltoidea
Aurinia saxatilis
Baptisia australis
Campanula glomerata
Cerastium tomentosum
Ceratostigma plumbaginoides
Clematis heracleifolia
Dianthus deltoides
Fragaria 'Pink Panda'
Geranium
Monarda didyma
Nepeta
Phlox stolonifera
Phlox subulata
Ranunculus repens 'Pleni-
    florus'
Telekia speciosa
Tiarella cordifolia
Viola odorata

25. Perennials To Cut Back After Flowering for Aesthetics in the Spring

Aquilegia hybrids
Arabis caucasica
Aubrieta deltoidea
Aurinia saxatilis
Brunnera macrophylla
Cerastium tomentosum
Clematis recta
Dianthus barbatus
Dianthus deltoides
Dianthus gratianopolitanus
    'Bath's Pink'
Hesperis matronalis
Iberis sempervirens
Iris, bearded
Lamium maculatum

Nepeta mussinii
Paeonia hybrids
Papaver orientale
Phlox divaricata
Phlox subulata
Polemonium caeruleum
Pulmonaria saccharata
Saponaria ocymoides
Stylophorum diphyllum
Thermopsis caroliniana
Thymus
Valeriana officinalis
Veronica austriaca subsp.
    teucrium
Viola odorata

26. Perennials To Cut Back After Flowering for Aesthetics in the Summer

Acanthus spinosus
Aegopodium podagraria
    'Variegatum'
Alchemilla mollis
Amsonia tabernaemontana
Artemisia abrotanum
Artemisia absinthium
    'Lambrook Silver'
Artemisia 'Powis Castle'
Artemisia schmidtiana 'Nana'
Baptisia australis
Centaurea montana
Centranthus ruber
Coreopsis grandiflora
Coreopsis verticillata
Crocosmia 'Lucifer'
Digitalis purpurea
Euphorbia polychroma
Filipendula rubra 'Venusta'
Geranium endressii 'Wargrave
    Pink'
Geranium ibericum 'Johnson's
    Blue'
Geranium sanguineum
Geum hybrids
Helianthemum nummularium
Heliopsis helianthoides

Hemerocallis
Heuchera micrantha 'Palace
    Purple'
Kniphofia hybrids
Lavandula
Linum perenne
Nepeta ×*faassenii* 'Six Hills
    Giant'
Phlox maculata
Phlox paniculata
Ranunculus repens 'Pleni-
    florus'
Ruta graveolens
Salvia nemorosa
Sanguisorba obtusa
Santolina chamaecyparissus
Sisyrinchium angustifolium
Solidago hybrids
Teucrium chamaedrys
Thalictrum aquilegiifolium
Tradescantia ×*andersoniana*
Trollius ×*cultorum*

27. Perennials To Deadhead to a Lateral Leaf, Bud, or Flower and Then Cut Back to Basal Foliage

Achillea
Aconitum napellus
Adenophora liliifolia
Alcea rosea
Anaphalis triplinervis
Anchusa azurea
Anthemis tinctoria
Aquilegia hybrids
Artemisia lactiflora
Astrantia major
Campanula
Centaurea montana
Coreopsis grandiflora
Corydalis lutea
Delphinium
Digitalis grandiflora
Echinops ritro
Eryngium planum
Filipendula ulmaria

Gaillarida ×*grandiflora*
Gypsophila paniculata
Helenium autumnale
Hesperis matronalis
Iris, bearded
Leucanthemum ×*superbum*
Linaria purpurea
Lupinus hybrids
Lychnis coronaria
Malva alcea 'Fastigiata'
Monarda didyma
Oenothera fruticosa subsp.
  glauca
Onopordum nervosum
Patrinia scabiosifolia
Penstemon barbatus
Physostegia virginiana
Salvia nemorosa
Sidalcea malviflora
Solidago hybrids
Stokesia laevis
Tanacetum coccineum
Tanacetum parthenium
Telekia speciosa
Tradescantia ×*andersoniana*
Veronica spicata
Veronicastrum virginicum

28. Summer- and Autumn-Flowering Perennials To Cut Back Before Flowering for Height Control

Achillea millefolium
Aconitum napellus
Adenophora liliifolia
Alcea rosea
Anthemis tinctoria
Artemisia
Aster
Asteromoea mongolica
Boltonia asteroides 'Snowbank'
Chrysopsis villosa
Dendranthema ×*morifolium*
Echinacea purpurea
Eupatorium maculatum
  'Gateway'

Gaura lindheimeri
Helenium autumnale
Helianthemum nummularium
Helianthus salicifolius
Heliopsis helianthoides
Hibiscus moscheutos
Hypericum calycinum
Lavandula
Linum perenne
Lobelia cardinalis
Lychnis coronaria
Macleaya cordata
Malva alcea 'Fastigiata'
Monarda didyma
Perovskia atriplicifolia
Phlox maculata
Phlox paniculata
Physostegia virginiana
Platycodon grandiflorus
Rudbeckia
Ruta graveolens
Santolina chamaecyparissus
Sedum 'Autumn Joy'
Solidago hybrids
Tanacetum parthenium
Teucrium chamaedrys
Tradescantia ×*andersoniana*
Vernonia noveboracensis
Veronica spicata
Veronicastrum virginicum

29. Perennials That Will Not Flower If Their Terminal Flower Buds Are Removed

Acanthus spinosus
Aruncus dioicus
Astilbe ×*arendsii*
Dictamnus albus
Filipendula rubra 'Venusta'
Filipendula ulmaria
Geum hybrids
Hemerocallis
Heuchera micrantha 'Palace
  Purple'
Hosta
Iris, bearded

Iris sibirica
Kniphofia hybrids
Lupinus hybrids
Papaver orientale
Stachys byzantina

30. Perennials That Can Be Pinched

Achillea millefolium
Adenophora liliifolia
Alcea rosea
Anthemis tinctoria
Artemisia
Aster
Begonia grandis var. *evansiana*
Boltonia asteroides 'Snowbank'
Campanula persicifolia
Chelone lyonii
Clematis heracleifolia
Dendranthema ×*morifolium*
Eupatorium maculatum
  'Gateway'
Helenium autumnale
Helianthus salicifolius
Leucanthemum ×*superbum*
Linaria purpurea
Lobelia cardinalis
Lychnis coronaria
Malva alcea 'Fastigiata'
Monarda didyma
Penstemon barbatus
Perovskia atriplicifolia
Phlox maculata
Phlox paniculata
Physostegia virginiana
Platycodon grandiflorus
Rudbeckia
Sedum 'Autumn Joy'
Solidago hybrids
Tanacetum coccineum
Tanacetum parthenium
Vernonia noveboracensis
Veronica spicata
Veronicastrum virginicum

31. Perennials That Do Not Respond Well to Pinching

Acanthus spinosus
Alchemilla mollis
Aquilegia hybrids
Armeria maritima
Aruncus dioicus
Astilbe ×*arendsii*
Crocosmia 'Lucifer'
Delphinium
Dianthus
Dictamnus albus
Digitalis
Filipendula rubra 'Venusta'
Filipendula ulmaria
Gaillarida ×*grandiflora*
Geranium
Geum hybrids
Hemerocallis
Heuchera
Hosta
Iris
Kniphofia hybrids
Ligularia dentata
Limonium latifolium
Lupinus hybrids
Papaver orientale
Polygonatum odoratum 'Variegatum'
Rodgersia
Telekia speciosa
Verbascum

32. Perennials That Require Deadleafing

Acanthus spinosus
Achillea 'Coronation Gold'
Achillea 'Moonshine'
Ajuga reptans
Alcea rosea
Alchemilla mollis
Anaphalis triplinervis
Angelica gigas
Aquilegia hybrids
Arabis caucasica
Artemisia 'Powis Castle'

Arum italicum 'Marmoratum'
Aruncus dioicus
Asarum europaeum
Aster novi-belgii
Astilbe ×*arendsii*
Astrantia major
Aurinia saxatilis
Begonia grandis var. *evansiana*
Bergenia cordifolia
Brunnera macrophylla
Chrysogonum virginianum
Cimicifuga racemosa
Clematis heracleifolia
Crocosmia 'Lucifer'
Dianthus barbatus
Dicentra formosa 'Luxuriant'
Digitalis purpurea
Fragaria 'Pink Panda'
Gaillarida ×*grandiflora*
Geranium macrorrhizum
Geum hybrids
Helleborus orientalis
Heuchera micrantha 'Palace Purple'
Heuchera sanguinea
Hibiscus moscheutos
Hosta
Ligularia dentata
Limonium latifolium
Lychnis coronaria
Phlox paniculata
Rodgersia aesculifolia
Sanguisorba obtusa
Stachys byzantina
Stylophorum diphyllum
Telekia speciosa

33. Perennials That Normally Do Not Need Pruning for the Winter

These perennials normally do not need pruning before winter, assuming that other recommended pruning has been performed during the season.

Acanthus spinosus

Achillea
Aconitum napellus
Adenophora liliifolia
Aegopodium podagraria 'Variegatum'
Ajuga reptans
Alchemilla mollis
Amsonia tabernaemontana
Anaphalis triplinervis
Anchusa azurea
Angelica gigas
Anthemis tinctoria
Aquilegia hybrids
Arabis caucasica
Armeria maritima
Artemisia
Arum italicum 'Marmoratum'
Asarum europaeum
Asclepias tuberosa
Aster ×*frikartii* 'Monch'
Aster tataricus 'Jin Dai'
Asteromoea mongolica
Astilbe ×*arendsii*
Astrantia major
Aubrieta deltoidea
Aurinia saxatilis
Baptisia australis
Belamcanda chinensis
Bergenia cordifolia
Boltonia asteroides 'Snowbank'
Campanula
Centaurea montana
Centranthus ruber
Cerastium tomentosum
Ceratostigma plumbaginoides
Chelone lyonii
Chrysogonum virginianum
Chrysopsis villosa
Cimicifuga racemosa
Clematis heracleifolia
Coreopsis grandiflora
Coreopsis verticillata
Crocosmia 'Lucifer'
Delphinium
Dendranthema ×*morifolium*
Dianthus

Dictamnus albus
Digitalis
Echinops ritro
Epimedium ×rubrum
Eryngium
Eupatorium maculatum
 'Gateway'
Euphorbia polychroma
Filipendula
Fragaria 'Pink Panda'
Gaillarida ×grandiflora
Gaura lindheimeri
Geranium macrorrhizum
Geranium platypetalum
Geranium sanguineum
Geum hybrids
Gypsophila paniculata
Helianthemum nummularium
Helianthus salicifolius
Helleborus orientalis
Hemerocallis
Heuchera
Hibiscus moscheutos
Hypericum calycinum
Iberis sempervirens
Iris sibirica
Kniphofia hybrids
Lamium maculatum
Lavandula
Leucanthemum ×superbum
Liatris spicata
Limonium latifolium
Linaria purpurea
Linum perenne
Liriope spicata
Lobelia cardinalis
Lupinus hybrids
Lychnis coronaria
Oenothera fruticosa subsp.
 glauca
Onopordum nervosum
Papaver orientale
Patrinia scabiosifolia
Penstemon barbatus
Perovskia atriplicifolia
Phlox divaricata

Phlox stolonifera
Phlox subulata
Polemonium caeruleum
Pulmonaria
Pulsatilla vulgaris
Ranunculus repens 'Pleniflorus'
Rudbeckia
Ruta graveolens
Santolina chamaecyparissus
Saponaria ocymoides
Scabiosa
Sedum 'Autumn Joy'
Sisyrinchium angustifolium
Stachys byzantina
Stokesia laevis
Tanacetum coccineum
Tanacetum parthenium
Teucrium chamaedrys
Thymus
Tiarella cordifolia
Valeriana officinalis
Veronica austriaca subsp.
 teucrium

34. Perennials That Require Maintenance in the Spring

Acanthus spinosus
Achillea
Aconitum napellus
Adenophora liliifolia
Aegopodium podagraria
 'Variegatum'
Ajuga reptans
Alcea rosea
Alchemilla mollis
Amsonia tabernaemontana
Anaphalis triplinervis
Anchusa azurea
Angelica gigas
Anthemis tinctoria
Aquilegia hybrids
Arabis caucasica
Armeria maritima
Artemisia
Arum italicum 'Marmoratum'
Asarum europaeum

Asclepias tuberosa
Aster
Asteromoea mongolica
Astilbe ×arendsii
Astrantia major
Aubrieta deltoidea
Aurinia saxatilis
Baptisia australis
Belamcanda chinensis
Bergenia cordifolia
Boltonia asteroides 'Snowbank'
Brunnera macrophylla
Campanula carpatica
Campanula glomerata
Centaurea montana
Cerastium tomentosum
Ceratostigma plumbaginoides
Chelone lyonii
Chrysogonum virginianum
Chrysopsis villosa
Cimicifuga racemosa
Clematis heracleifolia
Coreopsis grandiflora
Coreopsis verticillata
Crocosmia 'Lucifer'
Delphinium
Dendranthema ×morifolium
Dianthus
Dictamnus albus
Digitalis
Echinacea purpurea
Echinops ritro
Epimedium ×rubrum
Eupatorium maculatum
 'Gateway'
Euphorbia polychroma
Filipendula
Foeniculum vulgare
 'Purpureum'
Fragaria 'Pink Panda'
Gaillarida ×grandiflora
Gaura lindheimeri
Geranium macrorrhizum
Geranium platypetalum
Geum hybrids
Gypsophila paniculata

34. Perennials That Require Maintenance in the Spring, continued

Helenium autumnale
Helianthemum nummularium
Helianthus salicifolius
Helleborus orientalis
Hemerocallis
Hesperis matronalis
Heuchera
Hibiscus moscheutos
Hypericum calycinum
Iberis sempervirens
Iris sibirica
Kniphofia hybrids
Lamium maculatum
Lavandula
Leucanthemum ×*superbum*
Liatris spicata
Limonium latifolium
Linaria purpurea
Linum perenne
Liriope spicata
Lobelia cardinalis
Lupinus hybrids
Lychnis coronaria
Macleaya cordata
Malva alcea 'Fastigiata'
Monarda didyma
Patrinia scabiosifolia
Penstemon barbatus
Perovskia atriplicifolia
Phlox
Physostegia virginiana
Polemonium caeruleum
Pulmonaria
Ranunculus repens 'Pleniflorus'
Rudbeckia
Ruta graveolens
Santolina chamaecyparissus
Saponaria ocymoides
Scabiosa
Sedum 'Autumn Joy'
Sisyrinchium angustifolium
Solidago hybrids
Stachys byzantina

Stokesia laevis
Tanacetum coccineum
Tanacetum parthenium
Teucrium chamaedrys
Thymus
Tradescantia ×*andersoniana*
Tricyrtis hirta
Valeriana officinalis
Veronica austriaca subsp. *teucrium*
Veronicastrum virginicum
Viola odorata

35. Perennials That Require Maintenance in the Summer

Acanthus spinosus
Achillea
Aconitum napellus
Adenophora liliifolia
Aegopodium podagraria 'Variegatum'
Ajuga reptans
Alcea rosea
Alchemilla mollis
Amsonia tabernaemontana
Anaphalis triplinervis
Anchusa azurea
Anemone ×*hybrida*
Angelica gigas
Anthemis tinctoria
Aquilegia hybrids
Arabis caucasica
Armeria maritima
Artemisia
Arum italicum 'Marmoratum'
Aruncus dioicus
Asclepias tuberosa
Aster ×*frikartii* 'Monch'
Aster novi-belgii
Astilbe ×*arendsii*
Astrantia major
Aurinia saxatilis
Baptisia australis
Begonia grandis var. *evansiana*
Bergenia cordifolia
Boltonia asteroides 'Snowbank'

Brunnera macrophylla
Campanula
Centaurea montana
Centranthus ruber
Cephalaria gigantea
Cerastium tomentosum
Ceratostigma plumbaginoides
Chelone lyonii
Chrysogonum virginianum
Chrysopsis villosa
Cimicifuga racemosa
Clematis heracleifolia
Clematis recta
Coreopsis
Corydalis lutea
Crocosmia 'Lucifer'
Delphinium
Dendranthema ×*morifolium*
Dianthus
Dicentra formosa 'Luxuriant'
Digitalis
Echinacea purpurea
Echinops ritro
Eryngium
Eupatorium maculatum 'Gateway'
Euphorbia polychroma
Filipendula
Foeniculum vulgare 'Purpureum'
Fragaria 'Pink Panda'
Gaillarida ×*grandiflora*
Gaura lindheimeri
Geranium
Geum hybrids
Gypsophila paniculata
Helenium autumnale
Helianthemum nummularium
Helianthus salicifolius
Heliopsis helianthoides
Helleborus orientalis
Hemerocallis
Hesperis matronalis
Heuchera
Hibiscus moscheutos
Hosta

Iberis sempervirens
Iris, bearded
Iris sibirica
Kniphofia hybrids
Lamium maculatum
Lavandula
Leucanthemum ×*superbum*
Liatris spicata
Ligularia dentata
Linaria purpurea
Linum perenne
Lobelia cardinalis
Lupinus hybrids
Lychnis coronaria
Macleaya cordata
Malva alcea 'Fastigiata'
Monarda didyma
Nepeta
Oenothera
Onopordum nervosum
Paeonia hybrids
Papaver orientale
Patrinia scabiosifolia
Penstemon barbatus
Phlox
Physostegia virginiana
Platycodon grandiflorus
Polemonium caeruleum
Pulmonaria saccharata
Pulsatilla vulgaris
Ranunculus repens 'Pleniflorus'
Rodgersia
Ruta graveolens
Salvia nemorosa
Sanguisorba obtusa
Santolina chamaecyparissus
Saponaria ocymoides
Scabiosa
Sidalcea malviflora
Sisyrinchium angustifolium
Solidago hybrids
Stachys byzantina
Stokesia laevis
Stylophorum diphyllum
Tanacetum coccineum
Tanacetum parthenium

Telekia speciosa
Teucrium chamaedrys
Thalictrum aquilegiifolium
Thermopsis caroliniana
Thymus
Tradescantia ×*andersoniana*
Trollius ×*cultorum*
Valeriana officinalis
Verbascum
Vernonia noveboracensis
Veronica
Viola odorata

36. Perennials That Require Maintenance in the Autumn

Adenophora liliifolia
Alcea rosea
Anemone ×*hybrida*
Artemisia ludoviciana 'Silver King'
Aruncus dioicus
Aster novi-belgii
Begonia grandis var. *evansiana*
Brunnera macrophylla
Centranthus ruber
Cephalaria gigantea
Clematis recta
Corydalis lutea
Delphinium
Dicentra formosa 'Luxuriant'
Echinacea purpurea
Foeniculum vulgare 'Purpureum'
Geranium endressii 'Wargrave Pink'
Geranium ibericum 'Johnson's Blue'
Helenium autumnale
Heliopsis helianthoides
Hosta
Iris, bearded
Kniphofia hybrids
Ligularia dentata
Malva alcea 'Fastigiata'
Monarda didyma
Nepeta

Paeonia hybrids
Papaver orientale
Phlox maculata
Phlox paniculata
Platycodon grandiflorus
Polygonatum odoratum 'Variegatum'
Ranunculus repens 'Pleniflorus'
Rodgersia
Salvia nemorosa
Sanguisorba obtusa
Sidalcea malviflora
Solidago hybrids
Telekia speciosa
Thalictrum aquilegiifolium
Thermopsis caroliniana
Tradescantia ×*andersoniana*
Tricyrtis hirta
Vernonia noveboracensis
Veronica spicata
Veronicastrum virginicum
Viola odorata

U.S. Department of Agriculture Plant Hardiness Zone Map

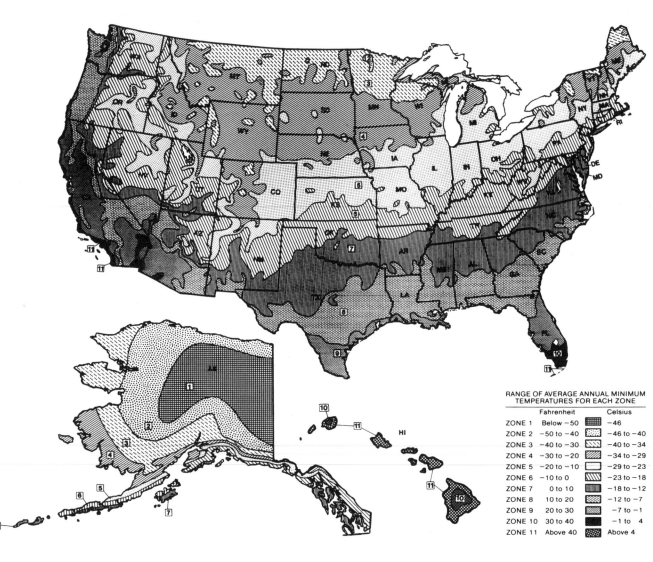

RANGE OF AVERAGE ANNUAL MINIMUM
TEMPERATURES FOR EACH ZONE

	Fahrenheit		Celsius
ZONE 1	Below −50		−46
ZONE 2	−50 to −40		−46 to −40
ZONE 3	−40 to −30		−40 to −34
ZONE 4	−30 to −20		−34 to −29
ZONE 5	−20 to −10		−29 to −23
ZONE 6	−10 to 0		−23 to −18
ZONE 7	0 to 10		−18 to −12
ZONE 8	10 to 20		−12 to −7
ZONE 9	20 to 30		−7 to −1
ZONE 10	30 to 40		−1 to 4
ZONE 11	Above 40		Above 4

Metric Conversion Chart

INCHES	CENTIMETERS	FEET	METERS
⅛	0.3	¼	0.08
¼	0.6	⅓	0.1
⅓	0.8	½	0.15
½	1.25	1	0.3
⅔	1.7	1½	0.5
¾	1.9	2	0.6
1	2.5	2½	0.8
1¼	3.1	3	0.9
1⅓	3.3	4	1.2
1½	3.75	5	1.5
1¾	4.4	6	1.8
2	5.0	7	2.1
3	7.5	8	2.4
4	10	9	2.7
5	12.5	10	3.0
6	15	15	4.5
7	17.5	20	6.0
8	20	25	7.5
9	22.5	30	9.0
10	25	35	10.5
12	30	40	12
15	37.5	45	13.5
18	45	50	15
20	50		
24	60		
30	75		
36	90		

$$°C = 5/9 \times (°F - 32)$$
$$°F = (9/5 \times °C) + 32$$

Glossary

acidic soil: a soil having a pH of less than 7.

adventitious root: a root that originates from a stem or other part of the plant where roots do not normally occur.

aerating soil: loosening the soil to allow better air circulation, accomplished by mechanical methods.

alkaline soil: a soil having a pH of greater than 7.

amendment: any material, such as compost, lime, or synthetic conditioners, that is worked into the soil to improve its conditioning properties.

annual: a plant that completes its life cycle in one growing season and then dies.

apical bud: a bud located at the tip of a stem or branch.

apical dominance: a condition wherein the terminal or apical bud inhibits the development of lateral buds on a shoot.

auxin: a plant growth hormone that controls shoot growth and root formation. Generally produced in actively growing (meristematic) regions of the plant.

axil: the upper angle between a petiole and stem.

axillary bud: a bud formed in an axil.

backfill: soil used for filling in the area around a plant's roots in the planting hole.

bareroot: a plant that is sold without any soil around its roots.

basal foliage: the leaves that grow from the base or crown of a plant.

bed: a garden area that has definite measurements and is a separate part of the landscape.

beneficial insect: an insect that eats or parasitizes harmful garden insects.

biennial: a plant that completes its life cycle in two growing seasons and then dies.

bloom sequencing: cutting back part of a plant or planting to delay flowering on that portion.

border: a garden area similar to a bed, usually containing more than one type of plant, that may be backed by walls, fences, or taller plants such as trees or hedges.

bulbil: a small bulb located in the axil of a leaf.

catwalk: a small path behind a border, which allows the gardener to reach the back without stepping in the bed.

compost: an organic material rich in *humus* that is formed by decomposed plant material and other *organic matter* and is effective as a soil conditioner.

crown: the location on a plant where the stem meets the roots, usually found at soil level.

cultivar: a contraction of *cultivated variety*, it refers to a group of cultivated plants within a species that are distinguishable by one or more characteristics, which are retained when the plant is propagated.

cutting back: pruning off foliage and possibly flower buds or deadheads to renew a plant's appearance or to encourage a new flush of growth and flowering, or to control the plant's height or flowering time.

cutting garden: a garden planted especially for producing cut flowers.

cytokinin: a plant growth hormone that stimulates cell division.

deadhead: an old or spent flower.

deadheading: removing spent flowers or flowerheads for aesthetics, or to prolong bloom or promote rebloom, or to prevent seeding.

deadleafing: removing dead leaves to improve the appearance of a plant, or in an effort to prevent or reduce the presence of pests or diseases.

disbudding: removing side buds to encourage larger terminal buds, or removing terminal buds to produce smaller but more numerous side buds.

division: a method of increasing plants by separating or splitting them apart.

drift: a long-shaped planting of perennials, as opposed to a rigid patch or block.

edging plant: a plant similar to a low-hedge plant that is usually mounded and provides softness to the margins of a bed or border.

evergreen: a perennial that retains its foliage for more than one growing season.

existing soil: the soil at a site before any amendments have been added.

eyes: dormant growth buds.

fertilizer: an organic or inorganic material, such as manure or chemicals, that is put on or in the soil to improve the quality of the soil and encourage better plant growth.

fibrous root system: a root system that does not rely on a *taproot* but consists of many branched and lateral rootlets.

foliar feeding: the fertilizing of a plant by spraying liquid fertilizer directly on the surface of the leaves.

formal garden: a landscape or garden design that usually consists of straight lines, complex bed designs, hedges, and/or topiaries, usually arranged symmetrically.

frost date: the approximate date of the last killing frost in the spring or the first killing frost in the autumn.

glaucous: covered with a blue-green, grayish-blue, or white waxy bloom or material that easily rubs off, often used in describing plant foliage.

groundcover: a plant, usually one that is low growing, that spreads laterally to quickly cover the soil surface. Groundcovers are useful for suppressing weeds and protecting against soil erosion.

habit: the general form or shape of a plant.

hardening: the process of slowly acclimating plants that were grown under shelter to outdoor climates.

herbaceous: a non-woody plant that dies back to the ground every year.

humus: the chemically complex organic matter in soil made up of decaying plant material; it is usually black or dark brown in color.

hybrid: a plant that is the result of a cross between two or more genera or species.

invasive plant: a plant that, when grown in the right environmental conditions, readily spreads and reproduces to the extent that it can take over the garden and become a nuisance.

island bed: a garden bed that is surrounded on all sides by lawn, groundcover, or stone and does not have a background border of shrubs or fencing.

lateral: a side growth that branches from a shoot or root.

loam: a soil of medium texture that contains a moderate amount of sand, silt, and clay.

massed planting: a planting in which large plants or large groups of plants are incorporated to provide mass, visual bulk, landscape balance, and/or to serve as fillers or specimens.

melting out: a condition where the center of a plant dies out, normally due to rot caused by excessive moisture or humidity.

microclimate: the climate of a small area, be it shady, sunny, moist, dry, etc.

mulch: a material that is applied to the soil surface to discourage weed growth, help retain moisture in the soil, and maintain a uniform root temperature; some materials used as mulch include manure, bark, and pine needles.

native plant: a plant that naturally occurs in a given area.

naturalized setting: an environment that is native or contains native plants; also, an area that has been designed to look as though it was naturally occuring.

neutral soil: a soil having a pH of 7.

nitrogen (N): the nutrient that promotes vigorous growth of the stem and leaves; nitrogen needs to be added regularly to most soils.

node: the point on a stem where leaves are attached.

organic matter: mulches, compost, and similar materials that are derived from living organisms, such as decomposed plant material.

overwinter: to pass the winter, used when discussing a plant's survivability or care during the winter months.

panicle: a branched group of flowers on a single stem in which the center flowers open last and the growth and elongation of the main stem does not stop with the opening of the first flower.

palmate: lobed or divided as in the shape of a fan, with all divisions originating from the same point; used to describe the arrangement of a plant's leaves.

pea staking: the use of short, twiggy sticks to support bushy perennial plants (technique was originally used to support pea plants); see Figure 5-2.

peony hoops: metal circular staking material used to support peonies and other bushy perennials.

perennial: a plant that normally survives for three or more seasons.

pH: an indication of the hydrogen-ion concentration in soil, used to measure a soil's alkalinity or acidity.

phosphate: a form of phosphorus (P) that assists in strong root growth in plants; one of the three basic nutrients in fertilizers.

photoperiod: the amount of daylight hours that best promote plant growth and flowering.

pinching: removing the growing tips and first set of leaves (approximately ½–1 in.) of a plant to promote the production of side shoots; a finger and thumb are used for pinching. Used to create fuller, shorter plants often with more numerous but smaller flowers.

potash: a form of potassium (K) that is included in fertilizers to improve flowering and fruiting.

prolong bloom: to extend the bloom period of a plant or planting.

pubescent: covered with short, soft hairs.

rebloom: a second bloom phase that is usually characterized by smaller, often shorter and less numerous flowers than the intial bloom period. Sometimes induced by *deadheading*.

reseed/self-seed: to drop fertile seeds that will produce seedlings.

rhizome: a horizontal underground stem that has nodes, buds, or scalelike leaves and often is enlarged for food storage.

rogue: a plant that varies from the rest of the planting and is not wanted; also used to describe the removal of an unwanted plant or plants, often due to their aggressive tendencies.

rootbound: a condition in which a plant's roots have filled the area that they are confined to, whether a pot or an area in the soil, and can no longer funtion to their capacity.

rosette: a crown of leaves radiating from approximately the same point at or close to the surface of the ground.

scape: a leafless stem that arises from the ground, usually bearing a flower or flowers and possibly scales or bracts, such as on *Heuchera* and *Iris*.

secondary flowering: the flowering of lateral buds after the terminal bud has flowered, and usually after the terminal flower has been pruned off.

seedheads: ripe seeds that have dried in a cluster.

sewage sludge: an organic fertilizer that is made up of dried processed sewage.

shaping: shearing a plant in a rounded or mounded fashion to form structure in the garden.

shearing: pruning or *cutting back* with hedge shears.

soil fertility: the quantity and balance of light, heat, water, air, and nutrients needed to fortify the soil so that it can support plant growth.

soil structure: the capability of the soil to form aggregates, which is the natural grouping together of individual particles of sand, silt, and clay to form larger units.

soil texture: the classification of soil types based on the relative proportions of sand, silt, and clay.

soluble salts: the salts found in compost, which if present in too high a concentration will hinder plant growth and development.

spike: generally a group of flowers borne on a single upright stem.

spreader sticker: a substance that can be mixed with another substance to prevent it from washing off; dish detergent is commonly used for this purpose.

staking: using a piece of wood, metal, or plastic to provide support to a tall flower stalk.

stalk: the stem of a plant that supports the leaves, flowers, and fruit.

stolon: a horizontal stem above or just below the ground that forms roots at its tip to produce new plants.

stoloniferous: bearing stolons.

subshrub: a plant that has a woody base but has herbaceous shoots above ground that die back annually.

taproot: the main root of a plant; it usually grows straight down.

terminal: growing at the tip of a branch or stem.

thinning: removing shoots, leaves, flowerheads, or seedheads to improve the growth habit or overall appearance of a plant, or in an attempt to reduce the incidence of disease by removing infected parts and/or by increasing light and air circulation around a plant.

tillering: the growth habit of a groundcovering grass or monocot.

tip burn: the scorching of a plant's leaf tips by the sun.

top-dressing: an application of fertilizer, compost, manure, or other soil amendment to the soil surface around a plant to replenish nutrients.

transpiration: water loss by evaporation from leaves and stems.

transplanting: moving a plant from one place to another.

variegated: a term used to describe a plant that is striped, spotted, or otherwise marked with a color other than green; usually for describing foliage.

variety: a subdivision of a species that exhibits inheritable characteristics.

vernalization: to promote flowering by exposing a plant to a cold treatment.

whorled: the arrangement of leaves or flowers in circular clusters around a stem.

woody perennials: perennials that have hard and thickened stems or trunks and do not die back to the ground.

woolly: having long and entangled soft hairs.

Bibliography

Armitage, A. M. 1989. *Herbaceous Perennial Plants*. Athens, GA: Varsity Press.

Bakalar, E. 1994. *A Garden of One's Own*. New York: William Morrow.

Best, C. 1992. Natural pesticides: are they really safer? In *The Environmental Gardener*. New York: Brooklyn Botanic Garden.

Best of Fine Gardening. 1995. *Healthy Soil*. Newtown, CT: Taunton Press.

Brickell, C., ed. 1993. *The American Horticultural Society Encyclopedia of Gardening*. London: Dorling Kindersley.

Chinery, David. n.d. *Annuals, Biennials, Perennials, Groundcovers and Vines Useful When Gardening With Deer*. New York: Cornell Cooperative Extension of Westchester County.

Coombs, Duncan, Peter Blackburne-Maze, Martyn Cracknell, and Roger Bentley. n.d. *The Complete Book of Pruning*. England: Ward Lock.

Cresson, C. 1993. *Charles Cresson on the American Flower Garden*. New York: Prentice Hall.

Daughtrey, M. L., and M. Semel. 1992. Herbaceous perennials: diseases and insect pests. Cornell Cooperative Extension Bulletin 207.

DiSabato-Aust, T. 1991. Pruning herbaceous plants. In *Pruning Techniques*. New York: Brooklyn Botanic Garden.

———. 1992. Pruning perennials for peak performance. *Proceedings, Perennial Plant Association*. Steven M. Still, ed. Hilliard, OH.

———. 1994. Deadheading and cutting back. *The Best of Fine Gardening: Plant Care*. Newtown, CT: The Taunton Press.

EPA. 1994. Characterization of municipal solid waste in the United States: 1994 update. EPA Bulletin 530-R-94-042.

Greenlee, J. 1992. *The Encyclopedia of Ornamental Grasses*. Emmaus, PA: Rodale Press.

Hansen, R., and F. Stahl. 1993. *Perennials and Their Garden Habitats*. Portland, OR: Timber Press.

Harper, P., and F. McGourty. 1985. *Perennials: How to Select, Grow and Enjoy*. Tucson, AZ: HP Books.

Hebb, R. S. 1975. *Low Maintenance Perennials*. Jamaica Plain, MA: Arnold Arboretum of Harvard University.

Hoitink, H. A. J., M. A. Rose, and R. A. Zondag. 1995. Properties of materials available for formulation of high quality container media. *The Buckeye* (June): 1–7.

Jelitto, L., and W. Schacht. 1985. *Hardy Herbaceous Perennials*. 2 vols. 3rd edition. Portland, OR: Timber Press.

Kashmanian, R. M., and J. M. Keyser. 1992. The flip side of compost: what's in it, where to use it and why. In *The Environmental Gardener*. New York: Brooklyn Botanic Garden.

Keys, D. 1992. *Canadian Peat Harvesting and the Environment*. Ottawa: North American Wetlands Conservation Council.

Lovejoy, A. 1993. *The American Mixed Border*. New York: Macmillan.

Lovejoy, A., ed. 1991. *Perennials: Toward Continuous Bloom*. Deer Park, WI: Capability's Books.

McGourty, F. 1989. *The Perennial Gardener*. Boston: Houghton Mifflin.

Ney, B., ed. 1990. *Ornamental Grasses*. Kennett Square, PA: Longwood Gardens.

Patterson, J. C., J. J. Murray, and J. R. Short. 1980. The impact of urban soils on vegetation. *M.E.T.R.I.A. Proceedings* 3: 33–56.

Perennial Plant Association. *Standards*. Steven M. Still, ed. Hilliard, OH.

Phillips, E., and C. C. Burrell. 1993. *Rodale's Illustrated Encyclopedia of Perennials*. Emmaus, PA: Rodale Press.

Price, S. F. 1995. Snip, shape and shear: deadhead perennials for a second flush of blooms. *Fine Gardening* (July/August): 54–57.

Reinhardt, M. 1991. Landscaping with perennials—the organic way. In *Proceedings, Perennial Plant Association*. Steven M. Still, ed. Hilliard, OH.

Sheldon, E. 1989. *A Proper Garden*. Harrisburg, PA: Stackpole Books.

Smith, E., and S. Treaster. 1990. Application of composted municipal sludge in the landscape. Columbus: The Ohio State University Department of Horticulture.

———. 1991. Production of herbaceous perennials in mineral soil amended with composted municipal sludge. Columbus: The Ohio State Unversity Department of Horticulture.

Sunset Books. 1978. *Pruning Handbook*. Menlo Park, CA: Lane Publishing.

Still, S. M. 1994. *Manual of Herbaceous Ornamental Plants*. Champaign, IL: Stipes Publishing.

Tyler, R. W. 1991. Organic matter: the life blood of soils. *The Buckeye* (October): 25–37.

———. 1993. Calculating compost capacity. *Lawn & Landscape* (March).

———. 1993. Cashing in on compost. *Lawn & Landscape* (March).

———. 1996. *Winning the Organics Game*. Alexandria, VA: ASHS Press.

van de Laar, H. J., G. Fortgens, M. H. A. Hoffman, and P. C. de Jong. 1995. *Naamlijst van vaste planten*. Boskoop, Netherlands: Proefstation voor de Boomkwekerij.

Woods, C. 1991. Notes on the propagation and maintenance of herbaceous perennials. In *Perennials: A Gardener's Guide*. New York: Brooklyn Botanic Garden.

Index of
Plant Names

Page numbers in **boldface** indicate a main text entry.